Constitutional Law
FOR
DUMMIES®

by Glenn C.Smith, JD, LLM, and Patricia Fusco, JD

WILEY

John Wiley & Sons, Inc.

Constitutional Law For Dummies®

Published by
John Wiley & Sons, Inc.
111 River St.
Hoboken, NJ 07030-5774
www.wiley.com

For general information on our other products and services, please contact our Customer Care Department within the U.S. at 877-762-2974, outside the U.S. at 317-572-3993, or fax 317-572-4002.

For technical support, please visit www.wiley.com/techsupport.

Wiley publishes in a variety of print and electronic formats and by print-on-demand. Some material included with standard print versions of this book may not be included in e-books or in print-on-demand. If this book refers to media such as a CD or DVD that is not included in the version you purchased, you may download this material at http://booksupport.wiley.com. For more information about Wiley products, visit www.wiley.com.

Library of Congress Control Number: 2011942767

ISBN 978-1-118-02378-5 (pbk); ISBN 978-1-118-21413-8 (ebk); ISBN 978-1-118-21367-4 (ebk); ISBN 978-1-118-21376-6 (ebk)

Manufactured in the United States of America

10 9 8 7 6 5 4 3 2 1

WILEY

About the Authors

Glenn Smith, JD, LLM, is a full-time constitutional law professor at California Western School of Law in San Diego, California. He also regularly teaches as a visiting professor of political science at the University of California, San Diego (where in 1996 he was named as a Professor of the Year by graduates of the university's Marshall College). At California Western School of Law since 1985, Professor Smith teaches a nationally recognized course in which students reenact Supreme Court cases, taking on the roles of justices and attorneys arguing and deciding constitutional issues. He regularly teaches other constitutional law courses and has published numerous articles on constitutional law for scholarly journals and for publications aimed at more general audiences. Professor Smith regularly speaks about constitutional controversies in media interviews and speeches.

A Root-Tilden scholar at New York University School of Law, Professor Smith received his juris doctorate in 1978. He earned a master of laws degree from Georgetown University Law Center. From 1979 to 1983, he served as a legal counsel to the United States Senate Governmental Affairs Committee.

When Professor Smith isn't teaching or writing, he enjoys the company of friends and family — especially when travelling, wining, and dining are involved. He is mad for strong espresso and cappuccino!

Patricia Fusco, JD, Deputy Attorney General, California Department of Justice, currently prosecutes complex white-collar felony crimes in Southern California and has been a practicing attorney in San Diego for 13 years. She has extensive experience as a criminal prosecutor and civil litigator, including prosecuting domestic violence, code enforcement, and other criminal cases, and handling construction litigation and personal-injury defense. A graduate of Southern Connecticut State University (with a bachelor of science in journalism) and California Western School of Law, Attorney Fusco was a paralegal and a legal secretary prior to entering law school in 1995. She enjoys cooking, entertaining, wine tasting, playing tennis, and spending time with friends and family, including her two pups, Rudy and Auggie.

Dedication

Glenn Smith dedicates this book to his wonderful wife, Diane. Without her constant inspiration and expert editing, the book would not have been written.

Patricia Fusco dedicates this book to Mom and Dad. Wish you were here to see this. I miss you both!

Authors' Acknowledgments

We would like to thank Colleen Monaco and Margot Hutchison for opening up the opportunity for us to write this book. Also, many thanks go out to our editors at John Wiley & Sons, Inc., in New Jersey and Indiana, for their encouragement and expert guidance throughout the writing process.

Publisher's Acknowledgments

We're proud of this book; please send us your comments at http://dummies.custhelp.com. For other comments, please contact our Customer Care Department within the U.S. at 877-762-2974, outside the U.S. at 317-572-3993, or fax 317-572-4002.

Some of the people who helped bring this book to market include the following:

Acquisitions, Editorial, and Vertical Websites

Senior Project Editor: Christina Guthrie

Acquisitions Editor: Tracy Boggier

Copy Editor: Caitlin Copple

Senior Copy Editor: Danielle Voirol

Assistant Editor: David Lutton

Editorial Program Coordinator: Joe Niesen

Technical Editor: Dr. Darren Wheeler

Editorial Manager: Christine Meloy Beck

Editorial Assistants: Rachelle Amick, Alexa Koschier

Cover Photos: © iStockphoto.com / onur ersin

Cartoons: Rich Tennant (www.the5thwave.com)

Composition Services

Project Coordinator: Patrick Redmond

Layout and Graphics: Carl Byers, Timothy C. Detrick, Corrie Socolovitch

Proofreader: Bonnie Mikkelson

Indexer: Valerie Haynes Perry

Publishing and Editorial for Consumer Dummies

    Kathleen Nebenhaus, Vice President and Executive Publisher

    Kristin Ferguson-Wagstaffe, Product Development Director

    Ensley Eikenburg, Associate Publisher, Travel

    Kelly Regan, Editorial Director, Travel

Publishing for Technology Dummies

    Andy Cummings, Vice President and Publisher

Composition Services

    Debbie Stailey, Director of Composition Services

Contents at a Glance

Table of Contents

Introduction

*F*ew subjects affect your everyday life more than constitutional law. From how your government is organized to whether you have a right to speak freely or when police can search your house, what the Constitution says and means has a big impact on you. Constitutional law, with all its complexity and range, may at times be maddening, but it's a fascinating subject to delve into.

We think that after exploring the topics in this book, you'll find constitutional law as interesting as we do. And whatever your purpose in getting this book, you will find it a useful reference in the future. It will give you the foundation to better understand hot topics discussed in the news — and even give you ammunition to win those debates at the water cooler!

About This Book

We wrote this book with a focus on undergraduate students taking classes on constitutional law. This book is a good supplement that will ease students' understanding of course material. But the book is also a good reference guide that will prove useful to law students, journalists, and eve just plain inter- ested citizens. We wrote the book with an eye toward explaining complex concepts so that everyone can understand them. You don't necessarily even need to read the entire book — you can easily reference different sections on an as-needed or as-interested basis.

Constitutional Law For Dummies helps you realize like never before the impor- tance of the Constitution and the ways it is interpreted. In this book you see how the courts analyze whether you have a right to have a gun in your house or to yell obscenities in a public place, for instance. You find out how the United States government is structured (and why) and just what the Supreme Court's role and importance are. It has been said that Supreme Court justices are some of the most powerful people in the world. When you read this book, you will see why.

In this book, you find that we regularly reference legal tests and doctrines. (For example, in Chapter 11's discussion of freedom of speech, we partly organize the discussion around the key distinctions between *unprotected* and *protected* speech and the different levels of scrutiny for content-based versus content-neutral regulation.) We're not trying to make a constitutional lawyer out of you (although it's fine with us if you become one). Instead, our empha- sis on legal tests and doctrines reflects both an educational and practical strategy.

Educationally speaking, being familiar with the applicable legal rules is critical because these rules are the lenses courts and other Constitution interpreters use to see their way to the essence of the Constitution and its meaning in the 21st century. If you want to understand modern constitutional law, you need to understand the legal tests and doctrines critical to shaping it. Plus, legal tests and doctrines are a great way to organize a series of case results that could seem confusing and arbitrary without presenting the organizing principle underlying them.

Practically, we give legal tests and doctrines their due so that we can be sure this book serves the needs of as many readers as possible. You may be a law student, or be thinking about becoming one. If so, you absolutely will want to soak up the rules and doctrines explained in this book. If you're an undergraduate constitutional-law student, we want to make sure that our book helps you prepare for class. Even if your professor doesn't emphasize legal tests and doctrines, *our* doing so will help you deeply understand the materials — and maybe even ace the exam!

Conventions Used in This Book

We generally abandon the technical ways lawyers write about cases in briefs for courts or legal publications. When we talk about a case decided by the Supreme Court or a lower court, we give you the official case name and the citation to where it can be found in the hard-bound volumes of published cases. We're not expecting you to immediately run out to your nearest law library! But if you want to read more from the case, you can usually find info online by entering the case name and/or citation in a search engine.

Following is the explanation of what the parts in a Supreme Court case citation mean. We use *Jones v. Adams,* 222 U.S. 11 (1999), which we made up, as a sample.

- ✔ ***Jones:*** The first party is almost always called the *petitioner,* the person who lost in the lower court immediately below the Supreme Court in the judicial pecking order. Generally, as cases wend their way through state or federal courts, the party named first is referred to as the *plaintiff* (the person bringing the suit). But in U.S. Supreme Court cases, this first-named party is petitioning the Court to review and reverse a matter decided in a lower court, in which he may or may not have been the instigator of the case.

- ✔ ***Adams:*** The second name (the one after the *v.*) usually signifies the *respondent,* who had the more favorable ruling in the immediately lower court. When a case first starts out, the second named party is the *defendant,* the person being sued. But in U.S. Supreme Court cases, this second person may or may not have been the defendant in the lower case. (Very much liking the opinion immediately below, the *respondent* is countering, or responding to, the petitioner's request that the Court hear and possibly reverse the case.)

✔ **222:** This number refers to the volume of collected cases from the court (in this case, the U.S. Supreme Court) in which the opinion in this case is found.

✔ **U.S.:** These letters refer to the court deciding the case — here, the U.S. Supreme Court. Generally, these letters reference a series of books that report cases from different courts. You can tell from the abbreviation which series of books, and which court, the case comes from. Different courts have different abbreviations that would appear in this place in a case cite, which signals where the case was heard.

✔ **11:** This number refers to the page number on which the reported decision in the case begins in that volume (in this example, 222).

✔ **(1999):** The year listed is when the case was decided. Because the wheels of justice sometimes turn slowly, it may be years after the case was initiated.

When discussing cases and theory, we use the words *precedent, rule, decision,* and *doctrine* interchangeably. These words have technically distinct nuances. But they (and other similar terms we use, like *governing law*) basically mean the same thing in this book. They all signify the current "rules of the road" used by courts and other Constitution interpreters in implementing the letter and spirit of the document.

We periodically use other words or concepts that may be unfamiliar to you. Where this occurs, we italicize the word or phrase to point out its importance, along with providing an easily understandable definition to help your reading. We don't assume specialized knowledge or experience on your part.

What You're Not to Read

We'd love for you to read every single word we wrote, but we're realistic people. If you just want the bare-bones info, you can skip certain elements that enhance the text but aren't essential for understanding.

Sidebars, which are the gray boxes, contain material that provides an interesting aside to a given topic. We may present an especially intriguing or cutting-edge case that helps illustrate a concept discussed in that chapter. Or we may comment on the practical importance of a legal rule under study.

Paragraphs marked with the Technical Stuff icon contain more-detailed information that will only fascinate the true constitutional-law geek. (If you find it interesting, we promise not to tell anyone.)

Foolish Assumptions

We wrote this book with the assumption that most readers are enrolled in an undergrad-level Constitutional Law course. Therefore, we cover essential topics that we think a college student (and even a law student) needs to grasp. However, you may also like this book if any of the following statements apply to you:

✔ You are considering becoming a lawyer and want to get a taste of one of the critical topics that will be covered in law school.

✔ You are a journalist covering stories about high-profile cases, and you need a better understanding of what the Supreme Court is all about and how to evaluate cases based on precedent.

✔ You are an interested citizen who wants to better understand the pivotal role constitutional law plays in how this country runs (or doesn't!).

✔ You are considering going into politics and would like a better grasp on governmental structure and divisions of power.

✔ You are just a geek who loves to read about complicated subjects because you have a lot of brain power left after getting home from work and taking care of your house, your family, and your dogs.

We also assume that you know the following about the U.S. legal system:

✔ The U.S. Supreme Court is the highest court in the land, has the last word on cases appealed to it, and is the ongoing interpreter of the U.S. Constitution — though other courts, officials, and citizens get into the act a lot!

✔ A majority of justices (usually five or more) is needed to create a binding *precedent* (a decision that must be honored by lower courts and others). Even when a majority of justices agrees on who wins a lawsuit, however, no true majority opinion may be formed if the justices use different rules *(doctrines)* or theories in coming to a common result.

   A *plurality opinion* is the leading view of legal issues shared by fewer than a majority of justices.

   Whether or not a given constitutional challenge results in a binding majority opinion, one or more justices often writes *concurring opinions* elaborating on their reasoning.

✔ Justices disagreeing with the majority result or reasoning usually write *dissenting opinions* pointing out why they disagree and what conclusion they wanted. Dissenting opinions often help point to what the majority means. One era's dissent can become tomorrow's majority.

How This Book Is Organized

This book is logically organized by types of issues. It concentrates mostly on *civil* (noncriminal) constitutional issues, although the last part covers constitutional law as it relates to certain rights in the criminal arena. And sometimes topics overlap. Following are the general categories and a bit about what you find in each part of the book.

Part I: Studying Constitutional Law: The Foundations

Before really being able to master any subject, you need a foundation. You can better understand constitutional law if you first have an understanding of the document itself. So in this part we start with a brief history surrounding the Constitution. We then break down the document into five major facets. We also discuss some key aspects of constitutional law, including the different Constitution-interpreting theories and how constitutional issues differ from nonconstitutional ones.

Part II: Allocating Governmental Roles

The most important feature of the original Constitution adopted in 1791 is how it defines the parameters of the new government. It forms the federal government, allocates its powers among three branches, and establishes checks and balances on each branch. In this part, we explain modern understandings about the powers and limits of the federal government. We chart the resulting limitations on state power and we also explain current realities and uncertainties in the relationships among Congress, the president, and the federal courts.

Part III: Protecting Property Rights and Avoiding Arbitrary Action

Important to the framers of both the original Constitution, the Bill of Rights, and later constitutional amendments was making sure that property rights were adequately protected under the new government. You see in this part how the courts have interpreted the several constitutional clauses dealing directly with property rights over the years. A related framer focus was protecting liberty from arbitrary deprivation and people from discriminatory action; in this part we also examine how the framers' efforts have fared for different rights and groups.

Part IV: Rights to Self-Expression and Political Participation

In these chapters, we discuss the controversial topics of freedom of speech and religion. We bring you up-to-date on these issues and explain how courts have determined what laws government can and cannot adopt, and the way Americans exercise these rights. When is speech protected, and how much? How separate must church and state really be? And how does the Constitution shape the rules of engagement in the political arena — on a variety of matters ranging from voting and running for office to establishing electoral districts? The answers to these questions are the subjects of Part IV.

Part V: Understanding Privacy Rights

The Constitution's framers had major problems with how British and colonial governments invaded privacy rights, especially in the criminal process. This part explores the strong "privacy" protections modern courts have found to be an integral part of the way the Constitution's due-process provisions protect "liberty." We also devote two chapters to the constitutional rights of Americans not to incriminate themselves and not to have their homes or other property searched arbitrarily.

Part VI: The Part of Tens

In keeping with how all *For Dummies* books are written, here we give you our top ten lists. Hundreds of constitutional-law cases are important, but we have done our best to narrow them down to ten of the most important cases involving government power and individual rights. We give you some of the details of the cases and explain how they came out. These are cases you may often hear mentioned as laying the groundwork for certain rights or concepts discussed in the news or magazines or periodicals.

Icons Used in This Book

We use the following icons in this book to point out certain information.

This information brings certain topics to life for you. We discuss real case examples so that you can see how a concept plays out in real legal, political, or social forums. Understanding actual examples helps you remember the concepts.

This icon is a reminder of some important information that you should keep in mind when dealing with constitutional law. Reading the information accompanying these icons helps you understand the surrounding text and larger aspects of constitutional law.

Paragraphs marked with this icon give you shortcuts for understanding Court decisions or predicting what the Court will do in the future.

At times, we make technical distinctions of interest to sticklers, but these paragraphs go beyond the basics and aren't necessary for you to read if you don't want to.

Where to Go from Here

Where you go from here really depends on what your purpose was in getting this book. If you are a student, you may want to consult it on a subject-by-subject basis, reading certain chapters or parts before you delve into textbook reading assignments so you can understand the material more easily. If you're new to this subject, very curious about all sides of constitutional law, or an overachiever, then you may just want to read the whole book from start to finish. But otherwise, a subject-by-subject approach should work for just about anyone, so check out the table of contents and see what interests you most. Either way, adjust your seat belt as we take you on a flight through the most important aspects of a fascinating subject.

Part I

Studying Constitutional Law: The Foundations

In this part . . .

The basis for constitutional law is the U.S. Constitution, and it has multiple facets. So before you approach learning about constitutional law, you need a foundation — you need to know what the Constitution aims to do. This part gives you that foundation, starting with a history of the document itself. Several chapters address its main aspects, and then we give you some details on key overall features so you can gain a better general understanding of the Constitution and related law. We also discuss where many people go astray in analyzing the Constitution so you won't fall prey to common mistakes.

Chapter 1

Understanding the Constitution

In This Chapter

▶ Summarizing the Constitution's historical background

▶ Taking a look at distinguishing characteristics of the Constitution

▶ Appreciating the five components that make up the Constitution as a whole

*C*onstitutional law is the study of how courts and other interpreters have given life and meaning to the United States Constitution. The Constitution and related law define the powers and limits of the national government — including how its three branches interact with each other and relate to state and local governmental authorities. Constitutional law also limits in many significant ways how governments at all levels interact with the people living within their boundaries. It protects key civil and criminal rights, including rights to avoid arbitrary and discriminatory treatment, protection for freedom of speech and religion, and guarantees of personal privacy.

In this book we explain the key details of constitutional law through summaries that make complicated legalese and technical details easily understandable and get right to the core of how the Constitution affects people in meaningful, practical ways. But before you delve into the specific topics in the following chapters, we give you an overview of that all-important document itself, the U.S. Constitution.

A country's (or a state's) constitution provides a framework for how governmental institutions will operate and how they will treat people. In a country like the United States, where the national constitution is the supreme legal authority, the U.S. Constitution becomes the yardstick against which to measure the validity of all other governmental actions — be they laws passed by Congress, the policies of local school boards, or the actions of an individual police officer.

Knowing a bit about the U.S. Constitution's history and why and how certain clauses were put in the document in the first place will help you make sense of the ways it has been interpreted. For instance, you can better understand search-warrant requirements or checks and balances if you know why the framers thought to include them.

This chapter begins with a brief summary of the historical background leading up to the proposal in 1787 of the constitutional plan we still use today. This brief bit of context makes clear that the Constitution's framers did not write on a clean slate — they started with what was already familiar, and they had specific ideas in mind as to what was needed. We then summarize nine key features making the U.S. Constitution distinct from the constitutions of other governments and even many other democracies. The last and most extensive section provides a tour of the five basic topics addressed by the various articles and amendments known collectively as the Constitution.

Looking at the Constitution's Creation

Many volumes of history and political commentary address the historical background leading up to the proposal of a new governing arrangement in 1787. Scholars fiercely debate whether the framers of the U.S. Constitution were uniquely learned and inspired visionaries, reactionary elites bent on looking out for themselves rather than protecting the masses, or something in between. Lucky for you, you don't need to know all the ins and outs of these ongoing discussions (though you may, like us, find them interesting if you look them up sometime).

Rather, to give you the essential historical perspective for understanding where the framers were coming from (which is an important factor in many areas of constitutional law), we present you with the following turbo-summary of the conventional account of the Constitution's historical background — in 373 words:

During and after the American Revolution (whose hostilities ended in 1781), American leaders recognized that they needed some kind of overarching national authority to undertake key activities. For six years, the states functioned in a loose confederation under a document called the *Articles of Confederation*. Almost immediately, the defects of the Articles became apparent:

- Each state had an equal vote in the legislative body operating under the Articles, which the states with the greater populations resented.

- Laws resulting from the Articles reflected awkward political compromises, and the lack of any executive authority made effectively carrying out legislative directives difficult.

- The government created by the Articles lacked taxing authority; it had to depend on voluntary financial contributions from states.

These defects couldn't be easily remedied, because the Articles of Confederation said that all 13 states had to unanimously agree to make fundamental changes in governmental procedures.

Meanwhile, states began to act in ways that alarmed the country's leaders. At times, inspired by popular uprisings, state legislatures interfered with the enforcement of debts and discriminated economically and legally against nonresidents. Some states engaged individually in foreign policy with England, France, and other powerful countries whose influence was feared by the leaders of the national government.

As disenchantment with the Articles of Confederation grew, states authorized delegates to meet to draft amendments. After an awkward start, the delegates at the 1787 Constitutional Convention ultimately decided to scrap the Articles of Confederation completely and instead propose a new Constitution, consisting of seven articles, for state ratification. Among other things, the new Constitution methodically responded in an almost checklist fashion to perceived defects in the Articles of Confederation. For example, the first power the framers gave to the new Congress was the power "To lay and collect Taxes." And the new document explicitly forbade the states to "enter into any Treaty, Alliance, or Confederation."

While they were at it, the framers also expressly forbade the new national government from engaging in many of the activities practiced by the despised English monarchy or their colonial representatives. As the following sections explain, the framers had certain specific areas of rights and governmental organization they felt needed to be addressed. They did so in pointed, though brief, fashion.

Understanding the Constitution's Key Features

The U.S. Constitution has certain key features that distinguish it from the constitutions of other countries (or even, for some of its key features, from those of U.S. states). In general, you can split these features into three categories: characteristics of the document itself, features relating to government power, and features pertaining to rights of the people. Different observers may disagree about the number and relative importance of these features, but we think all the following aspects belong on the short list. (We discuss several of these features in detail in Chapter 4, which covers the structure of the federal government.)

Setting up the document

The way the U.S. Constitution positions itself, words its provisions, and provides for its amendment set it apart from many other constitutions around the world (and even from some state constitutions):

✔ **Constitutional supremacy:** In the U.S., the provisions of the Constitution are the "supreme law of the land" and the ultimate benchmark for judging the validity of all laws adopted by Congress — and, indeed, all actions by government officials at the national, state, and local level.

Relatively few countries — and even relatively few democracies — give their constitutions that power. For example, although England and the other former commonwealth countries have deeply rooted democratic traditions and are moving toward constitutional supremacy as part of European Union membership, these countries still emphasize "parliamentary supremacy." Under this theory, the laws passed by a country's legislature are preeminent, and their legality or constitutionality can't be questioned.

✔ **Relatively brief and general provisions:** Compared to the more modern constitutions of other countries and most American states, the provisions of the U.S. Constitution allocating governmental power and establishing individual rights are quite brief and general. This brevity fuels the ongoing issues about constitutional interpretation that we highlight in Chapter 2 and throughout this book. For instance, as you see in Chapter 8, the Supreme Court decided a number of cases turning the brief and general constitutional language guaranteeing that "life, liberty, and property" not be deprived "without due process of law" into detailed specifications for constitutionally adequate notice and hearings and powerful protections for some liberty rights related to privacy. In so doing, the Court has triggered some of the biggest fights over the legitimacy of its rulings.

As one of many examples of its relative brevity and generality, the U.S. Constitution has three short provisions addressing taxation. In a single sentence, Article I, Section 8 gives Congress the power "To lay and collect Taxes, Duties, Imposts, and Excises." Article I, Section 9 prohibits Congress from taxing exports from any state. And the Sixteenth Amendment clarifies that the requirement in Article I that federal taxes be "uniform" does not rule out the current method of federal income taxation. Even though thousands of pages of law govern federal taxation, these details reside in tax statutes passed by Congress, regulations and other guidance issued by the Internal Revenue Service, and judicial decisions construing those statutes and regulations.

By contrast, the 105-page California Constitution contains 32 articles, running some 18 pages, specifying a variety of details about state taxation. A California constitutional provision even provides special rules for the taxation of fruit and nut trees.

✓ **A relatively stable, but still changeable, constitution:** Article V of the U.S. Constitution allows the document to be amended only when a supermajority supports constitutional change over a sustained time period. Specifically, it takes two-thirds margins either in Congress or in the states to propose an amendment, which must then be ratified by three-fourths of the states.

Requiring sustained support for constitutional change promotes the stability and supremacy of the Constitution. Constitutional values are immunized from normal majoritarian upheavals and short-term political pressures (a major reason why only 27 amendments have been created in our 220-plus years of experience with the Constitution). On the other hand, if the Constitution were not amendable (or, like the Articles of Confederation, could be amended only when the states *unanimously* concurred), pressures for change would eventually build up to the point where scrapping the existing Constitution in lieu of a new one would seem to be the only viable alternative. (After all, this is why the Articles of Confederation were ended, not amended, in 1789!)

The difficulty of amending the Constitution

In the 220-plus years since the framers replaced the Articles of Confederation with the Constitution, only 27 amendments have been adopted. Ten of these (the Bill of Rights) were adopted in one installment in 1791, and the remaining 17 were adopted between 1794 and 1992.

Some indication of the difficulty of adopting constitutional amendments is shown by the very low percentage of proposed amendments adopted. As many as 200 amendments are proposed in each two-year congressional term. Few, if any, of these proposals even make it out of a congressional committee — much less receive the two-thirds vote margin necessary to propose them for state ratification.

Another dimension of the difficulty of amending the Constitution is the number of high-profile and initially popular amendment proposals ending up in the dustbin of constitutional history. These scrapped proposals include a 1924 amendment that would have abolished child labor and the 1972 equal-rights amendment that would have explicitly prohibited gender discrimination. Over 300 amendments to overturn or significantly cut back on abortion rights recognized in *Roe v. Wade* have never made it out of Congress.

Yet the experience with the most recent constitutional amendment shows that good things come to those who wait. The Twenty-Seventh Amendment, which limits the power of members of Congress to raise their own salaries, was adopted 202 years after its initial proposal in 1790. (Most modern amendments put a time limit on ratification, but older amendments may not. It is, for example, theoretically possible that the 1924 child labor amendment could be adopted some day.)

Dividing and allocating government power

The U.S. Constitution is majorly concerned with how governmental power is allocated among competing power centers. It is not surprising, therefore, that the following key features of the Constitution relate to who exercises what governmental powers and what safeguards prevent abuse of government powers:

- ✔ **Popular sovereignty (power from the people):** The constitutional plan proposed in 1789 assumed that the true source of political power was the American people. As any school child knows, the preamble to the Constitution begins with the phrase "We the People . . . do ordain and establish this Constitution. . . ." The manner in which Articles I, II, and III proceed to vest legislative, executive, and judicial powers in the relevant institutions also emphasizes how power originates with the American people. The *vesting* metaphor implies that the people are the principal power holders, temporarily loaning power to act on their behalf to legislators, the president, and federal judges.

  This concept of "people power" may seem commonplace today. But it was radical in 1789, when political power was thought to originate from God, from divinely inspired kings, or from competing warlords.

- ✔ **Separation of national government powers:** Again departing from many of the world's democracies and other governments, the Constitution's framers separated legislative from executive functions (and judicial functions from both, for good measure). In most parliamentary government systems, by contrast, the political party or parties in the legislative majority also run the executive branch. Changing the status quo in a parliamentary democracy is easier than in the U.S., but power is concentrated.

  As you can see from our more detailed discussion on power allocation in Chapters 5 and 6, power concentration was something the U.S. Constitution's framers feared. Their decision to separate national powers and provide multiple means for the three federal government branches to "check and balance" each other generated ongoing disputes about divvying up a wide range of domestic and foreign-affairs powers.

- ✔ **Federalism:** Another key feature of the U.S. constitutional system is *federalism* — the system in which a strong national government shares powers with a competing level of strong state governments, headed by political officials chosen from different constituencies and reflecting different sets of interests. Again, federalist systems are relatively rare among the world's political systems. More common, even in populous democracies, is a system in which a strong central government is the main authority. This system doesn't face strong competing subnational political units; at most, one or more large cities exercise substantial powers delegated by the national government.

  The framers' decision to allocate power in a federalistic manner generated extensive disputes about the scope and limits of national-government power (as we cover in Chapter 5) and ongoing efforts to protect states' rights (the subject of Chapter 7).

Protecting people's rights

The entire Constitution (and the key features discussed in the preceding section) ultimately aims to protect the rights and liberties of the American people. "We the people" are the ultimate beneficiaries, for example, of assuring the Constitution's stability over time and limiting federal-government power.

The following three other key features of the Constitution are even more directly related to the rights of individuals and groups of citizens:

- ✔ **The rule of law:** The U.S. Constitution embodies "equal justice under law," a concept related to (but broader than) constitutional supremacy. This ideal, certainly not always realized in practice, holds that every American should be treated the same by government officials, regardless of their race, gender, income status, religion, or party affiliation. This commitment that America be "a nation of laws and not of men" (and women) assumes that governmental authorities will apply the same neutral legal principles in all similar cases. The commitment to equality under law has influenced many areas of constitutional interpretation, including the body of case law preventing governments from acting arbitrarily (as discussed in Chapter 8) or discriminating on the basis of race or gender (as detailed in Chapter 10).

- ✔ **Balancing majority rule and minority protection:** The governmental system established by the U.S. Constitution generally assumes that public policy should be what a majority of citizens wants. This commitment to majority rule is reflected in the commonplace constitutional provisions as to how a bill becomes a law. Ordinarily, a majority of legislators in the House and Senate (each of whom is, in turn, chosen by a majority of voters) can adopt legislation that becomes "the law of the land" with the active approval or at least grudging acquiescence of the president (also usually reflective of an electoral majority).

Still, the U.S. Constitution balances this strong commitment to majority rule in several important ways:

- • Several supermajority requirements — for example, two-thirds vote margins for convicting officeholders of impeachable offenses, for overriding presidential vetoes, and for proposing constitutional amendments — give a determined minority the power to hold up significant action.

- • The Constitution (and especially the post-1789 amendments) significantly departs from majority rule by enshrining constitutional protections for unpopular minorities (such as criminal defendants) and equipping an independent, life-tenured federal judiciary to declare unconstitutional actions taken in the name of a strong majority. (Chapter 6 examines the many interesting and important issues surrounding judicial review and the general interaction among the federal courts, Congress, and the president. And Parts II, III, and IV of this book are full of constitutional rules protecting minority rights — many of which would probably be opposed by a majority of Americans if put to a vote.)

✔ **Negative rights:** The U.S. Constitution generally prohibits governmental officials from doing bad things rather than requiring them to do good things. Unlike most modern constitutions of other countries, the U.S. Constitution is not a source of positive benefits or rights that Americans can expect from their government. You will not find in the U.S. Constitution a requirement that governments actively promote access to healthcare, guaranteed employment or housing, or any of the many positive guarantees associated with the modern welfare state. Instead, the Constitution gives the national government the power to create positive benefits if the people demand them from their officials.

Most of the individual-rights provisions added to the Constitution after 1789 are phrased in the negative. (For example, governments may not abridge freedom of speech or deny equal protection of the laws). Even rights seemingly phrased in the positive boil down to prohibitions on governmental *interference* rather than an affirmative requirement that government spend money or otherwise act to assure the effective exercise of the right. (For example, for most of the time since its adoption in 1791, the Sixth-Amendment provision giving defendants "the assistance of counsel" merely meant that government could not thwart participation by counsel a defendant could afford to hire on his own. Only in the last several decades has a limited right to government-provided counsel been afforded to indigent defendants.)

The daring framers: Turning a philosopher's dream into a constitutional cornerstone

Until the American Constitution framers used the separation of powers as the key organizing principle for the federal government, it was mainly an Enlightenment-era philosopher's good idea. Specifically, it was a theory popularized by French social critic and political thinker Charles-Louis de Secondat, generally referred to as *Montesquieu*. Montesquieu's multivolume treatise published in the 1740s proposed separation of powers as an antidote to the corrupting tendencies he found inherent in various forms of government.

That the American framers were willing to stake the success of the national government on an idea that had not been tried on a large scale or in the modern era is some indicator of their visionary thinking and risk-taking propensities.

Appreciating the Five Main Topics Addressed by the Constitution

Even though the U.S. Constitution is usually thought of and printed as one document, its various provisions really address five distinct topics. Your understanding of the Constitution and the law that has sprung up around it will benefit from the following discussion, which identifies and elaborates a bit on these five main topics:

- ✔ **The seven articles:** Proposed in 1789 and ratified by the states in 1789, the articles establish a powerful, but also limited, national government and rules for the states.

- ✔ **The Bill of Rights:** Proposed as a package in 1789 by the first Congress to meet under the new Constitution, these first ten amendments establish important individual rights and declare two important principles about how the Constitution works.

- ✔ **The great post–Civil War amendments:** Ratified in 1868, the Thirteenth, Fourteenth, and Fifteenth Amendments abolish slavery and establish rights for newly freed slaves.

- ✔ **Voting-rights amendments:** The Seventeenth, Nineteenth, Twenty-Third, Twenty-Fourth, and Twenty-Sixth Amendments, ratified from 1913 to 1971, expand voting rights by establishing certain groups' rights to vote.

- ✔ **Other amendments altering political procedures and power arrangements:** The other nine amendments (ratified as long ago as 1795 and as recently as 1992) reform other electoral and political practices or "clean up" perceived problems with previous constitutional provisions and interpretations.

In later chapters you get acquainted with the details of many of these constitutional provisions and amendments. For now, we want you to get familiar with the overall lay of the constitutional land.

Although almost every school-age child memorizes the preamble to the Constitution, it isn't considered a distinct topic. The preamble helps point to the intent of other constitutional provisions and memorably notes the framers' intent to "form a more perfect Union, establish Justice, insure domestic Tranquility, provide for the common defence, promote the general Welfare, and secure the Blessings of Liberty to ourselves and our Posterity." However, it isn't an independent source of legally enforceable rights. It's probably a good thing for some national officials that they can't be sued for sowing disunion or detracting from our "domestic Tranquility!"

Hardly a slam-dunk: The tough and contentious fight to ratify the new Constitution

Because of its enduring power, the Constitution is sometimes mistakenly thought to be the product of an easy and obvious ratification process. Yet the fight to establish a substantially more powerful federal government was anything but easy. Shortly after the new constitutional plan was unveiled, a determined and brilliant group called the *Antifederalists* organized to oppose ratification. They wrote strong anonymous essays, published in colonial newspapers, comprehensively critiquing the proposed constitutional plan and warning that the new federal government would become too powerful. These criticisms were answered by leading constitutional proponents Alexander Hamilton, James Madison, and John Jay, in a series of 85 anonymous essays later collected as the *Federalist Papers.* (Modern Constitution interpreters often turn to these essays to determine "the intent of the framers," as we discuss in Chapter 2.)

The debate at the ratification conventions and in pamphlets and newspaper columns was heated. And the vote margins in some key states were very close. For example, a switch of 2 votes among New York's 57 delegates would've defeated that key state's ratification drive. Had 6 out of 168 delegates voted differently in the largest state, Virginia, the constitutional adoption drive would've been mortally wounded.

Even more interesting is that New York's close vote was achieved only by a promise that the first Congress meeting under the new Constitution would immediately set to work to adopt a bill of rights to limit the new government's potential to abuse individual liberties. In a very real sense, the promised amendments saved the day in a very fractious period.

The original seven articles: Establishing a new national government

The Constitution of 1789 consisted only of seven articles, with a variety of provisions. The first three articles establish a new national government composed of the familiar three branches (legislative, executive, and judicial). The fourth article sets forth how the states are to function with respect to each other and to the new national government in the new constitutional order. The remaining three articles establish the supremacy and legitimacy of the new Constitution.

Planting a strong federal oak with three branches (Articles 1–III)

The framers proposing their bold constitutional experiment in 1787 intended to create a substantially more powerful, but nevertheless meaningfully limited, national governing entity. Both of these goals can be seen in the first three constitutional articles, which establish and empower governmental structures to exercise legislative, executive, and judicial powers sufficient to carry out the new duties entrusted to the federal government. But the very division of the federal government into three separate and competing branches (and further splits of authority *within* the legislative and judicial branches) shows how the framers wanted to prevent governmental authority from becoming too concentrated (and, hence, too powerful).

The first three articles of the Constitution share significant things in common. They each begin with an initial section placing a portion of national-government power (legislative, executive, and judicial) in a different branch (the House and Senate, the president, and the federal courts). They then grant specific powers to the established branch, while imposing limitations on those powers.

Each of the three articles also protects the independence of the branch it establishes in two ways:

✔ First, each of the articles protects the branch it creates from retaliation by the others. For example, members of Congress can't be put in jail or required to pay damages for slanderous official statements, and Congress is disabled from reducing presidential or federal-judge salaries.

✔ Second, each of the articles provides ways for the branch it creates to check and balance the other two branches. Congress can, for example, impeach the president, other executive branch officials, or federal judges. The president, in turn, can veto legislation passed by Congress and pardon persons convicted in federal courts.

Prescribing state-to-state and state-to-federal government relationships (Article IV)

The pre-1789 world involved states relating to, and often competing with, each other in a loose confederation. Merely introducing a new federal government into the mix created issues about how the states would relate to the big new kid on the block. Beyond that, the framers of the new Constitution included provisions to reform state-to-state relationships.

To deal with how states would relate to the new federal government, Article IV protects existing states from having their boundaries changed without their permission and provides a mechanism for the admission of new states (Section 3). Article IV also obligates the new federal government to protect states from invasion by foreigners or Native Americans or domestic unrest within state borders, and to guarantee the states "a Republican Form of Government" (that is, one broadly representative of majority will).

The general lack of "individual rights" provisions in the Constitution of 1789

You would be forgiven if you associate *constitutional* with protection of individual rights. Most modern students are more familiar with the Constitution as a protector of freedom or against discrimination than as an allocator of government power.

So constitutional-law students are sometimes surprised that establishing individual rights was not a key concern to the framers drafting the constitutional reform proposal of 1789. True, the original seven articles did include a few important individual liberties. For example, Article I prevents Congress from suspending the *writ of habeas*

corpus (a centuries-old English protection against arbitrary incarceration) and forbids both federal and state legislatures from passing *ex post facto* laws (that is, laws that unfairly go back in time and make something illegal that was legal when the defendant engaged in it). Article I also forbids state governments from impairing contract obligations; we cover the modern cases interpreting this important individual-liberty protection in Chapter 9.

Still, the vast majority of important individual-rights protections normally associated with the Constitution came after the original seven articles were adopted.

Article IV also addresses the pre-1789 problem of state-versus-state conflict. Article IV obligates each state to give "Full Faith and Credit to the public Acts, Records, and judicial Proceedings" of other states (Section 1), to grant out-of-state citizens "all Privileges and Immunities" a state provides to its own citizens (Section 2), and to return runaway slaves and fleeing felons to the state with a legal claim on them (also Section 2).

Promoting the supremacy and legitimacy of the new government and Constitution (Articles V–VII)

The last three articles of the initial Constitution contain several provisions addressing issues of federal and constitutional supremacy and legitimacy. To go a bit out of numerical order, the most important and direct of the supremacy provisions is the *supremacy clause* of Article VI, Clause 2. A single sentence declares three critical propositions:

- ✔ The Constitution is "the supreme Law of the Land" — trumping contrary provisions in state constitutions or laws.

- ✔ Federal laws and treaties (and, by later extension, administrative regulations adopted under federal laws) must also be consistent with the Constitution; if they are, they also trump state constitutions and laws.

- ✔ State judges are specifically required to enforce federal supremacy. The framers fully expected, and the modern reality bears out, that federal legal issues often arise and are vindicated in state proceedings with little or no involvement by the federal judiciary.

Other important provisions in the last three articles accomplish the supremacy and legitimacy of the federal government and new Constitution less directly:

- The relatively brief Article V provides two alternatives by which constitutional amendments can be *proposed* and two options for state *ratification* (that is, approval) of proposed amendments. Making it quite difficult but not impossible to amend the Constitution promotes the Constitution's supremacy (by making it largely immune from the politics and whims of temporary majorities) and legitimacy (by providing a mechanism for fundamental constitutional change when a supermajority consensus lasts over time).

- Article VI, Clause 1 states that the new government assumes all debts and prior engagements of the previous Articles of Confederation government. (After all, how legitimate would the new national government be if it shirked its predecessor's obligations?)

- Article VI, Clause 3 requires that all legislative, executive, and judicial officials of the national and state governments take oaths to support the new Constitution (and, therefore, the new national government it establishes).

- Article VII declares that the new Constitution became effective when two-thirds (9) of the 13 states ratified it. This requirement establishes the legitimacy of the new government by setting a requirement of supermajority support while at the same time fixing the old Articles of Confederation problem of requiring unanimity for constitutional change. (In reality, the Constitution's supporters did not just declare victory when they reached the 9-state margin; they pressed for and achieved ratification by all 13 original states.)

A meaningful difference among Articles I, II, and III

Articles I, II, and III differ significantly in their length and detail. In creating, empowering, and limiting Congress, Article I is the most extensive and detailed. Article II uses substantially less detail and verbiage in creating the presidency and executive branch, and the Article III provisions creating the federal judiciary are even more sketchy.

This difference reflects both the framers' perception that the legislative branch would be the most powerful and important one and the greater difficulty the framers had in achieving consensus about the design of the presidency and the federal courts. Indeed, until late in the Constitutional Convention the framers weren't sure that the new government needed lower federal courts. Many framers thought it would be enough to have state courts enforce federal legal rules under the supervision of the United States Supreme Court — the only federal court actually created by the Constitution.

The pragmatic framers: Fashioning protections against abuse

The framers of the Constitution of 1787 were not just big-picture visionaries. They were also savvy observers of the capacity of political officials to abuse power and act in self-serving ways, and they made sure that the Constitution would prevent some of that bad behavior.

For example, the framers penned several provisions dealing with financial abuse and conflict of interest. Article I, Section 6 prohibits any member of Congress from being appointed to an executive office that was created or given a salary increase during the member's legislative service. This provision obviously prevents legislative self-dealing, by preventing a powerful legislator from feathering his or her own nest. But, more subtly, the provision also helps legislators resist temptation from legislative leaders and the president, who might offer plum appointments as the price for supportive votes.

The constitutional-amendment provisions of Article V are a great example of how the pragmatic framers imposed more subtle, interlocking protections against a different kind of power abuse. Recognizing that the Congress would be unlikely to propose constitutional amendments undermining legislative powers, the framers provided a mechanism by which the states could hotwire around an uncooperative Congress (that is, by calling for a constitutional convention). Similarly, the framers recognized that state legislatures would not likely ratify constitutional amendments running contrary to their narrow power interests. That appears to be why the framers empowered Congress to choose to have constitutional amendments ratified in state conventions rather than in state legislative halls.

The Bill of Rights: Ten amendments against federal tyranny

Early in their efforts to secure ratification of the 1789 constitutional proposal, supporters ran into strong states-rights-based suspicions that the new federal government would become an instrument of oppression. A bill of rights was needed, skeptics argued, to guard against this abuse.

Initially, Constitution supporters argued that a bill of rights was unnecessary, dangerous, or both. The bill of rights was unnecessary, the argument went, because the federal government was limited to its enumerated powers. (Because nowhere in the Article I powers of Congress or elsewhere were any officials given power to suppress the rights of American citizens, disclaiming such a right was seen by some to be unnecessary.) Opponents of a bill of rights also argued that trying to list rights that could not be abridged by the federal government would create the dangerous implication that rights not listed were not intended to be protected and, therefore, could be suppressed!

Whatever the logic of these arguments, it became clear that several key states would not ratify the Constitution without a promise that a strong and detailed bill of rights would be added to the new Constitution as a series of amendments. Showing their practical streak once again, key framers (the most important of whom was James Madison) switched from being bill-of-rights opponents to instrumental players in the drafting and passage of the first ten amendments.

After months of successive rounds of committee drafts, congressional debates, and state-ratification deliberations, the Bill of Rights was added to the Constitution's original seven articles. We devote several chapters of this book to fully detailing the landmark cases and constitutional rules generated by its provisions, so for now we just provide a bare-bones breakdown of the protected rights and understandings, organized in three categories.

Protecting key civil rights and liberties against federal government encroachment

In order of their appearance in the new Bill of Rights amendments (ratified in 1791), the Constitution:

- ✔ Prohibits laws "respecting an establishment of religion" (First Amendment)

- ✔ Prevents laws prohibiting "the free exercise" of religion (First Amendment)

- ✔ Forbids restriction of "the freedom of speech, or of the press" (First Amendment)

- ✔ Outlaws impairing the rights of Americans to assemble "peaceably" and to petition government for "redress of grievances" (First Amendment)

- ✔ Protects the "right of the people to keep and bear Arms" (Second Amendment)

- ✔ Prevents Americans from being forced to give room and board to soldiers (Third Amendment)

- ✔ Prohibits depriving persons of "life, liberty, or property, without due process of law" (Fifth Amendment)

- ✔ Forbids the confiscation of private property for public use "without just compensation" (Fifth Amendment)

- ✔ Protects rights relating to trial by jury in civil cases (Seventh Amendment)

Preventing abuse of the criminal justice power

The Bill of Rights also obligates federal law-enforcement officials to afford distinct but interlocking protections to criminal suspects. Again, in numerical order, the Bill of Rights:

✔ Bans "unreasonable searches and seizures" and requires "probable cause" for search warrants (Fourth Amendment)

✔ Requires indictment by a grand jury before prosecution can begin for a capital or "otherwise infamous" crime (Fifth Amendment)

✔ Forbids "double jeopardy" (essentially, retrying a defendant "for the same offense" after having been found innocent) (Fifth Amendment)

✔ Outlaws self-incrimination (Fifth Amendment)

✔ Requires "speedy and public" trials (Sixth Amendment)

✔ Assures defendants of an impartial jury in the state and district where the crime was committed (Sixth Amendment)

✔ Requires that defendants be informed of accusations against them and be able to confront adverse witnesses and subpoena favorable ones (Sixth Amendment)

✔ Mandates that people accused of crimes "have the assistance of counsel" for their defense (Sixth Amendment)

✔ Forbids excessive bail and fines and "cruel and unusual punishments" (Eighth Amendment)

Clarifying important understandings about rights

The last two amendments in the Bill of Rights don't specify rights to be protected. The Ninth and Tenth Amendments instead act more like "rules of the road" for rights interpretation.

Specifically, the Ninth Amendment directly addresses the concern of the original Bill of Rights opponents that specifying some rights would inevitably leave others out in the cold. The Ninth Amendment reads in its entirety as follows: "The enumeration in the Constitution, of certain rights, shall not be construed to deny or disparage others retained by the people." Thus, the Ninth Amendment presupposes that Americans enjoy other "natural rights" or implied fundamental rights beyond those expressly stated in the previous eight amendments or elsewhere in the Constitution.

Despite the clear intent of the Ninth Amendment to recognize non-express (implied) constitutional rights, the modern Court has not generally relied on the amendment when it has recognized implied rights. Some observers say that the Court doesn't rely on it because although the Ninth Amendment clarifies that there *are* implied rights beyond those textually stated, it doesn't explain *which* rights are preserved or even *which standards* to use in identifying them.

Slavery: One very important omission in the initial constitutional plan

In at least one sense, the Constitution's seven articles and the Bill of Rights are noteworthy for what they did *not* do — resolve deep-seated divisions over the keeping of human beings as slaves (primarily, but not completely, in the Southern states).

Despite the obvious inconsistency between slavery and the ringing phrase in the Declaration of Independence that "all men are created equal," the framers couldn't resolve the political stalemate over this hot-button issue. They therefore contented themselves with preserving the status quo (existing state of affairs).

Article I, Section 9 of the Constitution gave the federal government the power to abolish the importation of slaves — but not until 1808. Article IV obligated states to return runaway slaves to their masters. And the most callous-seeming provision relating to slavery is the "three-fifths" compromise of Article I, Section 2, which counts slaves as worth three-fifths of a free person for purposes of taxation and representation in the House of Representatives.

Instead, implied rights have been recognized on bases other than the Ninth Amendment. Chapter 13 shows how the Court has used Fifth- and Fourteenth-Amendment rights to "equal protection of the laws" to afford strong protection to fundamental implied rights to vote. Chapter 14 demonstrates that the Court strongly protects implied rights to privacy under the distinct "due process of law" language of these amendments.

The Tenth Amendment says that any powers not delegated to the federal government are given to state governments. This amendment may just clarify what's already implicit in the Constitution's approach to federal-government authority (as explored in Chapter 5). But the fact that the framers went to the trouble to emphasize residual state powers in the Bill of Rights shows the importance they placed on preserving strong state governments. (In Chapter 7, we detail the various judicial doctrines designed to protect the role of states as important policymakers in the American system.)

The Tenth Amendment ends by emphasizing that powers the Constitution does not grant to the national government yet specifically denies to the states are "reserved . . . to the people." Again, given the way the Constitution allocates power, this feature may be implicit and obvious, but its explicit inclusion in the Bill of Rights provides yet another reminder of the importance the framers placed on popular sovereignty (which, as noted earlier, is the principle that political power originates from the American people).

The great post–Civil War amendments: Limiting state governments

Before the Civil War, the U.S. Constitution was largely a scheme for establishing and controlling national power. But a major cause — if not *the* major cause — of the Civil War was the fight between Southern slave owners and Northern abolitionists. In the immediate aftermath of the Civil War, therefore, abolishing slavery and preventing the defeated slave-owning states from perpetuating racial discrimination became the focus of three constitutional amendments, acceptance of which became the price of readmission to the Union of the defeated Southern states.

As Chapter 10 explains, these Civil War Amendments continue to provide important protection for the voting and other rights of racial minorities. And, as Chapter 8 points out, the due-process clause in one of these amendments has become the basis for expanding to state and local governments almost all the individual-liberties protections of the Bill of Rights.

A detail of the post–Civil War amendments that's critical to the evolution of modern antidiscrimination law is that each of the amendments ends with a section giving Congress "the power to enforce, by appropriate legislation" the amendment's protections. This power makes the Congress a potential co-partner in establishing and perfecting constitutional protections. In fact, in the areas of school desegregation and voting rights, landmark congressional statutes have been more instrumental in ending discrimination as a practical matter than Court decisions have.

Prohibiting slavery

In one brief but profound sentence, the Thirteenth Amendment abolishes slavery and involuntary servitude in the United States. (Interestingly, the Thirteen Amendment is one of the few constitutional provisions interpreted to apply to private, nongovernmental behavior. As a result, it has some potential application to employer sweatshops and other extreme private working arrangements.)

Preventing mistreatment of newly freed slaves — and of many other Americans

The Fourteenth Amendment includes some one-time provisions designed to reintegrate the rebellious Southern states into the Union. For example, Section 3 prohibits persons from holding federal office if they violated a previous oath to support the Constitution; Section 4 deals with Civil War debts.

The lasting legacy of this amendment, however, are its broadly phrased provisions seeking to prevent state governments (and all local-government units operating under state authority) from perpetuating the racially discriminatory practices that had accompanied American slavery. In the modern era, these provisions have bloomed into robust and multifaceted protections against race discrimination. Beyond that, the modern Court and many public officials have used two Fourteenth Amendment provisions to erect numerous protections transcending the race-discrimination context. Specifically, the Fourteenth Amendment accomplishes the following:

- ✔ **It makes "all persons born or naturalized in the Unites States" citizens of the U.S. and the state in which they reside.** Originally intended to make freed slaves citizens, this language has become controversial in a different context, as a source of "birthright citizenship" for the children of undocumented aliens.

- ✔ **It forbids a state from making or enforcing a law "which shall abridge the privileges or immunities of citizens of the United States."** This language was a potentially fertile basis for making states give their citizens all the individual protections the Constitution requires from the national government. Narrow judicial readings of the language in the early post-ratification period, however, stunted this potential growth.

- ✔ **It prevents a state from depriving "any person of life, liberty, or property, without due process of law."** As Chapter 8 details, this due-process clause protects important procedural and substantive rights on its own say-so; further, the clause's protection of "liberty" also provides the basis for judicial decisions applying most of the Bill of Rights to state and local governments.

- ✔ **It outlaws state denials of "equal protection of the laws."** The source of strong modern protections against racial discrimination (including in affirmative-action programs), the equal-protection clause has spawned important barriers to other kinds of discrimination, including that based on gender, alienage, and paternal legitimacy.

Protecting minorities' right to vote

The Fifteenth Amendment, the last great post–Civil War amendment, focuses on protecting the voting rights of the newly freed slaves and other racial minorities. The Reconstruction Congress recognized that the best ongoing protection against state and local officials reverting to their old racist ways would be to make their political futures dependent in part upon the electoral muscle of racial minorities.

Voting-rights amendments: Expanding voting rights in other ways

Five later constitutional amendments expand voting rights by giving previously disenfranchised voters the right to vote or by eliminating practices standing in the way of their fully exercising voting power. In chronological order, these amendments of the Constitution

- ✔ Provide that U.S. Senators are chosen directly by their state's voters in general elections, rather than the previous practice of having Senators chosen by state legislatures (Seventeenth Amendment; 1913)

- ✔ Grant women the right to vote (Nineteenth Amendment; 1920)

- ✔ Give residents of the District of Columbia the right to name three electors, whose votes help elect the president and vice president (Twenty-Third Amendment; 1961)

- ✔ Prevent government from conditioning the right to vote in federal elections on payment of a "poll tax or other tax," eliminating a practice that some states used to indirectly deny African Americans and other minorities the right to vote due to their inability to pay the tax (Twenty-Fourth Amendment; 1964)

- ✔ Lower the voting age in federal and state elections to 18 (Twenty-Sixth Amendment; 1971)

Other amendments reforming political procedures or power arrangements

A variety of other constitutional amendments adjust power arrangements, especially between federal and state governments. Several of these power-altering amendments fix problems created by Court interpretations of other constitutional provisions, and one amendment cleans up problems from a previous constitutional amendment. Two of these nine amendments were adopted a few years after ratification of the Bill of Rights; the remainder was ratified during various reform periods in the 20th century.

All these amendments share a common theme of altering politics and power. And all these amendments show the ability of Americans to learn from experience (and sometimes from past constitutional mistakes).

Changing presidential elections

Four amendments reform perceived problems in the election of the president. This set of amendments makes the following changes:

- **Provides for the separate election of the president and vice president (Twelfth Amendment; 1804):** This amendment prevents a repetition of earlier, awkward elections in which the president and vice president were from different political parties (1796) and an upstart candidate almost took the presidency from his party's leader (1800).

- **Moves up the date on which a newly elected president assumes office (Twentieth Amendment; 1933):** This change reduces the time in which a "lame duck" current president who has not been reelected can continue to pursue policies that may not be representative of current political preferences.

- **Limits any president to two terms of office (Twenty-Second Amendment; 1951):** Although crucial to American recovery from the Great Depression of the 1930s and victory in World War II in the 1940s, Franklin Roosevelt's four terms as president created concerns that a popular president could extend his hold on power longer than is good for American democracy.

- **Provides for an orderly process for replacing a sitting president or vice president who dies or resigns in office or for temporarily replacing a president unable to fulfill presidential duties (Twenty-Fifth Amendment; 1967):** Cleaning up some ambiguities in the Constitution's Article II, this amendment provides that the vice president takes over in the case of presidential death, resignation or temporary incapacity; that a vacancy in the office of vice president can be filled by the president subject to congressional approval; and that the vice president and a majority of the cabinet can certify that the president is temporarily unable to serve, in which case the vice president takes over in the interim.

Limiting congressional prerogatives

The most recent amendment to the Constitution was proposed early in the country's founding but wasn't ratified until by 1992 by the requisite number of states. The Twenty-Seventh Amendment prevents members of Congress from raising their salaries until the voters have had a chance to react to proposed salary increases at the next election for members of the House.

Adjusting federal and state powers

Four amendments alter federal government powers, directly or indirectly affecting the balance of power between federal and state governments. This group of amendments

✔ **Reduces the ability of litigants to sue state governments in federal court (Eleventh Amendment; 1795):** Interestingly, this amendment directly reverses an early and unpopular Supreme Court decision.

✔ **Allows Congress to impose a federal income tax, even if state-by-state wealth differences mean that it is not apportioned by population (Sixteenth Amendment; 1913):** This amendment also reverses a Supreme Court decision invalidating a previous income tax as unconstitutional.

✔ **Established a national "Prohibition" policy banning "the manufacture, sale, or transportation of intoxicating liquors" (Eighteenth Amendment; 1919):** Leaders of the post–World War I temperance movement grew annoyed with the slow pace of nonconstitutional reform efforts and so pushed through this experiment in substantive national policy by constitutional amendment.

✔ **Repealed Prohibition and gave state governments special powers to regulate alcohol use within their jurisdictions (Twenty-First Amendment; 1933):** This amendment brought to a close America's 14-year experiment with alcohol prohibition. The policy, which did little to reduce alcohol abuse and sparked the growth of organized crime, is widely regarded as a failure — although some revisionist analysts disagree. Although Americans regularly propose constitutional amendments to adopt seemingly necessary social policies, opponents argue that experience with the Eighteenth and Twenty-First Amendments provides a cautionary tale about the inflexibility and wrongheadedness of this method.

Chapter 2

Constitutional Law: A View from 30,000 Feet

....

....

*E*ven students with a good grasp of the Constitution's historical background, key features, and main topics aren't yet ready to dive into the details of the law involving the document. To help you get started, in this chapter we take you on a flight over the constitutional-law landscape. So buckle your seat belt, and we'll cruise at a high enough altitude to get the big picture of some key territories. If you're a student in a constitutional-law course, it will likely cover at least some of these topics directly. But beyond helping you get through a class, this orientation shows how to bring an all-important multidimensional approach, involving both legal and nonlegal aspects, to every constitutional doctrine you study.

Seeing how the Constitution's legal and nonlegal facets interact prepares you for the nuanced approach professors usually bring to the subject. Being forewarned, you won't make the mistakes many students and other Americans make by naïvely assuming that constitutional law is an objective exercise in purely legal reasoning under an agreed-upon approach (such as "strict construction") to constitutional interpretation. Nor will you reduce constitutional law to "just politics."

Another misconception you have a chance to shed is that constitutional law is something only judges practice. Certainly, judges (especially the U.S. Supreme Court Justices) have the most impact on how constitutional powers and rights develop. But nonjudicial officials, from the president of the United States and the Congress down to the local cop on the beat, invoke and impact constitutional law as part of their duties. And millions of Americans without official titles are regularly called upon to vote and otherwise act based on their best understanding of the Constitution.

This chapter also acquaints you with the major difficulties in interpreting the Constitution. You see that, although a number of interpretive theories have been tested over the Constitution's 220-plus year run, two competing theories are the main contenders today. We cover these dueling theories, originalism and the evolving-Constitution theory, in some depth.

Substantial uncertainty and controversy now and probably always will attend the core question "How should the Constitution be interpreted?" But with the overview in this chapter, you can hit the ground running in understanding constitutional law in class and in your everyday life.

Getting to Know the "Law" Part of Constitutional Law

You may think it's a little obvious to begin with the observation that constitutional law is significantly about, well, law. Yet constitutional decision making — even when practiced by life-tenured, relatively apolitical federal judges — is often characterized as simply an extension of the ongoing political fights between liberals and conservatives and among Democrats, Republicans, Greens, Tea Partiers, and other partisans. As we openly admit in the next section, constitutional law includes substantial aspects of policy and politics. However, you need to understand at the outset that it is not just politics. *Law* informs constitutional law at three levels:

✔ **The U.S. Constitution presents judges and others with words to be read in light of various accepted rules of construction.** When constitutional interpretations make their way into judicial decisions or opinions from other public officials (such as the U.S. Attorney General and state attorneys general), *stare decisis,* the legal system's assumption that precedents will be followed unless formally overruled, kicks in. *Stare decisis* means that no constitutional interpreter — not a Supreme Court Justice, nor the president, nor the House majority leader — is free to simply ignore agreed understandings about the Constitution or past judicial precedents in the interests of "good politics."

✔ **Legal-system assumptions about proper methods and roles may limit constitutional interpreters.** Modern constitutional interpretation reflects certain understandings about when constitutional interpreters should defer to other decision makers or to overarching legal principles. Doctrines of judicial restraint and deference to elected policymakers may, for example, cause a Supreme Court justice with generally conservative leanings to vote to uphold a liberal social policy passed by Congress. So too may a liberal jurist decline to endorse a new constitutional interpretation, even though it would achieve a progressive social result, because of the legal-philosophical norm against disturbing long-settled assumptions about property ownership or expectations written into business contracts.

✔ **Law can constrain pure politics in constitutional interpretation through a legal-system version of peer pressure.** Judges and public officials are members of elite professional communities whose members enforce legal-system norms. Judges care how their judicial colleagues, other public officials, law professors, and the media evaluate their performance (including how they honor judicial precedents and accept the presumed limits on their role). Presidents and legislators want to be seen as on the correct side of the American political culture, including its belief in "the rule of law."

That desire probably explains, for example, why during the political wrangling over raising the federal debt ceiling in summer 2011 President Obama declined to even *threaten* to act alone to ease the crisis. Whatever the political advantages to such a move, which would have required an unorthodox expansion of obscure language in Section 4 of the Fourteenth Amendment (protecting Civil War debts), the president likely worried that going too far out on a constitutional limb would invite criticism — and maybe even impeachment charges — from his political peers.

The norms for following the proper judicial role are not just annoying platitudes judges and other officials give lip service to as they vote their politics. Judicial opinions and political speeches regularly contain examples of people interpreting the Constitution in ways that are contrary to their politics but based on legal constraints. For example, Justice Anthony Kennedy felt such personal distaste in joining a majority of his colleagues to uphold the free-speech rights of protesters burning the American flag, *Texas v. Johnson,* 491 U.S. 397 (1989), that he penned a separate concurring opinion. It stated, "The hard fact is that sometimes we must make decisions we do not like. We make them because they are right, right in the sense that the law and the Constitution, as we see them, compel the result."

The justices' differing views on following precedent

Not all judges (and particularly Supreme Court Justices) adhere to precedent as strictly as you might think. Justice Clarence Thomas is widely regarded as more willing than other justices to abandon the rulings of past cases if he thinks they're wrong. Thomas has reportedly said, "When faced with a clash of constitutional principle and a line of unreasoned cases wholly divorced from the text, history, and structure of our founding document, we should not hesitate to resolve the tension in favor of the Constitution's original meaning" (Jeffrey Toobin, *The Nine: Inside the Secret World of the Supreme Court* [Random House]).

Thomas's position on *stare decisis* sometimes puts him at odds even with Justice Scalia, a fellow conservative and comrade-in-decisions. In Toobin's book, Scalia is quoted as saying, "[Thomas] doesn't believe in *stare decisis,* period [...] if a constitutional line of authority is wrong, he would say let's get it right. I wouldn't do that." Scalia follows *stare decisis,* but he believes that the only practical way to correct an erroneous constitutional interpretation is for the Court to overrule its previous precedent. With that in mind, Scalia believes that the Supreme Court is freer when addressing constitutional questions (as opposed to statutory interpretations and other nonconstitutional questions) to depart from precedent and overturn a prior decision.

But don't get the idea that the Supreme Court frequently overrules past cases. On average, it's happened less than once per Court term — 150 times in the 172-year period (from 1810 to 1992) covered by "Supreme Court Decisions Overruled by Subsequent Decisions," a report on the Government Printing Office website entitled "The Constitution of the United States." More frequently, the Court doesn't officially overrule, but merely "distinguishes," past precedents (that is, the Court narrows case impacts by reading new limitations into their logic and scope).

Grasping the "Non-Law" Part of Constitutional Law

Trying to explain constitutional law without discussing politics and policy preferences would be as incomplete as an account that focuses *exclusively* on them. In this section we explain several ways in which politics and policy preferences influence constitutional law. We also point out several factors limiting their impact.

Identifying how politics and policy preferences affect decision making

Even when judges and other interpreters try to avoid injecting politics and policy into constitutional decision making, it inevitably enters in several ways, which we explain in this section.

Influence of life experiences

Because humans, not coldly logical robots, must interpret and apply the Constitution, all decision makers bring their policy preferences and values learned from life experiences.

Justice Harry Blackmun was the author of the decision in *Roe v. Wade,* 410 U.S. 113 (1973), which declared that women have a "fundamental right" to choose abortion during the first six months of pregnancy. (We discuss *Roe* and later abortion-rights cases in Chapter 14.) Before taking the bench, Blackmun served as the chief lawyer for the prestigious Mayo Clinic. Blackmun worked with and valued doctors. It was therefore no surprise that his *Roe* majority opinion emphasized the *medical* history of abortion and linked a woman's decision to have an abortion to her "consultation" with "her responsible physician."

By contrast, Justice Sandra O'Connor came to the Court as a woman who had experienced gender discrimination and paternalism. Her pivotal opinion reaffirming the abortion right against an increasing onslaught on and off the Court is less doctor focused. Rather, O'Connor's opinion in *Planned Parenthood v. Casey,* 505 U.S. 833 (1992), emphasized that the abortion decision is an "intimate and personal" decision at the heart of a woman's "conception of her spiritual imperatives and her place in society" that "to a large extent" "shape[s]" a woman's "destiny."

Group dynamics and personality politics

Another way that politics comes into constitutional law is the fact that decisions are usually made by collective bodies (for example, the nine-member U.S. Supreme Court, three-judge federal courts of appeals, or congressional bodies and their committees). This arrangement brings into play a wide range of group dynamics. Especially at the U.S. Supreme Court, where individual justices know that their best legal analyses mean nothing unless at least four other colleagues join to make a majority, compromise is a necessity. Supreme Court watchers note the potential for justices to "bring along" their colleagues through personal persuasion and negotiation. Some justices are notoriously better at the gentle art of persuasion than others.

Planned Parenthood v. Casey provides a useful example of group dynamics at work in the Supreme Court. As you can explore in Chapter 14, where we discuss privacy rights, Justice O'Connor's *Casey* opinion turned two little-noticed words ("undue burden") from previous abortion decisions into the standard by which all abortion regulations have been reviewed since 1992. Many commentators agree with Justice Scalia's dissenting argument that the O'Connor standard is a mere political compromise "created largely out of whole cloth" and having "no principled or coherent legal basis." Yet whatever its flaws in logic and precedent, O'Connor's formulation turned out to be the most abortion-protective standard a majority of justices could agree to.

Political partisanship and ideology

No one can deny that political partisanship and ideology significantly influence constitutional law. The political parties have markedly different positions on many key constitutional questions, ranging from states' rights to the proper balance between public safety and defendants' rights. These partisan differences show up in the constitutional decisions presidents and legislators make, the attitudes they bring to judicial confirmation hearings, the ways they characterize and react to judicial decisions, and so on.

Political partisanship and ideological polarities repeatedly show up in judicial decisions. The rulings of federal trial-court judges appointed by Republican presidents often, but certainly not always, take more conservative views about federal-government power and civil liberties than opinions from judges appointed by Democratic presidents. Rulings from state and federal courts across the nation show some variations based on dominant regional attitudes and which political party chose the judges.

Political ideology and partisanship also make regular appearances at the nation's highest Court. Conservative justices and justices appointed by Republican presidents — two categories that typically overlap — often vote together on many constitutional questions. So do their liberal and Democrat-appointed counterparts. For example, studies of decisional patterns show that, during the 2010–2011 Court term, Justice Scalia, who is generally regarded as conservative, voted 90 percent of the time with fellow conservative Chief Justice Roberts. By contrast, Scalia only voted 65 percent of the time with liberal Justices Breyer and Ginsburg. (Still, note that these ideologically mismatched justices voted together a majority of the time!)

Understanding the limits of politics and policy preferences

Always be wary of reducing constitutional law to "just politics." The main thing you should keep in mind about ideology and political partisanship is that, for the following reasons, they provide only a limited explanation for constitutional law:

✔ **Not all constitutional issues cut clearly along ideological lines.** This is shown by the substantial percentage of constitutional decisions on which most if not all judges agree. For example, in the 2010–2011 Supreme Court term, 48 percent of all constitutional cases were decided unanimously; another 28 percent saw only one or two justices dissenting.

Even in more controversial cases, the patterns of voting don't cleave along ideological lines. Some free-speech decisions, for example, show conservative justices voting on principle to achieve very liberal results — and vice versa.

Texas v. Johnson, 491 U.S. 397 (1989), posed the highly controversial question whether political demonstrators had a First-Amendment right to burn the American flag. Defying what simple ideology would suggest, conservative justices Scalia and Kennedy (who in 1989 was less of the centrist he now is) joined liberal Justice Brennan's majority opinion that flag burners were immune from prosecution. By contrast, liberal Justice John Paul Stevens joined the dissenters.

✔ **Different concepts of what is liberal and conservative abound.** Classic conservatives believe in judicial restraint — the theory that judges should minimize the extent they invalidate the actions of elected officials or otherwise disturb the legal status quo. Yet to establish conservative results (for example, to protect property rights from commonly accepted government regulation), judges would have to be "activists" in altering established precedents and imposing novel constraints on elected officials. It's far from clear in which of these directions conservatism would or should lead a judge of that stripe. A comparable uncertainty faces liberal judges.

✔ **Various ideological or political factors may pull constitutional decision makers in offsetting directions.** Decision makers may reconcile offsetting ideological and political signals by using legal factors, such as norms about following precedent and staying within the proper judicial role (see the earlier section "Getting to Know the 'Law' Part of Constitutional Law"). Ideology and politics do not function as simple shot-callers.

Both liberal and conservative justices were put in a quandary by *Gonzales v. Raich,* 545 U.S. 1 (2005). The *Raich* controversy grew out of previous Supreme Court decisions (which limit Congress's ability to regulate local *noneconomic* activities through its interstate-commerce-regulation power, as discussed in Chapter 5). When seriously ill patient Angel Raich grew marijuana in her backyard for her own "medical marijuana" use (as permitted by a ballot proposition adopted by California voters), officials enforced federal antidrug laws against her. Raich sued, arguing that she didn't grow marijuana for economic gain or participate in the illegal drug trade; Raich claimed her local, non-economic activity was exempt from federal regulation.

REAL WORLD EXAMPLE

A post-9/11 case of very strange judicial allies

One of the most important recent examples of how constitutional-law decisions are not just about ideology and politics is *Hamdi v. Rumsfeld,* 542 U.S. 507 (2004). *Hamdi* grew out of the 9/11 terrorist attacks and challenged the authority of President Bush to indefinitely detain an American citizen (alleged to be an "enemy combatant") in a military brig. A number of justices sympathized with the president's position in whole or in part. Yet the two most anti-presidential-power justices were the most liberal (Justice Stevens) and among the most conservative (Justice Scalia). Stevens joined an opinion written by Scalia. The opinion noted that the Constitution gives *Congress* the power to indefinitely suspend the writ of habeas corpus, the main line of defense against indefinite incarceration, in times of war. Congress had not suspended the writ of habeas corpus. So Scalia and Stevens reasoned that the executive branch could not achieve that result in effect by a presidential order. *Hamdi* is a very useful reminder that reducing constitutional law to a simple ideological battle between conservatives and liberals fails to see important nuances.

The *Raich* case put conservative justices in a real bind. Their support for states' rights pointed toward upholding the right of California voters to use the democratic process to pursue a social policy at variance with federal law. Yet conservatives are also antidrug, so they sympathized with arguments that creating a loophole in federal drug laws could undermine enforcement. Two states'-rights conservatives (Scalia and Kennedy) let their presumed antidrug impulse trump their states'-rights concern in *Raich,* voting with the majority to uphold federal law. Liberal justices faced similar conflicts.

Defining (Federal) Court Primacy in Constitutional Law

Most constitutional-law courses explore the meaning and application of the Constitution by studying *judicial* decisions. Judges are by no means the only constitutional-law players in town (more on this in the next section), but we can't deny that they're "first among equals" in constitutional decision making.

A variety of factors explain the primacy of judges in constitutional interpretation. First, as noted by the "Great Chief Justice" John Marshall in the landmark case of *Marbury v. Madison* (1803), "it is emphatically the province and duty of the judiciary to say what the law is." If the natural role of judges is to decide legal questions and the Constitution is such an elemental part of American law, then the fact that constitutional questions abound in legal controversies coming before the courts is no surprise. (We further discuss *Marbury* and judicial review in Chapter 6.)

Additionally, whereas elected officials can often safely ignore or underplay constitutional issues, judges usually (although not always) must decide all questions presented to them. Litigants have the greatest incentive and ability to raise and emphasize constitutional issues; convicted defendants and corporate conglomerates often seek strategic goals (overturning a sentence; escaping costly government regulation) simply by having a judge, who must seriously consider their constitutional arguments, rule in their favor.

And even though state-court judges decide many more civil and criminal cases overall than their federal counterparts, the modern reality is that the *federal* judiciary does more of the constitutional-law interpreting than state courts. (In part, this is because lower federal courts contribute most of the cases decided by the Supreme Court; 73 percent of the cases decided by the Court in its 2010–2011 term came from lower federal courts.) Although both federal and state judges have authority to decide U.S. constitutional questions, the preferences of constitutional litigators, the greater willingness of life-tenured federal jurists to take on controversial questions, and a number of other factors are behind federal judicial primacy.

Realizing How Everyone Practices Constitutional Law

As important as judicial Constitution interpreters are, they are by no means the whole story. This section identifies the full range of nonjudicial decision makers and summarizes some factors limiting the influence of judges in constitutional decision making.

Identifying the nonjudicial constitutional decision makers

Nonjudicial officers make many important decisions that expand or retract constitutional rights.

To start at the top, the president and his advisers must weigh many constitutional questions in deciding what kind of legislation to propose and how to react to legislation passed by Congress. They must consider many constitutional issues while weighing options to deal with foreign-policy crises. And they must weigh constitutional and other values to determine how the executive branch will implement judicial decisions.

Members of Congress face constitutional questions in many of their tasks, from the typical (for example, in drafting and enacting legislation) to the extraordinary (for example, in deciding constitutional issues attending presidential impeachment proceedings!).

State governors, mayors, and other executives — and legislators at the state, county, and city levels — face similar constitutional matters.

If you move from government *officials* to the much wider range of government *employees,* a wide array of potential constitutional-law practitioners appears. The individual police officer on the beat who must decide whether to search an arrested defendant, the teacher in a classroom who must decide whether a student may bring a religious icon to show and tell, and the Social Security administrator who must decide whether a disability-benefits claimant deserves further hearing procedures are, among many others, the first deciders of numerous constitutional questions.

Finally, the swarm of constitutional practitioners swells by the millions when you add American voters to the mix. Political candidates at all levels take positions on constitutional matters relating to states' rights, the rights of immigrants, and a host of other salient issues; voters are called upon to weigh competing constitutional claims in exercising their franchise. Proposals to amend state constitutions or adopt legislative proposals, placed directly on the ballot in the 27 states with initiative or referendum procedures, sometimes raise federal constitutional questions.

Recognizing why judges may not decide constitutional controversies

Many constitutional decisions are never reviewed judicially, and many more aren't reviewed for a number of years after they're made.

Many people who believe that they have been the victims of unconstitutional government action don't have the incentive or means to bring a legal challenge. Even when matters are taken to court, a delay of several years is usual, during which time the initial constitutional decision usually "sticks." (Not infrequently, events in the meantime may make the case no longer a live controversy for judicial resolution, thus insulating the initial decision under the mootness doctrine we discuss in Chapter 6.)

Yet another barrier to judicial supervision of the constitutional-law decisions of others is a sheer question of numbers. There are only so many federal and state judges. And the only court in a position to harmonize conflicting judicial decisions — the U.S. Supreme Court — only writes opinions deciding 80 to 90 cases a year (fewer than half of which are constitutional cases).

Other key constitutional questions of great importance to Americans will likely never be judicially supervised for another reason. As we explore in Chapter 6, "justiciability" doctrines designed to reduce friction between unelected federal judges and elected officials will likely prevent courts from ever providing definitive guidance on key questions of war and peace, tax and budget policy, and the like.

The take-away point here is that lots of people who never wear black robes influence, for better or for worse, the quality of constitutional protection Americans enjoy.

Identifying Constitutional Interpretive Theories

Constitutional decision making poses many difficult legal and nonlegal challenges. The decision maker has to understand and reconcile vague and, at times, contradictory constitutional language. A person interpreting the Constitution has to make sense of broad and inconsistent statements from the different framers (drafters) of constitutional language. The decision maker must also harmonize past case decisions pointing in different directions. And all this brain work must promote a variety of political, social, and economic values in the short term and the long term.

Not surprisingly, then, many judges and legal scholars try to simplify the process of constitutional interpretation by using overarching theories about how the Constitution should be interpreted. Such interpretive theories are important guides for resolving individual questions, and they offer three main benefits:

- ✔ Armed with a unifying theory, the Constitution interpreter doesn't have to deal with every new question in isolation and on a blank slate.

- ✔ Interpretive theories promote uniformity and predictability in constitutional matters, which all Americans who follow constitutional decisions (especially lawyers) appreciate.

- ✔ Constitution interpreters can also use mega-theories to lend an aura of legitimacy to their decisions. Decisions about the Constitution look less like the result of individual politics and personal whim — and perception is especially important for unelected and less politically accountable federal judges, who are supposed to stand above politics.

Many interpretive theories are out there, but two main ones have taken the forefront in the modern era:

- ✔ **Originalism:** Interpreters who subscribe to this theory see their basic task as applying the Constitution in a manner faithful to the original understanding of its drafters. To fit this theory, interpretations should be true to the words the framers used and the assumptions of the era in which they wrote.

- ✔ **Evolving-Constitution theory:** Evolving-Constitution theorists agree with originalist theorists that the intent of the Constitution's framers is the relevant starting point. But evolving-constitutionalists think the document was intended to, and should, reflect changes in law and society since its founding.

The dispute between advocates of these two theories is, unsurprisingly, long-standing and ongoing. The framers left behind no decisive instructions about how to interpret the document they wrote. No provision of the Constitution says "Read me broadly" or "Don't look beyond the traditions of the eras in which I was written." And given the high stakes involved in modern constitutional interpretation, and the close connection between constitutional law and politics, disputes over interpretive theory inevitably reflect ongoing political fights.

We discuss these two disputing theories in more depth in this section. Keep in mind that distinguishing the nuances in the theories is sometimes not as easy as it may seem. Tighten your seatbelt!

A leading scholar of the two main theories gave them easy-to-confuse names: *interpretivism* and *non-interpretivism*. For clarity — not to mention pronounceability! — we use the other popular labels (*originalism* and *evolving-constitutionalism,* respectively), but other sources may stick with interpretivism/non-interpretivism.

Some interpreters use other approaches to constitutional interpretation rather than or in addition to the two theories we explore in this section. Some of these less-prominent theories are based on broad critiques of law and seek to achieve a particular vision of a better American society. Others are based on politics or government structure. (For example, the *representation-reinforcing* approach holds that constitutional provisions should be interpreted to enhance the accessibility of political institutions.)

Understanding the search for original intent

The biggest difference between the two main theories of interpretation really boils down to how "stuck on the framers" the interpreter should be. Originalists see the Constitution as embodying certain fundamental conceptions about governmental power and individual freedom that are not supposed to change, except by a supermajority consensus acting through the constitutional-amendment process the framers provided. Originalists see their task as accurately reading the "original intent" of the framers and then applying it as new constitutional questions arise.

Interpretive theories in the real world

Although constitutional-law courses and professors emphasize the originalist and evolving-Constitution theories, don't be surprised if you don't always see these theories in the real world. Some past and present Supreme Court justices haven't really tried to articulate guiding theories. Even justices who try to develop theories seem to desert them in individual cases. Their reasoning in particular cases seems to just get them to the outcome they want. And nonjudicial officials who interpret the Constitution are especially free in changing theories because their constituents may care less about theoretical purity than practical results.

Knowing where originalists look to find framer intent

Originalists think that the best evidence of the framers' original intent is the constitutional text they wrote. Beyond that, originalists believe that interpreters should look to direct indicators of framer intent, such as notes from the 1789 Constitutional Convention or other indicators of what the drafters of constitutional language desired. (Especially important "other indicators" are the *Federalist Papers,* which as noted in Chapter 1 are essays written by Constitution supporters during the push for ratification.)

Which framers are the focus of originalist interpretation depends on the constitutional provisions at issue, because not all provisions were drafted by the same people:

- ✔ The framers of Articles I through VII of the original Constitution of 1789 were the men who met at the Constitutional Convention in Philadelphia.

- ✔ The framers of the Bill of Rights (the first ten constitutional amendments) were James Madison and others in the First Congress meeting in 1789.

- ✔ The framers of the Thirteenth, Fourteenth, and Fifteenth Amendments abolishing slavery, assuring due process of law, and protecting against racial discrimination were members of the post–Civil War Congress in 1868.

- ✔ Similarly, the framers of the other 14 individual amendments adopted between 1795 and 2002 were members of the Congress proposing that amendment.

Constitutional interpreters need to keep these timing issues in mind so they know which historical documents to turn to for indicators of framer intent.

If neither the text nor framer-intent indicators provide a clear answer, original-intent proponents see the only other legitimate source as the legal and social traditions of the framing period. Because the era of the framers was in some cases quite different from the present age, using the framers' traditions as an interpretive guide can have very significant implications.

Avoiding misconceptions about originalism

Originalists don't necessarily think that the framers had to be able to foresee the particular social or technological changes we've seen over the years. They don't, for example, refuse to apply Fourth Amendment warrant requirements to the telephone or Internet because James Madison didn't anticipate them. Rather, the question is whether Madison and the other framers had a more general intent about privacy that is relevant in the high-tech age.

Also, originalist interpretation should not be equated with *strict construction,* the theory that constitutional terms should be read narrowly to limit government power and individual rights. By contrast, if an originalist finds that the intent of the framers was to provide broad protection for, say, trial by jury, then a faithful originalist should read rights broadly in favor of criminal defendants. Indeed, in *United States v. Booker,* 543 U.S. 220 (2005), originalist Justice Antonin Scalia agreed to strike down sentencing schemes he deemed to violate the Sixth Amendment trial-by-jury rights of defendants because judges, not jurors, determined critical facts affecting sentence length.

Originalism in action

One of the Supreme Court's most controversial recent decisions (one we discuss in Chapter 9) is also a great illustration of originalism in action. The Constitution's Second Amendment states that a "well regulated Militia, being necessary to the security of a free State, the right of the people to keep and bear Arms, shall not be infringed." This amendment generates ongoing and loud political passions. Yet for decades many observers assumed, based on iffy cues from old Supreme Court opinions, that the amendment doesn't grant rights to individual gun owners outside of the "militia" context. Many were surprised when a 5–4 Supreme Court majority held, in *District of Columbia v. Heller,* 554 U.S. 570 (2008), that a gun owner could assert Second-Amendment rights against the District's tough gun-control law.

The *Heller* majority opinion (written by the Court's leading originalist, Justice Scalia) relied heavily on the Second Amendment's wording and other indicators about what the framers intended to accomplish. The opinion emphasized historical sources, such as court opinions written during the framing period, and similar provisions in state constitutions, journals, legal treatises, and news articles of the day. To Scalia and company, these indicators showed a tradition of colonial-era Americans taking their gun rights very seriously, for home protection and other purposes — not just for militia service. The majority even referenced the kind of guns owned by early Americans in determining which modern firearms are protected against the kind of excessive regulation the majority found that the District had perpetrated. The Court concluded that laws banning Americans' most preferred form of protection, handguns, do not pass constitutional muster.

Contrasting the evolving-Constitution alternative

Evolving-Constitution fans agree with originalists that the Constitution's text should be consulted for answers. However, evolving-Constitution interpreters also look to the consensus of modern American society, advances in scientific and social-scientific knowledge, accepted social norms, and fundamental human-rights principles.

Understanding how evolving-Constitution interpreters reason — and why

The evolving-Constitution approach doesn't dismiss the framers as a bunch of irrelevant old fogies. Evolving-constitutionalists find framer intent relevant and deny any desire to warp the Constitution into something its drafters rejected.

Evolving-Constitution interpreters think that looking only at the original intent of the Constitution's framers (or the traditions of the era in which they wrote) is inappropriate and dangerous. These theorists believe that the framers recognized that each generation would need to adapt constitutional principles to a new legal, political, economic, and social environment. Evolving-Constitution advocates say that the Constitution was framed in such brief and general language in order to accommodate future adaptations. To support this idea, they also point to the Ninth Amendment, which recognizes implied rights beyond those expressly stated.

Avoiding misconceptions about evolving-constitutionalism

As with originalism, misconceptions and unfair criticisms arise about the evolving-Constitution approach. Because most modern examples of evolving-constitutionalism tend to support "liberal" political results — such as expanded rights to reproductive freedom and protection against discrimination based on gender and sexual orientation — some people wrongly assume that evolving-constitutionalism is inherently liberal. But just as originalism is not inherently conservative, evolving-constitutionalism can also justify expansion of property rights and other liberties prized by political conservatives, based on modern economic and social realities and more-advanced perceptions of fundamental rights.

Critics of evolving-constitutionalism also wrongly condemn it as seeing the Constitution as an "empty vessel" into which to pour whatever desires and aspirations the interpreter desires. In fact, the approach initially credits the constitutional text and the intentions of its framers, and it bases constitutional evolution on specific indicators. Properly undertaken, evolving-constitutionalism is not a mere license to change the Constitution; rather, it reads framer intentions in the light the framers arguably expected modern generations to do so — how those intentions make sense given modern realities.

Evolving-constitutionalism in action

A five-justice Supreme Court majority used a evolving-Constitution approach to find in *Roper v. Simmons,* 543 U.S. 551 (2005), that the juvenile death penalty violated the Eighth Amendment ban on "cruel and unusual punishment." Examining "the evolving standards of decency that befit a maturing society," the majority credited declining use of the juvenile death penalty by American legislatures and juries, modern social-science findings about the neurological and psychological development of juveniles, and — especially controversial to originalists both on and off the Court! — anti-death-penalty sentiments in other countries.

Chapter 3

Mapping Out Key Concepts and Distinctions in Constitutional Law

● ●

In This Chapter

▶ Recognizing the difference between constitutional and nonconstitutional law

▶ Understanding how state constitutions work with the U.S. Constitution

▶ Remembering that being constitutional doesn't make something right

● ●

*T*his chapter completes your "preflight orientation" by visiting some key concepts and distinctions that help you avoid confusion as you travel extensively in constitutional-law land (via the remaining chapters). This chapter first discusses in detail key differences between constitutional and nonconstitutional law sources and issues. We then differentiate the U.S. Constitution from the constitutions of the 50 states and remind you that questions about the constitutionality of government action are not the same as debates on whether that action is wise or appropriate.

Sorting Out Constitutional and Nonconstitutional Law

Many of the laws and policies governing Americans have both constitutional and nonconstitutional sources. In this section, we distinguish constitutional from nonconstitutional law sources, and in so doing make an important point about where many of the legal rules governing most aspects of American life come from. We also explain how both constitutional and nonconstitutional issues can arise when government actions become controversial, and we explain how courts and lawyers analyze those types of issues differently.

Getting policies and individual rights from nonconstitutional sources

Article VI of the Constitution made the Constitution the "Supreme Law of the Land" (see Chapter 1 for details). All federal laws and treaties, all executive and judicial orders, and all federal regulations authorized under them derive their authority from — and must comply with — the U.S. Constitution. All state and local laws, regulations, and court decisions must also comply with it. Article VI even provides that the U.S. Constitution wins out over *state* constitutions when they conflict.

However, the U.S. Constitution's place at the top of the legal heap doesn't mean it's where you find most of the legal rules and rights relevant to American citizens, corporations, and nonprofit organizations. As Chief Justice John Marshall famously noted in *McCulloch v. Maryland,* 17 U.S. 316 (1819), the Constitution merely sets out the "great outlines" and the "important objects" of governmental power and restraint. The detailed mosaic of laws determining the rights, duties, and benefits enjoyed by Americans is mostly found in a wide variety of nonconstitutional sources.

Of thousands of potential examples, here are three types of policies and laws not detailed in the Constitution:

✓ **Federal taxation:** Most Americans care a lot about (and every once in a while complain about!) federal taxes. Yet the U.S. Constitution has precious little to say about the kinds or rates of taxes Americans face. The only provisions relating to federal-government taxation in the original Constitution are the 44 words in Article I, Section 8, Clause 1 giving Congress the power to "lay and collect Taxes" and the even shorter prohibition in Article I, Section 9, Clause 5 against Congress taxing state exports. The only explicit mention of federal taxation in the later constitutional amendments is the Sixteenth Amendment, which overturned a Supreme Court ruling to allow a federal income tax.

The relevant details surrounding the federal income, gasoline, Social Security, Medicare, estate, and other taxes paid by Americans can be found in thousands of provisions in the Internal Revenue Code (a compilation of statutes enacted by Congress), even more voluminous guidance in Internal Revenue Service rules, interpretations, and guidance documents, and thousands of pages of tax-court cases.

✓ **Antidiscrimination laws:** Federal law prohibits various forms of discrimination based on race, gender, religion, age, disability, and other protected bases in important economic transactions and life activities. These activities include getting and keeping a job, buying or renting housing, accessing banking services and credit, and enjoying restaurants, hotels, sports arenas, and the like.

The Constitution's only contribution to these important legal rights and privileges is to *allow* the federal government to establish such laws. The specific parameters of the right to avoid discrimination, or remedy it when it rears its ugly head, are found in the following sources: numerous federal statutory provisions (including Titles VII and IX of the Civil Rights Act of 1964, which deal with discrimination on the job and in sports programs at educational institutions); several important presidential executive orders; numerous rules, regulations, guidelines, and case-by-case decisions of the many federal agencies (such as the U.S. Civil Rights Commission, the Equal Employment Opportunity Commission, and the Justice Department) with jurisdiction over various forms of discrimination; and thousands of judicial decisions applying and interpreting these myriad sources of legally binding anti-discrimination law.

✔ **Voting rights:** Even where the U.S. Constitution is the *source* of important rights, many of the *details* regarding the scope of those rights and the procedures governing their exercise are found in federal statutes, agency rules, and court decisions interpreting and applying them.

Several U.S. Constitution provisions protect the right to vote in federal, state, and local elections. (For example, as we explored in Chapter 1, the Fifteenth, Nineteenth, and Twenty-Sixth Amendments protect voting rights for racial minorities, women, and 18- to 20-year olds. And as Chapter 13 develops in detail, modern Court rulings find that a fundamental right to vote — one that trumps restrictions on who can vote and become a candidate — is implicit in the Constitution's command to afford "equal protection of the laws.")

Yet, many of the most important guarantees of American voting rights are found not in the Constitution but in federal legislation and regulations. The Voting Rights Act, which protects against discrimination in the drawing of election districts and the conduct of elections, the Help America Vote Act, passed after the disputed 2000 presidential election and designed to limit future election snafus, and the network of federal campaign-finance laws and regulations are just three examples. Although the Constitution contains a few words *authorizing* these federal laws, the details are in the nonconstitutional sources.

Seeing how one dispute can have constitutional and nonconstitutional issues

A legal controversy (in court or out) about any governmental policy or individual right can involve both constitutional and nonconstitutional issues. To help us show in the next section how different perspectives and sources apply to the two issue types, we give a concrete illustration here of how the same controversy can generate constitutional and nonconstitutional issues.

A politically hot dispute arose in 1988 when the U.S. Secretary of Health and Human Services (HHS) issued a regulation imposing significant new restrictions on family-planning clinics receiving federal funds under Title X of the 1970 Public Health Service Act. Popularly known as the *gag rule,* the HHS regulation forbade Title X clinics and doctors from counseling women about or otherwise advocating "abortion as a method of family planning." Critics of the gag rule argued that the regulation was invalid because it went beyond the authority Congress gave to HHS in the 1970 Act. Alternatively, critics argued that the gag rule was invalid because it inhibited access of pregnant women to abortion in violation of their substantive-due-process right to choose abortion (as discussed in detail in Chapter 14) and interfered with the professional right to speak (as detailed in Chapter 11) of doctors and other healthcare professionals.

Although the two criticisms in the preceding sentence are clearly constitutional issues (because they implicate constitutional rights under the Fifth and First Amendments), the earlier argument that the gag rule was inconsistent with Title X raises a nonconstitutional issue for which the U.S. Constitution had no special relevance. (Instead, as you see in the following section, the issue about the scope of Title X raises a question of statutory interpretation.) The Constitution's only contribution to the Title X issue is to give Congress a broad general power to spend federal tax dollars (as it did in Title X) on programs Congress thinks will promote "the general welfare" (such as family planning).

Comparing the modes of analysis for constitutional and nonconstitutional issues

Resolving a controversy over constitutional issues requires assuming a different perspective from what's required to resolve nonconstitutional issues. From those different perspectives, different sources become the relevant ones to consult. And the standard order requires that all the nonconstitutional issues should be decided before turning to the constitutional ones.

In this section we use the gag-rule example to underscore the various considerations that any analyst — judicial or otherwise — faces when looking at constitutional and nonconstitutional issues arising in the same controversy.

Looking at the controversy from the right perspective — and using the right sources

A person analyzing whether a statute permits Rule X or Result Y is serving as the agent of the Congress that adopted the statute. For example, a court or other analyst trying to determine whether Title X permits Health and Human Services to adopt the gag rule seeks to determine what the 1970 Congress adopting the Public Health Service Act intended. Therefore, that analyst wants to consult the statutory text adopted in that year, the legislative history (committee reports, floor debates, statements at legislative hearings, and so on) of the bill's progress toward enactment, and evidence about Congress's purpose in adopting Title X.

A person instead addressing the constitutional questions about the gag rule — whether it violated the First-Amendment rights of doctors or the Fifth-Amendment rights of pregnant women — is serving as the agent of the framers and ratifiers of the Bill of Rights (adopted in 1791). A constitutional-issue decider has the job of bringing the intent of the Bill of Rights framers into the modern era. The court or other analyst would have to interpret the brief and general textual language proposed in 1791 and read the tea leaves of Bill of Rights consideration in the first Congress that proposed the amendments and in the state ratification conventions approving them.

Only confronting constitutional issues if the nonconstitutional issues can't resolve the controversy

A court or other analyst investigating a controversial law or policy raising both constitutional and nonconstitutional issues takes those issues in a definite order. Under standard rules of judicial restraint, all nonconstitutional issues are decided before reaching any constitutional ones. This rule of priority flows from the reality that deciding that government action is unconstitutional interferes maximally with the ability of elected officials and their agents to continue to exercise power. Such ultimate interferences with discretion are avoided if possible.

Using the example presented in "Seeing how one dispute can have constitutional and nonconstitutional issues," if the gag rule violates the First or Fifth Amendments, the HHS secretary cannot enforce it (and Congress can't remedy the constitutional violation by merely passing a new statute). The meaning of the First or Fifth Amendment would have to be changed through a constitutional amendment or revised Supreme Court decision.

Deciding that the government is acting illegally for *nonconstitutional* reasons, by contrast, leaves more options for elected and appointed officials. If the problem is that the act as passed by Congress in 1970 did not authorize the gag rule, a new Congress can amend the act to allow such a rule. Or, the HHS secretary can just amend the gag order to bring it into line with the 1970 act.

The rule of priority becomes an important rule of restraint when the analyst deciding constitutional and nonconstitutional issues is an unelected federal court. Unnecessary interference with the prerogatives of the national political branches is a first-order separation-of-powers concern going to the heart of the judicial branch's legitimacy (as we detail in Chapter 6). Therefore, a core canon of judicial restraint, most famously invoked by Justice Louis Brandeis in an influential concurring opinion he wrote in *Ashwander v. Tennessee Valley Authority,* 297 U.S. 288 (1936), holds that courts should exhaust all nonconstitutional avenues for resolving a dispute before reaching the ultimate strong medicine of constitutional review.

Civil constitutional law versus *criminal* constitutional law

A key distinction in American law in general, and constitutional law in particular, is between *civil* rights and *criminal* rights. (In fact, constitutional-law courses at the undergraduate and graduate levels are often split along this line.)

Criminal constitutional law refers to the constitutional protections afforded to individuals (or entities) when they come into conflict with governmental law-enforcement authorities. Some criminal constitutional-law doctrines apply to all citizens of the United States — for example, the limits on the random sobriety checkpoints that can be encountered by any motorist. But most of the boundaries established by criminal constitutional law kick in whenever an individual (or entity or its officials) comes under suspicion for having committed a crime, is arrested, is charged with a crime, pleads guilty or is tried and convicted, is sentenced, or has the prescribed sentence carried out. Classic examples of criminal constitutional law include

✔ The requirement that police officers read arrested defendants their Miranda rights

✔ The general need for law-enforcement authorities to get a warrant to search a home

The higher stakes at issue in criminal trials — the defendant can, after all, have his liberty and maybe even his life taken away if convicted! — generally lead to stricter and more elaborate protections in that area of government action.

Civil constitutional law refers, essentially, to everything else. It's a broad collection of doctrines applicable when individuals or entities interact with any governmental authority in any capacity other than as a criminal suspect. Classic examples involving civil constitutional law include

✔ When a protest group is denied a permit to march on a city street

✔ When an individual or entity claims arbitrary or discriminatory treatment at the hands of a government official

The distinction isn't always clear. For example, involuntary civil commitment (such as sending persons judged to be insane to a psychiatric facility) can resemble criminal confinement in constitutionally important ways. In terms of parties and goals, the standard divide is that *civil law* is used to redress injuries caused by other individuals (or entities). *Criminal law* pits the members of a community (as represented by public prosecutors) against individuals (or entities) accused of wrongs the legislature has defined as wrongs against the community as a whole.

Understanding How the 50 State Constitutions Fit In

Even though this book is devoted to the *United States* Constitution, we should consider here how the constitutions of the 50 states fit into the picture. Appreciating the interaction between federal and state constitutions is useful in preventing you from becoming confused when studying political and legal controversies. Also, if you live in one of the many states in which amending the state constitution is relatively easy (because it doesn't require the supermajority consensus over time that the U.S. Constitution requires), you're likely to be asked to vote for or against proposed constitutional changes on important issues of economic, social, or political policy. Understanding how your state constitution can be an important part of enabling or limiting government power makes you a better voter and citizen.

The U.S. Constitution doesn't create or empower state and local governments. State constitutions — some of which were around before the U.S. Constitution and significantly influenced it — do that. Although state constitutions are not allowed to contradict the provisions of the U.S. Constitution, they are certainly free to give *additional* governmental powers or rights exceeding those provided in the U.S. Constitution's 7 articles and 27 amendments.

Here are some examples of how additional powers play out in some state constitutions:

- ✔ **Additional governmental powers:** State constitutions may grant powers that the federal Constitution cannot. In *United States v. Lopez,* 514 U.S. 549 (1995), the Court held that the federal government lacked authority to make carrying a gun within 1,000 feet of any public school a federal crime. (For more information about the case, see Chapter 5.) But *Lopez* in no way prevents state constitutions from authorizing their legislatures to enact, and their executive officials to enforce, *state* bans on gun toting near schools. Although escaping federal charges, the defendant in *Lopez* still faced state charges under Texas law. Many other states have similar laws as permitted by their state constitutions.

- ✔ **Additional individual rights protections:** State constitutions are often important sources of individual rights protections over and above those provided by the U.S. Constitution. For example, as provisions in the California state constitution have been interpreted by California courts, residents of the Golden State have these rights, which the U.S. Supreme Court has held are *not* protected by the U.S. Constitution:

    - A broader requirement of separation between government and religion

    - State-funded abortions for poor women enrolled in public health programs

    - A broader right to keep sensitive personal information secret

A related point is that *state* courts and other state officials responsible for interpreting state law (such as a state's attorney general) are the experts — and provide the last word — on what their state constitution means.

For example, interpreting how a "three-strikes" sentencing provision in the California constitution (that is, one giving extra-harsh penalties for offenders who reoffend three times or more) should apply to a particular defendant is a state-law issue. A federal court wouldn't generally decide that question (and if it did decide it in the context of other issues, it would do its best to put itself in the shoes of California state courts and decide consistently with California court decisions). Only if a *federal*-law issue were raised about the three-strikes provision — for example, if the harsh sentences arguably violated the Eighth Amendment's prohibition on cruel and unusual punishment — would a federal court get involved in deciding the matter under the *federal* Constitution. (And at that point, the framers also gave state courts the authority to "play federal court" and decide federal-law issues like this, subject to ultimate Supreme Court review.)

Seeing That "Constitutional" Isn't the Same as "Right" or "Logical"

We close this chapter with one last distinction causing mischief to students of constitutional law — not to mention public officials, pundits, and any Americans engaging in good ol' fashioned political arguments. These people often forget that whether Law X, Policy Y, or Action Z is *constitutional* is not the same question as whether the law, policy, or action is enlightened, moral, or even common-sensical.

Just because the federal government has the constitutional *power* to subsidize tobacco farmers (under its broad authority to spend tax funds for purposes it thinks serve the general welfare) doesn't mean that it should. (You wouldn't be the first person to suggest that the federal government works at cross-purposes by encouraging tobacco production and then spending billions of dollars to convince Americans not to buy tobacco products!) And just because the federal government is not *required* by the Constitution to ensure that every American gets enough to eat (as we note in Chapter 1, the Constitution is largely a "negative constitution" not obligating the government to act) doesn't mean that failing to provide this basic human necessity makes economic or humanitarian sense.

Similarly, assuming that the current Supreme Court majority is correct that the Constitution *permits* public high schools to randomly drug test student athletes and participants in extracurricular activities, but not other students, that doesn't make the practice right or good educational policy. If this anti-drug policy (the legal basis of which is discussed in Chapter 15) seems perverse — it ends up *exempting* from testing the nonparticipatory "slackers" most likely to do drugs — that argument is against the logic or validity of the policy, not its legality.

So as you read the remainder of this book, please keep in mind that just because something is unconstitutional doesn't make it otherwise wrong. And just because something is constitutional doesn't make it right. For better or for worse, the Constitution's framers left government officials and the voters who elect them substantially free to make dumb decisions!

Part II

Allocating Governmental Roles

In this part . . .

When many people think about the Constitution, they think about things like freedom of speech, freedom of the press, or the right to bear arms. But the Constitution includes so much more. One of the framers' main purposes was to create a strong national government, but not without meaningful limits. In this part, we discuss how the Constitution maps out the three branches of the federal government, creating checks and balances and limits on power. We discuss each branch and the powers and limits on each in detail.

Chapter 4

"Constituting" a New Federal Government

....

In This Chapter

▶ Exploring the new kind of government envisioned by the Constitution's framers

▶ Setting up a two-branch Congress to legislate

▶ Putting a president in charge of the executive branch

▶ Establishing a judicial system with life-tenured justices

....

*T*he basic purpose of the Constitution ratified in 1789 (consisting of Articles I through VII) was to create a substantially more powerful federal government that would nevertheless be meaningfully limited. In this chapter, we first overview the framers' decisions to make the new national government supreme, place it within an existing structure of powerful state governments, limit it to enumerated powers, and separate national powers among three independent and competing branches.

Then we detail how the constitutional plan for the new federal government successively created, empowered, and limited the legislative, executive, and judicial branches. We detail many constitutional provisions frequently studied in constitutional-law courses — both because the provisions are important in their own right and because they lay the foundation for many of the controversies and unresolved questions still percolating today.

Grasping the Constitution's Main National Governmental Innovations

The framers used four innovative devices to accomplish their intention to "constitute" a new federal government. They made the national government supreme, upheld the power of the states, limited the national government to powers named in the Constitution, and set up a system of checks and balances so that none of the three branches of government would wield too much power. We consider each of these innovations briefly in this section.

Making the new national government supreme

The framers of the Constitution of 1789 didn't start writing with a clean slate. Thirteen state governments had operated for six years in a "firm league of friendship" under the Articles of Confederation (see Chapter 1). Part of what made life and government under the Articles unworkable was the absence of a sufficiently strong, unifying national government to exercise such important functions as raising and supporting a standing army, engaging in diplomacy with foreign nations, and ensuring that interstate commerce was conducted under minimally fair and harmonious rules.

So the first order of constitutional business was to establish a new national governmental entity with sufficient power. Following are the key elements establishing the national government's supremacy:

✔ A direct statement in Article VI that the Constitution (and the legislation and treaties adopted pursuant to it) is "the supreme Law of the Land"

✔ A corresponding Article VI obligation on all federal and state officeholders to take an oath to "support this Constitution"

✔ A specific Article VI charge to state judges to enforce constitutional supremacy in their decisions, ignoring "any Thing in the Constitutions or Laws of any State to the Contrary"

✔ Specific prohibitions (in Article I, Section 10) against state governments' coining money, making treaties with foreign governments, taxing interstate commerce, and otherwise acting like a national sovereign

Federalism: Giving the national government state rivals for power

The framers intended the new national government to function within the existing framework of state governments. The framers did not abolish the states. Nor did they reconstitute them under the new Constitution. State governments continued to be organized and to exercise powers under their own constitutions and as guided by their own citizens. For example, states were free to depart from the national model of a two-house legislature. (At present, Nebraska has only one legislative chamber.) And whether a state could, say, charter corporations depended on what its own constitution said, not the U.S. Constitution.

Overlaying the new national government on top of existing state governments was more than a practical, political necessity. The framers thought that robust state governments would be an important check on abuse of national government powers. That's why the framers made federal officeholders dependent in several ways on state-government officials. U.S. senators were originally chosen by state legislators, not directly by voters. (Adoption of the Seventeenth Amendment changed that.) The Constitution also makes states responsible for drawing House legislative-election districts every ten years, and states are initially responsible for the "Times, Places, and Manner of holding Elections for Senators and Representatives."

We discuss a number of important contemporary controversies involving federal/state relations in Chapter 7. For now, the point is that positioning relatively powerful states to exercise power with, and to check, the new national government is a crucial part of keeping the national government in its appropriate place.

Limiting the national government to specific enumerated powers

To curb the ability of the new national government to abuse its powers, the framers limited the new federal government to enumerated (expressly specified) powers. Specifically, the framers did not intend the federal government to be like state governments, which retained general "police powers" to promote the health, safety, morals, and welfare of their citizens through any laws not prohibited in their own constitutions or the national one.

Articles I, II, and III list specific powers given to the national legislature, the executive branch, and the federal judiciary. We explore these powers in the later sections "Granting legislative power," "Granting executive power," and "Granting judicial power."

Several provisions in the other articles in the Constitution also grant specific powers to Congress or to the federal government generally. An example of the former is Article IV, Section 3, which gives Congress the power to govern "the Territory or other Property belonging to the United States" — a very important power, given the millions of acres of national parks and other public lands! An example of an enumerated power given to the federal government as a whole is the obligation in Article IV, Section 4 to protect states against invasion and guarantee them a representative government.

The framers explained in the *Federalist Papers,* written to support the ratification of the Constitution, that the national government would only exercise powers specifically granted. The framers clearly intended, as later clarified in the Tenth Amendment in the Bill of Rights, that "powers not delegated to the United States by the Constitution" are reserved to the states and their citizens.

The noble intentions of the framers stated in the Constitution's preamble are not power grants. So although it says (among other things) that they intended the new national government to "insure Domestic Tranquility, provide for the common defence, promote the General Welfare, and secure the blessings of Liberty to ourselves and our Posterity," the national government can't, for example, justify a measure solely on the grounds that will make Americans feel more tranquil. That aspiration is important, but it's not a constitutionally granted national power, as is, say, the power to tax.

Check(s), please! Separating national powers into three independent branches

One of the most important and innovative constitutional design features is the division of national authority into three independent branches. The United States was the first modern government to divide legislative, executive, and judicial branches into separate branches with independent selection processes, constituencies, and responsibilities — on the theory, as James Madison put it in "Federalist No. 51," that "the separate and distinct exercise of the different powers of government" would "be essential to the preservation of liberty."

But separation of powers is only part of the framing equation to prevent a dictatorial national government. An absolute assignment of all legislative powers to Congress, all executive powers to the president, and all judicial powers to the federal courts could've created three mini-tyrannies.

Instead, the framers provided a number of interlocking and offsetting ways for each branch to "check and balance" the powers primarily lodged in the other branches. The following discussion covers most of these checks and balances, which set the stage for ongoing constitutional-law challenges:

- ✔ **Legislation:** Congress takes the lead in enacting legislation, but the president participates in the process by having veto power over legislation (or more typically, by threatening to veto bills to force Congress to accommodate his views). Congress can in turn "check" this presidential check on its power by overriding the presidential veto (which takes a two-thirds majority of each house). The courts can check and balance both of the other branches by declaring statutes to be unconstitutional.

- ✔ **Executive functions:** The president has primary authority to appoint federal officials, make treaties, and send troops to war. But this presidential power is checked by constitutional requirements that the Senate must agree by majority vote. The president is generally responsible for executing or enforcing congressional laws and policies, but Congress possesses a number of powers to control that responsibility, including its budgetary and appropriations powers and its ability to conduct oversight hearings.

Checking and balancing: Bills, vetoes, and the power to override

You're probably familiar with the Article I, Section 7 provisions about how a legislative "bill" becomes an official national law. (At least, maybe you know the *Schoolhouse Rock* song about it!) But you may not have considered how this commonplace constitutional provision is the most intricate and extensive example of how the framers provided checks on national powers and then sought to check and balance the problems created by each of those checks.

The framers worried that the national legislative power would be abused to adopt laws benefiting narrow "factions" (their word for what we would call "special interests") or otherwise failing to serve the public good. The framers' first check is that a bill can't emerge from Congress until it commands a majority in both the House of Representatives and the Senate. Thus, the status quo could change only when a majority of Americans *and* a majority of states assented.

But what if legislation that went against the public interest managed to emerge from both houses? Not to worry. The president, who represents the majority of Americans but is elected through a different process, can veto such evil legislation.

And what if the president exercises his veto not for noble reasons but as a tool of special interests or as a personal vendetta? As an answer, the framers empowered Congress to override the presidential veto by a two-thirds vote of both houses.

However, if the president didn't like a bill but knew that the Congress had the votes to override a veto, he might stall the proceedings by just doing nothing. (This inaction is commonly called a *pocket veto* because the president metaphorically sticks the bill in his pocket.) So to prevent the president from stymieing a supermajority in favor of policy change, Article I, Section 7 provides that a bill becomes a law in ten days if the president doesn't sign it.

But that creates a new legislative abuse angle! Suppose the Congress knew that it didn't have the two-thirds margin to override a presidential veto. Could it send the bill to the president and then adjourn so as to prevent the president from vetoing and returning it — thus making the bill become law after the ten days pass? Unacceptable, said the framers, who provided that the provision making a bill a law ten days after the president fails to sign or veto it is inoperative if "the Congress by their adjournment prevent [a bill's] Return, in which Case it shall not be a Law."

This example of five interlocking, offsetting limits on actors in the legislative process is a prime instance of how the framers took "checks and balances" seriously. It's also an example of how the framers were not just big-picture visionaries but were also savvy men schooled in the practical realities of political officials tending to abuse power.

✔ **Judicial power:** Federal courts do the heavy lifting in deciding cases, but Congress can shrink or expand court jurisdiction (as long as it doesn't exceed the overall constitutional jurisdictional limitations). Congress can also enhance or retard the judicial branch by creating or declining to create necessary courts and judgeships and by granting or withholding necessary operating funds. Congress may even be able to use its power to make "Exceptions and Regulations" to the jurisdiction of the Supreme Court to strip the justices of jurisdiction over controversial categories of cases (such as those involving abortion rights, school prayer, and same-sex marriage, for example). Federal courts can issue rulings, but they depend on Congress to appropriate funds to execute those decisions and on the president and federal law enforcers to carry out the letter of the decisions. Specifically, the president may pardon or grant clemency to defendants convicted by federal courts.

We explain in Chapter 6 how overlapping and uncertain power grants have created a number of difficult modern controversies over separation of power.

Article 1: Creating, Empowering, and Limiting a Two-Branch Congress

This section details how the framers of the new Constitution "constituted" an important government branch: the legislature. Among other things, you see the legislature's enumerated powers, specific power limits, and checks and balances at work. We also note some of the constitutional-law issues arising from the manner in which the Constitution of 1789 establishes Congress.

The House and Senate: Creating a bicameral legislature

The framers' decision (expressed in Article I, Section 1) to vest "All legislative Powers" in a Senate and a House of Representatives, elected for different terms and reflective of different political interests (as fleshed out in Article I, Sections 2 and 3), was a truly momentous one. It put into play the following different dynamics:

✓ **Representation of states and the general population:** Legislative policy cannot be made without the concurrence of two very different majorities:

- The states, whose interests are reflected in the Senate, because each state is entitled to the same number of Senators (two)

- The U.S. population as a whole, whose perspective is mirrored in the House of Representatives, where each state's membership varies according to its population

What was so great about the Great Compromise?

Historians call the framers' decision to divide legislative powers between two houses (bicameralism) the *Great Compromise*. Presidents, legislators, and citizens witnessing legislative gridlock when the House and Senate can't come to agreement may legitimately wonder what's so "great" about this constitutional feature and just what it "compromised" (besides ease of governance!).

Bicameralism finessed a deep disagreement among two competing visions of legislative representation at the Constitutional Convention of 1789. Not surprisingly, small states (propounding the *New Jersey plan*) desired equal representation in the legislature. Larger states, by contrast, supported the *Virginia plan,* which tied legislative power to population.

When the Convention deadlocked and threatened to dissolve over bickering among different state delegates, they agreed in classic compromise form to split the difference. Small states would achieve their equal representation in the Senate, and the interests of large states would be protected by the population-based House of Representatives. This compromise was great in the sense that it allowed the Constitution to be adopted.

This incident helps to underscore the extent to which the Constitutional Convention was a typical political gathering. Although also visionary and admirable, the framers were not above jockeying for political advantage. And as with any legitimate political enterprise, compromise was often necessary to grease the wheels of progress.

✔ **Term lengths and changing perspectives:** Legislative policy reflects different temporal perspectives. All members of the House need to seek reelection every two years, so the House reflects the latest political trends. By contrast, Senators have six-year terms, and in each national-election year, only one-third of the Senators are newly elected (or reelected); the remaining two-thirds reflect different perspectives and degrees of legislative experience and can stem a popular movement.

✔ **Competing interests:** The House and Senate, which need to work together to pass legislation, can be of different political parties and be dominated by different interests.

Empowering the new Congress

Article I of the Constitution deals with congressional power in three different senses. First, Section 8 gives Congress 17 specific powers and 1 residual authorization to make other "necessary and proper" laws. Second, other Article I provisions give Congress the power to establish rules and practices to govern itself. Third, Article I gives members of Congress some potent tools by which to prevent the other two national branches from elbowing their way into the legislative arena.

Granting legislative power

The Constitution's Article I, Section 8 catalogs the major powers of the national legislature. Following is a summary of Congress's 17 substantive powers:

- ✔ **Fiscal powers:** Responding to perceived deficiencies in government under the previous Articles of Confederation government (see Chapter 1), Article I gives Congress the following powers:

  - Levying taxes (Clause 1)

  - Borrowing money on behalf of the U.S. (Clause 2)

  - Coining and regulating the value of money (Clause 4)

  - Punishing counterfeiting (Clause 5)

- ✔ **Economic development and regulation:** The framers sought to correct the states' tendency to go it alone economically. Article I grants the new legislature the following important new powers to establish a new framework for a national commercial marketplace:

  - Regulating interstate and foreign commerce (including commerce with "Indian Tribes," which had many of the attributes of foreign countries) (Clause 3)

  - Establishing uniform laws to govern bankruptcies so that people can emerge from financial distress and get a "fresh start" as productive economic participants (Clause 4)

  - Establishing legal structures to protect intellectual property through copyrights and patents (Clause 8)

  Other congressional powers have substantial economic components, as well as broader significance:

  - Establishing a "uniform Rule" for immigration and naturalization, which was especially important when the U.S. needed immigrants to settle new territories and fuel economic expansion (Clause 4)

  - Establishing post offices and "post Roads" (Clause 7)

  - Punishing piracy and other crimes against shipping (Clause 10)

- ✔ **Military and national-security powers:** Responding to difficulties Americans faced in fighting the Revolutionary War and seeking to assure security in a dangerous post-Revolution era, the framers gave Congress the following powers pertaining to the military and national security:

  - Organizing and funding an army (Clause 12) and a navy (Clause 13)

  - Making rules to govern these forces (Clause 14)

  - Organizing, governing, and calling out state militias (the historical predecessors of today's national-guard units) to "suppress [domestic] Insurrections and repel [foreign] Invasions" (Clauses 15 and 16)

(A related power in another article entirely is the Article III power given to Congress to "declare the Punishment of Treason.")

✔ **Powers to complete the national government:** Two other clauses give Congress the following powers to complete important aspects of national governmental design:

- Creating special-purpose federal courts (Clause 9). (These courts add to the general-jurisdiction, lower federal courts Congress can create under the Article III provisions relating to the judicial power.)

- Creating a national capital district, thereby leading to the creation of Washington, D.C. (Clause 17)

Article I, Section 8 completes its laundry list of congressional powers with a broader residual power "To make all Laws which shall be necessary and proper for carrying into Execution the [17 specific substantive] Powers, and all other Powers vested by the Constitution in the Government of the United States, or in any Department or Officer thereof." As we discuss in Chapter 5, this "necessary and proper" clause gives Congress ample authority to use a wide range of implied means for accomplishing powers specifically enumerated in Article I or granted elsewhere in the Constitution.

Congress gains one other important source of power from the adoption of constitutional amendments after the Constitution of 1789. The great post–Civil War amendments (the Thirteenth, Fourteenth, and Fifteenth Amendments) and later amendments include language authorizing Congress to "enforce" their substantive protections through "appropriate legislation." Interpreting, expanding, and contracting this congressional power has been a major staple of modern Supreme Court decision making.

Empowering Congress to function as an institution

Article I of the Constitution also gives the branches of Congress powers permitting them to function institutionally. Section 5 gives each house of Congress the power to establish its own internal rules and several powers relating to members of Congress. Section 5 also lets each house judge the "Elections, Returns, and Qualifications of its own members," discipline (and, with a two-thirds vote, expel) its members, compel the attendance of absent members, determine procedures for daily adjournment, and decide when proceedings should be secret.

Equipping Congress to resist encroachment from the other branches

To promote checks and balances, the framers gave Congress important resources for preserving its independence and resisting encroachment from the executive and judicial branches. Three short, direct clauses in Section 6 provide these important protections:

✔ **A requirement that legislators be paid:** The framers shrewdly assumed that if the executive branch could withhold congressional salaries, the president or other executive officials could bend members of Congress to their desires. The Constitution requires that Congress "shall receive a Compensation for their Services [. . .] paid out of the Treasury of the United States."

✔ **A privilege against arrest:** Members of Congress are generally "privileged from Arrest during their Attendance at the Session of their respective Houses, and in going to and returning from" legislative sessions. This provision is one of many examples of provisions directly reacting to, and preventing, an abuse practiced in England — where kings and parliamentarians found that a good way to change the outcome of a legislative vote was to arrest enough opposition members on trumped-up charges!

✔ **Immunity for congressional speeches and debates:** Another provision outlawing a disfavored English practice, the so-called *speech-or-debate clause* insulates members of Congress from both executive-branch prosecutors and federal judges. To assure congressional independence of action, this clause gives legislators absolute immunity from civil or criminal actions based on their official pronouncements and other actions. (Among other consequences, the clause gives members of Congress a right, unique among American citizens and other officials, to basically libel or slander others in statements on the floor of Congress.)

The modern Supreme Court has had to interpret the deceptively simple language of the speech-or-debate clause on several occasions. The Court has, for example, extended legislative immunity to more than just "speeches" and "debates" in their narrow sense; instead, the immunity protects a broader group of official actions that are an "integral part of the deliberative and communicative processes by which members participate in committee and House proceedings," as the Court put it in *Gravel v. United States,* 408 U.S. 606 (1972). Gravel also extended constitutional immunity to congressional staffers performing functions that would be privileged if performed by their bosses themselves. On the other hand, the Court in *United States v. Brewster,* 408 U.S. 501 (1972), found that the speech-or-debate clause doesn't protect members of Congress from prosecution for bribery and other misconduct as long as prosecutors don't introduce evidence of legislative acts or the motives of members of Congress.

Limiting the new Congress

Although the framers gave the new national legislature substantial powers, they also limited congressional authority in important ways. First, the requirement that members of Congress stand for regular reelection is an important political limit on members of Congress, who realize that on an ongoing basis they must account to voters for their acts and omissions.

How the limits on congressional power have led to some high-profile challenges

The substantive limits on congressional legislative powers have generated a number of Supreme Court cases noteworthy in part because of the high political drama behind the decisions. Following are some prominent examples:

✔ *Nixon v. Administrator of General Services,* **433 U.S. 425 (1977):** This case resulted from post-Watergate restrictions imposed on President Richard Nixon in the aftermath of his resignation from office under threat of impeachment. Nixon challenged a federal law mandating that he turn over all the records, notes, and tape recordings he made as president to the General Services Administration, for eventual release to the public. He unsuccessfully claimed that the law singled him out for adverse treatment in violation of the ban on legislative bills of attainder. (The Court held that the act did not single out the president wrongly or punitively.)

✔ *Hamdi v. Rumsfeld,* **542 U.S. 507 (2004):** This high-profile post-9/11 case considered President Bush's right to indefinitely detain in a military prison a U.S. citizen suspected of being a terrorist "enemy combatant." A divided Court majority held against the president. Central to the case was whether Congress had effectively suspended habeas corpus in the narrow circumstances allowed by Article I, Section 9 when it passed antiterrorist legislation after the September 11 attacks.

✔ *United States v. Richardson,* **418 U.S. 166 (1974):** *Richardson* raised the dicey question of whether Congress's long-standing practice of hiding CIA expenses in other parts of the federal budget violated Article I, Section 9, which requires that "the Receipts and Expenditures of all public Money shall be published from time to time." The Court avoided ruling on the merits by finding that plaintiffs lacked proper standing to argue the issue.

Second, limiting Congress to enumerated powers prevents Congress from successfully asserting powers not delegated.

Third, some of the Article I, Section 8 grants of substantive power to Congress (discussed earlier in "Granting legislative power") themselves contain limits. For example, the Clause 12 power to fund armies expressly limits appropriations to two-year terms.

Fourth, Article I provisions about how Congress functions also include limits on each branch's prerogatives. Section 5 provides that a majority of members is a necessary quorum for doing business, and this section requires each house to keep and publish a journal of proceedings. Section 5 also ties each house to the other by prohibiting either from adjourning for more than three days without the other house's consent. Most significantly, the strong power of the House of Representatives to bring articles of impeachment against other federal officials is checked by the fact that impeached officials are only removed from office if a supermajority of Senators concurs during an impeachment trial.

Finally, Section 9 of Article I specifies these additional limits on the legislative authority:

✔ Three important limits (in Clauses 2 and 3) prevent the legislature from oppressively wielding its criminal-law powers. Congress may not generally suspend the writ of habeas corpus, the "Great Writ" that since the time of the Magna Carta has remedied arbitrary and indefinite incarceration. Congress also can't do two other hated practices of English oppressors — pass a bill of attainder (that is, a law singling out the activities of an individual or small group) or an ex post facto law (a statute reaching back in time to impose criminal penalties on something that was legal at the time it was done).

✔ Clauses 4 through 7 limit Congress's taxation and fiscal powers. In successive order, these clauses prevent disproportionate taxes, forbid taxes on state exports, outlaw preferential treatment of any state's ports or maritime commerce, and require that federal funds be spent only when Congress has officially appropriated the money and the spending is publicly disclosed.

Article II: Creating, Empowering, and Limiting the Executive Branch

The framers of the Constitution of 1789 had experienced the difficulties of trying to win a revolution and run a national government by Congress without a strong administrative function. Yet, with recent memories of abuses by English kings and royal governors, the framers had mixed feelings about creating a strong executive office.

The blueprint for a separate executive branch established by Article II is less extensive and less fully conceived than the substantially longer article creating the legislative branch (see the earlier section "Article I: Creating, Empowering, and Limiting a Two-Branch Congress"). In part, this difference is because the framers envisioned, as James Madison wrote in "Federalist No. 51," that in a representative democratic government like the United States, "the legislative authority necessarily predominates." In part, the framers remained divided throughout most of the constitutional convention between alternative plans for structuring the executive. Finally, the framers probably were reassured that they could trust George Washington, who was universally assumed to be the likely first president.

Still, in creating the rudiments of what has grown into the modern powerful American presidency and executive bureaucracy, Article II follows the format of the previous article by creating the office of the presidency and vice presidency (and providing for the appointment of inferior officers), empowering executive officeholders, and correspondingly limiting them.

Creating the executive branch

Article II vests "The executive Power" in a president and vice president elected to four-year terms. In addition to laying down age, citizenship, and residency requirements for the president, Section 1 of Article II creates the presidency and vice presidency as officers clearly distinct from, and with different constituencies and power sources than, Senators and House members. Following are some key highlights of presidential selection:

✔ The president and vice president are the only federal officials elected by a constituency broader than any one state. Specifically, the person elected president is the candidate who puts together a majority of electoral votes from many states.

A related point is that only the president and vice president can claim to have won the support of a distinct cross-section of voters across the nation. Senators were selected by state legislatures, not voters, when the Constitution was adopted. Except for in the smallest of states, House members are elected from sub-units within individual states.

✔ The election of a president and vice president registers national sentiments at four-year intervals, whereas all members of the House and one-third of the Senate must face voters every two years. Among its many implications, this term length means that an executive administration reflects a longer-lived set of policy views.

Article II did not establish subordinate executive offices below the president and vice president. Instead Article II, Section 2, empowers the president to appoint "Inferior officers" and allows the president to "require the Opinion, in writing, of the principal Officer in each of the executive Departments." (Notably, this is the only, albeit implicit, recognition in the Constitution that the federal executive branch would need bureaucrats to do its work.)

Empowering the new president and executive branch officials

Article II of the Constitution deals with executive power in two main ways. First, Sections 2 and 3 give the president (and subordinates) a number of specific powers and one more general power to "faithfully execute" U.S. laws. Second, Article II gives the president tools for checking and balancing the other national branches. We explore these two topics in this section.

Granting executive power

The specific Article II grants of executive power can be categorized by substantive area. The following list helps you understand the big picture of presidential power and breaks each area into specific powers:

✔ **Appointment and personnel powers:** Article II gives the president powers relating to the appointment of national government officials — and not just in the executive branch. Following are two of these powers:

- Article II, Section 2, Clause 2 states that, with the "advice and consent" of the Senate, the president nominates and appoints "Ambassadors, other public Ministers and Consuls, Judges of the supreme court" and "other Officers of the United States."

- Section 2, Clause 3 lets the president make "recess appointments" — that is, to fill vacancies occurring when the Senate is in recess. These appointments last until the end of the next session of Congress, which could mean that appointees stay in office for more than a year without Senate approval.

✔ **Military and foreign-policy powers:** Several powers give the president and the executive branch powers to assert U.S. military power and conduct diplomacy overseas — and sometimes even at home.

- The first power given to the president by Article II, Section 2 is the power to serve as "Commander in Chief of the Army and Navy of the United States, and of the Militia of the Several States" when performing United States functions. (A memorable example of the latter command is President Dwight Eisenhower's sending the National Guard to Little Rock, Arkansas, to enforce a federal court's order to desegregate city schools.)

  Section 2, Clause 2 gives the president the power to make treaties (again, with Senate concurrence) and name U.S. Ambassadors. This power allows the president to conduct diplomacy, with the goal that, hopefully, exercise of his war powers will be unnecessary.

- Section 3 includes a power to "receive Ambassadors and other public Ministers" from foreign countries.

✔ **Powers to impact government policy:** Several Article II powers give the president leverage for affecting domestic policy.

- Presidential powers to influence congressional lawmaking include the president's authority in Section 3 to call Congress into session "on extraordinary occasions," to adjourn Congress when the two houses are at an impasse on adjournment, and to recommend appropriate legislation to Congress.

- The president can also alter the direction of judicial decision making by granting "Reprieves and Pardons" to defendants convicted of violating federal law (as allowed by Section 2).

✔ **A general "faithful execution" power:** Section 3 gives the president the residual power to "take Care that the Laws be faithfully executed." (This power is similar to the legislative "necessary and proper" default power discussed in the earlier section "Empowering the new Congress.")

The landmark decision in *Youngstown Sheet & Tube Company v. Sawyer,* 343 U.S. 579 (1952), discussed in more detail in Chapter 6, held that this power is not authority for the president to "be a lawmaker" or make "a presidential policy." Rather, the president must direct the execution of "a congressional policy."

In reality, however, the line between policy execution and policy formation is a thin one, and often more of the practical impacts of a policy stem from the details of execution.

In passing the International Emergency Economic Powers Act of 1977, Congress set the policy that in circumstances of "national emergency," the assets of foreign governments should be frozen. Yet the act gave the president the power to determine when such a "national emergency" had arisen and to set the scope and circumstances of asset freezing under very generic guidelines. Thus, President Carter's 1979 decision to freeze Iranian assets after the seizure of the American embassy in Tehran and taking of American hostages — and President Reagan's 1981 decision, as part of an agreement to free the American hostages, to nullify the freeze and direct disputes into an international tribunal — had much greater real-world significance than Congress's initial passage of the act.

Equipping the pres to resist encroachment from the other branches

The framers perfected the separation of powers by equipping the executive branch to fight encroachment from Congress. In addition to the president's power to veto legislation, which allows the chief executive to thwart laws threatening presidential powers and prerogatives, these Article II provisions specifically seek to protect the president against Congress:

- ✔ **Protection against salary reprisal:** As part of the framers' general concern that games not be played with salary, Article II, Section 1 includes a protection, similar to that afforded to Congress by Article I, that the president receive compensation for services and that the salary may not be diminished during his term.

- ✔ **Limiting impeachment of the president and other executive officials:** Congress's ability to remove the president and other executive officials is an important *limit* on executive power. But limiting impeachment to "Treason, Bribery, or high Crimes and Misdemeanors" rather than, say, garden-variety political unpopularity, and requiring a two-thirds vote in the Senate to remove the impeached official from office, permit presidents to resist attacks from a hostile Congress. (Anyone doubting this protection is welcome to check with former-president Bill Clinton, whose impeachment by the House of Representatives reached nowhere near a two-thirds vote in the U.S. Senate.)

Recess appointments: A modern way to end run a hesitant Senate

When the Constitution was originally drafted, the "recess appointment" provision (allowing appointments by the president while Congress is in recess) reflected the expectation that Congress would meet for only a limited portion of each year. In the modern era of largely year-round Congresses, the "recess appointment" provision has taken on a quite different significance in the tug of war often taking place between presidents and Senate majorities (especially when the political party of the majority isn't that of the president!).

Modern presidents have sometimes gotten around Senate majorities that won't approve nominees by instead naming them as recess appointments. For example, President George W. Bush responded to Democratic Senate inaction on the nomination of controversial judicial nominee Charles Pickering to be a circuit-court judge by making Pickering a "recess" appointee.

This use of executive power is one of many potential reminders about how the Constitution's power-granting provisions can have unanticipated consequences, or take on a different significance, in light of changing institutional dynamics and political realities.

The Article II power permitting the president to issue pardons and reprieves to persons convicted in federal court is one example of how the Constitution equips presidents to stop perceived judicial arrogance. In the early 1800s, for example, President Thomas Jefferson pardoned several persons convicted of violating the notorious Alien and Sedition Laws, in prosecutions seen as tainted by heavy-handed presiding judges loyal to the opposition party.

Limiting the executive branch

The Constitution framers included important limits on executive authority:

- ✔ Just as the need to run for reelection is an important method of promoting legislative accountability, the fact that presidents seeking second terms will, under the provisions of Article II, have to stand for reelection is an important limit on presidential authority.

- ✔ The threat of impeachment is a serious potential limit on misbehavior by presidents, vice presidents, and other executive-branch officials.

- ✔ The theory of enumerated powers means that presidents must find authority in their expressly granted powers or reasonable extensions of those powers. Various modern presidents have claimed "inherent powers" implicit in the office of president or in the notion of "executive power," but no modern Supreme Court has validated these assertions.

✔ Presidential powers granted by Article II contain limits. For example, Congress can reduce presidential control by transferring the power to appoint lower-ranking federal officials ordinarily exercised by the president to "the Courts of Law, or in the Heads of Departments."

✔ Article II contains other specific limits on the president's room for action. Section 1 provides that presidents may not have their salary increased during their term of service and may not receive any other "Emolument" from the U.S. government or any state. Section 3 obligates the president to report to Congress on "the State of the Union" (although the Constitution does not require that Republicans refuse to applaud when the president introduces Democrat-supported proposals, and vice versa!).

Article III: Creating, Empowering, and Limiting a Life-Tenured Judiciary

The framers of the Constitution of 1789 had experience with the lack of a sufficiently independent judiciary in England and the colonies. On important occasions, jurists were too much under the thumbs of kings and legislative officials to be able to control abuses of power.

To remedy that problem, the framers wrote a Constitution creating an independent Supreme Court. However, they were significantly divided about whether to create lower federal courts or to depend on state courts to enforce constitutional rules under Supreme Court guidance. Also, the framers generally gave less thought to the judicial function than to the legislative and executive functions, so the blueprint for a separate judicial branch established by the Constitution's Article III is comparatively short and incomplete.

Still, in creating the rudiments of what has grown into a powerful and independent judiciary that jurists around the world envy, Article III follows the format of the previous articles by creating one court and the possibility of others, empowering federal judges, and correspondingly limiting them.

Creating a distinct judicial branch

Article III's only sentence addressing court creation vests judicial power in a Supreme Court and "in such inferior Courts as the Congress may from time to time ordain and establish." ***Note:*** Regardless of whether Congress created federal courts to enforce supreme national law, the Article VI supremacy clause (see "Making the new national government supreme" at the beginning of this chapter) obligated state courts to give predominance to the Constitution and federal laws and treaties consistent with it.

Article III may, in fact, be most noteworthy for the many seemingly important details of federal-court operation it omits. Nowhere does the Constitution specify the number of justices to serve on the Supreme Court. (Congress set this number by statute, and it varied from six to ten until settling on the current figure of nine in the 1880s.) Unlike its treatment of members of Congress and the president, the Constitution does not specify minimum ages or qualifications of federal jurists.

Empowering the new federal judiciary

Article III of the Constitution deals with judicial power in two main ways. First, Section 2 enumerates seven categories of federal-court jurisdiction and divides those categories between *original jurisdiction* (cases that can start out in the U.S. Supreme Court) and *appellate jurisdiction* (cases that start out in lower federal or state courts and go to the Supreme Court on appeal). Second, Article III gives federal judges substantial tools for preserving their independence against the onslaught of the other branches.

Granting judicial power

Article III, Section 2, Clause 2 limits the federal judiciary to the following specific categories of cases, each of which is of special concern to the supremacy and legitimacy of the new Constitution and federal government:

- **Federal questions:** The first and most important jurisdictional grant is for "all Cases, in Law and Equity, arising under" the Constitution, federal law, and treaties. State courts also hear so-called federal questions as they arise in normal civil and criminal litigation. But the framers wanted to ensure that legal questions important to federal-government power could go up on appeal to the Supreme Court and could be heard by any lower federal courts Congress created.

- **Cases in which the status of one or both parties deserves a federal-court forum:** To the framers, appeal to the Supreme Court and recourse to lower federal courts seemed appropriate for these case categories:

  - **"Cases affecting Ambassadors, other public Ministers, and Consuls":** Because foreign sovereigns are on an equal footing to the United States and the issues they raise are of national significance, their cases merit a federal forum.

  - **"Controversies to which the United States shall be a Party":** Clear federal interests suggest the availability of a federal forum, in a lower court initially or on appeal to the Supreme Court.

  - **Cases involving a state sued by another state, a state sued by citizens of another state, or "Citizens of the same State claiming Lands under Grants of different States":** The common state-versus-state thread of these case categories makes it wise to provide a federal forum not associated with any particular state.

- **Cases "between Citizens of different States":** This "diversity jurisdiction" ensures that federal courts are available as relatively neutral alternatives when trying cases in the state courts of either plaintiffs or defendants would seem to give one side a home-court advantage. Diversity jurisdiction is the only exception to the general rule that federal courts do not decide state-law questions. In diversity cases, a federal judge "plays state-court judge," applying the relevant state law and following state court precedents, although from a supposedly less biased perspective.

- **"Cases of admiralty and maritime jurisdiction":** Federal court involvement here is consistent with the new national government's predominance over foreign commerce and international shipping.

Notice that none of these grants of federal-court jurisdiction expressly authorizes the federal courts to engage in the all-important power of judicial review — the authority to declare acts by other officials, including Congress and the president, illegal. Early in the nation's history, the Supreme Court claimed this power by implication.

Equipping the federal judiciary to independently resist encroachment from the other branches

The framers gave federal judges a degree of independence from electoral accountability unheard of before or since. True, the initial nomination and confirmation of federal justices and lower-court judges reflects presidential and Senatorial politics. But after confirmation, federal judges hold their jobs for life as long as they discharge their duties with "Good Behavior." (The precise meaning of the term has never been decisively defined.)

Following are three other aspects of judicial independence:

- **Protection against salary reprisal:** The judiciary is the third branch benefitting from the framers' sense that controlling the salaries of officials might practically control their hearts and minds. So Article III, Section 1 requires that federal judges receive compensation for their services, and it outlaws diminishing their salary.

- **Limiting impeachment to "Treason, Bribery, or high Crimes and Misdemeanors" and requiring A Two-Thirds Vote in the Senate" to remove an impeached judge from office:** Impeachment has generally been limited to the occasional bad judicial apple committing actual crimes. No Supreme Court justice has ever been removed from office.

- **The absence of any provision by which Congress or the president can veto or otherwise directly invalidate a judicial decision:** In contrast to the president and Congress, who have offsetting weapons to check and balance each other about legislation, government spending, and appointments, the judiciary is not subject to any direct check on its basic activity of deciding cases. No other official can veto a federal judge's decision or order. Outright defiance of judicial orders is rare and universally condemned.

Why state judges should be envious of their life-tenured federal colleagues

Compared to their federal colleagues, state judges are much more subject to electoral and other political pressures. No state grants life tenure to its state Supreme Court judges. All state high-court judges are appointed to fixed terms, renewable at the pleasure of political officials or voters.

Twenty-three states elect their Supreme Court judges. Even in other states, where governors or legislative officials appoint Supreme Court judges, such "merit selected" judges are subject to electoral pressures in retention elections or through recall petitions. The judges on intermediate state courts of appeal and on state trial courts are even more subject to election and reelection. Thirty states choose judges below the Supreme Court level in partisan and nonpartisan elections.

Ultimately, of course, the judiciary's major weapon against abusive legislative or executive action is the judiciary's awesome power of judicial review, claimed in the 1803 decision of *Marbury v. Madison,* 5 U.S. 137. *Judicial review* is the power to review actions of Congress and the executive branch and declare them unconstitutional or otherwise illegal based on the judiciary's independent judgment. This power plays a major role in promoting checks and balances — as well as in generating ongoing controversy about the proper judicial role! We discuss judicial review in more detail in Chapter 6.

Limiting the judicial branch

As with all branches of the federal government, the Constitution's framers also provided multiple limits on judicial authority. First, judges can be impeached if they engage in criminal behavior or obvious misconduct. Second, the theory of enumerated powers (as backed up by the Tenth Amendment) also means that federal judges may only take cases falling within one of the seven expressly granted jurisdictional categories. Barring a genuine issue involving the national Constitution or federal laws, federal courts may not, for example, decide what elements make a contract valid under the laws of a particular state.

Third, as with the legislative and executive powers granted previously, Article III itself establishes a few limits on federal judicial power. Article III, Section 2 requires federal criminal trials to be by jury and held in the state in which the crimes were allegedly committed. Section 3 prevents courts from allowing a person to be convicted for treason "unless on the Testimony of two Witnesses to the same overt Act, or on Confession in open Court."

Finally, the following powers the Constitution gives to Congress and the president can be used to limit judicial power:

- **The appointments power:** The president and Senate's power to appoint judges can affect the ideological direction of federal judges.

- **Congress's power to propose constitutional amendments:** The Eleventh and Sixteenth Amendments overturned Supreme Court decisions, and this power can be used in the future for the same end.

- **The power to overturn a seemingly incorrect judicial ruling about what a federal law, executive order, or regulation mean:** The president and Congress can change the law, executive order, or regulation.

- **Powers related to the enforcement of judicial decisions:** Judicial decisions are not self-executing. Outright defiance of court decisions (say, passing a law stating that no federal funds may be used to enforce a court decision requiring prisoners to have more cell space) is rare and generally condemned, but the president and Congress do have a range of valid actions they can use to give less-aggressive enforcement of decisions they don't like.

- **Congress's power in Article III, Section 2 to make "Exceptions" and "Regulations" to the Supreme Court's appellate jurisdiction:** This most-important and still-unresolved limit on federal-court jurisdiction seems to permit Congress to manipulate Supreme Court jurisdiction by not allowing the Court to make potentially unpopular, significant decisions. For example, Congress could arguably prevent the Court from recognizing same-sex marriage rights by "excepting" cases asserting such rights from review by the Court. And because Congress arguably has at least the same "jurisdiction-stripping" power over lower federal courts it brought into being in the first place, Congress could use the power to entirely disallow constitutional-rights cases from federal court. (The implications of this constitutional provision receive fuller treatment in Chapter 6.)

In addition, Congress's power to establish lower federal courts and to enact laws "necessary and proper" for the fulfillment of the judicial role means in practice that Congress (and presidents weighing in on legislation) control many aspects of regular judicial business. These aspects include which courts hear cases and in what order, what judicial remedies are available, when recourse to federal court is and is not available, and what procedures will be used in federal criminal and civil trials and appeals.

Chapter 5

Charting the Reach of National Government Powers

. . . .

In This Chapter

▶ Identifying express and implied national powers

▶ Using the commerce power as a jumping-off point for regulation

▶ Checking out four other important powers given to the federal government

▶ Including the president: Legislating through the executive branch

. . . .

*B*ecause Congress is the nation's chief lawmaker, the story of federal-government power is initially a story of *congressional* power. Since the landmark 1819 case of *McCulloch v. Maryland,* congressional powers have been understood as an interaction among express constitutional powers, implied powers, and other constitutional limits.

As this chapter details, the classic *McCulloch* formula provided the framework for a marked expansion in the size and scope of national-government activities in the modern era. Nowhere is this expansion — and the concerns and tensions it created — clearer than with the federal government's power to regulate interstate commerce. For that reason, we devote a lengthy section to the ways the Court has in general expanded national powers beyond the likely initial expectations of the Constitution's framers.

We also explore other federal legislative powers that have spurred expansions and limitations of their own, including taxation and federal spending. We end the chapter with a brief discussion of how the executive branch is a significant player in the game of federal power, even affecting legislative matters.

Seeing the Big Picture: Congress's Express and Implied Powers

This section introduces the basic three-part test the Court developed in *McCulloch v. Maryland,* 17 U.S. 316 (1819), for determining when federal laws are constitutional. The *McCulloch* formula first looks at whether Congress is fulfilling one or more of the powers the Constitution expressly gives it. Second, *McCulloch* allows a generous range of "implied" means for achieving express powers; the operative test is whether the implied means are "appropriate and plainly adapted" to achieving the enumerated means. Third, *McCulloch* requires that the exercise of federal power not violate any other provision.

Looking at express congressional powers

The Constitution gives Congress a number of express legislative powers. The main source of these powers is Article I, Section 8, which lays out a laundry list of 17 powers, such as the power to tax, to establish post offices, to regulate immigration, and to establish an army and navy. (An 18th power granted at the end of the laundry list — the authority to pass laws that are "Necessary and Proper" to carry out the other express powers — is a different kind of power grant entirely. We discuss it in the next section.)

Congress also exercises authority granted elsewhere in the Constitution, such as the Article IV power over federal land and property and the power various constitutional amendments give Congress to "enforce, by appropriate legislation" the protections those amendments establish.

Many of the thousands of federal laws in statute books today are there simply because Congress exercised its explicitly stated powers. Federal laws against piracy in international waters, for example, are a direct result of Congress exercising its power in Clause 10 of Article I, Section 8 to "define and punish Piracies and Felonies committed on the high Seas." The extensive federal laws governing trademark, copyright, and patent protection fulfill Congress's express power (in Clause 8) to "secur[e] for limited Times to Authors and Inventors the exclusive Right to their respective Writings and Discoveries."

Congress's express powers are normally referred to as *plenary* powers. (In this context, *plenary* means whole and complete in itself, requiring no further justification.) When Congress exercises its plenary powers, as long as it fulfills the terms of the express constitutional text (for example, as long as its copyright grant is for a limited time), it doesn't have to make any showing that its lawmaking actions are appropriate or otherwise justified by the benefits they will achieve. This showing is normally associated with *implied* congressional powers (see the next section for details).

For example, if Congress passed a law raising military salaries, this law would be seen to meet Congress's explicit power to "raise and support Armies," without proof that current salaries are inadequate to attract the needed number of soldiers, that the pay raises are the most cost-effective use of national-security funds, and so on. These justifications might be prudent *politically,* to prevent complaints about wasting taxpayer dollars. But Congress's Article I power doesn't read "to raise and support Armies by paying soldiers sufficiently ample salaries to achieve recruitment." Congress has the power to "raise and support" armies, and as long as Congress didn't violate other constitutional rules in the process, the Constitution is satisfied.

Using tools to put express powers into effect: Implied congressional powers

A federal government restricted to exercising the express congressional powers — that is, one able to tax, regulate interstate commerce, establish armies, and set up specialized lower courts — would be a credible, powerful government. Yet the modern U.S. national government pursues a much broader range of activities (and has the employees and budget to fulfill them!) because of the recognition by Chief Justice John Marshall early in the nation's history that the framers intended the new federal government to have "ample" implied means — which is to say, plenty of breathing room — for effecting its express powers.

The landmark case recognizing implied congressional powers is *McCulloch v. Maryland,* 17 U.S. 316 (1819). On its way to settling a question of intergovernmental tax immunity, the *McCulloch* Court had to decide whether Congress had the constitutional authority to pass legislation establishing a national bank in 1815. Because the express powers of Congress don't include authority to establish a banking entity, or any corporation for that matter, the power had to be implied as a valid means of fulfilling one or more enumerated ends.

In the process of upholding the national bank as a proper exercise of congressional authority, *McCulloch* answered these two key questions:

✔ **Did the framers intend to grant implied powers to Congress?** Chief Justice Marshall's decision answered yes and gave two main reasons:

   • Written constitutions, such as the United States Constitution, are only bare-bones blueprints. They can only mark "the great outlines" and designate "important objects"; the "minor ingredients which compose those objects" must be *implied* from "the nature of" the important power grants.

- The framers of the Constitution were practical men who intended that the new federal government would have sufficient power to get the job done. Marshall noted that the framers had "experienced the embarrassments resulting from" a more restrictive federal-power formulation in the previous Articles of Confederation. He reasoned that, having set up the national government "with such ample powers, on the due execution of which the happiness and prosperity of the nation so vitally depends," the framers intended to provide "ample means for [those powers'] execution."

✔ **What degree of connection must be shown between Congress's implied means and the relevant enumerated end(s)?** Marshall chose a forgiving standard requiring that the implied means merely be "appropriate" and "plainly adapted" to achievement of one or more express powers. In answering the question this way, Marshall rejected the argument made by the state of Maryland and long favored by Thomas Jefferson and other states-rights advocates. These supporters of a limited national government would have restricted implied means to ones that were necessary or essential for express powers to be fulfilled.

The importance of Chief Justice Marshall's decision to choose *appropriate and plainly adapted* over *necessary* as the connective tissue between implied means and express ends cannot be overstated. A much smaller and less-powerful federal government would've resulted from the latter choice. It would, for example, be much harder to argue that the federal government had to have a national bank — that without one the national government would be wholly unable to manage tax revenues, borrow funds, fuel westward expansion, or pay soldiers. After all, state banks could be pressed into service. Much easier is the argument that a national bank is "appropriate and plainly adapted" to exercising these enumerated federal powers.

The bottom line: A federal government without the generous choice of means *McCulloch* allows would be a much more modest entity. Its post offices would have employees, sell one type of stamp for each kind of mail service, and enforce laws against mail theft; these elements are necessary to run an established post office. But the post office would not be able to sell the current wide array of commemorative stamps and incidental merchandise and probably wouldn't offer boutique mailing services such as Express Mail. These frills are clearly "appropriate and plainly adapted" to raising postal revenue and encouraging postal patrons to visit their neighborhood post office, but they're hardly necessary to a bare-bones postal operation.

A frequent but inaccurate view of *McCulloch*

Curiously, many writers attribute *McCulloch*'s implied-powers theory solely or mainly to the last "catchall" provision in Article I, Section 8, which gives Congress the power to "Make all laws which shall be necessary and proper for carrying into Execution" the previous congressional power grants and the other authority provisions elsewhere in the Constitution. This typical shorthand oversimplification ignores the fact that Marshall spent substantial time defending national implied powers through the two reasons explained above before he even mentioned the "necessary and proper" clause. The clause was actually cited by the opponents of the national bank in arguing that the national government was severely restricted in its choice of means.

Far from being Marshall's main line of argument, the clause (and its possible suggestion that implied means had to be truly *necessary*) was a hurdle the Chief Justice had to overcome. He did so. (Always the clever wordsmith, he noted that the framers placed the clause in the power-*granting* Section 8 of Article I, rather than the power-*limiting* Section 9. He also argued that reading *necessary* in a restrictive sense would render the accompanying word *proper* unnecessary extra wording.)

Still, *McCulloch*'s rationale would've justified generous implied legislative powers even in the absence of the necessary and proper clause.

Constitutional limits: Exercising powers without breaking the rules

McCulloch v. Maryland held that the manner in which Congress is exercising its express and implied powers must be "consist[ent] with the letter and spirit of the constitution." This limit has three main applications:

✔ **Congress must follow any limits included in the express-power grants themselves.** A few of the express-power grants have words of limitation built into them. For example, the copyright and patent power allows Congress to provide such protection for "Limited times." So although Congress doesn't generally have to justify the correctness of its copyright laws, to survive constitutional scrutiny it would have to establish that those laws appropriately limit the copyright and patent time frame. For example, the Court had to decide in the 2003 case of *Eldred v. Ashcroft*, 537 U.S. 186, whether a law extending copyright protection for 90 years after an author's death was sufficiently limited to be pronounced constitutional. (The Court held that it was.)

✔ **Congress can't violate the various structural limits the Constitution imposes on lawmaking.** For example, Congress can't validly raise revenue through a bill starting out in the Senate. The origination clause in Article I, Section 7, Clause 1 requires that revenue bills start out in the House of Representatives, the legislative branch the framers thought would more directly represent the views of American voters and therefore make taxation more acceptable. Nor can Congress exercise its powers in ways undermining states-rights protections embodied in such constitutional provisions as the Tenth Amendment. (We discuss states' rights in Chapter 7.)

✔ **Congress can't pass laws violating any of the Constitution's individual-liberties protections.** To use a hopefully far-fetched example, if Congress set up a new post office to be used only by male patrons — a sort of postal "man cave" — it would obviously violate Congress's equal-protection obligations under the Fifth Amendment. When challenged, Congress couldn't just say, "Hey, our power to establish post offices is plenary." Under prevailing constitutional theory, Congress must exercise its legislative powers consistent with the individual-liberties protections in the constitutional articles and in the amendments later adopted. (How these protections restrict the powers of Congress, as well as those of state and local governments, is pursued in Parts III, IV, and V of this book.)

Observing Express and Implied Powers in Action: The Commerce Power

Courses in constitutional law typically use the decisions and doctrines surrounding part of the congressional power (stated in Article I, Section 8, Clause 3) "to Regulate Commerce with foreign Nations, and among the several States, and with the Indian Tribes" as the prime focus for understanding the scope and limits of congressional powers. We agree that the interstate-commerce portion of this power deserves special attention for the following three reasons:

✔ Regulating interstate commerce provides the basis for many of the extensive and important federal laws designed to promote the health, economic status, social welfare, and morals of the nation.

✔ The case decisions and legislative actions under the interstate-commerce power provide especially vivid and complete examples of how the *McCulloch* federal-power formulation works.

✔ The twists and turns in interstate-commerce decisions over time show the ongoing difficulty the Court faces in balancing the need to provide ample federal power with the importance of preserving enough of a role for state regulation.

As this section explains, the interstate-commerce clause is important both as an express grant of important federal authority and as a basis for the federal government to insert itself into areas traditionally dominated by state governments in earlier eras.

Regulating interstate commerce directly

Many federal laws do nothing fancier than literally "regulate Commerce . . . among the several States." These laws, spanning a broad range of economic, social, and moral concerns, fall into two basic categories: laws regulating commerce across state lines and laws regulating connected activities.

Laws regulating commerce across state lines

Classic examples of interstate-commerce laws include prohibition on shipping goods from one state to another or receiving goods originating from another state. But thanks to Chief Justice Marshall's expansive reading of the interstate-commerce clause in *Gibbons v. Ogden,* 22 U.S. 1 (1824), Congress has the following abilities:

- ✔ Congress can allow but restrict (or even encourage) commerce across state lines.

- ✔ Congress can regulate commerce that is illegal and nefarious (for example, transporting illegal drugs) as well as commerce that is legal and legitimate.

- ✔ Congress can regulate the movement of people as well as goods. An illustration of both points is the appropriately named Mann Act of 1910, which successfully used the express interstate-commerce-regulation power to make it illegal to transport any person across state lines for the purpose of immoral sex or prostitution.

Today the Court tends to defer to Congress's regulation of commerce across state lines. This attitude is markedly different from that expressed almost a century ago in *Hammer v. Dagenhart,* 247 U.S. 251 (1918). *Hammer* struck down a 1916 law Congress adopted, after a decade of lobbying, to prohibit the interstate shipment of goods produced by child labor. Distinguishing the 1916 law from past bans on dangerous or unhealthy goods (such as tainted eggs), the *Hammer* Court viewed child-made goods as "themselves harmless." (A pencil made by a child is no more dangerous to users than a pencil made by an adult.) Citing a states-rights concern animating earlier and later efforts to restrict the federal commerce power, the *Hammer* majority worried that upholding the 1916 law "would sanction an invasion by the federal power" into "a matter purely local in its character, and over which no authority has been delegated to Congress."

The Court officially overturned *Hammer* in a World War II–era case upholding a federal ban on the interstate shipment of goods made by employees paid substandard wages or worked for an excessive number of hours. The Court in *United States v. Darby,* 312 U.S. 100 (1941), saw *Hammer* as an unjustified departure from the principle that "[t]he motive and purpose of a regulation of interstate commerce are matters for the legislative judgment . . . over which the courts are given no control."

Laws regulating activities "in" or integrally connected to the "instrumentalities" of interstate commerce

As with regulation of movement across state lines, Congress can regulate particular activities taking place in interstate-commerce *instrumentalities* (that is, in the channels or facilities through which interstate commerce occurs). Federal laws prohibit, allow yet restrict, or promote a wide array of activities that take place

- ✔ On interstate highways
- ✔ On modes of interstate transportation (such as buses and trains)
- ✔ Through interstate communication avenues (such as the U.S. mail, interstate telephone and telegraph lines, and even the Internet)

For example, Congress has the power to make bringing a weapon into an airport serving interstate passengers — or even possessing a weapon close to the airport — a crime. Congress can do this even though the weapon isn't itself being toted across state lines; it is a localized activity. As the Court recently phrased it in *United States v. Lopez,* 514 U.S. 549 (1995) — a major decision we discuss later in "Limiting regulation of many non-economic activities" — Congress can "regulate and protect the instrumentalities of interstate commerce, or persons or things in interstate commerce, even though the threat may come only from intrastate activities."

The express power to regulate interstate commerce, as with all express powers, is plenary. To establish that interstate regulatory laws are constitutionally (as opposed to politically) valid, Congress does not have to show that they are beneficial or needed to deal with real economic, social, or moral problems. As the Court underscored in upholding a federal ban on the interstate transportation of foreign lottery tickets in *Champion v. Ames,* 188 U.S. 321 (1903), the interstate-commerce-regulation power is "complete in itself, and is subject to no limitations except such as may be found [elsewhere] in the Constitution."

Using interstate commerce to justify broad regulation of local activities

The interstate-commerce power is more than a powerful tool for federal regulation of commerce among states, the instrumentalities serving it, and local activities threatening it. It is also the green light for the modern era of across-the-board regulation of industries, crimes, and social practices.

Following is a partial list of significant federal laws at issue in modern Supreme Court decisions construing the interstate-commerce power's reach to local activity:

- ✔ The 1935 National Labor Relations Act, the New Deal–era comprehensive system for regulating labor/management relations, protecting workers from unfair labor practices and ensuring rights to collective bargaining (upheld in *National Labor Relations Board v. Jones & Laughlin Steel Corporation,* 301 U.S. 1 [1937]).

- ✔ The Civil Rights Act of 1964, including prohibitions on racial discrimination in hotels, restaurants, and other places of public accommodation (upheld in *Heart of Atlanta Motel v. United States,* 379 U.S. 241 [1964] and *Katzenbach v. McClung,* 379 U.S. 294 [1964]).

- ✔ Comprehensive federal bans on the possession, transportation, and sale of illegal drugs — including a ban on the sale and possession of privately cultivated medicinal marijuana even when state law allows it (coverage of medicinal marijuana okayed in *Gonzales v. Raich,* 545 U.S. 1 [2005]).

This section explains how modern Supreme Court doctrines expanded congressional power over commerce "among" states into a powerful tool to regulate activities generally *within a single state* (that is, intrastate or local activities). Then this section examines the modern Court's mixed success in trying to put the brakes on farther reaches of the interstate-commerce power.

Starting with formalistic limits on Congress's regulation of local activities

Court decisions before 1937 generally used formal, categorical distinctions between local activities *directly* related to interstate commerce (such as local shipping and selling of products) and local activities only *indirectly* related to interstate commerce (such as production and manufacturing). The Court saw regulation of direct local activities as an appropriate implied means of regulating interstate commerce. Regulation of indirect local activities seemed highly inappropriate. For example, in *United States v. E. C. Knight,* 155 U.S. 1 (1895), the Court struck down a federal attempt to break up a monopoly over 98 percent of the country's sugar production on grounds that sugar refining was "production" only indirectly related to interstate commerce. The Court rejected federal regulation even while characterizing refined sugar as a "necessity of life" bought by almost all American consumers.

By design, the drawing of a distinct line between direct and indirect effects didn't lead the Court to consider the *practical economic effects* of local activities. The clearest example is the Depression-era case of *Carter v. Carter Coal Company,* 298 U.S. 238 (1936). In its last use of the direct/indirect test before entering a more pragmatic era, the Court struck down the Bituminous Coal Conservation Act of 1935, a major piece of New Deal legislation that regulated product pricing and labor relations in the coal industry. Given the scale and importance of this critical national industry, labor strife clearly would have had a dramatic and adverse effect on the national economy.

But the *Carter* majority essentially said, "Don't talk to us about how practically important coal production is!" Because coal mining and the labor practices associated with it are only indirectly related to interstate commerce, the *Carter* Court held that Congress could not reach it. As the majority put it: "[The] distinction between a direct and an indirect effect turns, not upon the magnitude of either, but entirely upon the manner in which the effect has been brought about. [I]f the production by one man of a single ton of coal . . . affects interstate commerce indirectly, the effect does not become direct by multiplying the tonnage, or increasing the number of men employed."

Expanding the local reach of the interstate-commerce power

Before 1937, Supreme Court decisions reined in federal authority when Congress tried to reach local commerce (see the preceding section). But in the aftermath of President Roosevelt's controversial 1937 proposal to "pack" the Supreme Court with justices more sympathetic to Roosevelt's policies — and as part of a more general retreat from second-guessing government regulation of the economy — the Court became much more friendly toward federal regulation of local commerce.

Acknowledging that local activities practically affect the national economy

In one of the first major developments in this expansion, the Court became more pragmatic. The Court held that national regulation of local activities is appropriate and plainly adapted to regulating interstate commerce when local activity has a substantial effect on the national economy. In the *Jones & Laughlin* decision cited earlier, the Court found that because the nation's fourth-largest steel company was a "completely integrated enterprise" owning and operating mines and transportation facilities in several states and on the Great Lakes, the effect of labor conflict at the company "would be immediate and might be catastrophic."

Considering the cumulative effect of local activities on interstate commerce

In 1942, the Court began to allow activities that were not "substantial" in their effect on the national economy when viewed in isolation to be grouped (or "aggregated") together. If as a "class" these activities are substantial, that justifies regulation in the name of interstate commerce. This innovation dramatically opened up the potential range of local activities subject to federal regulation, as the following example illustrates.

Wickard v. Filburn, 317 U.S. 111 (1942), upheld 1930s legislation designed to help farmers bounce back from the economic ravages of the Great Depression. The law assured farmers a stable crop price in exchange for their agreement to control production. Farmer Filburn got into legal trouble by producing 141 more bushels of wheat than allowed under the federal program. (Filburn fed the extra wheat to his dairy cattle.) Filburn eventually claimed that the federal agricultural law was unconstitutional. Filburn argued that he wasn't a large steel company, so his law violation couldn't alone have a substantial effect on the farm economy.

But add all the Farmer Filburns together, the *Wickard* Court held, and you have a distortion in the demand or supply of wheat across the nation. Playing armchair economist, the Court noted two possibilities. If many farmers grew and consumed more wheat than federal law allowed, they wouldn't need to buy as much wheat on the market. Lower the overall demand for wheat, while supply remains constant, and you drive down prices. Alternatively, said the Court, if a large group of wheat farmers sold their excess production illegally, this would increase the overall wheat supply. Raise supply while keeping demand the same and, again, you lower overall prices.

By letting the government add the impacts of localized individuals together, and show an *aggregate* substantial adverse effect on the national economy, the *Wickard* Court allowed federal agricultural laws to reach very small potatoes (to bring in another agricultural reference!). This theory allows federal regulation to reach small-time producers and sellers of a wide array of products and services.

The Civil Rights Act cases provide another example of how "small fish" can get caught up in the net of federal interstate-commerce regulation. *Katzenbach* upheld application of federal antidiscrimination laws to a small barbecue restaurant far from the interstate highway and with no real connections to interstate commerce other than that the restaurant bought some of its meat from out-of-state sources. By itself, Ollie's Barbeque clearly didn't affect interstate commerce significantly. But add all the little restaurants together, and you have the necessary basis for concluding that discriminating restaurants collectively have a substantial effect.

Deferring to Congress's rational basis for action

The Court further increased Congress's interstate-commerce power by holding that the legislature's judgment that aggregated activities will have a substantial economic effect should be upheld as long as Congress had a "rational basis," based on evidence it developed or borrowed from state legislatures, for thinking that the aggregated activities have a substantial effect. Even if some evidence is contrary to Congress's economic judgment, Congress should be deferred to. These easy-to-meet standards emerge from the Civil Rights Act cases of *Heart of Atlanta Motel v. United States,* 379 U.S. 241 (1964), and *Katzenbach v. McClung,* 379 U.S. 294 (1964). They further expand the scope of congressional regulation by giving the benefit of the doubt to Congress in doubtful cases.

In enacting the Civil Rights Act of 1964, Congress amassed anecdotal evidence that racial segregation in public accommodations in the South discouraged travel by African Americans, suppressed business relocation decisions, and depressed the overall level of hotel bookings, restaurant revenues, and associated supply purchases. It is virtually impossible to call this evidence not "rational," even though others argued that desegregation would make the economic situation worse because a greater number of whites would refuse to stay at hotels and patronize restaurants.

Declining to assess Congress's real motivation for action

The Court's final step in liberalizing Congress's use of the interstate-commerce power came from another aspect of the Civil Rights Act cases. The Court held that if Congress develops the necessary rational basis for an aggregated substantial effect, it doesn't matter that the substantial-effect justification is just a "pretext" for a deeper moral or social concern.

Of course, Congress didn't pass the Civil Rights Act because it was vitally interested in the *economics* of racial discrimination; legislators latched on to interstate commerce as the justification for civil-rights reform most likely to succeed in court. Not a problem, held the *Heart of Atlanta/Katzenbach* Court. The true motive of Congress is irrelevant. This holding opened the way for wide-scale use of the interstate-commerce power to enact federal regulation of local morals and crime.

The combined effect of these liberalizing cases was that in the modern era it seemed that any real limits on the interstate-commerce power were political, not constitutional. Very few, if any, areas of local activity would be so economically trivial that, when combined, they could not plausibly have a substantial effect on the national economy.

Limiting regulation of many non-economic activities

With Congress's interstate-commerce powers largely expanded by 1964, the stage seemed set for widespread federal muscling in on activities traditionally regulated by state and local governments. For almost 60 years after the Court began to expand the interstate-commerce power in the 1937 *Jones & Laughlin* case, the Court never met a commerce-clause-based law it didn't like — or at least was willing to declare unconstitutional. But a couple of recent cases raise major questions about extending the interstate-commerce power to non-economic local activities.

In 1995 and again in 2000, a Court concerned about states' rights tried to draw a line in the constitutional sand. In *United States v. Lopez*, 514 U.S. 549 (1995), a 5–4 majority invalidated the Gun-Free School Zones Act of 1990, which outlawed possession of a firearm within 1,000 feet of any school. In *United States v. Morrison*, 529 U.S. 598 (2000), the same justices struck down the Violence Against Women Act, which provided a special civil-damage remedy for victims of gender-motivated violence.

Did the *Lopez/Morrison* limit go up in smoke? Medical marijuana and federal antidrug laws

The Court's latest foray into the interstate-commerce power, *Gonzales v. Raich,* 545 U.S. 1 (2005), put the justices in a quandary. *Raich* raised the question of the constitutionality of applying federal antidrug laws to patients growing marijuana for their own personal use in compliance with California's "medical marijuana" law.

From one perspective, growing medical marijuana seemed like a classic non-economic activity beyond the reach of federal regulation. After all, patients weren't selling marijuana or participating in the illegal marijuana trade in any way. They didn't even buy the marijuana plants in interstate commerce.

But the majority of the Court used various theories to justify federal regulation. The dominant view emphasized that Congress could rationally worry that "the high demand in the interstate market will draw [medical] marijuana into that market." (Translation: Patients or caregivers will be tempted to sell their homegrown marijuana, which is indistinguishable from the non-medical kind.)

Some observers (including the dissenting *Raich* justices) see *Raich* as the Court watering down the *Lopez/Morrison* limits. Others instead see a more conventional application of the exceptions the *Lopez* opinion itself contains. Whoever is right, the legal situation is now even hazier.

(We can't resist reminding you of a point we make in Chapter 2: *Raich* shows how justices deciding constitutional cases are often subject to contradictory policy concerns. *Raich* put both conservative and liberal justices in binds. Conservatives generally champion states' rights, which would cause them to sympathize with supporting California's medical-marijuana experiment by telling the federal government to butt out. But conservatives are also antidrug. Liberals, in turn, sympathize with patients' rights but also support federal regulation. Yet another example of why constitutional adjudication should not just be reduced to a political or ideological battle!)

The problem wasn't that Congress lacked sufficient justification for concluding that the activities reached by the laws substantially affected interstate commerce. The substantial, aggregate effect was more than clear. Having guns at or near schools — distracting from the educational climate, producing graduates less qualified to compete economically, lowering neighborhood property values, and so on — clearly has a substantial economic effect. The cumulative cost of absenteeism and medical and psychological treatment for victims of violence imposes a large drag on the national economy.

No, said the *Lopez* and *Morrison* Courts, the problem was more basic. Arguments such as those in the previous paragraph "pile inference upon inference in a manner that would . . . convert congressional power under the commerce clause to a general police power of the sort retained by the States." While not overturning the previous line of cases from *Jones & Laughlin* on, the Court held that the substantial-effect rationale can't save federal regulation of local activities having "nothing to do with 'commerce' or any sort of economic enterprise, however broadly one would define those terms." (The laws at issue were unconstitutional because they were not explicitly limited to economic activities. The law in *Lopez* was not limited to people bringing guns to school to commit economic crimes such as selling drugs, and many of the violent crimes against women covered by the *Morrison* law were sexual and physical assaults not done for economic reasons.)

The *Lopez/Morrison* doctrine threw settled legal doctrines about the interstate-commerce power into great uncertainty. Lower courts had to sort through new legal challenges to federal laws long thought to be valid.

After *Lopez,* opponents of the federal "superfund" law, which requires the cleanup of abandoned hazardous waste sites and tries to bill the parties responsible for the pollution, argued that the law was now unconstitutional. In eventually upholding the superfund law, federal courts had to wade through such questions as whether pumping toxic chemicals into the ground was a non-economic, physical activity and whether the fact that the chemicals were at *one time* part of a commercial enterprise was relevant now.

The current meaning of *Lopez* and *Morrison* is still hard to pin down. The cases included several complicated exceptions from their general principle that non-economic local activities were beyond the reach of federal power. And in a more recent case concerning medical marijuana (see the related sidebar), the Court may have backed away from its effort to limit Congress. Still, the *Lopez/Morrison* limit looms over any current dispute over the ability of Congress to "go local" in commerce-based regulation.

Understanding Rules of Engagement for Other Federal Government Powers

The interstate-commerce power is definitely the "800-pound gorilla" in terms of congressional powers. Whether in terms of practical impact, number of Court decisions, or degree of ongoing controversy, it stands out. (You can read about the commerce power in the earlier section "Observing Express and Implied Powers in Action: The Commerce Power.")

However, four other congressional powers have generated their fair share of controversy: taxing, spending, war, and enforcing constitutional protections. Lest you think that the commerce power is uniquely important or problematic, we briefly canvass these four additional powers here. They led to specialized constitutional-law doctrines in their own right. And these powers provide other examples of the express/implied power framework in operation.

Deduc (t)ing the taxing power

The first power the framers gave to the new federal government in Article I, Section 8 was the power "To lay and collect Taxes, Duties, Imposts and Excises, to pay the Debts and provide for the common Defence and general Welfare of the United States." Providing the new government with its own independent source of revenue not dependent on state governments voluntarily honoring their tax obligations was a key priority to the framers.

The taxing power is the express basis for the many and varied federal income, Social Security, Medicare, gasoline, and other excise taxes modern Americans and their businesses now pay. It broadly and explicitly justifies a number of taxing methods for a variety of purposes. The Sixteenth Amendment eliminated Supreme Court concerns about how the original constitutional requirement that taxation be proportional would affect a federal income tax; ever since, income taxes have been a major source of federal revenue (and ongoing political controversy!).

In the modern era, the Court largely defers to legislative judgments about the legitimate levels and targets of taxation. Current case law directs complaints to the political process, not the courts. Although theoretically possible, it's highly unlikely that the Court would strike down a tax measure clearly not serving any of the purposes explicitly stated in the constitutional language.

The many requirements imposed on individuals and other taxpaying entities (such as making taxpayers retain copies of W-2 forms and requiring people who claim a tax credit for business use of a personal car to keep written trip records) are good examples of measures not expressly stated in the Constitution but justified by the *McCulloch* test, which asks whether a government action is a valid implied means to an enumerated end. (We discuss *McCulloch* in the earlier section "Seeing the Big Picture: Congress's Express and Implied Powers.") Whether such requirements are necessary or essential to ensuring an effective taxation system, they clearly are "appropriate and plainly adapted" to do that. *McCulloch* explains, therefore, why the tax statutes and IRS regulations can be chock-full of such procedures.

The only real area of potential trouble for Congress in using its taxing power is in potentially running afoul of other constitutional restrictions. This last step in the *McCulloch* analysis — that is, whether the otherwise valid exercise of the federal power is "consistent with the letter and spirit" of other constitutional provisions — may be a snag in taxation schemes touching on the First-Amendment right to keep political associations confidential or providing funds to religious organizations, thereby possibly violating First-Amendment prohibitions on establishment of religion.

Scrutinizing the sin tax: Discouraging bad behavior through tax schemes

Before the modern era of giving great leeway to congressional taxation, the Court tried to distinguish federal-tax plans authentically raising revenue from schemes that were really seeking to discourage activities by penalizing them. The Court was concerned that Congress might try to use the power to tax to bypass restrictions on Congress's interstate-commerce power. For example, after the Court struck down the Child Labor Act in *Hammer v. Dagenhart,* 247 U.S. 251 (1918), Congress decided to slap a 10 percent tax on goods manufactured with child labor.

Seeing this child-labor tax as an attempt by Congress to regulate in the guise of a tax, the Court struck it down in *Bailey v. Drexel Furniture Company,* 259 U.S. 20 (1922). The Court recognized that all taxes have an "incidental" regulatory effect, because they encourage or discourage behavior. But the Court found that "there comes a time in the extension of the penalizing features of [a] so-called tax when it... becomes a mere penalty with the characteristics of regulation and punishment." When it does, according to the *Bailey* ruling, Congress exceeds its taxing power.

When it abandoned its more-restrictive approach to the congressional interstate-commerce power, the Court also resigned from the business of distinguishing taxes from penalties.

In *Marchetti v. United States,* 390 U.S. 39 (1968), the taxing power came into potential collision with the Fifth-Amendment right against self-incrimination. The *Marchetti* Court struck down a federal tax on the income of professional gamblers because it would, in essence, require gamblers to report their activities in violation of state antigambling laws. Without adequate protections to assure that the tax man didn't rat out gamblers to law-enforcement officials, the Court held that the federal government could not prosecute gamblers for failure to report their illegal income.

Spending a little time with the spending power

Technically, the federal government has no express power to spend money. But the Court has drawn the logical conclusion that the express powers to raise taxes and to borrow money (the latter power the framers put in Article I, Section 8, Clause 2 — immediately after the taxing authority) make no sense unless the federal government can spend funds to accomplish its constitutionally specified purpose. (Speaking of not making sense, many taxpayers probably have their own ideas of some nonsensical federal spending!)

Congress's power to spend public funds for debt payment, defense, and promoting the "general welfare" is the basis for the many federal grants, loan guarantees, benefits, and procurement activities widely impacting so many areas of the national economy and life. The spending power is like both the interstate-commerce power and the taxing power in that the Court has now backed down from its previous view that it could invalidate spending for certain subjects as involving too much federal interference in economic policy matters better decided by states and local officials.

An example of the previous less-spending-friendly approach is *United States v. Butler,* 297 U.S. 1 (1936). *Butler* struck down provisions in the Roosevelt-era Agricultural Adjustment Act of 1933 using federal funds to subsidize farmers who agreed to restrict crop production. Assuming that the federal government could not directly regulate agricultural output — an assumption rejected in *Wickard v. Filburn,* as discussed earlier — the Court concluded that Congress could not do so indirectly via federal spending. A year later, as part of generally loosening up the reins on federal power, the Court abandoned the *Butler* doctrine.

The many requirements imposed on individuals, companies, other entities, and governmental units receiving federal funds are good examples of how the *McCulloch* implied-means-to-an-enumerated-end test works outside the commerce-power context. (Turn to the earlier section "Using tools to put express powers into effect: Implied congressional powers" for more on *McCulloch.*) Requiring student-loan applicants to fill out long forms and disclose financial data to show that they are eligible recipients, insisting that organizations and governments getting federal funds go through independent financial audits, and a host of other typical requirements for receiving federal financial support are clearly appropriate and plainly adapted to ensure that federal spending accomplishes its purposes. *McCulloch* explains, therefore, why many sections of the federal code and numerous regulations of various beneficiary agencies are so full of such incidental procedures.

The Court developed a special four-part test to determine when the federal government can require a state or local government to change its laws as a condition of receiving federal funds. The most important new elements of the test laid down in *South Dakota v. Dole,* 483 U.S. 203 (1987), are that the condition must be expressly stated in the federal grant law and that the condition imposed on grant recipients not be "unrelated" to the interests prompting the federal government to provide the grants in the first place. (Specifically, *Dole* upheld a requirement that states wanting to continue to receive full federal-highway funding had to require residents to be 21 years of age in order to drink alcoholic beverages. The Court thought that the drinking-age condition related to federal interests in highway safety.)

Stretching war powers to cover domestic regulation

Congress has several powers relating to the successful undertaking of a war. Congress has the power to declare war, to raise and support armed forces and to make rules to govern them. The explicit terms of these "war powers," supplemented by the implied power to use means "appropriate and plainly adapted" to fulfill them, provide ample basis for the federal government to fight and win even a major war.

But what about winning the peace? *Woods v. Cloyd W. Miller Company,* 333 U.S. 138 (1948), raised interesting questions by holding that the bundle of congressional war powers may be used to regulate a U.S. domestic problem "of which the war is a direct and immediate cause."

Woods challenged the constitutionality of a 1947 law freezing rents. Even though World War II had officially ended by then, the Court concluded that "the war power does not necessarily end with the cessation of hostilities." The Court accepted Congress's judgment that the war caused an acute housing shortage by diverting raw materials for military use and then returning large numbers of soldiers to American soil in a relatively short time. The housing shortage threatened a big price spike; hence, the rent-control law was valid.

The task of meaningfully limiting the expansive holding and rationale of *Woods* remains unresolved to this day. The *Woods* Court itself recognized "the force of the argument that the effects of war under modern conditions may be felt in the economy for years and years, and that if the war power can be used in days of peace to treat all the wounds which war inflicts on our society," it could "swallow up" all meaningful constitutional restrictions on federal power. But the Court has not revisited *Woods,* and expansion of other congressional powers has made justification of domestic regulation through war powers largely unnecessary. (Part of the reason why the Court turned to the war powers in *Woods* was because, at the time, the Court had more doubt about whether Congress could justify regulating housing prices through the interstate-commerce power.)

Limiting congressional power to enforce constitutional protections

Section 5 of the Fourteenth Amendment gives Congress express power "to enforce, through appropriate legislation," the amendment's requirements that state and local governments provide equal protection of the laws and afford due process to their residents. Especially as this due-process provision has become the vehicle for applying most of the Bill-of-Rights protections to the states and their subdivisions (as we explain in Chapter 8), the "Section 5" power has become a potent tool for Congress to regulate how these governments treat people under their authority.

Current Supreme Court doctrines place these two important limits on congressional power to enforce the constitutional protections embodied in the Fourteenth Amendment:

✔ Congress may only enforce an existing Fourteenth Amendment right, not "chang[e] what the right is" or "determine what constitutes a constitutional violation."

✔ Even when only enforcing existing rights, the congressional remedy must be "congruent" and "proportional" to the problem under attack (that is, Congress's action must be appropriate in direction and breadth).

These hardly self-evident limitations need an example to flesh them out, and no illustration is better than the case articulating the limits, *City of Boerne v. Flores,* 521 U.S. 507 (1997). *City of Boerne* challenged the constitutionality of the 1993 Religious Freedom Restoration Act (RFRA). Congress passed RFRA in response to the Court's decision in *Employment Division, Department of Human Resources v. Smith,* 494 U.S. 872 (1990). As we explain in Chapter 12, *Smith* significantly changed the law involving the free-exercise clause of the First Amendment. Pre-*Smith* decisions gave laws substantially burdening religious exercise an exacting "strict scrutiny" (which requires that the government's interest be "compelling" and that its law be "narrowly drawn" to accomplish that compelling interest). *Smith* defaulted to an easy-to-meet rational-basis test. In RFRA, Congress sought to bring back the good-old-days of strict scrutiny.

Foul!, cried the *City of Boerne* Court — as concerns Congress's ability to reimpose a strict-scrutiny regime on state and local governments. First, instead of enforcing rights as now in place, RFRA appeared to the *City of Boerne* Court to be a congressional effort to "decree the substance of Fourteenth Amendment restrictions on the States." Congressional pretensions to "alter the meaning of the Free Exercise Clause," said the Court, threaten the judicial-review function and the supremacy of constitutional rights.

A second and independent problem with RFRA, said the *City of Boerne* Court, was that Congress's remedy was way out of proportion to the disease. Thus, "imposing a heavy litigation burden on the States" and "curtailing their traditional regulatory power" without proof of widespread state and local trampling on religious freedom was not "congruent" with or "proportional" to the problem RFRA sought to address.

Boerne was a dramatic departure from earlier court/congress cooperation. In the years before *City of Boerne,* justices gave Congress lots more room to protect individual rights in ways the Court had been unwilling to.

Executive orders: Continuity and controversy

The practice of issuing executive orders began with the first president, George Washington. Presidents vary significantly in their use of executive orders; President Theodore Roosevelt took the practice to a high art, issuing more than 1,000. Presidents in office during wartime (such as Abraham Lincoln and Franklin Roosevelt) or other national emergencies (Franklin Roosevelt gets mentioned here as well, as a Great Depression–era president) have established especially important national policies through executive order.

The importance of and controversy surrounding executive orders as sources of national policy formation are graphically illustrated by the executive orders President Barack Obama issued soon after assuming the presidency in January, 2009. Fulfilling campaign promises, Obama's executive orders declared that the terrorist detention center at Guantanamo Bay military base — a detention center itself established by executive orders from President George W. Bush issued after 9/11 — would be shut down within a year. Another Obama order also banned harsh interrogations (which critics said amounted to official torture) of terrorist suspects.

These executive orders fanned significant controversies in Congress and among the public. Concerned that suspected terrorists held at Guantanamo military base might be held (or even released) on American soil because the U.S. government wouldn't be able to convince other countries to take them, Congress included language in a 2011 defense-appropriations bill limiting the Obama administration's options. This complication and others led President Obama to issue a substantially amended new executive order in March of 2011. The order backpedaled on the time frame for closing Guantanamo and in other ways harmonized Obama's policy with Bush's original approach; the new order indicated that the Administration might proceed with trying terror suspects in military courts after all.

So, just as one piece of congressional legislation doesn't prevent further legislative changes, issuance of an executive order doesn't necessarily end the matter — especially when the subject is highly charged politically.

Years before *City of Boerne,* in *Katzenbach v. Morgan,* 384 U.S. 641 (1966), the Court reviewed the constitutionality of part of a federal voting-rights law prohibiting states from requiring voters to be proficient in the English language. Challengers argued that because the *Court* had declined in a previous case to impose such a prohibition, *Congress* could not do so now. The Court approved Congress's expansion of voting rights, generously deferring to the legislative body's fact-finding capacities and declaring that "it was for Congress [to] assess and weight the various conflicting considerations" at issue. The *Katzenbach* majority modestly declined to second-guess, saying "it is enough that we be able to perceive a basis upon which the Congress might resolve the conflict as it did."

This hands-off, can-we-perceive-the-basis approach contrasts dramatically with the intrusive two-step inquiry *City of Boerne* later established. Why did the *Boerne* Court change its tune so much? More than likely, the Court thought that RFRA was a bigger challenge to judicial authority because it sought to *reverse* a recent Court decision. Whatever the reason, the move from *Katzenbach* generosity to *City of Boerne* stinginess leaves Congress less able to protect the rights of Americans through protective legislation.

Getting the Executive Branch in the Act of Lawmaking

From the standard civics-textbook perspective, bringing the executive branch into a discussion of federal lawmaking may seem inappropriate (other than to point out that the president participates in legislation through the veto power). After all, the Congress *legislates;* the president and his underlings *execute.*

But for two main reasons briefly explained in this section, any discussion of national power would be incomplete without considering the significant role of the president and other executive branch officials in determining how the exercise of national lawmaking power impacts individuals, businesses, organizations, communities, and ultimately American society as a whole.

Issuing executive orders

One reason why the president needs to be considered as a lawmaker in reality is the long-standing practice of presidents issuing executive orders to implement the powers they are granted by Article II of the Constitution. When the president issues an executive order setting forth how the armed forces will participate in NATO war games (in furtherance of his Section 2, Clause 2 commander-in-chief power), or when he issues an executive order establishing procedures to be followed by applicants for pardons or reprieves (in furtherance of his power to grant such relief, also in Section 2, Clause 2), he is in a very real sense legislating — that is, he is setting forth generically and for the future what standards will govern a highly interested group of government employees or benefit applicants.

Constitutional analysis of executive orders shares the following similarities with laws passed by Congress and signed by the president or passed over his veto:

✔ Executive orders are valid and binding to the extent that they are consistent with one or more expressly granted presidential powers.

✔ Presidential powers are generously interpreted as allowing implied extensions beyond their express terms.

✔ Executive orders must be consistent with all other constitutional requirements. (Of course, executive orders can't contradict existing federal statutes, either.)

Executive orders also share with statutes the reality that, even though they are often about relatively technical or trivial details, they can also be very important sources of governing law. President Truman's 1948 executive order desegregating the U.S. military was controversial in some circles at the time, but it set the stage for other civil-rights victories and assured today's racially integrated military. Executive Order 10925, issued in 1961 by President Kennedy and continued in substantially similar form since, establishes groundbreaking affirmative-action policies for federal employees and contractors. It is still one of the major sources of antidiscrimination "law" to this day.

Delegating legislative powers to the president and executive agencies

The president and executive-branch officials figure prominently in lawmaking in another, very important sense, besides executive orders (see the preceding section). As the Supreme Court put it in *Mistretta v. United States,* 488 U.S. 361 (1989), "in our increasingly complex society, replete with ever changing and more technical problems, Congress simply cannot do its job absent an ability to delegate power under broad general directives" to the president and lesser executive-branch officials.

This means that for many important regulatory or government-benefit statutes, Congress merely sketches in the broad outlines of its desired policy objectives and then passes responsibility on to the president or executive underlings to fill in the details. Under current Court decisions summarized in *Mistretta,* as long as Congress writes into its statute "an intelligible principle to which the person or body authorized to [act for Congress] is directed to conform, such legislative action" is constitutional.

Given the generous way in which this "intelligible principle" standard has been implemented — allowing Congress, for example, to authorize a wartime price administrator in the executive branch to fix commodity prices that would be "fair and equitable" (*Yakus v. United States,* 321 U.S. 414 [1944]) — the reality is that for many major regulatory and government-benefit laws, most of the legal requirements and details of interest to individuals and entities are established by executive delegates rather than by Congress. In a very real sense, administrators authorized to make implementing rules having "the force and effect of law" are the more important lawmakers much of the time.

Indeed, because Congress often delegates lawmaking authority initially to the president — for example, authorizing the president to determine that another country is discriminating against American goods and impose an appropriate counter-tariff on the goods of the offending country — this arrangement is another real way in which the president and not Congress can be the more important lawmaker.

Chapter 6

Sorting Out National Powers: Inter-Branch Conflict and Cooperation

*O*ne of the key features of the U.S. Constitution is separation of national powers among three distinct yet codependent branches. This setup, in which the legislative, executive, and judicial branches "check and balance" each other, was an important part of the framers' prescription for preventing the federal government from becoming oppressive.

This chapter examines the ongoing tension resulting from the positioning of the three national governmental branches. We first explore different aspects of the central separation-of-powers issue in constitutional law — deciding who is responsible for interpreting the Constitution. We trace the Supreme Court's landmark claim, in the 1803 case of *Marbury v. Madison,* of the power to declare acts of Congress unconstitutional. We then examine the power that Congress and the president still have to influence constitutional decision making. A section on inter-branch rivalry in constitutional interpretation briefly explains the rules of judicial restraint the Supreme Court has made for itself and other federal judges in an effort to avoid needless conflict with other elected officials.

We then turn to how the Court has refereed other important power disputes between Congress and the president. This section distinguishes the formalistic and pragmatic approaches the Court brings to modern separation-of-powers cases. The chapter concludes with a final section underscoring some key areas of inter-branch conflict that remain unresolved — constitutionally and politically — to this day.

Establishing Judicial Review: The Power to Declare Official Acts Unconstitutional

The Constitution's framers probably intended some form of *judicial review* (the power to review laws and actions of Congress and the president and declare them unconstitutional). But they didn't say so directly in the Constitution. Not until the landmark decision of *Marbury v. Madison,* 5 U.S. 137 (1803), was the Court's judicial-review power established. And although how the *Marbury* Court reasoned its way to judicial review remains controversial today, its validity and enduring importance are subjects of widespread agreement.

Understanding the framers' expectations

Most scholars think that the Constitution's framers expected federal courts to engage in some kind of judicial review of laws passed by Congress. One bit of evidence is how the Constitutional Convention handled a proposal to have Supreme Court justices join the president in a Council of Revision to review legislation passed by Congress. In rejecting the proposal, the framers apparently recognized that federal courts would later review the validity of legislation in cases coming before them; thus, the justices' attendance at the Council was unnecessary. Explaining the judiciary's role to Constitution ratifiers in Federalist Paper No. 78, Alexander Hamilton wrote that "the courts were designed to be an intermediate body between the people and the legislature, in order . . . to keep the latter within the limits assigned to their authority."

Still, neither the English nor American colonial judges with whom the framers were familiar engaged in anything like the aggressive judicial review performed today by federal courts. This fact, plus the relative lack of attention framers gave to the organization of the federal judiciary, may explain why they didn't expressly provide for judicial review in the constitutional text. Even the Article III language giving federal courts the power to decide "all cases and controversies arising under the Constitution" raises the question of whether a lawsuit asking courts to rule against a law or decision of Congress or the president is a case "arising under" the Constitution.

Establishing judicial review with Marbury v. Madison

In the following sections we summarize the situation leading to *Marbury v. Madison,* explain the Court's basic logic, and identify several reasons why that logic remains not fully convincing to this day.

Setting the stage for Marbury's momentous holding

The Supreme Court took judicial review from iffy implication to clear holding in the landmark case of *Marbury v. Madison,* 5 U.S. 137 (1803). *Marbury* arose when newly elected President Jefferson instructed his secretary of state (James Madison) not to deliver commissions of appointment to 41 persons (including William Marbury) appointed as justices of the peace in the last days of the administration of former president John Adams. (The appointments were confirmed by the Senate but not delivered by the time the Jefferson Administration assumed office. Jefferson preferred to see political plums go to *his* loyalists.)

Marbury and his fellow appointees invoked a provision in Section 13 of the Judiciary Act of 1789. The provision allowed aggrieved parties to sue directly in the Supreme Court for *writs of mandamus* — orders requiring government officials to perform legally required duties. The Court held that Marbury and colleagues had a right to their commissions, the law afforded them a remedy, and mandamus was the appropriate order for accomplishing that. Only one issue, said the Court, denied Marbury and his buddies the relief they sought: The Supreme Court had no jurisdiction to issue the requested mandamus writ.

As the *Marbury* Court saw it, the Judiciary Act's grant of mandamus power was inconsistent with the way Article III of the Constitution divided the federal judicial power between the Supreme Court's original and appellate jurisdiction. Article III limited original jurisdiction — that is, cases that could be brought directly to the Court without first going to a lower federal or state court — to only the two case categories the framers expressly provided for. Chief Justice John Marshall and his colleagues saw Section 13's grant of mandamus power as contradicting Article III by in essence adding a third category of original jurisdiction (namely, cases against federal officials), which would be, well, unconstitutional!

Identifying the two basic principles invoked in Marbury

Now facing an act of Congress with a clause seemingly "repugnant to the constitution," the *Marbury* Court asked whether it still "bind[s] the courts, and oblige[s] them to give it effect." The Court decided no, they were not required to follow Section 13, *because in the Court's view it was contrary to the supreme constitutional plan.*

The *Marbury* Court didn't rely primarily on either express constitutional language or indications of the framers' intent (see the earlier section "Understanding the framers' expectations"). Instead, Chief Justice Marshall found it "only necessary to recognize certain principles, supposed to have been long and well established." Here are his two principles:

- ✔ **Constitutional supremacy:** Marshall argued that judicial review was implicit in the kind of constitution that Americans had adopted — namely, a "supreme paramount law" not "alterable when the legislature shall please to alter it."

✔ **Nature of the judicial role:** Marshall saw judicial review as implicit in the judicial role, which was to "apply the rule to particular cases" by deciding which of two or more conflicting law sources governs.

Understanding the weaknesses of Marshall's reasoning

Few modern analysts disagree with the holding of *Marbury*. Judicial review is an accepted (and as argued, essential) bulwark in the constitutional structure. But many scholars find Chief Justice Marshall's *reasoning* dubious today. Following are their main concerns:

✔ **The inconsistency of Section 13's grant of mandamus power with Article III of the Constitution is debatable.** Critics think that the *Marbury* Court made too much of the fact that the framers listed two categories of cases that could go originally to the Supreme Court and provided that other case categories would go to the Court on appeal. Critics point out that the judicial-power provisions of Article III are sketchy and the framers otherwise gave Congress a big role to play in defining federal-court structure. Why assume, critics ask, that the framers (many of whom were members of the Congress that passed the 1789 Judiciary Act!) didn't want Congress to add to the Court's original jurisdiction in worthwhile cases?

✔ **The *Marbury* Court never adequately justified why existing "express checks" on unconstitutional congressional action needed to be expanded.** Much of the rhetoric Chief Justice Marshall used to develop his first principle (that judicial review is inherent in a supreme constitution) appears misdirected. That is, Marshall spent most of his argument stating that the Constitution is supreme and that Congress may not violate it. That point is indisputable; it flows directly from the Article VI supremacy clause.

What Marshall instead needed to establish was that the framers intended for the *judicial branch* to participate in ensuring congressional compliance with the Constitution. The two most important arguments made by critics of *Marbury* are these:

- Why assume that the framers would want an implied judicial check added to the multiple specific checks on Congress listed in the Constitution (the presidential veto and making members run for reelection, for example)?

- Why give the Court the freedom to act unconstitutionally, which was denied to Congress? Marshall pointed out that the Constitution is undermined if the limits it established "may, at any time, be passed by those intended to be restrained." Marshall was referring to the Congress, but his description of persons able to ignore the Constitution "at any time" seems even more applicable to federal judges. Without an immediate check on their decisions and with no need to face reelection once appointed for life, the federal judiciary seems even less subject to correction than Congress.

Tough luck for Marbury the litigant

You may think that the mistake Marbury and his fellow appointees made was to start in the wrong court, bringing an *original* action in the Supreme Court. Because a mandamus action against Secretary of State Madison clearly fell within the Court's *appellate* jurisdiction over cases "arising under" U.S. laws, readers often conclude that the disappointed office seekers could just refile their challenge in a lower court and take it up to the Supreme Court if they lost.

Unfortunately for Marbury and friends, no lower federal or state court had jurisdiction to issue a mandamus writ against a high-ranking federal official. The Supreme Court was the only game in town. Although the *Marbury* opinion didn't dwell on the point, denying access to the Court meant that the office seekers never got their commissions — in practice making a lie out of *Marbury*'s famous line, "For every right there is a remedy."

✔ **Some critics say that Chief Justice Marshall never adequately explained his leap from the typical role of judges to the extraordinary role assumed when the federal judiciary corrects Congress (or the president).** Critics argue that judicial review of Congress (and, by extension, the president) involves an *extraordinary* exercise of judicial power. After all, it involves one branch telling a coequal that its actions are invalid, arguably becoming superior in the process. Assuming the legitimacy of this power from the *ordinary* judicial role — in which federal judges correct inferior federal officials or subordinate state and local judges and elected officials — is arguably like assuming that because the first-year resident in the emergency room can stitch up a cut finger, she can perform complex brain surgery.

Appreciating the upside of judicial review

Whatever its logical fallacies, *Marbury* provides an enduring legacy that has well served (and, many would argue, primarily guaranteed) the Constitution's longevity.

Here are some advantages of — and justifications for — judicial review:

✔ **Protecting constitutional values through a branch that's less sensitive to political change:** *Marbury* ensured that the least politically responsive of the national-government branches could strongly protect constitutional values. Although the federal courts haven't always stood up to temporary political passions, especially in times of economic or national-security stress, they've done better than their electorally accountable counterparts. And, although the legal training and role expectations of judges are no guarantee of "equal justice under law," they certainly help.

> ✔ **Supporting checks and balances:** Judicial review of congressional and presidential actions also promotes checks and balances by making federal courts more-or-less equal partners in the tripartite government.

Many observers say that these rationales more convincingly justify the modern importance of judicial review than Chief Justice Marshall's *Marbury* reasoning.

Clarifying the Role of Elected Officials in Interpreting the Constitution

Marbury didn't necessarily claim that the Constitution's framers intended federal courts to be the supreme constitutional interpreters. A different Court opinion more than 150 years later did that. Still, Congress and the president retain substantial direct and indirect power to shape constitutional interpretation and to advance or undermine constitutional values.

Judicial supremacy: Binding the other branches to Supreme Court decisions

As great a landmark as it was, the *Marbury* decision didn't necessarily establish that the Supreme Court had a special role to play in constitutional interpretation. All that the *Marbury* Court had to decide (and all it arguably did decide) was whether the justices got to do the same thing Congress and the president could do in their areas of power — namely to use their own interpretation of the Constitution in fulfilling their official duties.

Even after *Marbury,* the three branches could be coequal sharers in constitutional interpretation, checking and balancing each other and fulfilling the framers' general separation of powers. President Andrew Jackson said as much in 1832 when he vetoed a bill reestablishing a national bank. Explaining why he was acting on his own assessment that a national bank was unconstitutional, and not deferring to the Court's view in *McCulloch v. Maryland* that such a bank *was* constitutional (as explained in Chapter 5), Jackson wrote: "The Congress, the Executive, and the Court must each for itself be guided by its own opinion of the Constitution. . . . The opinion of the judges has no more authority over Congress than the opinion of Congress has over the judges, and on that point the president is independent of both."

The Court implicitly rejected the view that the Court is merely equal to the other branches in *Cooper v. Aaron,* 358 U.S. 1 (1958). *Cooper* rejected the assertion that Arkansas officials were not formally bound by the Court's school-desegregation decision in *Brown v. Board of Education* until a new court ruling specifically found *Brown*'s constitutional interpretation applicable to them. In rendering a decision declaring the Court's supremacy over state and local officials, *Cooper*'s reasoning seems to apply as well to Congress and the president.

Cooper claimed that *Marbury* "declared the basic principle that the federal judiciary is supreme in the exposition of the law of the Constitution" and that this basic principle "has ever since been respected by this Court and the Country as a permanent and indispensible feature of our constitutional system." *Cooper* concluded that the *Brown* decision, as much as the Fourteenth Amendment it interpreted, was "the supreme law of the land" binding everyone who takes an oath to support the Constitution. Presumably, Congress and the president, who take a similar oath, are also bound by Supreme Court decisions.

Cooper's take on judicial *supremacy* — the view that federal courts play a special and even supreme role in interpreting the Constitution — is now in vogue. Members of Congress and presidents often criticize rulings by the Supreme Court and lower federal courts, who make easy targets because traditions of judicial demeanor prevent them from responding in kind. But elected officials rarely assert the right to legislate or execute in ways directly contrary to the Court's constitutional pronouncements. In this way, Congress and the president get to talk a big game while leaving the truly controversial constitutional decisions to federal jurists.

What's left for Congress and the president?

Assuming that Congress and the president cannot directly defy the Court's constitutional rulings — and remembering that the Constitution limits other direct reprisals against judges and justices (such as preventing salary diminution and limiting impeachment to "high Crimes and Misdemeanors") — the question remains: What authority is left for Congress and the president to check and balance the federal courts and actively shape constitutional and nonconstitutional law?

The answer is, a lot. The modern realities of governing (together with the judicial-restraint doctrines considered in the next section) mean that many important areas of domestic and foreign policy with big constitutional dimensions never, or only slowly, reach the federal courts. Congress and the president have a crucial impact on protecting or undermining constitutional values when they fulfill their core legislative and executive duties.

Congress and the president also have a number of means at their disposal to influence constitutional and nonconstitutional values indirectly by checking and balancing the federal judiciary. To give you a taste of this large and important subject, we provide two non-exhaustive lists of key things elected officials *clearly* can do and things that officials *arguably* can do.

Clearly legitimate ways to influence the work of federal courts

One area in which Congress can impact the courts is through appointments and the allocation of judicial resources. Here are the actions that Congress can take:

- **Appoint and confirm federal judges and justices to fill existing judicial vacancies.** The president and the Senate can seek to appoint judges who will rule the "right" way (that is, consistently with the views of the president or Senate).

- **Create (or not create) new district-court or court-of-appeals vacancies, including by dividing up existing court-of-appeals circuits.** These decisions affect both the workload and the overall ideological tenor of the federal judiciary.

- **Determine how much money and attention will be devoted to the full enforcement of particular Court rulings.**

- **Enhance (or contract) federal-court jurisdiction and remedial powers, thus expanding (or contracting) the cases federal courts can take and the remedies they can provide.** Although Article III of the Constitution defines "the judicial Power of the United States," the Court has long held that the Article established the greatest *potential* reach of that power. How much of that power is realized depends upon laws passed by Congress.

Arguably valid ways to check and balance the federal courts

The "jury is still out" on the constitutionality and legitimacy of several other potentially important checks on judicial power. The following two means of influence are especially subject to ongoing argument:

- **"Packing" the Supreme Court by adding enough new members to allow the current president and Senate to appoint a working majority:** Critics branded President Franklin Roosevelt's 1937 proposal to pack the Court a dangerous interference with the independence the framers intended for the federal judiciary. Yet the Constitution sets no fixed number of justices. The number has varied from six to ten. Plus, the express provisions on judicial appointment and confirmation contain no limits. In fact, they don't even require minimum ages or other qualifications!

✔ **Making exceptions to the Supreme Court's appellate jurisdiction to disable the Court from ruling on constitutional questions:** If Congress sensed that the Court was about to rule that the Constitution requires states to recognize gay marriages, could Congress pass legislation stripping the Court of jurisdiction over appeals on this issue? For decades, such "Court-stripping" bills have been proposed; some have come close to passage. A trio of cases taking varying positions on different jurisdiction-limiting bills adopted after the Civil War fail to provide definitive guidance. Thus, even today proponents can claim that Article III, Section 2, Clause 2 expressly grants this power without reservation. Opponents can also plausibly respond that icing the Court out of constitutional decision making, under the cynical hope that lower courts will interpret the Constitution differently, is completely contrary to judicial and constitutional supremacy.

Limiting Judicial Power through Doctrines of Self-Restraint

Some very important limits on the federal judiciary's Constitution-interpreting power come not from sources outside the judicial branch but from the judiciary itself. The modern Court has developed a number of *justiciability* doctrines, which often prevent federal courts from deciding constitutional and nonconstitutional issues.

In theory, the justiciability limits derive from Article III's language limiting the federal judicial power to actual "cases or controversies." But in reality, these judicial-restraint doctrines reflect an awareness of how the judicial-review power puts federal courts into potential tension with many public officials — especially at the national level. The doctrines are also highly discretionary, meaning that judges may apply them rigorously or loosely in particular cases, given other important values besides judicial restraint.

Because Article III only applies to *federal* courts, the rules of justiciability do not technically bind state courts. However, many state courts have interpreted similar self-restraint rules from their state constitutions. In fact, many state courts copy or substantially re-create federal justiciability rules.

Lawyers and law students need detailed knowledge of the justiciability doctrines because they often make the difference between winning or losing a lawsuit. This knowledge is usually gained from reading and parsing stacks of cases! Here we provide an overview of the major different categories of self-restraint doctrines, with particular attention to the justiciability rule most clearly reflecting basic concerns over separation of powers.

Restricting judicial forums to especially injured parties: Standing to sue

Some justiciability doctrines seek to reserve judicial forums for *proper parties.* Motivated by concerns that federal courts not become, in the words of *Valley Forge Christian College v. Americans United,* 454 U.S. 464 (1982), "debating societies" for the ventilation of abstract grievances by members of the public, the Court has developed a number of rules to ensure that a party challenging government action has proper "standing" to sue. Generally, that means the person making the challenge is someone who actually suffered a specialized injury. A litigant must claim more than the rights of any U.S. citizen (and, except in rare cases, any taxpayer) not to have their government act illegally. The Court has identified three standing requirements from Article III of the Constitution and two additional "prudential" standing limits.

Three constitutional requirements

These Article III–standing requirements — the minimum requirements to assure that the lawsuit is a constitutionally recognizable "case or controversy" — require the challenge to have the following characteristics:

- **Injury in fact:** The plaintiff alleges an injury that is *distinct* from the citizenry at large, *palpable* (that is, real and concrete rather than speculative or abstract), and *actual or imminent* (as opposed to occurring someday in the future).

- **Causation in fact:** The plaintiff's alleged injury is "fairly traceable" to governmental actions or omissions, not to the way that third parties react to governmental actions or omissions.

- **Redressability:** The plaintiff's alleged injury can be remedied by favorable judicial action.

Additional prudential standing limits

Additional requirements are called the *prudential* limits because they aren't constitutionally required but rather stem from additional discretion in avoiding inappropriate judicial decision making. Following are some prudential limits:

- **A general ban on third-party standing:** Except in unusual cases, plaintiffs mounting federal-court challenges must assert their own rights and interests, not those of others.

- **The *zone of interests* test:** Litigants who challenge governmental action on the ground that it violates a congressional statute must show that they (the litigants) are "arguably within the zone of interests meant to be protected" by that law. The language is from *Air Courier Conference of America v. American Postal Workers Union,* 498 U.S. 517 (1990), which held that postal workers who would arguably lose jobs because postal regulatory authorities loosened international mailing restrictions could not challenge the rule change under the relevant federal postal statutes. The *Air Courier* Court interpreted those laws as intending to protect postal patrons and the Postal Service itself, but not postal workers.

Ensuring that judicial review is timely

Several justiciability doctrines aim to ensure that the time is appropriate for challengers to mount a federal-court lawsuit.

Following are two doctrines denying a federal court hearing for scenarios in which it's too early to bring a lawsuit:

- ✔ Because a challenged governmental policy has not yet become final, the litigant essentially seeks an *advisory opinion* (that is, nice advice about the correct view of the law that will not really provide relief to a party).

- ✔ The litigant's claim of injury is not yet "ripe" for judicial resolution because, among other possible reasons, further developments are needed to make the challenger's injuries more than a hypothetical threat, or the effects of further administrative action haven't run their course.

Mootness, another important justiciability doctrine, is concerned about the other side of litigation timing. A challenge can become moot, or no longer worthy of argument and decision, when no live controversy is taking place between the parties. Typically, mootness occurs when the plaintiffs may no longer be suffering any injury or the defendants may have ended their arguably illegal action. Mootness analysis raises a number of subtleties, including the following points:

- ✔ **Even if the plaintiff's main injury has ceased, her lawsuit is not moot if she still faces collateral consequences.** For example, even if she is no longer illegally detained in jail, if her arrest will appear on her employment record, her case is not moot.

- ✔ **The courts can still hear a technically moot case if its issues are "capable of repetition" with respect to this plaintiff and "evasive of review."** That is, if the same events could occur and become moot again before reaching court, the case can be brought to court.

In the highly controversial abortion-rights case *Roe v. Wade,* 410 U.S. 113 (1973), Texas tried to avoid a Court ruling against its strict anti-abortion law by arguing that Roe's constitutional claim was moot because she was no longer pregnant. The Court granted an exception, because Roe could get pregnant again and seek a legal abortion, only to have the nine-month gestation cycle of pregnancy again defeat her claim. The Court was unwilling to zone most reproductive-rights cases out of federal court.

Staying out of it: Keeping especially troubling issues out of federal court

One justiciability doctrine more directly reflects special concerns about the tough position in which judicial review puts unelected federal judges. The *political-question doctrine* prevents cases from being heard in federal courts (regardless of the litigant or the basis or timing of the lawsuit) for any of the following reasons (as formally laid down in *Baker v. Carr,* 369 U.S. 186 (1962):

✔ **The Constitution gives another federal official, not the federal courts, final authority to decide the issue.** For example, in *Nixon v. United States,* 506 U.S. 224 (1993), the Court held that the language of Article I, Section 3 giving the Senate the "sole Power to try all Impeachments" disabled federal courts from deciding a challenge by impeached federal-district judge Walter Nixon. Judge Nixon had claimed that it was unconstitutional for the Senate to allow one of its committees, rather than the full Senate, to hear the relevant evidence, with other Senators merely relying on the committee's summary report.

✔ **Judges lack "judicially discoverable and manageable standards."** In *Colegrove v. Green,* 328 U.S. 549 (1946), the Court held that the Article IV obligation of the national government to "guarantee to every State in this Union a Republican Form of Government" is not subject to judicial resolution because federal courts would have to wander into questions of governmental philosophy and practical politics to define the minimum requirements of Republicanism.

✔ **Other special concerns make judicial involvement unwise, such as in the following situations:**

- When federal judges can't decide a case until a political official makes "an initial policy determination" not appropriate for judges. (For example, perhaps money claims can't be resolved until the president formally recognizes the official representative of a foreign country.)

- When federal judges can't decide without "expressing lack of respect due" Congress or the president. (For instance, courts would not likely referee a dispute between the president and a top aide.)

- When the situation requires "an unusual need for unquestioning adherence to a political decision already made." (For example, in cases of national emergency, a questionable presidential lead may need to be followed without challenge.)

- When conflicting "pronouncements by various departments on one question" would be inappropriate. (For an example, read on.)

Goldwater v. Carter, 444 U.S. 996 (1979), not only illustrates the special political-question concerns in action but also points to a still-unresolved separation-of-powers controversy. The *Goldwater* Court faced a lawsuit by several senators, who, having voted initially to ratify a defense treaty with Taiwan, argued that the Senate also had to approve President Carter's later decision to cancel the treaty. The Court declined to decide the constitutional question the Senators raised, with four justices finding it a nonjusticiable political question. (Another justice found the challenge unripe because Congress and President Carter had not yet exhausted the *political* avenues for contesting the question.) The political-question concerns of the four justices likely included a desire not to disrespect the president's preeminence in foreign affairs or undermine the importance of dealing consistently with other countries.

Sorting Out Other Separation-of-Powers Disputes

Because the framers deliberately chose to have three independent and competing national-power centers, it isn't surprising that throughout the nation's history the three branches — and especially Congress and the president, the key national policymakers — have jockeyed for advantage.

In this section, we introduce two approaches the courts take in deciding separation-of-powers cases. We look at how some modern cases use the approaches, and we tell you how to predict which approach courts will take.

Distinguishing formalistic and pragmatic approaches

The modern Court employs two basic approaches in deciding separation-of-powers disputes:

✔ **Formalism:** As the name implies, this approach involves rigorous loyalty to the Constitution's provisions and structural formalities. When the Court is being formalistic, it tends to see the categories of legislative, executive, and judicial power as separated by relatively clear lines that should not be blurred by newfangled innovations dishonoring the framers' carefully formed limitations. The formalistic approach values preventing dangerous power concentrations over allowing the national government to deal efficiently with unanticipated challenges.

✔ **Pragmatism:** When the Court uses a pragmatic (practical) approach to separation-of-powers disputes, it recognizes that the framers didn't create three "hermetically sealed" national-power centers. The powers are shared and overlapping. The framers intended the branches to work together to take on important initiatives in a changing world. Pragmatists see constitutional formalities as creating an important framework for inter-branch cooperation and innovation.

Examining the results of modern separation-of-powers decisions

Until the last several decades, courts generally (but not completely) avoided refereeing disputes between the two elected branches. Historically, judges and legal scholars tended to see power disputes as best resolved through the political process. After all, Congress and the president possessed ample tools (such as the power to pass and veto legislation and the ability to grant and withhold appropriations and appointments) to protect their powers against threats from the other branch. Besides, courts recognized special dangers in getting involved in highly political and often partisan power struggles, because a federal judiciary is dependent on being perceived as above politics.

The Court overcame its general reluctance to decide separation-of-power controversies in a few cases, such as the landmark decision in *Youngstown Sheet & Tube Company v. Sawyer,* 343 U.S. 579 (1952), which we discuss in the following section. And since the early 1980s, the Court has decided a number of cases challenging acts of Congress that blurred the traditional lines between legislative, executive, and judicial powers. Sometimes formalism reigned, and the congressional experimentation was ruled unconstitutional. At other times, the Court interpreted the Constitution as allowing their perceived need for innovation or category blurring. We summarize these major separation-of-powers decisions here.

Formalism and pragmatism in play in Youngstown

Youngstown Sheet & Tube Company declared unconstitutional an executive order by President Harry Truman "directing his Secretary of Commerce to take possession of and operate most of the Nation's steel mills." Steel workers were threatening to strike, so Truman ordered this highly unusual (although temporary) takeover of private enterprise to assure steel production deemed essential to U.S. success in the Korean War.

The Court concluded that the president's order raised serious questions about the line between the Congress's power to set policy and the president's power to execute it. Six justices agreed that President Truman's steel-industry-seizure order violated the Constitution, but some justices used formalistic reasoning and others used a pragmatic approach:

✔ **Formalistic:** Justice Black's lead opinion catalogued the categories of power the president possesses under the Constitution. Black first noted that President Truman was not acting as the authorized agent of Congress. (See Chapter 5 for an explanation of the relevant modern constitutional doctrines.) Justice Black then concluded that Article II's enumeration of presidential powers did not justify the steel seizure under the commander-in-chief power. Nor was Truman "faithfully executing" a congressional policy; instead he was "direct[ing] that a presidential policy be executed in a manner prescribed by the President." Perceiving that the framers chose to entrust Congress, not the president, with enacting policies affecting domestic industries, Black said that "the historical events, the fears of power and the hopes of freedom that lie behind that choice" have to be honored "in both good and bad times."

✔ **Pragmatic:** Two different opinions were pragmatic:

- Justice Felix Frankfurter agreed that Truman's order was unconstitutional, but his influential concurring opinion pursued a practical, not abstract, analysis of separation of powers. Emphasizing that the framers created a "framework for *government*" involving "partly interacting" branches, Frankfurter admitted that "a systematic, unbroken, executive practice, long pursued to the knowledge of Congress and never before questioned" could in reality end up giving the president powers not formally and explicitly granted in the Constitution.

- Justice Jackson wrote a pragmatic concurrence that has also loomed large in later decisions. Rejecting formalism as inconsistent with "the actual art of governing," Jackson wrote, "While the Constitution diffuses power to secure liberty, it also contemplates that practice will integrate the dispersed powers into a workable government." Jackson noted that the president is likely to increase his power in the face of "congressional inertia, indifference, or acquiescence." The justice warned legislators that "any actual test of power is likely to depend on the imperatives of events and contemporary imponderables rather than on abstract theories of law."

Looking at laws formalistically held unconstitutional

In the following decisions, a majority or individual justices used a formalistic approach to invalidate a congressional or presidential power assertion:

✔ **Legislative veto provisions:** In nearly 200 statutes enacted over several decades before the Court ended the practice, Congress reserved for itself the power to reverse actions taken by executive officials under delegations of power from Congress. For example, in the legislative-veto provision at issue in *Immigration and Naturalization Service v. Chadha,* 462 U.S. 919 (1983), Congress allowed the attorney general to suspend the deportation of an alien who had violated federal law. But Congress reserved for either house of Congress the power to reject the attorney general's decision and put the planned deportation back on schedule.

Six justices in *Chadha* viewed the congressional veto of a deportation suspension as akin to a new legislative act (because it altered the rights and duties of people outside Congress). This view put the legislative veto in direct conflict with the "finely wrought" procedures the framers intended for legislation — which require both houses and the president to weigh in before changing the legal status quo.

✔ **Attempts to influence law execution through congressional agents:** In *Bowsher v. Synar,* 478 U.S. 186 (1986), the Court rejected a crucial provision in a complicated balanced-budget statute. The provision said that if Congress and the president couldn't agree on how to balance the federal budget, the controller general of the United States would ultimately determine the budget cuts. But the power to make budget cuts was viewed as "executive," and the controller was considered to be Congress's agent because Congress could remove the controller and thus control his loyalty. Therefore, the majority saw the interjection of the controller as totally at odds with the constitutionally required separation of executive from legislative powers.

✔ **A presidential line-item veto:** U.S. presidents often complain about not having the power most state governors do to "line out" particular items of the budget (that is, to simply draw a line through an item in a state budget listing, ending funding for that category). When Congress passed a statute in the 1990s giving the president a limited version of line-item authority, the Court balked. The Court in *Clinton v. City of New York,* 524 U.S. 681 (1998), held that giving the president power to change budget authorizations basically gave the president power to single-handedly amend federal law. This violated the "finely wrought" formalities to which the *Chadha* Court had decreed careful adherence.

✔ **Indefinite presidentially ordered detention of American citizens suspected of terrorism:** In *Hamdi v. Rumsfeld,* a 542 U.S. 507 (2004), a Supreme Court majority held that the U.S. government violated the Constitution by indefinitely detaining an American citizen suspected of being a post-9/11 "enemy combatant" without giving him "a meaningful opportunity to contest the factual basis for that detention before a neutral decisionmaker." The Court was split significantly on several important issues, including how much practical leeway the president should have to deal with a national-security threat. Justices Scalia and Stevens (usually on opposite sides of civil-liberties issues) formalistically concluded that only Congress could suspend the writ of habeas corpus pursuant to Article I, Section 9 of the Constitution.

Blurring the lines: Laws seen as acceptable power transfers

Other separation-of-powers decisions are anything but formalistic. The modern Court has upheld the blurring of the formal legislative/executive/judicial categories in the following decisions.

These decisions continue in the spirit of the delegation-of-legislative-power decisions we discuss at the end of Chapter 5 — decisions that since the 1930s have consistently upheld large-scale delegations of legislative authority to executive-branch agents.

- ✔ **Shifting federal-court claims to administrative forums:** In *Commodity Futures Trading Commission v. Schor,* 478 U.S. 833 (1986), the Court upheld a federal statute allowing disputes between commodity traders and their clients to be resolved by a federal administrative agency. This statute diverted legal claims and counterclaims that would ordinarily be heard in federal court into an executive-branch agency. Even though moving these legal disputes from the judicial box into the executive one also had the effect of denying disputants their Seventh-Amendment right to a jury trial, the *Schor* Court upheld the power transfer. Sounding eminently pragmatic, the Court worried that "formalistic and unbending rules" might "unduly constrict Congress' ability to take needed and innovative action." After examining the practical effect of the law on the federal judiciary's power — and confirming that the judiciary still preserved ample authority — the Court upheld the law.

- ✔ **Allowing important prosecutorial duties to be performed by a significantly independent counsel:** After the Watergate scandal in the 1970s forced President Nixon to resign in the face of threatened impeachment, Congress passed an independent-counsel law. The law sought to reduce the conflict of interest that Justice Department prosecutors face when deciding whether to prosecute high-ranking executive officials. The law provided that an independent counsel could be appointed by a three-judge panel; the panel would define the counsel's overall authority and approve their budgets, but the counsel would be largely unsupervised day to day and could independently decide how to handle the many strategic and legal issues prosecutors routinely face.

  Prosecution of federal criminal laws is a classically executive function overseen by the attorney general and, ultimately, the president. Sharing the power with judicial officials and removing the president's usual power to fire prosecutors at will significantly blurred traditional national-power dividing lines. Still, the Court in *Morrison v. Olsen,* 487 U.S. 654 (1988), upheld the independent-counsel law on the theory that the attorney general and president still could sufficiently control the appointment and work of an independent counsel and avoid improper interference with executive authority.

- ✔ **Allowing federal judges to serve on a national sentencing commission:** Having federal judges meet with other elected officials to establish guidelines for the length of federal criminal sentences seemed to significantly blur several categories. It arguably involved judges in inappropriate policymaking and threatened to undermine the judiciary's independence. But in *Mistretta v. United States,* 488 U.S. 361 (1989), the Court approved this power sharing, citing "Justice Jackson's *Youngstown* admonition that the separation of powers contemplates the integration of dispersed powers into a workable government."

Predicting when formalism or pragmatism will reign

Predicting whether courts will bring a more restrictive or permissive approach to future separation-of-powers controversies is helpful both to savvy students of constitutional law and other legal-system participants. Luckily, there does seem to be method to the madness, and we're here to help you interpret it:

- ✓ **Restrictive:** When courts think that Congress is adding to its own powers, they tend to be formalistic. This generalization explains the *Chadha* Court's rejection of the legislative veto and the later cases stopping other congressional attempts to intrude into law execution (see "Looking at laws formalistically held unconstitutional").

- ✓ **Permissive:** When Congress is not (in the words of the *Morrison* Court) "predatory" — when its transfer of powers does not "involve an attempt . . . to increase its powers at the expense of the Executive Branch" — the Court is usually pragmatic. As long as power sharing not directly benefiting Congress isn't too dramatic, it is constitutional. For that reason, the justices allowed the shifts of functions in the cases discussed in the preceding section.

The one case not easily fitting this pattern is the line-item-veto decision in *Clinton* (discussed in the previous section "Looking at laws formalistically held unconstitutional"). Congress giving the president sole authority over budgetary powers it usually guards jealously hardly looks like a predatory move. Yet the Court was high-mindedly formalistic, not pragmatic. What *Clinton* probably shows is that the Court won't tolerate innovations in separated powers — *regardless of who benefits* — when power transfers strike at core functions of national authority *central* to the framers' concern about concentrated power. When central constitutional understandings seem at risk, formalism still triumphs.

By any measure, taxing and spending are core national functions. The framers envisioned that participation by Congress (and especially a popularly elected House of Representatives) would legitimize fiscal decisions. Just as the Court would not likely allow the Senate to give away its formal power to declare war, it did not allow the Congress to abdicate its budgetary authority.

Identifying Areas of Unresolved Conflict

Despite the greater willingness of federal courts in the last several decades to referee fights between Congress and the president, many important separation-of-powers questions remain unanswered — at least in definitive Court decisions. In this section we highlight several of the prominent issues.

Although one or more of these unresolved questions may come before the Court in the future, many are unlikely to ever receive definitive judicial resolution. (One or more of the justiciability doctrines canvassed earlier would likely always frustrate challengers wishing for their day in the Court.)

Controlling war and military powers

The Constitution clearly assigns to Congress the formal power to declare war. In such a declared war, the president is the commander in chief. But what is the constitutional division of authority for undeclared wars (either unilateral or as part of a multinational force) or for ongoing "cold" wars or wars on terror? Many murky areas abound.

In the shadow of dissatisfaction with how Congress and the president functioned in the undeclared Vietnam War, in 1973 Congress passed the War Powers Resolution, which obligates the president to consult with Congress "in every possible instance" before introducing U.S. troops into harm's way. The president is supposed to withdraw troops after 60 days if Congress has not specifically authorized the military operation. Presidents and constitutional-law scholars have disputed the constitutionality of the War Powers Resolution; presidents have often failed to comply fully with its requirements. It has never been tested in court, and may never be.

Protecting the nation with presidential national-security powers

The 9/11 terrorist attacks put in stark debate ongoing uncertainties about the extent of the president's powers to protect the nation against attack and other emergencies. Many uncertainties remain. What are the limits on moving national-security prosecutions from civilian to military tribunals? Can the president order wide-scale interception of suspicious telephone conversations and e-mail communications?

As with other foreign-affairs controversies, a number of barriers — including standing, ripeness, and political-questions doctrines examined in the section "Limiting Judicial Power through Doctrines of Self-Restraint" — mean that the federal courts are unlikely to definitively resolve these questions soon.

Pondering foreign-affairs authority

Much uncertainty surrounds issues of the president's authority in matters of treaties, executive agreements, and foreign affairs. Because the Court never resolved the constitutional arguments raised in *Goldwater v. Carter* (discussed in "Staying out of it: Keeping especially troubling issues out of federal court"), the question of whether the Senate must agree to later cancel a treaty it originally ratified remains unresolved. Also unresolved is the status of less-formal diplomatic agreements entered into via "executive agreements" not submitted to the Senate. Indeed, much remains unclear about foreign affairs in which only the president has the right to represent the country.

"Impounding" budget appropriations

Does the president's general power to faithfully execute the law include the power to refuse to spend appropriated funds? Despite broad arguments by presidents bent on promoting budget discipline, the Court has not definitively decided how to reconcile presidential execution and congressional budgeting. Congress filled the power vacuum by passing the Budget and Impoundment Control Act of 1974. Among many other key budget procedures, the act creates a system in which the president reports budget deferrals and rescissions and Congress has opportunities to push back.

Claiming executive privilege to withhold communications from Congress

Executive privilege is the right of the president to withhold certain confidential information. During the dramatic events surrounding the Watergate cover-up and President Nixon's ultimate resignation, the president claimed an implied executive privilege to withhold confidential Oval Office tape recordings that government lawyers needed to prosecute high-ranking Nixon Administration officials. In *United States v. Nixon,* 418 U.S. 683 (1974), the Court unanimously ruled that the need for sharing relevant evidence "specific and central to the fair adjudication of a particular criminal case" trumped a generalized claim "of confidentiality of Presidential communications in performance of the President's responsibilities." (Nixon was ordered to produce the tapes for confidential review by the district court.)

Nixon didn't clarify the rules applicable in a more typical Congress-versus-president tussle over confidential internal documents. The *Nixon* Court called the president's need to keep confidential the advice he gets from key subordinates and the records of internal deliberations "weighty indeed and entitled to great respect." Whether that respect outweighs a congressional committee's need for information to oversee the execution of law and policy remains a source of political and legal contention. Although lower courts have rendered some decisions, most disputes between Congress and the executive branch are worked out through negotiation and political give and take.

Chapter 7

The Constitution and Federalism

In This Chapter

▶ Seeing what the Constitution says about state power

▶ Making the federal government top dog

▶ Preventing states from hurting out-of-state commercial activity

▶ Giving states power to resist congressional coercion

----

*T*he framers' decision to preserve strong state governments, even while overlaying a stronger national government at the top of the heap, is a key design feature of the Constitution. And as we introduce in Chapter 4, concerns for preserving state-government powers and prerogatives have led the modern Court to place limits on federal-government powers.

In this chapter, we explore in more detail several constitutional-law doctrines seeking to maintain the proper balance of power between federal and nonfederal governmental units. For example, we explore the nuances of the *preemption doctrine,* the several rules seeking to protect national supremacy while at the same time promoting a "cooperative federalism" in which both national and state/local laws deal with typical economic and social problems.

We also summarize the two-pronged approach the Court pursues to make sure that state and local laws don't inappropriately restrict out-of-state interests. These *dormant-commerce-clause* rules promote an integrated national economy by preventing state and local governments from discriminating against or unduly burdening business concerns outside their borders.

Having sketched in the major constitutional doctrines used to limit the states, the last section turns the tables, examining the rise of rules restricting the national government's ability to force states to do its bidding.

Understanding the Constitution's Basic View of the States' Role

In this section, we discuss why preserving state power is important and summarize the major legal rules limiting and protecting state power.

Asking the key question: Why have state and local governments, anyway?

In a 21st-century, globalized world in which modern Americans are accustomed to a large federal government employing millions of workers and pursuing a dizzying array of policies, state and local governments could seem unimportant. But having strong state governments still matters, and understanding why is especially important these days.

Among the most important rationales for having strong state (and, by extension, local) governments are the following reasons:

- ✔ **To provide a check on inappropriate expansion of federal-government power:** The framers intended that strong state governments, headed by officials with their own independent political-power bases, could foil efforts by federal officials to overrun their enumerated federal powers.

- ✔ **To better protect individual liberties:** To the Constitution's framers, keeping the federal government within its intended bounds was not just about government power. Because the national government was thought to be the biggest threat to the rights and prerogatives of U.S. citizens, states able to check federal abuse of power could also prevent federal abuse of individual rights.

- ✔ **To better represent the diverse needs and varying viewpoints of different parts of the nation:** A national one-size-fits-all strategy isn't always appropriate. Issues vary in intensity and specifics in different regions. State and local officials are closer to their people and therefore better able to understand and respond to their needs.

- ✔ **To let states serve as "laboratories of federalism":** This famous phrase, penned by Justice Brandeis in an otherwise unimportant 1932 case, points to the fact that states with substantial policymaking power can experiment with innovative laws and policies. Failed experiments can be dropped, and successful innovations can spread to other states and, eventually, to the nation as a whole.

✓ **To give Americans a broader choice of policy mixes:** Having 50 different sources of important health, social-welfare, and economic choices, rather than one, increases the odds that individual Americans will be able to find a mix of policies that is maximally satisfactory. Some states can provide high levels of social services and pay for them by higher taxes. Other states can pursue a low-service, low-tax model. To the extent possible, individual Americans can "vote with their feet" and move to their preferred state.

We don't want to romanticize state and local governments or overstate their abilities to solve national problems. These governments have enacted backwards and at times even discriminatory policies. A particular political party or ideology can more easily capture them. And some problems of national and international scope, such as air and water pollution transcending state and even national boundaries, are difficult for individual states to attack. Still, for good or bad, the Constitution preserves them as important power centers. And you need to know just how the Constitution does that.

Summarizing the Constitution's basic federal/state power-allocation devices

The Constitution's framers committed future generations to an ongoing federal/state balancing act. The framers intended that the existing system of state governments, then serving as the predominant source of social and economic legislation, would remain. The new level of national government they created was superimposed on top of current state governments. The framers intended that this federal government would be limited in its activities but supreme when operating in its legitimate sphere.

The Constitution seeks to preserve this fine balance of federal-versus-state power in four main ways:

✓ **By limiting the national government to enumerated powers (and those means "necessary and proper" to fulfill those powers):** We discuss the limitations more fully in Chapter 5. Here, the point is that the natural flip side of limiting federal power is preserving state autonomy. For example, the result of decisions like *United States v. Lopez,* 514 U.S. 549 (1995) (striking down the federal Gun Free School Zones Act of 1990, which prohibited having a gun within 1,000 feet of a school) is that they preserve state governments as the main regulators of key types of local activity (such as school violence).

Additionally, the Tenth Amendment states that "The powers not delegated to the United States by the Constitution . . . are reserved to the States respectively, or to the people."

✔ **By granting the federal government supremacy:** In addition to making the U.S. Constitution "The Supreme law of the Land," the Article VI supremacy clause allows federal laws and regulations and the treaties the federal government enters into with foreign countries to preempt contrary state constitutions, laws, and other policies. But state laws not inconsistent with federal laws are allowed. The various "preemption" doctrines enforcing this balance are explored in the next section.

✔ **By limiting states through the dormant commerce clause:** Congress's power to regulate interstate commerce is a potent source of current federal social and economic regulation and a modern source of much federal/state tension on and off the Court (see Chapter 5 for details). What we explore in the section "Limiting States' Self-Favoritism: The Dormant Commerce Clause" is the modern Court's finding that an implied limit on state power is implicit ("dormant") in the express interstate-commerce power grant.

✔ **By protecting state rights through other specifically designed doctrines and interpretations:** In the later section "Protecting State Sovereignty When Congress Regulates State Governments," we pull together a couple of specialized doctrines and case decisions through which the modern Court further preserves states' rights.

Establishing National Supremacy by Preempting Contrary State Authority

In modern America, federal laws and regulations often coexist with state, regional, and local laws and regulations. For example, federal consumer-protection laws usually establish minimum national standards for fair commercial dealing and advertising, fully expecting that state and local governments will add laws offering enhanced or more extensive protection to the basic federal level of protection. This "regulatory federalism," in which two or more governmental levels exercise concurrent powers, is totally consistent with the Constitution's design.

What is not constitutionally kosher is when a governmental unit below the national government legislates in a way contrary to federal law. This practice runs counter to the supremacy clause and the concepts of national sovereignty it embodies.

To protect national supremacy, the modern Court has developed several complicated and interrelated doctrines going under the name *preemption.* Most undergraduate constitutional-law courses don't go into the details. And you won't need them to argue with your buddies over federal-versus-state power. However, your understanding of federalism and the controversies it regularly causes will be enhanced if you understand the basic mechanics of preemption. The rest of this section addresses that need.

Modern preemption doctrines assume that federal and nonfederal laws can coexist; that is, courts start with a *presumption against preemption.* But this "rule" against preemption is overcome, and federal-government power wins out, in these three basic situations: express preemption, implied field preemption, and implied conflict preemption.

Interpreting express preemption

Sometimes when Congress passes a federal law, it includes specific language indicating a desire to preempt state laws. Enforcing express-preemption provisions requires courts to evaluate the words, legislative history, and underlying purposes of the law to discover how Congress intended the law to apply.

In *Riegel v. Medtronic, Inc.,* 552 U.S. 312 (2008), the Court had to interpret preemption language in the federal Medical Device Amendments (MDA) of 1976. This language prohibited states from imposing any "requirement" on a medical device "which is different from, or in addition to" the obligations federal authorities impose when they approve medical devices for human use. Medtronic argued that the MDA's preemption clause meant that medical-device manufacturers couldn't be sued in state court by patients injured when federally approved devices are used in their treatment. But Medtronic argued that jury verdicts of liability force device manufacturers to alter how they make and market their devices; state court verdicts thus practically operate as "requirements" at least "in addition to" (and, often, "different from") federal legal limits. The *Riegel* majority agreed and found state-court claims preempted.

Implying field preemption

Even in the absence of express-preemption language, modern courts may imply that a particular state law or policy is preempted by federal law when (1) the scope or design of federal law suggests that Congress meant to exclusively control a particular regulatory field and (2) the state law or policy is found to be in that preempted field.

Courts are likely to infer an implied congressional desire for this *field preemption* when the details of federal law are so "pervasive" that, in the words of *Rice v. Santa Fe Elevator Corporation,* 331 U.S. 218 (1947), "Congress left no room for the state to supplement it"; when the national government's interest is especially "dominant" (such as in the areas of national defense, immigration control, or bankruptcy law); or when a special need for uniformity makes the usually desirable state-by-state variation inadvisable.

Determining that a field is implicitly preempted is not the end of the inquiry, however. State laws or policies are void only when they are found to be *in* the preempted field. State laws or policies outside the field are fine as long as they are authorized under the state's constitution and not subject to other constitutional concerns.

In *Pacific Gas & Electric Company v Public Utilities Commission,* 475 U.S. 1 (1986), the Court considered the multistage, across-the-board process Congress set up for designing and operating nuclear power plants. The Court concluded that by passing such a pervasive law, Congress signaled an intent that nuclear-power-plant safety would be an exclusive federal domain in which state intrusion was banned. But the Court found that the challenged California law, which imposed a moratorium on nuclear-power-plant construction in the state until a viable way was found for storing nuclear wastes, was *not* in the forbidden field of safety promotion. The Court instead saw California's moratorium as pursuing the distinct and traditional state regulatory goal of ensuring that power producers remained economically viable over the long run. (Exorbitant waste-handling costs down the line could, said the Court, make nuclear power prohibitively expensive.)

The "playing kids" analogy: Keeping field preemption and conflict preemption straight

If the distinction between *field* and *conflict* preemption isn't straight in your mind, consider this silly analogy:

A group of children are engaged in litter cleanup in a city park. Some children are "federal kids." (You can tell that because they're wearing red, white, and blue T-shirts with pictures of Uncle Sam on them.) Other frolicking children are "state kids," clothed in T-shirts with colors and emblems typical of your state.

If the state children are picking up litter in an exclusively federal "field," the park police will intervene and tell the state kids to leave. Even if the state kids are playing nicely and are actually helping improve the federal kids' cleanup effort, they can't stay. The police will point to the "State Kids, Keep Out — This Field for Federal Kids Only" sign and escort the state kids out of the area.

But if the field the children are cleaning is not an exclusively federal field, the state and federal kids can keep playing together as long as they don't "conflict." But if the state kids start fights or otherwise interfere with the important community-service work of the federal kids, the park police will make them stop.

Of course, you know who the park police are in this metaphor!

Recognizing implied conflict preemption

Courts sometimes infer another brand of preemption. In *implied conflict preemption,* courts assume that a state law or policy violates the supremacy clause when it is impossible to comply with both laws or when, even though both laws can be followed, state law "stands as an obstacle to the accomplishment and execution of the full purposes and objectives of Congress." (The language is from *Hines v. Davidowitz,* 312 U.S. 52 [1941], which struck down a state alien-registration law that the Court thought would frustrate Congress's desire to "protect the personal liberties of law-abiding aliens" and distinguish America from "inquisitorial" nations during wartime.)

A recent preemption case not only illustrates "conflict preemption" in action but also shows how seemingly technical preemption issues can be at the center of heated political controversies. In *Chamber of Commerce v. Whiting,* 131 S.Ct. 1968 (2011), a divided Court rejected claims that federal immigration laws preempted an Arizona law; the law let state authorities suspend and ultimately revoke the business licenses of any employer shown to intentionally hire unauthorized aliens. After considering and rejecting claims that the law ran afoul of express preemption language forbidding states from imposing "civil or criminal sanctions" on employers hiring illegal aliens, the justices focused on and rejected the Chamber of Commerce's arguments that Arizona's law conflicted with the goals of federal law. (Among several arguments, the Chamber asserted that the law upset the balance Congress achieved between deterring illegal hiring and avoiding burdens on employers and employees. The Chamber also argued that state law conflicted with federal law by *requiring* employers to use the "e-verify" Internet-based verification system Congress wanted to use as one of several voluntary options.)

Limiting States' Self-Favoritism: The Dormant Commerce Clause

One of the major reasons the framers strengthened the national government and gave it an express power to regulate interstate commerce was a growing unease with the favorable hometown advantage some states were giving their own commercial interests. By erecting trade barriers against goods and services from other states, and through other unfavorable treatment of out-of-state interests, some states threatened the cohesive national economy the framers desired.

Modern courts try to honor the framers' goal to grow integrated national markets in two ways. First, as we show in Chapter 5, post-1937 cases have generally expanded Congress's power under the commerce clause — to allow Congress to promote a nationalist vision of economic progress. This section examines the other side of the coin: modern judicial enforcement of *dormant-commerce-clause* limits on state laws.

Simply put, dormant-commerce-clause doctrines read the commerce power's affirmative grant of power to Congress as implying a restriction on state laws. Under dormant-clause case law, otherwise valid state laws are invalid if they treat out-of-state commercial interests inappropriately in either of two ways:

✔ State laws that *discriminate* against out-of-state commerce are presumed to be invalid unless they serve legitimate (nonprotectionist) purposes that can't be achieved by a less discriminatory alternative.

✔ State laws that merely *burden* out-of-state commerce (but do not discriminate against it) are presumed valid unless the burden is "clearly excessive" in light of the local benefits achieved.

In the following sections, we summarize how courts differentiate between burdensome and discriminatory laws, how they decide when discriminatory laws are justifiable, and how they try to keep states from enacting excessive burdens on other states.

Distinguishing discrimination from mere burdens on out-of-state interests

Because the discrimination-versus-burden distinction is so important as a practical matter — that is, discriminatory laws are invalid unless saved, whereas merely burdensome laws are valid unless shown to be clearly excessive — telling the two apart is the first step in any dormant-commerce-clause analysis.

Sometimes the presence of discrimination is clear on the face of the state law. The New Jersey law challenged in *City of Philadelphia v. New Jersey,* 437 U.S. 617 (1978), prohibited the deposit in New Jersey landfills of "solid or liquid waste which originated or was collected outside" the state's boundaries. Trash originating or collected inside the state could be deposited in landfills without limit. This discrimination against out-of-state trash was *facially discriminatory* — that is, clearly discriminatory from the text of the statute.

As is often true with constitutional law, however, situations that are less clear-cut are tougher to settle. Sometimes a law does not make a facial distinction between in-state and out-of-state interests, but it still has such a disproportionate *effect* on out-of-state interests that it will be treated as though it is overtly discriminatory.

One example of discrimination in effect is the North Carolina statute invalidated in *Hunt v. Washington State Apple Advertising Commission,* 432 U.S. 333 (1977). State law required that all fresh apple containers sold in or shipped into the state bear "no grade other than the applicable U.S. grade or standard." Although this policy applied equally to apples produced in North Carolina and outside the state, the Court found that the law discriminated against Washington State apple growers, who alone among the nation's apple growers had spent millions of dollars to develop their own apple-grading system. State law discriminated against interstate commerce, the Court held, because it raised the costs of doing business in North Carolina for Washington apple growers (who would have to specially package apples bound for the state) but not for in-state interests. The law also stripped the (out-of-state) Washington-apple industry of the "competitive and economic advantages it has earned for itself" — helping local producers in the process.

Considering whether discrimination is justified

After a court finds that a state law is discriminatory (whether overtly or in effect) against out-of-state commerce, the law usually fails. Even if it serves legitimate interests unrelated to giving a sweetheart deal to local commerce, the interests can usually be achieved by alternate means that don't discriminate against other states.

For example, New Jersey could have achieved the environmental goals it asserted in the *City of Philadelphia* case (discussed in the preceding section) by limiting the total amount of waste any disposal company — whether in state or out of state — could deposit in a given day. Or, the state could have charged a sliding-scale fee to both in-state and out-of-state waste collectors that increased with the volume of trash.

By contrast, *Maine v. Taylor,* 477 U.S. 131 (1986), provides a rare example of when a discriminatory law doesn't violate the dormant commerce clause. Maine's law prohibiting the importation of live baitfish into the state from other states was clearly discriminatory on its face. Nevertheless, evidence showed that parasites common to out-of-state baitfish, but not Maine's own in-state wild fish, threatened Maine's critical fishing habitats. Maine thus had a legitimate interest in protecting against environmental and economic risks. And because even a few infected baitfish introduced into Maine waters could wreak havoc (imagine no more "Live Maine lobsters!"), a ban was the only practical response.

Preventing extreme burdens on out-of-state commerce

Modern cases have opened up a second front against state legislation threatening the framers' desire for a well-integrated national economy: Even a nondiscriminatory state law is unconstitutional if it imposes burdens on out-of-state interests that are "clearly excessive" in light of the legitimate local benefits (that is, benefits other than protecting local industry from legitimate out-of-state competition).

Is determining whether burdens are "clearly excessive" inappropriate for judges?

The variety of dormant-commerce-clause analysis illustrated by the *Kassel* case (see the section "Preventing extreme burdens on out-of-state commerce") has its detractors, both on and off the Court. Critics say that deciding whether the burdens of state laws on out-of-state commerce are clearly excessive in light of the benefits asks federal judges (who are not elected) to make the kind of cost/benefit judgments that *elected* officials are supposed to make. For example, in the *Kassel* case, the justices had to second-guess traffic-safety officials, sort through conflicting engineering data, and ultimately determine whether the alleged

pluses of Iowa's law are a good "bargain," despite the costs on the trucking industry.

Similar appropriateness-of-role objections have been made about the second variety of conflict preemption — the doctrine that invalidates a state law if it "stands as an obstacle to the accomplishment and execution of the *full* purposes and objectives" of Congress (emphasis added). Here, too, the doctrine arguably gives courts too much room to weigh competing policies, determine at what point the fulfillment of federal purposes is now "fully" achieved, and assess how state laws will work in practice.

The Court found such a case of clearly excessive burden in *Kassel v. Consolidated Freightways Corporation,* 450 U.S. 662 (1981). The *Kassel* Court invalidated an Iowa law that, alone among neighboring states, forbade the use of 65-foot double-wide trucks on state highways. The *Kassel* Court found that Iowa's law "substantially burdens interstate commerce." As the Court explained, "Trucking companies that wish to continue to use 65-foot doubles must route them around Iowa or detach the trailers of the doubles and ship them through separately. Alternatively, trucking companies must use [smaller trucks for all states]. Each of these options engenders inefficiency and added expense."

In finding that the law's substantial burdens were "clearly excessive" in light of the benefits, the Court closely reviewed and discounted three arguments that shorter trucks were safer. The Court also reasoned that any safety gains earned by shorter trucks would be more than offset by the greater *number* of trucks necessary to haul the same amount of freight. (Common sense told the Court that greater numbers of trucks equaled more traffic accidents.)

Protecting State Sovereignty When Congress Regulates State Governments

A last set of federal-versus-state power issues arises when the federal government tries to exercise its powers directly with respect to state governments themselves. Suppose that Congress wants to extend to *state government* employees the minimum-wage and maximum-hour protections it already gives to employees of private companies. Is any additional consideration due state (and local) government employers because of their special sovereignty and constitutional status?

The modern Court's answer to the question of whether Congress faces any special constraints when it regulates state and local governments directly has varied. In the following sections we note four different "eras" in which the Court has given different answers in response to various commerce-power-based federal enactments. Then we identify an anticoercion principle generally affording added protection to states in the present era.

Identifying four eras of varying state-sovereignty protection

Maintaining the proper balance between federal and state power is both important and difficult. That's probably why the modern Court has seesawed between different eras of state-sovereignty protection. Organized chronologically, the following sections explain those different eras.

1937 to 1976: Treating the states like private parties

Federal power over major aspects of the American society and its economy expanded significantly from 1937 to 1976, during and after the 1930s New Deal era and the World War II years. At first, Congress tended to focus on private economic entities. But as state and local governments grew in size and importance, advocates began to press Congress to apply national regulatory laws to state and local governments.

A typical example of this regulation was the law at issue in *Maryland v. Wirtz,* 392 U.S. 183 (1968). When Congress amended federal minimum-wage and maximum-hour laws to include employees at hospitals, schools, and other institutions operated by state and local governments, they cried foul. State and local governments objected that they were on a different constitutional footing than private employers. (After all, private entities do not have a Tenth Amendment protecting their residual powers and were not who the framers counted on to restrain national-government excess). Yet, the *Wirtz* Court held that "valid general regulations of commerce do not cease to be [valid] because a State is involved." The *Wirtz* Court opined that "[i]f a State is engaging in economic activities that are validly regulated by the Federal Government when engaged in by private persons, the State too may be forced to conform its activities to federal regulation."

1976 to 1985: Treating the states as special

The Court's practice of treating states like private entities changed in 1976, marking a new era that lasted until 1985. In that year, a divided 5–4 Court held in *National League of Cities v. Usery,* 426 U.S. 833 (1975), that the Fair Labor Standards Act could not constitutionally be applied to the states under the commerce clause. *Usery* breathed new life into the theory that Congress must be more careful in regulating state and local governments "in areas of traditional governmental functions" (such as the wages paid to state and local government employees and the hours they work). After *Usery,* the Court handed down several decisions — some of which upheld Congress and some of which did not — seeking to devise a three-part formula for determining those state activities worthy of special judicial protection.

1985 to 1991: Reverting to a no-special-problem approach when Congress regulates the states

The *Usery* revolution was short lived. Nine years after that decision, in 1985, Justice Blackmun (a member of the earlier five-justice *Usery* majority) switched sides — and even wrote the lead opinion overturning *Usery* — in the case of *Garcia v. San Antonio Metropolitan Transit Authority,* 469 U.S. 528 (1985). In *Garcia,* a 5–4 majority held that federal minimum-wage and maximum-hour provisions could be applied to the states under the commerce clause. *Garcia* rejected *Usery*'s traditional-government-function test as "unworkable."

More important was Justice Blackmun's argument that "the principal means chosen by the Framers to ensure the role of the States in the federal system lies in the structure of the Federal Government itself." Blackmun and the *Garcia* majority meant by this that the framers wanted to protect state power and independence by equipping state and local officials to exert multiple kinds of *political* influence on national officials. As originally written, the Constitution instructed that Senators be elected by state legislatures. Those state officials also draw election districts for House members, control the selection of presidential electors, and in general regulate the "time, place, and manner" of all federal elections. According to the *Garcia* majority, these "procedural safeguards inherent in the structure of the federal system" generally ensure that federal politicians dance to the state-rights tune.

Especially pointed was the dim view the *Garcia* Court took about "judicially created limitations on federal power." Judges, the majority held, should generally get out of the business of "identify[ing] principled constitutional limitations on the scope of Congress' Commerce Clause powers over the States." These judicial attempts to ride to the rescue of states' rights were likely to be as ineffective as they were contrary to the framers' desires.

1991 to the present: The (partial) return of special judicial protection of state sovereignty

Because the *Garcia* majority wanted to keep courts out of the federal government-versus-states power struggle, you may naturally expect the Court to thereafter decline all invitations to design special protections for state sovereignty. Although the Court has in fact not reentered the field of finding new constitutional limits on Congress's *commerce-regulating* power specifically, the states'-rights impulse has moved the Court to render important and broad-reaching decisions protecting state sovereignty.

The first dent in the no-special-state-protection armor came in 1991 when the Court delved into the federal Age Discrimination in Employment Act (ADEA), which generally prohibited mandatory-retirement policies. In *Gregory v. Ashcroft,* 501 U.S. 452, the Court had to decide whether the ADEA barred states from requiring their judges to retire at specified ages. The *Gregory* Court called a state's decision about when its high-ranking officials should retire "a decision of the most fundamental sort for a sovereign entity." Given the strong state sovereignty interests at stake, the Court indicated that it would apply a "clear statement" rule of statutory interpretation: Unless Congress made abundantly clear that it intended the ADEA to bar mandatory state-judge retirement, the Court would not extend the statute that far.

Only a year later — in *New York v. United States,* 505 U.S. 144 (1992), the Court announced a broader constitutional doctrine at odds with the hands-off theory of *Garcia.* Five years after that, the Court reemphasized and extended the new doctrine in *Printz v. United States,* 521 U.S. 898 (1997). The *New York* and *Printz* decisions are important enough to merit more discussion in the next section.

Protecting state sovereignty through an "anticoercion" principle

The following sections discuss the anticoercion principle, which mandates that the federal government can't coerce states into following its legislation in certain circumstances.

Preventing compelled state regulation

In *New York v. United States,* 505 U.S. 144 (1992), the Court held that a provision of the Low-Level Waste Policy Amendments Act of 1985 went over the line in its treatment of state governments. Ironically, Congress adopted the act at the request of the National Governors' Association; after years of negotiations, the NGA produced a comprehensive plan to deal with the long-unsolved problem of how to dispose of "low-level" radioactive waste generated by medical and other industrial operations.

From the perspective of the *Garcia* decision, the act should have been proof positive that the procedural structures of the Constitution work to protect states' rights. After all, the act appeared to be a classic example of states using their political clout to get Congress to do their bidding.

Surprisingly, the Court took a very different (and dimmer) view of one provision of the act. This proviso essentially required states to either regulate low-level wastes according to congressional specifications or to "tak[e] title to and possession of the [waste] generated within their borders and becom[e] liable for all damages waste generators suffer." Under either scenario, Congress would have forced states to regulate the low-level waste problem.

The *New York* Court held that an important constitutional line has been crossed when "the Federal Government compels States to regulate." As the Court explained, "the accountability of both state and federal officials" is thereby "diminished." State officials normally decide whether and how to exercise power and their constituents appropriately hold them accountable for their decisions. The same is true for federal officials deciding to regulate or not. "But where the Federal Government directs the States to regulate," the *New York* Court warned, "it may be state officials who will bear the brunt of public disapproval," while federal officials causing the regulatory program "may remain insulated from the electoral ramifications of their decision."

Even beyond the accountability problem, the *New York* Court saw a violation of state sovereignty. "[T]he Constitution has never been understood," the justices wrote, to give Congress "the authority to require the States to govern according to Congress' instructions."

Extending the anticoercion principle to state law execution

In *Printz v. United States,* 521 U.S. 898 (1997), the Court extended the anticoercion limitation from *New York v. United States* (see the preceding section) to the executive branches of the states. *Printz* invalidated part of a major gun-control law enacted after the attempted assassination of President Ronald Reagan. The rejected provision temporarily required state and local law-enforcement officers to do background checks on applicants for gun permits. Because the instant-background-check system Congress required the federal government to develop was several years off, national legislators pressed state and local officials into service.

Enter two sheriffs from Montana and Arizona, who were anything but pleased to do the federal government's bidding. Agreeing with the sheriffs that "compelled enlistment of state executive officers for the administration of federal programs" is both unprecedented and unconstitutional, *Printz* worried that "[t]he power of the Federal Government would be augmented immeasurably if it were able to impress into service — and at no cost to itself — the police officers of the 50 States."

Understanding the bottom line in choice versus coercion

Both in stating new limits on Congress's power to restrict the States and in explaining why other more traditional federalism arrangements were acceptable, *New York* and *Printz* set forth a new coercion/choice polarity that future federal officials and constitutional-law students must come to terms with:

- ✔ **The federal government may not *coerce* state (or local) governments in any of the following ways:**

    - The feds can't tell state governments to pass specified laws.

    - The feds can't order states to be responsible for problems in ways that practically force them to exercise their regulatory powers.

    - The feds can't order states to execute federal laws.

- ✔ **The federal government can offer state (or local) governments a *meaningful choice* to participate in federal ventures.** Specifically,

    - Congress may offer the states federal funds and then impose "strings" (including that states change their laws or take specified enforcement actions). These offers preserve state sovereignty and accountability, said the *New York* Court, because "[i]f a State's citizens view federal policy as sufficiently contrary to local interests, they may elect to decline a federal grant."

    - Congress may regulate private activity pursuant to its powers but "offer States the choice of regulating that activity according to federal standards." Such "opt-out" provisions are periodically included in federal laws when Congress thinks that regulated entities might rather be regulated under a parallel state regulation alternative. These provisions are okay, said the *New York* Court, because "[i]f state residents would prefer their government to devote its attention and resources to problems other than those deemed important to Congress, they may choose to have the Federal Government rather than the State bear the expense of a federally mandated regulatory program."

The bottom line? When states can "just say no" to federal financial or regulatory incentives — when, in the words of the *New York* Court, "Congress encourages state regulation rather than compelling it" — state governments "remain responsive to the local electorate's preferences" and state officials "remain accountable to the people."

Part III

Protecting Property Rights and Avoiding Arbitrary Action

The 5th Wave   By Rich Tennant

"He said he's invoking eminent domain."

In this part . . .

The framers of the Constitution included important clauses to protect people's individual rights. The due-process and equal-protection clauses help protect many individual rights to varying degrees. In this part, we discuss the details of these clauses and see how challenges under them are analyzed by the courts. From eminent domain *(takings)* to the right to own a gun, these chapters help you understand the court's property-rights decisions.

Chapter 8

Avoiding Arbitrary Government Action: Due Process of Law

. . . .

In This Chapter

▶ Finding out the difference between procedural and substantive due process

▶ Exploring due-process challenges concerning liberty and property

▶ Deciding if process is due — and if so, how much and when

▶ Understanding how due process provides substantive protection

. . . .

*T*he Constitution's Fifth and Fourteenth Amendments forbid government officials from depriving persons of "life, liberty, and property without due process of law." This due-process command is used in many different applications, but at its core it prohibits arbitrary governmental action.

In this chapter, we introduce you to the core distinction between *procedural* and *substantive* due process and provide an overview of the major criminal and civil settings in which due-process challenges arise. The chapter then explores the key details of the legal rules and policies affecting procedural due process. We look at whether a property or liberty right exists to require *any* process, and then we examine the three-part balancing test used to determine when and how much process is due to protect a constitutionally recognized property or liberty right. The last section turns to substantive due process and summarizes the baseline rationality standard that applies in most cases when a challenger claims that government's deprivation of liberty and property is substantively arbitrary.

Distinguishing Procedural from Substantive Due Process

The Constitution's due-process-of-law clauses erect complicated procedural hoops governments must jump through — and substantive barriers they must not cross — before restricting liberty and property interests. The first step toward understanding this area of constitutional law is to distinguish a procedural due-process argument from a substantive one. At the heart of the question is whether someone is challenging the *way* government deprives people of liberty or property or is challenging the government's basic *ability* to deprive those rights.

Seeing why life isn't a due-process focus

This chapter discusses how the Constitution's due-process clauses protect liberty and property. Because the constitutional language identifies "life" as the first interest protected by due process, you may be thinking, "Hey, what about *life*?"

The death penalty is the only way that American governments are involved in depriving any persons of life. The only potential usefulness of due-process protections, therefore, is to protect against arbitrary imposition of the death penalty. As death-penalty jurisprudence evolved, however, different constitutional provisions became the basis for judging capital punishment.

The principal constitutional protection against arbitrary death-penalty imposition is the Eighth Amendment, which prohibits "cruel and unusual punishments." After several decades of evolving decisions, the Court has held that the Eighth Amendment limits the imposition of capital punishment in a number of ways, including the following three:

- ✔ **The death penalty is imposed only after defendants have been provided appropriate protections.** Modern Eighth-Amendment cases require a number of safeguards in an effort to "suitably direct and limit" sentencing discretion "so as to minimize the risk" that the death penalty will be imposed in a "wholly arbitrary and capricious" manner, in the language of *Gregg v. Georgia,* 429 U.S. 875 (1976). For example, *Gregg* limited the imposition of death to especially heinous crimes accompanied by at least one statutorily stated "aggravating

circumstance," permitted defendants to try to minimize their crimes by claiming all "mitigating circumstances," and required prompt and full appellate review.

- ✔ **The death penalty is only available when at least one victim was killed and when the defendant killed the victim directly or significantly participated in the scheme in which the victim died.**

- ✔ **The death penalty can't be given to defendants who are mentally retarded or who committed their crimes while under 18 years of age.** Recent Court decisions reason that these defendants can't fully appreciate the consequences of their actions, so execution is not appropriate, no matter what their crimes.

Other constitutional amendments also figure prominently in death-penalty cases. For example, the Sixth Amendment right to counsel (which includes the right to *effective* assistance of counsel) applies to both capital and noncapital cases (that is, cases that can involve the punishment of death and cases that can't). But the right to counsel can be especially important in death-penalty cases, given the heightened stakes and the specialized skills needed to try such a case. In capital-punishment cases, unlike other criminal cases, the defendant may even be entitled to co-counsel, given the serious and specialized nature of those types of cases. And although defendants rarely win cases claiming that they received ineffective assistance of counsel, in some cases counsel's conduct can be presumed to handicap the defendant.

Understanding procedural due process

Procedural due process addresses the *way* government deprives someone of liberty and property. A challenger claiming that a law or policy violates procedural due process is not challenging government's ultimate power to do so; rather, the challenger is saying that government cannot deprive him of liberty or property without affording him better procedures than it has.

In *Goldberg v. Kelly,* 397 U.S. 254 (1970), the Supreme Court decision many observers credit as giving birth to a modern due-process revolution, welfare recipients challenged the procedures used by New York City to revoke the welfare benefits they had legitimately qualified for and were receiving. (As you see in the later section "Identifying when a challenger can assert a due-process-protected property right," the recipients had a legitimate *property* right to due process because a New York statute gave poor people who met stated eligibility requirements a "legitimate entitlement" to welfare benefits.)

The welfare recipients argued — and the *Goldberg* Court largely agreed — that before New York City could revoke welfare benefits, it had to provide more-detailed notice and fairly elaborate hearing procedures so recipients could argue against the city's evidence and make their own case for continued eligibility. The recipients didn't claim, however, that the city could not ultimately deny them welfare — or even abolish the welfare system altogether. (As we discuss in Chapter 1, the Constitution generally doesn't require government to provide benefits or programs.) The recipients instead claimed that before the city could deprive them of welfare, it had to go through constitutionally required procedures.

Looking at substantive due process

When a challenger claims that a law or policy deprives her of liberty or property in excess of government's basic authority to do that, the issue is *substantive due process.* The challenger is saying that government doesn't have an adequate basis for the deprivation (and thus can't take their life, liberty, or property) — *regardless of how good the procedures are* that it uses in doing so. We discuss substantive due process at the end of the chapter.

In *Griswold v. Connecticut,* 381 U.S. 479 (1965), challengers argued that a Connecticut law criminalizing the use of contraceptive devices — even by married people — denied their right to privacy in making decisions about when and whether to get pregnant. (As we discuss in Chapter 14, the modern Court has found that an important aspect of the "liberty" due process protects is the right to certain kinds of privacy.) The challengers weren't arguing that Connecticut could deny access to birth control as long as it gave sufficiently adequate notice and a comprehensive enough hearing. The challengers instead claimed that, no matter how elaborate its procedures, Connecticut overstepped its power by arbitrarily depriving married persons of their *substantive right* to contraceptive access.

Identifying the Different Contexts in Which Due-Process Challenges Arise

You can better travel the world of due process if you understand the different contexts in which challenges involving it arise. In this section we provide an overview of the way due process protects liberty and property.

Distinguishing the ways liberty interests require due process

The due-process clauses of the Fifth and Fourteenth Amendments are important in protecting liberty interests in four ways. They require procedural protections for criminal defendants, mandate procedures before governments deprive others of liberty, set ultimate limits on government's power to restrict liberty, and apply the Bill of Rights to state and local governments. Here we discuss all four types of protection for liberty.

Requiring important procedural protections in criminal trials

Defendants convicted of criminal offenses face obvious limitations on their physical liberty when they're incarcerated or their freedom of action is limited as a condition of probation. The requirement that governments not deprive persons of liberty without due process is thus an important source of criminal-trial rights, supplementing the rights provided in several other relevant constitutional provisions.

Even when constitutional provisions specifically address criminal-trial rights (such as the Sixth Amendment right to counsel), due process and basic concepts of fairness flowing from these rights have influenced court decisions defining those constitutional provisions. Here are some important examples of how due-process requirements figure in criminal-trial rights:

> ✔ **The presumption of innocence and beyond-a-reasonable-doubt standard of proof:** Criminal defendants are presumed to be innocent; they don't have to prove their own innocence. Instead, the government must prove them guilty. (This seemingly obvious protection is among the most important guarantees the Constitution offers to a defendant. It

significantly affects a wide range of practical realities facing the prosecution and the defense.) An equally important requirement from due
process is that the highly-defendant-protective standard of proof for
criminal guilt, proof "beyond a reasonable doubt."

✔ **The right to be informed of the charges against the defendant:** A criminal defendant must be *arraigned* (brought before a judge to have the
charges against him read). The arraignment makes the defendant fully
aware of why he's accused so that a defense can be prepared.

✔ **The right to a fair trial:** The fair-trial concept includes the right to an
impartial jury (including the right to question potential jurors to make
sure that they have no prejudices in general or with respect to the specific case). Defendants also must receive fairness from other criminal-trial
participants (including a defense counsel without conflicts of interest, a
fair prosecutor, and an impartial judge). In high-profile cases, a fair trial
may involve issuing "gag orders" to attorneys and other trial participants not to talk to the media, closing court proceedings to the public
and media, sequestering the jury during trial, or even moving a trial to
a different place to avoid filling a jury with people who have already
formed an opinion due to extensive media coverage in their community.

Finally, due process of law influences other practically important protections
for defendants. Because jury members who see the defendant in a prison
uniform may associate the defendant with prison and therefore guilt, when
a jury is present, the defendant is always "dressed out" in plain clothes.
Shackles are removed before the jury is allowed into the courtroom (and
a sheriff's deputy is usually assigned to keep within a certain distance of
the defendant to prevent flight or other incidents). Nothing guarantees an
express right to be dressed out. But the requirement has evolved as part of
the defendant's basic right to a fair trial and to ensure that the jury's assessment of his guilt is not tainted by the fact that he is in jail.

Requiring important procedural protections before restricting physical freedom or limiting other liberties

Procedural due process requires the government to give adequate notice and
hold a meaningful hearing before adversely affecting a number of important
liberty interests with a wide range of governmental actions.

People who are already institutionalized by government — in jail or prison,
in custody pending deportation proceedings, or in involuntary civil commitment (for mental illness or other disability) — have successfully required
government to provide additional notice-and-hearing procedures before substantially altering their institutional conditions.

Members of society at large are at times protected by procedural due-process
doctrines when government takes actions disparaging personal reputations or
depriving parents of their rights with respect to their children, such as when
governments terminate parental rights for abusive or neglectful parents.

Limiting government's ultimate substantive power to restrict liberty

The *substantive* protections of the due-process clauses restrict government's ultimate ability to deprive a wide range of persons of a broad array of liberty interests. In *Meyer v. Nebraska,* 262 U.S. 390 (1923), the Court wrote expansively that the liberty protected by the due-process clauses

> . . . denotes not merely freedom from bodily restraint but also the right of the individual to contract, to engage in any of the common occupations of life, to acquire useful knowledge, to marry, establish a home, and bring up children, to worship God according to the dictates of his own conscience, and generally to enjoy those privileges long recognized at common law as essential to the orderly pursuit of happiness by free men.

Later developments limited or realigned this broad formulation of liberty. For example, the modern Court treats economic rights — that is, the right to contract, to own and use property, and to pursue a chosen career — as property rights, not liberty rights.

Even so, a number of liberty rights are still subject to substantive protection that varies from mere rational-basis review (for nonfundamental liberty rights) to strict scrutiny review (for fundamental liberty rights relating to some aspects of privacy). (The modern Court's cases elevating some privacy rights to a specially protected status are important and complicated enough to deserve their own chapter, so we discuss them in Chapter 14.)

Applying most Bill of Rights provisions to the states

The due-process clause of the Fourteenth Amendment serves as the medium for "selective incorporation" of the Bill of Rights — that is, making all but a few Bill-of-Rights protections applicable to state and local government.

The first ten amendments, collectively known as the Bill of Rights, directly limit only the federal government — not state or local governments. For example, the First Amendment only directly prevents the *national* government from abridging freedom of speech.

But in 1925 the Court "assumed" in *Gitlow v. New York,* 268 U.S. 652, that freedom of speech was "among the fundamental rights and liberties protected . . . from impairment by the states" under the post–Civil War Fourteenth Amendment's ban on deprivation of liberty without due process. Thus began a process of *selective incorporation* (that is, a decision-by-decision, constitutional-clause-by-constitutional-clause process of finding Bill of Rights protections included within the concept of due process).

Using a variety of formulations — such as fundamental fairness, whether the failure to provide a right "shocks the conscience," and the two-part *Palko* test (which, as we discuss in Chapter 14, focuses on whether a right is "deeply rooted" in American history and traditions and implicit in "ordered liberty") — the Court handed down more than two dozen decisions bringing almost all of the Bill of Rights under the due-process umbrella. Now that the Second Amendment's right to own guns is a fundamental due-process-protected right (see Chapter 9), only a couple of Bill-of-Rights protections — principally, the right to grand-jury indictment — remain inapplicable to state and local governments.

Triggering procedural and substantive protection in property-rights cases

The due-process clauses are important and distinct sources of protection against arbitrary deprivations of *property. Goldberg v. Kelly* (discussed in "Understanding procedural due process") shows how *procedural* due process can be an important bulwark against arbitrary deprivation of critical governmental social-welfare benefits. But welfare isn't the only benefit program whose administrators must afford substantial notice and hearing rights before terminating benefits. Several other benefits of special concern to low-income persons — including Social Security Disability and publicly funded housing — have spawned important cases defining the parameters of the procedural due-process right.

Procedural due process isn't of interest solely to financially challenged persons. A wide range of Americans has an interest in protecting a broad array of property rights — including the continued possession of a valid driver's license and the ongoing ability to work in a heavily regulated industry — from deprivation without constitutionally adequate procedures.

And even though rights to contract, pursue a chosen profession, and own and use property are no longer considered part of due-process-protected *liberty,* such rights still qualify as *property* rights subject to both procedural and substantive protection. For example, although the Court generally upholds most zoning laws (that is, laws limiting the uses individuals can make of their land and other real property), a local government changing the zoning status of property without providing notice and a hearing would face issues of procedural due process. And, the government can't go below a certain level of *substantive* arbitrariness when limiting land use — even if the government uses elaborate procedures in imposing the limits. As the Court stated in *Nectow v. Cambridge,* 277 U.S. 183 (1928), a zoning restriction "cannot be imposed if it does not bear a substantial relation to the public health, safety, morals or general welfare."

As discussed in Chapter 9, the Fifth and Fourteenth Amendment due-process clauses aren't the only constitutional provisions protecting property rights. The Fifth Amendment also forbids the "taking" of private property for public use "without just compensation." And among the relatively few individual-rights protections in the original Constitution is language in Article I, Section 10, Clause 1 forbidding states from passing "Laws impairing the Obligation of Contracts."

Determining Whether Process Is Due

In the usual procedural due-process challenge, a party feeling deprived of a valuable interest argues that government acted unconstitutionally because it provided no procedures or *inadequate* procedures. Before the challengers can have this objection taken seriously, however, they must establish that they have been deprived of an interest that qualifies as a property or liberty interest recognized by the Constitution's due-process clause.

This section notes the major sources of constitutionally recognized property and liberty rights, respectively. We also explain here the distinct doctrines used to define these rights.

Tracing property and liberty rights to their origins

Property and liberty interests can be created by many sources:

- **Statutes:** A statute passed by Congress, a state legislature, or a city council can create an interest triggering procedural due process. For example, in *Goss v. Lopez,* 419 U.S. 565 (1975), the Court held that state laws making public education available to all residents up to a certain age give students a constitutionally recognized "property" interest to go to school and receive the benefits of a public-school education — unless school authorities can show a valid reason (such as misconduct) for suspending students from school. (*Goss* also held, as we note below, that students have a "liberty" interest in not having their future career blighted by a false aspersion of misconduct.)

- **Legally binding equivalents of statutes**: Common-law court decisions, executive orders, administrative regulations, and other legally binding equivalents of statutes can also create constitutionally recognized property or liberty interests. For example, a presidential executive order governing security clearances for government contractors could create a constitutionally enforceable property right to due process before a security clearance is revoked. So too could regulations from a state prison authority create a liberty interest in not having parole revoked for alleged misconduct without appropriate procedures for proving inmate misdeeds.

- ✔ **Guidelines in government manuals:** Less-formal guidelines and sentiments in governmental manuals and memoranda can be the basis for a protected interest. For example, in *Perry v. Sinderman,* 408 U.S. 593 (1972), the Court found that, even in the absence of an official tenure system for state-college educators, a property right in continued employment was created by guidelines of the Coordinating Board of the state university system and an assurance in the college's internal manual that it "wishes the faculty member to feel that he has permanent tenure."

- ✔ **Established behavior patterns:** Even without a written basis, an ongoing pattern of behavior by governmental officials with authority to bind their agency can create a property or liberty interest.

- ✔ **The Constitution:** The Constitution itself can be a major source of liberty interests protected by due process. For example, as we explain in Chapter 14, parents have constitutionally based liberty interests in having a relationship with their children. And, in the later section "Defining when a challenger is asserting a due-process-protected liberty right," we note other due-process-protected liberty rights stemming from the Constitution. By contrast, the Constitution only recognizes property rights created outside of its boundaries. The Constitution is not a *source* of due-process-protected property rights.

Identifying when a challenger can assert a due-process-protected property right

Under modern procedural due-process case law, the key to being able to show a constitutionally protected property interest is to demonstrate that applicable laws, policies, or practices amount to a "legitimate entitlement" (a legally recognized right) and not just a "mere unilateral expectation" (an unenforceable, one-sided hope of fair treatment). The pair of cases the Supreme Court used to create the distinction best illustrates the practical and critical difference between a constitutionally protected entitlement and an unprotected expectation.

In *Board of Regents v. Roth,* 408 U.S. 564 (1972), the Court rejected the claim of a new professor at a state university that he had a property interest in continued employment; the professor claimed the university had to give him notice and a hearing before deciding not to renew his annual contract. The *Roth* Court cautioned that one claiming a protected property interest must have "more than an abstract need or desire" or a "unilateral expectation of it."

Professor Roth was on an annual contract. During the contract time period, he was protected by statutory language providing that he held his job "during efficiency and good behavior." Thus, had the university tried to remove him before the end of the contract period, it would have to provide notice as to its grounds for suspecting him of inefficiency or bad behavior.

Two practical realities about procedural due process: *Sinderman* as a prime example

The *Sinderman* case, described in "Identifying when a challenger can assert a due-process-protected property right," provides more than the Court's first illustration of what it takes to create a "legitimate entitlement" to property. It is also a very useful example of two practical realities surrounding procedural due-process arguments.

First, procedural-due-process analysis is influenced by more than just legal doctrines (such as, here, the distinction between *unilateral expectation* and *legitimate entitlement*). How much the court sympathizes with the challenger, as opposed to the government, can influence how legal doctrines are applied. This probably explains why the Court mentioned that Professor Sinderman was "successful enough to be appointed, for a time, the cochairman of his department" and only seemed to run afoul of supervisors when he became actively involved in "public disagreements with the policies of the college's Board of Regents." The Regents' decision to terminate Sinderman's contract for insubordination appeared to be punishing him

for exercising First-Amendment rights to discuss matters of academic policy. This unfair retaliation certainly diminished the college's credibility, and may have influenced the Court to consult and credit informal sources to find a protected property right.

Second, *Sinderman* illustrates the practical significance of winning a due-process claim. In theory, having a right to additional *process* does not guarantee a different *result*. Nothing actually prevented college officials from again terminating Professor Sinderman after giving him the required procedures. But college officials now had to provide an "official statement of the reasons for the nonrenewal of [Sinderman's] contract" beyond just branding him as insubordinate. Officials may have been more reluctant to officially admit their zeal to silence an academic dissenter. Although there's no guarantee that government officials will have a substantive change of heart, when procedural due process leads to greater information and deliberation, it may practically influence the outcome.

Roth failed to show, however, that any state laws or university policies entitled him to *renewal* of his contract. Instead, the Court found, "[s]tate law . . . clearly leaves the decision whether to rehire a nontenured teacher for another year to the unfettered discretion of university officials." At best Roth only hoped (or expected) that if he did a good job he would be rehired.

Conveniently, the Court decided a companion case to *Roth* showing the broad range of legal sources that can create the necessary "legitimate entitlement" to property. In *Perry v. Sinderman*, 408 U.S. 593 (1972), the Court found that a professor who had taught for ten years under year-to-year contracts at a state junior college had more than a one-sided hope to continued reemployment. Even though his junior college had no formal tenure system, the Court found that a combination of less-formal sources created a "no less binding understanding fostered by the college administration." This unofficial tenure program had been created by (1) a provision in the college's Faculty Guide that the administration "wishes the faculty member to feel that he has a permanent tenure as long as his teaching services are satisfactory and as long as he displays a cooperative attitude toward his coworkers and his superiors," and (2) state guidelines providing that a seven-year veteran of the college system has "a form of job tenure."

Defining when a challenger is asserting a due-process-protected liberty right

Unlike property rights, no one rule governs when liberty interests are sufficient to trigger procedural due process. A wide variety of liberty rights are established by provisions in the U.S. Constitution, in state constitutions, and in a variety of statutes, regulations, and court decisions. The best way to illustrate the protections is to provide a few examples of rights that do and do not qualify as constitutionally protected liberty interests triggering due process. In this section we explore liberty rights pertaining to reputation and to conditions in government institutions.

Rights relating to reputation

People's reputations can strongly affect their life and livelihood, but they can only claim due-process-protected liberty rights related to reputation in certain cases:

- ✔ **Without other factors, an interest in preserving one's reputation *is not* a liberty interest sufficient to require notice and hearing.** The Court so held in *Paul v. Davis,* 424 U.S. 693 (1976). Challenger Paul was arrested for shoplifting but never convicted. When his name and picture were placed on a list of "Active Shoplifters" compiled by a County Sheriff and circulated to local businesses, Paul claimed a liberty interest in not having his good name besmirched without a formal finding that he was guilty of the crime alleged. The Court disagreed.

- ✔ **An interest in preserving one's reputation *is* a sufficient liberty interest if the injury to a person's good name is accompanied by a "significant alteration" in their legal status or another independent injury.** Following are classic examples of this principle:

  - • **When a government-caused impairment of a person's good name will "seriously impair their chance to earn a living":** The quote is from *United States v. Lovett,* 328 U.S. 303 (1946), where three federal employees faced salary retaliation for "subversive activity," a label likely to jeopardize employment prospects.

- **When good-name impairment leads to the denial of an opportunity otherwise available under law:** *Wisconsin v. Constantineau,* 400 U.S. 433 (1971), ruled that notice and an opportunity for a hearing were required before a person's name could be included in a list of problem drinkers to whom it would be illegal to sell alcohol.

- **When charges of serious misconduct impair future educational opportunities:** In *Goss v. Lopez,* 419 U.S. 565 (1975), the Court noted that a wrongful suspension of a public-high-school student would create a black mark in the student's permanent file, perhaps hurting his college-admission prospects.

Rights relating to treatment in government-run institutions

People in school or prison have certain due-process-protected liberty rights:

✔ **School children *do* have a constitutionally protected liberty interest in avoiding arbitrarily inflicted physical punishment.** This right was announced by the Court in *Ingraham v. Wright,* 430 U.S. 651 (1977).

✔ **Convicted defendants put on probation as an alternative to incarceration — or paroled before the end of their prison terms — *do* have a protected liberty interest against having their probation or parole revoked without adequate notice and a hearing.** *Morrissey v. Brewer,* 408 U.S. 471 (1972), held this for revocation of parole. *Gagnon v. Scarpelli,* 411 U.S. 779 (1974), held this for revocation of probation.

✔ **Convicted defendants serving prison sentences *are* entitled to due process before the state revokes earned "good time" credits that would have led to their early release.** In *Wolff v. McDonnell,* 418 U.S. 539 (1974), the Court held that, although defendants have no constitutional right to early release, a statutory scheme for earning "good time" credits created a liberty interest to avoid having to endure unjustified prison time.

✔ **Prison inmates do *not* have a constitutionally protected liberty interest in avoiding changes in their conditions of incarceration — even if conditions are substantially more burdensome — if those changes are "within the normal limits or range of custody which the conviction has authorized the state to impose."** *Meachum v. Fano,* 427 U.S. 215 (1976), found no protected liberty interest for prisoners transferred from a medium-security to a maximum-security prison after suspicious arson incidents. Similarly, *Sandin v. Conner,* 515 U.S. 472 (1995), found no liberty interest for an inmate guilty of misconduct who was sentenced to "disciplinary segregation" in a special unit.

✔ **Prison inmates *do* have a liberty interest in avoiding changes in incarceration equating to an "atypical and significant hardship."**

- **When a prisoner is involuntarily transferred from a general-population prison to a mental hospital:** In finding a protected liberty interest, the Court in *Vitek v. Jones,* 445 U.S. 480 (1980), relied on a state statutory presumption of normal incarceration, on the mandatory quality of the transfer, and on the stigmatizing effect of a mental-illness allegation.

- **When a prisoner is given antipsychotic drugs without his consent:** *Washington v. Harper,* 494 U.S. 210 (1990), made this logical extension of *Vitek.*

Deciding How Much Process Is Due — and When

After you determine that the challenger is due *some* process — that is, after you find that the challenger is asserting a constitutionally recognized property or liberty interest — the next (and last) major questions are *what kinds* of processes government must provide and *when* it must do so.

Generally, courts answer these questions by using a three-factor balancing test — called the *Mathews balancing test* in honor of the case spawning it, *Mathews v. Eldridge,* 424 U.S. 319 (1976). Given the importance of the *Mathews* balancing test, we devote this section to generally laying out its basic design, explaining how it takes into account "emergency" situations (when government doesn't have the luxury of providing any process before acting), and illustrating the different kinds of results the *Mathews* balancing test can produce in nonemergency contexts.

Applying the Mathews balancing test

According to the *Mathews* balancing formula, the extent and timing of the procedures government must provide before depriving a person of constitutionally protected property or liberty are found by weighing all three of the following factors:

- ✔ The strength of the private interest that will be affected by the government's proposed action
- ✔ The strength of the government's interest, including the importance of the governmental function being performed and the fiscal or administrative burdens additional process could impose
- ✔ The risk of mistakenly depriving the individual of his interest via the current procedures, and the likely value of additional procedures

---

The other-remedies exception to *Mathews*

As with any good legal rule, procedural due process comes with an exception. Sometimes the Court has held that, even though challengers have protected liberty or property interests, they don't get the usually required notice and hearings because alternative legal remedies already serve the values procedural due process seeks to protect. For example, In *Lujan v. G&G Fire Sprinklers, Inc.*, 532 U.S. 189 (2001), the Court assumed for argument's sake that when a government agency withholds payments during a dispute with a private contractor, the contractor is deprived of a constitutionally protected property right. Still, the Court didn't require a hearing before payments were withheld because the state "makes ordinary judicial process" in the form of a typical contract-enforcement lawsuit available.

The *Mathews* balancing formula has a common-sense logic to it. When a property or liberty interest is especially important to the individual — and particularly when the government's interest in a speedy decision is not strong — relatively elaborate procedures are required before the deprivation becomes final. On the other hand, when the individual's interest is relatively low, or the countervailing government/public interest is especially strong, relatively less formal procedure is required.

Mathews's risk/benefit analysis of procedural adequacy also makes basic sense. If the current procedures are reliable and there is a low risk of error, then the case for requiring more procedures is weakened. ("If it ain't broke, don't fix it.") Or, even if current procedures are substantially likely to lead to error, but the risk can't be reduced as a practical matter by more elaborate procedures (that is, if what government is doing is just inherently risky), procedural due process doesn't order useless process. When current procedures run needless risks reducible through practically available additional procedures, government can't constitutionally act without them!

Presuming the need for predeprivation procedures except in emergencies

In general, when some process is due to protect against arbitrary deprivation of property and liberty interests, the procedures logically should come predeprivation (that is, *before* the final deprivation occurs). A true emergency or comparable need for expedition, however, excuses government from providing procedure before acting adversely. In such a case, later (postdeprivation) procedures have to mop up the damage.

The case establishing this emergency theory is *North American Cold Storage v. Chicago,* 211 U.S. 306 (1908), in which a poultry-processing company challenged governmental officials' seizure and destruction of meat suspected of being "putrid." Responding to the challenger's claim that failure to provide notice and a hearing before destroying the company's product violated its procedural due-process rights, the Court held that the serious danger to public health and safety from tainted poultry allowed government to act now and provide process later. The Court noted that the challenger could bring a later court action to recover damages for the destruction of its property.

Although *North American Cold Storage* presented especially dramatic (not to mention disgusting!) facts, its rationale is potentially useful to government officials wanting to resist arguments for predeprivation procedures in a variety of regulatory contexts (such as heavily regulated industries like airlines, banks, and drug manufacturers, where acts or omissions could threaten public safety or financial integrity).

Seeing the range of due-process scenarios produced by the Mathews balancing test

The best way to illustrate the *Mathews* balancing test in operation is to first explain the cases in which it required the most and the least extensive procedures. Then we illustrate other cases occupying midpoints on the extensiveness spectrum.

Reaching the high-water mark of required procedure

Goldberg v. Kelly, 397 U.S. 254 (1970), which ruled that New York City had to provide more-detailed notice of its reasons for revoking welfare benefits (see the earlier section "Understanding procedural due process"), still stands as the decision requiring the most extensive procedures in the name of due process. *Goldberg* held that, even though New York City gave extensive "fair hearing" procedures *after* terminating welfare benefits, the Constitution required the City to afford substantially more procedures *before* deprivation.

In explaining why the *Goldberg* Court found the city's existing procedures deficient, the *Mathews* Court explained that welfare recipients have especially strong interests because welfare is given to people "on the very margin of subsistence." Wrongfully cutting off welfare benefits could deprive *eligible* recipients of "the very means by which to live." On the other hand, the *Goldberg* Court said that the government also had an interest that welfare benefits not be "erroneously terminated" — an interest that clearly outweighed the increase in fiscal and administrative burdens (which the Court said could be minimized by "skillful use of personnel and facilities").

In evaluating the dangers in the procedures New York City already used (which included informal discussions between caseworkers and recipients and several levels of internal bureaucratic review), the *Goldberg* Court emphasized the following main deficiencies:

✔ **The process didn't give a recipient facing benefit termination "timely and adequate notice detailing the reasons for the proposed termination."**

✔ **The process unfairly limited recipients to presenting their position "in writing or secondhand through [their] caseworkers."** But most recipients needed to be heard orally because they generally lacked the educational sophistication to communicate in writing. Oral presentation also offered "flexibility" and allowed recipients "to mold [their] argument to the issues the decision maker appears to regard as important."

✔ **The process didn't allow deprived recipients to present evidence personally, call their own witnesses, or cross-examine adverse witnesses.** These limitations posed a particular risk of error because many welfare-termination proceedings turn on the "credibility and veracity" of live witnesses.

✔ **The process didn't require the decision maker to explain the basis for the decision, base it only on evidence presented at the recipient's hearing, or avoid direct participation in a previous procedural stage.**

When very informal procedures are enough

At the opposite side of possible outcomes is *Goss v. Lopez,* 419 U.S. 565 (1975). After strongly stating that a student suspended from school for more than ten days has both a constitutionally protected property interest (under state laws generally guaranteeing students the right to attend public school) and a protected liberty interest (because a suspension on false grounds besmirches the student's reputation *and* jeopardizes his chances for college acceptance), the Court provided a remarkably tame version of process due.

The *Goss* Court claimed to recognize the importance of the student's interest and the non-"trivial" risk of error in the school disciplinary process. But the Court was also concerned about not compromising the "vast and complex" job of administering the nation's schools by "elaborate hearing requirements." So the *Goss* Court found due process satisfied if the school official imposing the discipline advised the student of the charges and permitted him to tell his side of the story. (Few students facing determined and overworked school disciplinarians likely find much comfort in these *Goss* procedures!)

Making intermediate stops on the procedural due-process train

The following two cases are several of a number of cases at different points on the procedural-due-process spectrum between the *Goldberg* high point and the *Goss* low point. These cases show the balancing matrix in action:

✔ **Less elaborate procedures for terminating Social Security disability benefits:** In *Mathews,* the Court held that government officials are constitutionally allowed to terminate Social Security disability benefits through procedures much less elaborate than the *Goldberg* Court required for welfare-benefit terminations. Validating a predeprivation process emphasizing multiple opportunities for recipients to review medical records and submit additional evidence in writing, the 1976 *Mathews* Court weighed several factors differently than the *Goldberg* Court did six years earlier.

Most important, the *Mathews* Court theorized that, compared to the welfare context, less-formal procedures would work in the Social Security disability arena. Among the reasons cited were that disability determinations turn on supposedly more objective, focused, and easily documented medical questions, that medical records are "routine, standard, and unbiased" and do not need to have their "credibility and veracity" assessed at formal hearings via cross-examination, and that doctors easily communicate in writing.

✔ **Relatively modest procedures before firing a government employee:** In *Cleveland Board of Education v. Loudermill,* 470 U.S. 532 (1985), the Court again applied the *Mathews* matrix to hold that procedural due process required one relatively informal procedure beyond what government officials were already providing. *Loudermill* involved a security guard fired after school authorities discovered that he had not reported a felony conviction on an employment application asking the standard question, "Have you ever been convicted of a felony?" Board of Education officials insisted that they had a strong need to dismiss Loudermill without a hearing; they emphasized that he would get a post-termination hearing.

In requiring officials to let Loudermill appear before them in person before firing him, the Court found a substantial private interest (because most people are dependent upon their salary check for economic viability) and a reduced governmental interest (because "[i]t is preferable to keep a qualified employee on than to train a new one"). As to the risk of proceeding without an informal hearing, the Court noted that whether an employee deserves to be fired usually involves not just facts but also questions of discretion. For example, Loudermill claimed that he misunderstood the nature of his prior conviction and therefore did not deliberately lie on his application. His employers needed to hear from him directly to evaluate that claim.

Procedural due process and the post-9/11 detainees

One of the most recent and provocative applications of procedural due-process doctrines occurred in the post-9/11 case of *Hamdi v. Rumsfeld,* 542 U.S. 507 (2004). Hearing a challenge to the indefinite detention of a United States citizen as an alleged "enemy combatant," a four-justice plurality held that procedural due process required federal officials to give "a citizen-detainee seeking to challenge his classification as an enemy combatant . . . notice of the factual basis for the classification, and a fair opportunity to rebut the Government's factual assertions before a neutral decisionmaker." Without finally deciding other procedural questions, the plurality suggested that "the exigencies of the circumstances" permitted hearsay evidence not normally admissible in criminal proceedings to be used; the plurality suggested that the government's showing of "credible evidence" could put the burden on the detainee to rebut it.

Providing Low-Level Substantive Protection through Due Process

Substantive due process is a distinct branch of due-process analysis. It focuses not on the adequacy of the procedures government uses to deprive persons of liberty or property, but on whether governments can even restrict those rights.

Substantive due process is a very important area of constitutional doctrine. Constitutional-law courses at the undergraduate and law-school level typically spend several weeks on it. But for two reasons, we devote very few words to it in this last section.

First, for all property interests and most liberty interests, substantive due process affords a relatively low-level degree of protection against arbitrary deprivation. This baseline rational-basis standard is also applied to ensure that governmental line-drawing isn't discriminatory. Because the rational-basis case law is more fully developed with respect to the Constitution's equal-protection guarantees, we leave most of the details to Chapter 10. Here we simply want to point out that government may limit a person's property or liberty rights as long as the limitation in some way serves a "legitimate" governmental interest. Although governments usually meet the low-level rational-basis standard when they seek to limit property or liberty rights, the baseline limit does serve as a constant check on arbitrariness.

The second reason we don't provide much treatment of substantive due process here is that one aspect of that subject is important and complicated enough to deserve its own chapter. As we detail in Chapter 14, the modern Court has labeled some liberty interests relating to privacy rights as *fundamental* and subjected them to *strict scrutiny,* an exacting standard government usually fails to meet.

Chapter 9

Protecting Property: Land, Contracts, and Guns

....

In This Chapter

▶ Understanding the limits on governmental "taking" of private property

▶ Identifying when government actions unconstitutionally violate contracts

▶ Exploring the historical and newly emerging rights of gun ownership

....

*A*s we discuss in Chapter 8, due-process-of-law restrictions prevent governments from depriving persons of property. These restrictions provide important procedural protections (and less weighty substantive protections) to a wide range of entitlements to ownership. Yet the Constitution provides other important protections for other specific property rights. This chapter focuses on the three most important property-guaranteeing provisions.

The first section summarizes the major legal developments under the "takings" clause, which requires that governments not take private property for public uses without paying fair value for it. The clause has been extended to two contexts outside the classic eminent-domain power (for example, governments' right to condemn someone's house to build a freeway). The takings clause is implicated when governmental land-use restrictions significantly reduce the economic value of land without a sufficiently important reason; the clause is also in play if government imposes disproportionate conditions when granting approval to expand land uses. We also discuss how the Court got into hot water recently by refusing to limit the uses to which land could be put when compensation is paid.

The second section looks at how the Constitution prohibits the government from impairing contract obligations — one of the few individual-liberties provisions in the original Constitution of 1789. We note several related landmark decisions early in the nation's history and try to make sense of a meandering line of decisions potentially affecting government's ability to regulate important areas of national life, including cushioning the effect of economic distress on Americans.

The last section looks at the recent Supreme Court's revitalization of the Second-Amendment right to purchase and own guns. As we note, the Court has made two major decisions in the last several years reversing longstanding presumptions about gun rights. We close with a summary of several questions unanswered — and likely to be litigated soon — by the Court.

The Takings Clause: Protecting Private Property from Government

After the Fifth Amendment lists several civil and criminal rights that can't be violated by the federal government (including the protection against deprivation of life, liberty, or property without due process, the right to indictment by grand jury, and the right to avoid self-incrimination), the amendment concludes, ". . . nor shall private property be taken for public use without just compensation." This *takings clause* reflects the framers' view that a man's home was his castle and his property was sacred.

This section first illustrates the classic situations in which the takings clause is clearly relevant — when government takes property for public use as part of its *eminent domain* power. Then we explore the general rule that normal zoning and other land-use restrictions do *not* trigger a government obligation to provide compensation — a rule subject to an exception. Further, we examine the two-stage balancing test used to determine when laws placing conditions on further land use are "takings" requiring compensation. Finally, we note the legal and political fireworks caused by the Court's recent failure to meaningfully limit the range of public uses to which property can be put.

Illustrating how a "permanent ouster" clearly requires just compensation

The takings clause was intended to regulate the classic eminent-domain situation, which occurs when government permanently ousts a rightful owner from his land to use it for a purpose government regards as more important.

As long as it pays fair compensation, the government can take away property for a greater good, such as in any of the following typical examples:

- ✔ Condemning one or more houses sitting on the most cost-effective location for a freeway on-ramp
- ✔ Allowing a group of homes and businesses in a flood plain to go underwater to reduce a greater risk of flooding downstream
- ✔ Ordering the abandonment of a neighborhood that has been irrevocably tainted by toxic waste when that's the only way to protect public health

Fighting over "just" compensation

The government's views and the property owner's views about what is fair compensation may differ radically. Negotiations may be hot and heavy and feelings may run high. (In part, that may be because property owners feel an emotional attachment beyond mere economics.)

Government agencies whose typical functions require the confiscation of land try to ease the process by proactively offering comprehensive settlement packages and inducements for owners to surrender property without a fight. And disputes may be submitted for mediation. Still, failure to achieve an agreement on compensation may lead to successive rounds of costly litigation, with experts battling over the "fair market value" of the property (the estimated value of a property if subjected to its "highest and best use").

Yet not every "physical taking" is so complete. In *Loretto v. Teleprompter Manhattan CATV Corporation,* 458 U.S. 419 (1983), New York City's requirement that a landlord devote a small strip on the roof of his building to a cable TV box was found to be a taking that required fair compensation.

Noting when zoning laws are takings

The zoning and land-use laws most communities adopt — that is, laws limiting the kinds of development that can occur in certain areas of the community, and the like — keep landowners from making full use of their property as they see fit. These landowners may feel that valuable property rights have been taken from them and may expect compensation from public tax dollars. But governments can't afford to pay landowners every time their property value is affected by zoning laws. Such a "pay to play" rule could deter the government from making or enforcing zoning laws for the greater good.

Generally, the law finds reasonable land-use restrictions to be the price of living in a civilized community. Takings-clause law recognizes the infeasibility of triggering a compensation requirement every time some unit of government tells a homeowner he can't operate a home business or tells a land developer she can only build ½-acre single-family residences and not more lucrative high-density apartment towers. The courts give government land-use regulators substantial deference in disputed cases. (In the rare case when zoning restrictions are deemed to be arbitrary, the law is invalidated on grounds of substantive due process; it isn't a takings-clause problem triggering a compensation requirement.)

Still, limits are in place. Land-use restrictions stripping landowners of "all economically beneficial or productive use of land" are the functional equivalent of takings, requiring just compensation.

To illustrate where the line is drawn and how substantial reductions in property value must be endured before it is crossed, consider the following pair of cases:

- ✔ **No compensable taking:** In *Penn Central Transportation Company v. New York City,* 438 U.S. 104 (1978), the Court found no taking requiring compensation when the city's landmarks-preservation act stopped the owners of Penn Station from realizing ambitious plans to build a 50-plus story office building above or alongside its historic and iconic façade. Although the owners stood to lose millions of dollars from the thwarting of their development plans, the Court found no requirement to pay them compensation, because preserving important landmarks is "substantially related to the promotion of the general welfare" and the restrictions "permit reasonable beneficial use of the landmark site."

- ✔ **Compensable taking:** By contrast, *Lucas v. South Carolina Coastal Council,* 505 U.S. 1003 (1992), found a compensable taking when a state beachfront-management act prevented a landowner from "erecting any permanent habitable structure" on two residential lots he had paid almost a million dollars for. The *Lucas* Court sympathized with the state's interests in preserving coastal land from erosion. But the majority found that the state's unexpected restrictions, which went beyond the prohibitions imposed by common-law nuisance principles, inappropriately interfered with reasonable landowner expectations.

Unfortunately, the Court muddied the relative clarity in the "all-beneficial-uses" standard in a later case, *Palazzolo v. Rhode Island,* 533 U.S. 606 (2001). The *Palazzolo* Court wrote that even when some beneficial uses remain, "a taking nonetheless may have occurred, depending on a complex list of factors including the regulation's economic effect on the land owner, the extent to which the regulation interferes with reasonable investment-backed expectations, and the character of the government action."

Seeing when unreasonable conditions on further development are takings

One other takings issue arises when government allows a landowner to *further develop* his property on the *condition* that the landowner agree to other limits on property use. Even though government officials can completely deny zoning variances or other permits necessary for further land exploitation, saying yes to planned development doesn't give officials a completely free hand to impose any expensive conditions they want.

According to recent case law, to avoid being a taking requiring just compensation, government's conditions on development must further a "legitimate state interest" *and then* pass this two-part test:

✔ **The "legitimate state interest" and the permit condition imposed must have an "essential nexus" (a necessary link).** An example of the nexus not being met is *Nollan v. California Coastal Commission,* 483 U.S. 825 (1987). There, the Coastal Commission granted approval to property owners seeking to expand a beachfront house, with the condition that the homeowners provide public access through a path across their property (which separated two public beaches). The Court said that there wasn't an adequate connection between the condition and government's legitimate interest in preventing the new construction from blocking the view of the ocean. The Court said requiring public access had nothing to do with unblocking the ocean view.

✔ **The state interest achieved must be roughly proportionate to the extent of interference with private property rights.** Extracting too little benefit at too high a cost fails the "rough proportionality" concept. This is especially true when government seems to choose a more-property-rights-restrictive approach when a less burdensome one will do.

The case creating the "rough proportionality" test also provides two examples of when conditions don't measure up. In *Dolan v. City of Tigard,* 512 U.S. 374 (1994), city officials approved a business owner's plans to double the size of her retail site, but in exchange required her to dedicate roughly 10 percent of the overall property for a publicly accessible greenway and a pedestrian/bike path. The *Dolan* Court found that the city passed the first step in the nexus test: an "essential nexus" linked the conditions and the city's desire to prevent flooding (by leaving the greenway unpaved, to absorb rain runoff) and reduce traffic congestion (by encouraging walking and biking).

However, the Court found that leaving the greenway unpaved *without allowing public access to it* would have yielded just as much flood prevention. Because the right to exclude others from property is "one of the most essential sticks in the bundle" of property rights, forcing the business owner to forgo that "stick" was disproportionate. The pedestrian/bike path requirement, in turn, was disproportionate to the *Dolan* majority because the city could not demonstrate that increased pedestrian and bike activity would meaningfully ease traffic increases attributable to the retail expansion.

Declining to limit the public uses for which land can be taken

One of the most controversial recent Supreme Court cases is *Kelo v. New London,* 545 U.S. 469 (2005), in which a narrowly divided Court upheld a city's right to condemn houses in a neighborhood to redevelop land into a waterfront-resort area complete with conference hotel, marina, restaurants, and stores. Some homeowners, including an elderly longtime resident, didn't want to move. They objected that, because the condemnation would transfer their property to another *private* landowner who could restrict public access (rather than to a public entity itself), the land wasn't being seized for a "public purpose" as the takings clause requires.

The *Kelo* majority held that land condemned by government didn't literally have to remain open to the public to "serve a public purpose." The majority saw previous cases as consistently defining the public-purpose concept "broadly, reflecting our longstanding policy of deference to legislative judgments in this field." The majority found that the city had "carefully formulated an economic plan that it believes will provide appreciable benefits to the community, including — but by no means limited to — new jobs and increased revenue." It did not see its ruling as especially radical, despite claims by dissenting Justice O'Connor that it was "wash[ing] out any distinction between private and public use of property — and thereby effectively [deleting] the words 'for public use' from the Takings Clause."

More than a *Kelo* of controversy — and protecting constitutional rights outside the Supreme Court

The *Kelo* case has been highly controversial. Many people were upset that government was placing its power on the side of the rich and powerful, ousting marginalized but loyal residents of a nonblighted area in the process. Although the Court's constitutional interpretation can't be directly overturned without going through the lengthy and difficult process of amending the Constitution, public officials at every level of government and homeowner-rights advocates have searched for ways to limit the damage.

The most ingenious response was launched in the small New Hampshire town where then-Supreme Court Justice David Souter (part of the *Kelo* majority) had a small cabin. Critics of the decision started an unsuccessful move to have Souter's cabin condemned for another community use so that he would have a taste of his own medicine!

More seriously, *Kelo* led state legislatures to pass laws preventing state officials from engaging in *Kelo*-style condemnations. Congress placed limits on use of federal funds to support *Kelo*-type land seizures. In states permitting citizen initiative, reform proposals were put forward.

These developments reinforce three important points we emphasize throughout this book about constitutional rulings. First, constitutional questions in court usually arise over what government *can* legally do if it chooses to, not what its citizens or officials *should* or *will* do. Specifically, *Kelo* in no way *requires* states to allow similar property seizures. Second, just because no *federal* constitutional barrier prevents *Kelo*-style condemnations doesn't mean that the *state* constitutions can't be pressed into service to stop them. Third, *Kelo*'s aftermath shows the importance of nonjudicial avenues for promoting constitutional values. If the Supreme Court fails the Constitution (as many *Kelo* critics think it did), nonjudicial officials at the federal, state, local level — and ultimately, the people who elect them — can fill the void.

Not Impairing the Obligations of Contracts: The Contracts Clause

Individuals often acquire property through contracts, including land deeds. So a close connection exists between protecting contracts and protecting property (be it *real property,* such as buildings and land, or *personal property,* such as cars and computers). A provision of Article I, Section 10 declares that "No State shall . . . pass any . . . Law impairing the Obligation of Contracts." This "contracts clause" is among only a few provisions in the Constitution's original seven articles that directly protect individual rights. Why the framers' special concern about preserving contracts from state threat? What distinctions did the early Court draw under the contracts clause? What is the clause's modern relevance? We address each of these questions in turn.

Realizing why contract obligations mattered to the framers

The framers included the contracts clause to address a potentially worrisome economic situation. As a new national government began to take shape after the Revolution, economic stresses led state legislatures to pass a variety of "debtor-relief" laws. Some of these laws postponed the time for debt repayment; others offered debtors installment or partial-payment options that weren't part of the original debt arrangement. Still other laws required creditors to accept newly state-issued paper money of dubious value.

Creditors and other well-to-do interests disliked this interference by state governments. A number of framers found it troubling as well. Many believed that a key function of civilized government was to protect — not to undermine — the liberty to contract. (This view often went hand in hand with *laissez faire* economics, which holds that individual and collective prosperity is generally advanced by private markets relatively free of governmental interference.) Many framers worried that individual states sticking their noses into the creditor/debtor relationship would cause uncertainty interfering with the free availability of credit and the robust investment and economic activity needed to forge a national interstate economy.

The contracts clause sought to promote national economic integration and American prosperity. Provisions in the original Constitution forbidding states from coining money and giving the national Congress the power to regulate interstate commerce aided it.

Most individual-rights protections end up applying to all levels of government, either by express constitutional language or as expanded or interpreted by the courts. However, the contracts clause only limits impairments of contracts by *state* governments (and any regional or local subdivisions they empower). No equivalent prohibition applies to the federal government. Constitutional historians dispute whether this omission reflects a deliberate framer decision not to limit the federal government, an assumption that the federal government wouldn't impair contracts, or something else. (Note that highly arbitrary interferences with contract rights by the federal government would run afoul of the substantive limit against deprivation of property without due process added by the Bill of Rights' Fifth Amendment.)

Extracting the basic principles from early contracts-clause cases

In the 19th century, the contracts clause was the main source of Supreme Court litigation concerning the validity of state laws. After all, it was one of the few rights-enforcing constitutional provisions applicable to the states; the core Bill-of-Rights provisions didn't become "incorporated" and applied to the states until the Fourteenth Amendment was passed late in the century.

The Court decided a number of contracts-clause cases in the 1800s — several of which are regarded today as landmark cases. The following principles are among the most important issues decided in those cases:

✔ **The clause prevents state governments from passing laws that reach back to change the terms of contracts.** This prohibition applies both to contracts in which state governments are parties and contracts between purely private parties. The protection extends to individuals, corporations, and associations. And the protection runs to third parties succeeding to the rights of the original contracting parties.

The classic example of this principle is from the earliest contracts-clause case, *Fletcher v. Peck,* 10 U.S. 87 (1810). *Fletcher* struck down a law passed by a Georgia legislature to revoke an earlier public-land grant. The contract-revocation law sought to expunge from the state's records all deeds relating to those lands and the later sale of them — thereby invalidating a later sale from Peck to Fletcher. In crying foul, Chief Justice John Marshall invoked both the contracts clause and "general principles which are common to our free institutions."

The Court emphasized the way the contracts clause can apply to contract rights of non-individual entities in another classic case, *Dartmouth College v. Woodward,* 17 U.S. 518 (1819). After New Hampshire was formed into a state, the state government passed a law revoking the charter that the King of England had granted Dartmouth College. The

Supreme Court said the charter was a binding "contract" between the King and the trustees of the college and the state could not retroactively impair that contract.

✔ **The contracts clause does not prevent state governments from altering the environment in which future contracts will be concluded.** In *Ogden v. Saunders,* 25 U.S. 213 (1827), the Court held that the contracts clause only stops states from passing laws affecting contracts already in place; states can pass laws affecting contracts made after the laws are passed. In light of this distinction, the *Ogden* Court upheld a state bankruptcy law passed before the contract at issue was signed — because at the time they signed the contract, the parties likely took into account the possibility that circumstances could change (here, that the debtor would go bankrupt).

✔ **In deciding when state laws rise to the level of impairing existing contracts, a meaningful difference exists between canceling out a contract obligation and modifying the way the obligation can be fulfilled.** In *Sturges v. Crowninshield,* 17 U.S. 122 (1819), the Court found that a New York bankruptcy law unconstitutionally impaired an existing contract because it allowed the debtor to completely discharge the debt and leave the creditor holding the bag. But the *Sturges* Court said that a state could pass bankruptcy-type laws easing the circumstances of repayment without violating the contracts clause, so long as the law doesn't conflict with federal bankruptcy laws.

✔ **The contracts clause doesn't permit a state legislature "to bargain away the public health or the public morals."** This language is from *Stone v. State of Mississippi,* 101 U.S. 814 (1879), which challenged a Mississippi legislature's passage of an 1868 law making lotteries illegal throughout the state. The law conflicted with a permit the state granted the year before to a corporation to hold a lottery. When the Mississippi Attorney General later brought suit against the company for illegally operating a lottery, the company used the contracts clause as a defense. The *Stone* Court held that all the company had was a permit "that was good as against existing laws." The company had to live with the possibility that a future legislature would adopt laws reflecting a different view about what served its residents' moral and social welfare.

Reconciling the contracts clause with the emerging regulatory state

Even though the contracts clause was obviously important to the framers and the Constitution they created, they and later governing figures recognized that government still has to be able to operate, making and enforcing laws in the public interest. Especially as government expanded its regulatory presence in more modern eras, the Court was called on to reconcile the clause with the needs of expanded governance.

The Supreme Court's approach to contracts-clause questions also involves a balancing test, although a number of years passed before the Court articulated the test. In several major cases during the Great Depression, the Court implicitly used a balancing approach. Becoming acquainted with these cases helps you understand the transformation of this balancing act into an official three-part test.

Charting the Depression-era approach to contracts-clause protection

During the Great Depression of the 1930s, the government had an obligation to try to help the citizenry weather the dire economic climate. During this time frame, governments at all levels resorted to relatively drastic measures to ease pressures on the people and help the economy recover. And the Supreme Court reviewed cases with the emergency circumstances in mind, heavily crediting those concerns in the balance.

The classic Depression-era contracts-clause case is *Home Building & Loan Association v. Blaisdell,* 290 U.S. 398 (1934). After noting that "there has been a growing appreciation of public needs and of the necessity of finding ground for a rational compromise between individual rights and public welfare," the Court upheld, against a contracts-clause challenge by lenders (and also a substantive due-process challenge), a state law temporarily preventing mortgage companies from foreclosing on delinquent homeowners. The law, typical of the era's response to a wave of mortgage foreclosures and resulting social dislocations, allowed mortgage holders to seek court approval for extensions in the dates for mortgage payments and delays in foreclosures.

In holding that the law was a valid exercise of the state's police powers to protect its residents from economic collapse, the Court cited these factors as tilting the balance in favor of the government:

- The country was in a state of emergency that justified state protection of "the vital interests of the community."

- The law served the legitimate goal of protecting society's basic interests; it wasn't "for the mere advantage of particular individuals."

- The relief provided by state law was "appropriate to th[e] emergency and . . . granted only on reasonable conditions." In particular, the Court agreed that the period by which the mortgage obligation was extended was reasonable.

- The legislation was to be in effect temporarily.

Although *Blaisdell* was influenced substantially by the financial emergency, the Court clarified that, even in an emergency, the modification of contracts still had to be reasonable in scope and duration. The Court drove this home a year later in *Worthen v. Kavanaugh,* 295 U.S. 56 (1935), in which, after a more extensive and sophisticated balancing act, the Court struck down a different mortgage-extension law because the extensions were so long that they effectively destroyed the value of the collateral security.

A three-step analysis: Seeing how modern courts approach private contracts

Especially when a law intrudes into a contract between *private* parties, the Court pursues a three-step analysis that balances government's interests against the private party's contract right. As pulled together in *Energy Reserves Group v. Kansas Power & Light Company,* 459 U.S. 400 (1983), the Court examines the following issues (using language taken from the case):

1. **The Court determines the *severity* of government's impairment of private-contract obligations.**

   The Court is in part guided by whether the government has previously regulated the industry that the contract pertains to. (The Court's logic is that contracting parties in heavily regulated industries should know that further regulation is "foreseeable.")

2. **If substantial impairment has taken place, the Court asks the state to show "a significant and legitimate public purpose" proving that its contract impairment isn't a special-interest giveaway.**

   The Court has clarified that, although emergencies enhance the legitimacy of government's purposes, an emergency isn't necessary for governmental actions to be allowed under the contracts clause.

3. **If government satisfies the public-purpose showing, the Court questions "whether the adjustment of the rights and responsibilities of contracting parties is based upon reasonable conditions and is of a character appropriate to the public purpose."**

In *Allied Structural Steel Company v. Spannus,* 438 U.S. 234 (1978), the Court invalidated a state law significantly altering the financial costs a few private-sector companies faced from government-mandated changes in the pensions they offered to workers. Viewing the state law as severely impairing pension contracts, the Court doubted the significance of its public purpose based on the "extremely narrow focus" of the law and the absence of any "showing in the record" of "an important general social problem."

Showing some skepticism: Modern approaches to the government's own contracts

The modern Court seems to be more skeptical of midstream changes in contracts when state and local governments themselves are parties to them. No distinct test is applied for government contracts, but the Court seems to have a greater suspicion that the government may be pursuing its own narrow self-interest in avoiding financial obligations rather than pursuing a broader public interest.

Looking at contracts-clause issues and state budget crunches

Contracts-clause issues are a hot topic to watch these days. Budgetary crises will likely increase pressure on state and local governments to at least consider reducing generous pension plans for state employees or finding ways to free themselves from state contracts with private parties that seem questionable in leaner times. These pressures will only heighten the importance of contracts-clause considerations as states and private individuals calculate their next legal moves.

How will the Court likely respond to efforts by municipalities and states on the brink of bankruptcy to alter their financial obligations

to public employees and contractors? If the situation seems dire enough, the requisite emergency may appear to be at hand. But what about contracts already in place between the employees and entities, involving benefits already vested or which employees bargained for in taking employment? Altering these contracts seems to qualify as a severe impairment, raising questions about the reasonableness of any benefit/payment rollbacks. Plus, the courts have shown that in some instances they are more strict in analyzing laws that would change government's own obligations to the detriment of individuals.

United States Trust Company v. New Jersey, 431 U.S. 1 (1977), illustrates this more-skeptical approach. The Court took a very dim view of efforts by New Jersey and New York to void agreements they made just 12 years earlier when floating government bonds. (At that time, to provide financial assurances to major lenders, the states had agreed to bond provisions limiting their ability to use public funds to subsidize mass transit.) The Court warned that "a State cannot refuse to meet its legitimate financial obligations simply because it would prefer" to follow a different public policy. The Court viewed "total repeal" of public-funding restrictions as not essential in light of "less drastic" alternatives available (including contract *modification*).

Taking Aim at Rights of Gun Ownership: The Second Amendment

The right to bear arms — which immediately connects to the right to buy and own weapons — is perhaps one of the most hotly debated topics related to property ownership (and indeed, to constitutional law generally) in the modern era. Gun-control activists are constantly at odds with gun-ownership-rights activists. Some Americans think gun-control laws will reduce crime in this country, particularly in the wake of horrific crimes such as children taking guns to schools and killing other students and teachers. But other people hunt as a major hobby, and some people carry guns or keep them in their homes for protection.

The general belief of an individual gun-ownership right stems from the Constitution's Second Amendment, which states: "A well regulated Militia, being necessary to the security of a free State, the right of the people to keep and bear Arms, shall not be infringed." Although this provision may seem simple on its face, constitutional interpretation is rarely cut and dry; every word, every clause and every comma, semicolon and period is dissected to the point of exhaustion.

Before 2008, Second-Amendment rights — although undoubtedly a perennially hot political issue — seemed a relatively dormant area of constitutional law. The conventional understanding was that the constitutional prohibition against infringing the "right of the people to keep and bear Arms" didn't grant important individual gun-ownership rights (as compared to the right to own guns in order to participate in "[a] well-regulated Militia") and that the Second Amendment only limited the federal government.

Two Supreme Court decisions in 2008 and 2010 drastically changed the constitutional playing field for gun rights. This section sketches in the conventional understanding these decisions disturbed, explains the holdings and rationale of the Court's recent about-faces, and briefly summarizes issues the Court has not yet decided.

Understanding the previous era's limited view about gun rights

Although for years many people have adamantly claimed a strong constitutionally guaranteed right to own a gun, until very recently the Second Amendment was viewed for several reasons as a limited constitutional provision.

First, the Second Amendment remained one of the few Bill of Rights provisions not officially incorporated and applied to state and local governments. The Court declined to incorporate this amendment in two very old cases, *United States v. Cruickshank,* 92 U.S. 542 (1876) and *Presser v. Illinois,* 116 U.S. 252 (1886). Whatever the Second Amendment prohibited, then, it only did so for the national government and its instrumentalities (such as the District of Columbia).

Second, even at the federal level, the Court generally understood the Second Amendment to serve a rather limited purpose. For example, in *United States v. Miller,* 307 U.S. 174 (1939), the Court assumed that the amendment only forbade the federal government from interfering with a state's ability to effectively organize a militia. *Miller* and a later case relying on its interpretation (*Lewis v. United States,* 445 U.S. 55 [1980]) stopped short of finding a broadly applicable individual right to gun ownership.

Admittedly, these decisions could be challenged on a number of technical grounds. Early rejection of the Second Amendment's application to the states seemed rather casual; it may have reflected that the Court had not undertaken to apply individual provisions of the Bill of Rights to the states through "selective incorporation." And the cases appearing to reject an individual right to gun ownership outside of the militia context were cases interpreting statutes; constitutional issues were not the focus. Finally, in none of the cases had the Court confronted laws that substantially *prohibited* gun ownership (as opposed to imposing relatively minor registration restrictions on owning guns).

Summarizing the recent strong assertions of gun rights

Two landmark Supreme Court decisions in 2008 and 2010 (filling a total of 181 pages in the official reports and generating eight different judicial opinions) turned the tables on past understandings, breathing substantial new life into the Second Amendment.

Establishing a broader individual gun-ownership right

In *District of Columbia v. Heller,* 554 U.S. 570 (2008), a very divided Supreme Court struck down major portions of a gun-control law in the District of Columbia (which is generally treated as an organ of the federal government, and not a "state"). The law "totally ban[ned] handgun possession in the home" and "requir[ed] that any lawful firearm in the home be disassembled or bound by a trigger lock at all times, rendering it inoperable." In so doing, the majority exhaustively examined and credited historical arguments that a general right of self-defense and home protection unrelated to militia service was central to early Americans. The majority viewed this broad self-defense right as essentially what the Second Amendment was designed to protect.

The Court clarified that the preface in the amendment referring to the militia didn't limit or expand the operative clause, *the right to bear arms.* Calling the right to individual self-defense the "central component" of the Second Amendment — and viewing the Second Amendment as a central impulse for adopting the Bill of Rights — the *Heller* majority endorsed a strong constitutional right to gun ownership and use.

The *Heller* Court nevertheless explained that the Second Amendment gun-ownership right was limited like other constitutional rights. Specifically, the Court confirmed that the amendment allows laws prohibiting possession of firearms by felons and mentally ill people, restricting possession of guns in sensitive places such as schools, and limiting the commercial sale of firearms.

Extending this broader Second-Amendment right to state and local governments

The *Heller* decision broadened the bases for challenging national firearm regulations that were long thought to be beyond constitutional doubt. But on its own, *Heller* did not open up new Second-Amendment challenges against the many state and local gun-control laws sprinkled throughout the country. (Remember that D.C. is a federal entity, so *Heller* only expanded the meaning of rights of gun owners as against restrictive *federal* laws.)

State and local governments got involved in the upheaval two years later in *McDonald v. City of Chicago,* 130 S.Ct. 3020 (2010). *McDonald* involved several consolidated cases alleging that municipal ordinances banning handgun possession by almost all private citizens violated constitutional gun-property rights. The *McDonald* lower court had relied on the early string of cases we canvass in "Understanding the previous era's limited view about gun rights" to refuse to apply the Second Amendment to the states.

In *McDonald,* the same five justices who had enhanced the importance of Second Amendment rights as against the federal government in *Heller* took their expanded view of gun rights to its logical conclusion. Viewing "the right to keep and bear arms [as] fundamental to our scheme of ordered liberty" — for several reasons, including reading historical evidence as emphasizing how important gun rights were to Constitution drafters and the public alike — the *McDonald* majority found the Second Amendment to be applicable to the states and their political subdivisions.

Identifying important remaining questions on gun rights

As with many major alterations in constitutional law, the *Heller* and *McDonald* decisions left open many important questions to be sorted out in later litigation. The future answers to these questions will go a long way toward determining the scope of governmental powers to regulate guns and gun-related violence. The following questions seem especially significant:

- **What arms do Americans have the right to bear?** The *Heller* Court recognized that an important limitation on the Second Amendment was that it only justified keeping and carrying arms commonly used when the amendment was adopted. No right was granted to carry "dangerous and unusual weapons." Although the majority's expanded view of gun-ownership rights definitely protects handguns and ordinary rifles and excludes M-16 military rifles, many questions remain to be worked out in later court battles about the exact scope of arms protected.

- **What level of scrutiny should be used in evaluating laws limiting Second-Amendment rights?** The most important and outcome-determining question about most constitutional rights is how weighty they are — specifically, what level of scrutiny should be imposed on laws limiting them. Over strong objections from dissenters, the *Heller* majority declined to answer the question decisively.

- **To what extent are gun registration, background-check requirements, and general concealed-weapon bans safe from invalidation?** The *Heller* majority declared the presumptive validity of limitations on gun possession by felons and mentally ill people, bans on carrying firearms in sensitive places, and "laws imposing conditions and qualifications on the commercial sale of arms." But whether the latter phrase protects the full range of current federal, state, and local registration and background-check laws depends on the specific importance of the "laws imposing conditions." And whether bans on concealed weapons in "sensitive places such as schools and government buildings" include concealed weapons in all public places remains unclear.

No doubt, multiple gun-ownership rights cases will come before the Court in future years, so we may someday find out the answers to these and other questions.

Chapter 10

Preventing Government from Discriminating

*G*overnments often legitimately draw lines between groups. For example, tax and employment laws typically distinguish between large and small businesses. But some governmental discrimination — especially line-drawing based on race, gender, and other personal characteristics — generates major controversies pursued in constitutional-law classes and argued about in society. This chapter equips you to deal with this important issue by exploring the basic framework and important legal developments preventing governments from denying "equal protection of the law."

After highlighting the essence of the Constitution's main equality guarantee, we explain the baseline requirement that all government line-drawing be rational. Building on this rational-basis default standard, we then show how the courts apply a much more powerful level of review ("strict scrutiny") to laws discriminating based on race and national origin (including affirmative-action programs). We also chart the more-powerful level of review ("intermediate scrutiny") used for laws discriminating based on gender.

Another section explores how current doctrines treat laws that, while not overtly discriminating based on race or gender, have disproportionate discriminatory *effects* on those bases. Finally, we examine a doctrine that allows a more-than-rational level of review (at least in practice) when government action seems to reflect prejudice against a disfavored group.

Understanding the Essence of the Equal-Protection Guarantees

Several constitutional provisions relate to some form of government discrimination. The Fifteenth Amendment prohibits discrimination in voting. (We deal with this important dimension of discrimination in Chapter 13, which covers several constitutional doctrines relating to voting and electoral rights.) Article I, Section 9, Clause 6 forbids Congress from giving any "Preference . . . to the Ports of one State over those of another."

Still, the broadest and most important constitutional protections against governmental discrimination are the provisions in the Fifth and Fourteenth Amendments forbidding governments at all levels from "deny[ing] the equal protection of the laws." This section establishes three key points about the scope of equal-protection guarantees and explains how equal-protection issues arise in constitutional law.

If you want to sound like a constitutional-law expert, keep in mind that the Bill of Rights (which guarantees individual liberties with respect to the federal government) doesn't *literally* contain an equal-protection clause. Instead, the Supreme Court has ruled that the Fifth Amendment's prohibition against the federal government depriving Americans of "life, liberty, or property, without due process of law" contains an *implicit* equal-protection "component." This view partly reflects that later Fourteenth Amendment drafters included an explicit equal-protection clause in the same paragraph in which they required states to provide due process; this move arguably shows that due process and equal protection are related components of a broader right against arbitrary government treatment. Also, it would just seem illogical and bad policy for the federal government to be able to discriminate against Americans in ways the states and localities couldn't!

Considering the scope of equal-protection guarantees

The Fourteenth Amendment was adopted after the Civil War to prevent racial discrimination against newly freed slaves and other historically mistreated African Americans. However, modern constitutional doctrines have extended equality protections significantly beyond racial discrimination, so many other individuals are now protected by equal-protection guarantees.

The right to equal protection can be claimed by any "person" within the jurisdiction of the governmental entity passing a law. This right even protects persons who are not citizens. And, significantly, it includes corporations and associations, which are treated as fictional "persons" under the law.

Keep in mind that, as with other constitutional text, the equal-protection language is phrased in the negative. That is, the constitutional text *prevents* governments from acting unequally *when governments choose to act.* Equal protection does not impose any *affirmative* obligation on governments to fight inequality in American society (such as wealth disparities and the like).

Seeing how equal protection kicks in whenever government draws lines

Many federal, state, and local laws apply to all persons (including corporations) within the relevant government jurisdiction. Every person in the United States is subject to federal antidrug laws. No person within California is immune from the state's laws against driving negligently.

But many — perhaps most — governmental laws and policies apply more selectively. Minimum-wage and maximum-hour provisions exempt some small businesses and certain employees. Tax rates vary depending on the income of the taxpayer. Abortion regulations apply only to pregnant women.

Because governments often must draw lines between different categories of persons and entities to accomplish their policy goals, governments often face allegations that they violated the Constitution's equal-protection obligations. Specifically, an equal-protection challenge arises in the following situations:

✔ Government *benefits* certain persons or entities and declines to provide benefits to other persons or entities OR government *burdens* certain persons/entities and does not burden other persons/entities.

    AND

✔ The persons or entities on the burdened (or not benefitted) side of the line seem "similarly situated" to (that is, seem as deserving as) the persons or entities on the other side of the line.

One classic equal-protection case is *Railway Express Agency v. New York,* 336 U.S. 106 (1949). *Railway Express* challenged the constitutionality of a New York City ordinance generally banning from city streets vehicles bearing signs advertising products or services. The ordinance exempted vehicles advertising their own products or services. Challengers claimed that the ordinance unconstitutionally discriminated against vehicles that carried advertising for another business.

You find out in the next section why the *Railway Express* Court upheld the ordinance's distinctions under the "rational-basis" test. For now, notice how the ordinance is a classic example of governmental line-drawing. On the *burdened* side of the line are all vehicles advertising the products or services of businesses other than the ones owning the trucks. On the *not burdened* side of the line are vehicles advertising their own company's products or services. Following is a tabular representation of the ordinance:

Burdened (Or Not Benefited)	**Not Burdened (Or Benefited)**
Vehicles advertising for another business	Vehicles advertising a business's own goods or services

Setting the Equal-Protection Baseline against Government Discrimination

Whenever governments pass laws impacting a person's interests in life, liberty, and property, they at a minimum have to act "rationally" — that is, non-arbitrarily (see Chapter 8 for details). Modern constitutional-law doctrines enforce this requirement via a two-part rational-basis test.

A similar test kicks in whenever government draws lines between favored and disfavored (or burdened and not burdened) groups. Actually, Court decisions about equal protection have more thoroughly defined the rational-basis test.

Laws or other governmental policies pass the *rational-basis standard* as long as both of the following conditions hold:

✔ The scrutinizer of government action can conceive of at least one legitimate interest the government might be pursuing.

✔ A rational person would think that the law or policy in some way furthers the conceivable legitimate interest.

As you can see, the rational-basis standard generally cuts governments lots of slack. The standard seeks to preserve the proper balance between elected officials and unelected federal judges by preventing judges from straying into detailed assessment of the pros and cons of governmental policies. (Courts generally say that nonjudicial decision makers should do comparative policy analysis.) Specifically, this standard is easy to pass because

- ✔ **Even relatively trivial interests qualify as legitimate.** For example, the republic won't end if the shops and residences in a city's "old town" neighborhood aren't painted in a consistent, historically authentic color scheme. But that regulation is a "legitimate" end for local government to pursue as part of its zoning and land-use powers.

- ✔ **The interest deemed legitimate doesn't have to be one the government lawmaker or policymaker actually was guided by or stated when the law or policy was adopted.** A _post hoc_ (after the fact) rationalization can be suggested by government lawyers when the law is challenged later in court. As long as this creative suggestion could conceivably have been government's interest, it's enough.

- ✔ **As long as some part of the problem government seeks to solve is handled by the law or policy at issue, it doesn't matter if it is very overinclusive (it goes farther than necessary) or quite underinclusive (it is an incomplete, partial solution).** Legislatures often spread the regulatory net wider than strictly necessary in order to make sure that they deal with the problem, and courts don't find the inclusivity irrational.

  Legislatures are also allowed by courts to take half steps on the way to solving a problem. Experimenting with regulation on a limited basis or concentrating scarce regulatory resources on the biggest part of the problem can make sense. Politically, a legislative majority may not support a "full on" solution; often "half a loaf is better than none."

- ✔ **Because the government's regulatory solution to some part of the problem only has to be rational, the government's logic doesn't have to be very significant.** Specifically, even if most evidence is on the other side, it may still be "rational" for government to think what it thinks. (For example, even if the vast weight of evidence is that greenhouse gases cause global warming, as long as "rational" scientists think otherwise, government can too.) To quote the Court in one recent equal-protection case, as long as the government's position is "at least debatable," that's good enough.

In light of all the reasons why the rational-basis test is easy to pass, you can understand why the New York City advertising ordinance at issue in _Railway Express_ passed rational-basis scrutiny. The Court was willing to imagine that the ordinance sought to avoid visual distractions to drivers, thus enhancing traffic safety. (This is _clearly_ a "legitimate" interest — especially in New York City, where drivers and pedestrians take their lives into their own hands just by venturing out!) And certainly New York authorities were "rational" in thinking that some of the banned advertising vehicles would have been distracting. (The point was "at least debatable.") So the fact that the law was overinclusive (because it banned tasteful, low-key ads that weren't distracting) and underinclusive (because it failed to ban distracting ads by vehicles advertising a business's *own* goods and services) wasn't problematic.

Because baseline rational-basis scrutiny provides only moderate protection, courts feel the need to use higher levels of scrutiny for certain kinds of discrimination — including race, national origin, and gender. We focus on these issues and a few others in the rest of the chapter.

Strongly Fighting Discrimination Based on Race or National Origin

Modern equal-protection cases provide much more protection against governmental discrimination based on race and national origin (that is, the country of one's ancestry) than rational-basis scrutiny does (see the preceding section). After all, if the core purpose of the Fourteenth Amendment — including its requirement not to deny equal protection — was to protect racial minorities, stronger judicial medicine would seem to be called for.

This section traces the evolution of that stronger medicine, which is now expressed in an official *strict-scrutiny* standard. We explain how strict scrutiny differs from the mere rational-basis default standard, illustrate how in practice strict scrutiny dooms almost all laws discriminating based on race or national origin, and fit affirmative-action laws into the equation.

Suspicious minds: Judicial questioning of race and national-origin distinctions

Even before the rigorous strict-scrutiny standard was developed through case law, which is described in the next section, the Court decided several important cases indicating that discrimination based on race or national origin was highly suspect. The following three cases are especially worthy of note:

  ✔ *Strauder v. West Virginia*, **100 U.S. 303 (1880):** A dozen years after the Fourteenth Amendment's ratification, the Court struck down a state law limiting jury service to white male adults. Noting that the Amendment sought to deter predictable race discrimination after slavery's abolition, the Court declared that "the very fact that colored people are singled out . . . because of their color, though they are citizens, and may be in other respects fully qualified, is practically a brand upon them . . . , an assertion of their inferiority, and a stimulant to that race prejudice which is an impediment to securing . . . equal justice."

✔ *Korematsu v. United States,* **323 U.S. 214 (1944):** In this case, the Court upheld the mass internment during World War II of Americans of Japanese ancestry living on the West Coast. Despite the anti-equality *outcome* of the case, the Court spoke eloquently that "all legal restrictions which curtail the civil rights of a single racial group are immediately suspect." Declaring the need for "the most rigid scrutiny" to avoid "racial antagonism," the Court implicitly recognized that race and national origin, although distinct, are closely associated bases for unthinking prejudice. (Of course, critics of *Korematsu* at the time and now think that the Court overcredited national-security fears and underestimated the racist motivations behind the internment order.)

✔ *Brown v. Board of Education of Topeka,* **347 U.S. 483 (1954):** In overruling past precedent and declaring that racially segregated public schools throughout the South and elsewhere had to be desegregated, a unanimous Court found that separating students "of similar age and qualifications solely because of their race generates a feeling of inferiority as to their status in the community that may affect their hearts and minds in a way unlikely ever to be undone."

Understanding modern "strict scrutiny" of race or national-origin laws

Strong judicial suspicions about race discrimination and national-origin discrimination have matured into an official strict-scrutiny standard that's much more rigorous than the rational-basis test. As we discuss in the earlier section "Setting the Equal-Protection Baseline against Government Discrimination," the rational-basis standard is the equal-protection default rule and typically defers to the government. But unlike rational-basis review, the strict-scrutiny test requires the government law or policy to meet the following standards:

✔ **Actual interests:** The interests asserted to defend a law discriminating based on race or national origin must be the actual interests that really did motivate government. Unlike in rational-basis analysis, the court will not "conceive" of interests that "might" have motivated the government.

✔ **Compelling interests:** Government can't justify discrimination based on just any legitimate interest. Rather, the interest must be *compelling* (that is, of highest-order importance, such as protecting national security, avoiding deaths or injuries, or protecting the nation's economy).

✔ **A necessary law:** The discriminatory law must be *necessary* to achieve government's actual compelling interest(s). Unlike rational-basis scrutiny, a law simply advancing government's goal in some way is not enough. Rather, it must be true that *without this law* government would not be able to accomplish its compelling concerns.

✔ **Narrow tailoring:** Unlike rational-basis scrutiny, which tolerates substantial overinclusion and underinclusion, strict scrutiny requires that a law or policy be the most carefully calibrated alternative that will do the job. Unnecessary discrimination will be fatal to the law. (For this reason, narrow tailoring is often called the "least discriminatory alternative" rule.) And even if government avoids also discriminating against other racial or national-origin groups, the law won't pass scrutiny; selective racial discrimination is no better than more indiscriminate racial antagonism.

Strict scrutiny generally works to invalidate almost any law that stigmatizes or otherwise treats as inferior any member of a racial or national-origin group. Strict scrutiny is so effective that one well-known scholar called it "strict in theory and fatal in fact."

Many government interests, although legitimate or even important, don't rise to the highest level of a compelling interest. More often, even if courts rule (or at least assume for argument purposes) that governmental interests are compelling, they typically find that the interest could be achieved by more closely tailored means. Rarely, if ever, does anything other than government's most narrow pursuit of a critical priority survive the challenge.

This reality can be illustrated from two different directions:

✔ **(Supposedly) passing strict scrutiny:** As noted in the previous section, a divided *Korematsu v. U.S.* Court upheld — under scrutiny supposedly "most rigid" — a broad scheme of systematic discrimination against hundreds of thousands of Japanese Americans. But an extreme context was necessary to produce this rare judicial approval of national-origin discrimination. The U.S. was at war with a heavily armed Japanese enemy that had recently destroyed most of the Pacific Fleet during a surprise attack on Pearl Harbor. The government claimed serious concerns about Japanese sabotage and even an invasion on the country's West Coast. In these unusual circumstances, United States military commanders initially imposed a curfew on all persons of Japanese descent (including many who were U.S. citizens) living on the West Coast. This restriction was followed several months later by "exclusion orders" moving Japanese descendants to far-away "relocation centers."

The *Korematsu* majority didn't officially employ the elements we now call strict scrutiny. But we can overlay its reasoning on this modern template as follows: The high national-security stakes at issue clearly seemed compelling. And the Court's crediting of military judgments that "the need for action was great, and the time was short" implies that America did not have the luxury of pursuing more-narrowly tailored and less-inclusive means, such as excluding a smaller category of especially "high risk" Japanese descendants or assessing the loyalty of individual Japanese descendants most critical to the war effort. The majority implicitly saw the extreme measure of internment as regrettable but necessary in light of the "pressing public necessity."

✔ **Failing strict scrutiny:** At first blush, the race-based policy at issue in *Johnson v. California,* 543 U.S. 499 (2005), looks like it could have withstood strict scrutiny. *Johnson* considered a California Department of Corrections policy housing new inmates in cells with inmates of their same race for 60 days. State prison authorities claimed that temporary race-based assignments gave staff time to investigate gang affiliations and avoid violence caused by rival prison gangs of different races.

Even though avoiding gang violence seems to be a very compelling interest, especially in overcrowded prisons like California's — and even though the temporary nature of the racial segregation helped it seem narrowly drawn — a seven-justice majority held that California's policy was not necessary to achieve the state's goals.

Korematsu's modern legacy

Although the decision still has its defenders, *Korematsu* is widely seen today as a tragic mistake and a highly erroneous product of war hysteria and racism. Legal scholars agree that the decision wouldn't be a precedent for any remotely comparable program of national-origin discrimination today. Scholars see *Korematsu* as a prime example of how American courts are at their worst when trying to apply constitutional values when the country feels profoundly unsafe.

In 1988, the Congress passed a law providing for a presidential letter of apology and reparations to each survivor (or the survivor's heirs) of the World War II internment scheme. When the reparations program ended in 1999, $1.6 billion had been paid to over 82,000 Japanese Americans. Long before that, a majority of the justices who originally upheld the exclusion orders in *Korematsu* regretted their decision in public statements or private correspondence.

Although *Korematsu* isn't good legal support for racial or national-origin discrimination to advance national-security interests, its theory about the need for strict scrutiny stands.

Fitting "benign" discrimination (affirmative action) into the equation

Fitting affirmative action programs in with strict-scrutiny standards raises major theoretical and practical problems. After all, preferential treatment intended to help minorities by remedying the effects of past offensive discrimination still discriminates based on race in the provision of important government benefits, such as admission to undergraduate and graduate public education and eligibility for public contracts. But, unlike *invidious discrimination* (the term often used for old-style race discrimination seeking to *harm* racial minorities), affirmative action intends to be *benign* (beneficial) *discrimination*. (Of course, critics contend that affirmative action harms racial minorities by perpetuating stereotypes that they can't compete without government favoritism. But we keep our focus on its constitutionality.)

In this section, we explain why and how the Court now applies strict scrutiny to affirmative-action laws and policies.

Defending (and criticizing) strict scrutiny for affirmative action

From 1976 to 1989, the Supreme Court invalidated some race-based affirmative action (for example, holding in *Regents of the University of California v. Bakke,* 438 U.S. 265 (1978), that the U.C. Davis Medical School could not reserve 16 places in its 100-person entering class for African American applicants). During that time period, the Court upheld other affirmative-action programs. The Court agreed, for example, in *Fullilove v. Klutznick,* 448 U.S. 448 (1980), that the federal government could set aside 10 percent of its public-works contract funds for minority-owned subcontractors. In none of these cases could a majority of justices agree about the applicable standard of scrutiny.

Clarity (if not the end of controversy!) came in *City of Richmond v. Croson,* 488 U.S. 469 (1989), in which a majority of justices held that state and local affirmative-action programs had to survive strict scrutiny. The Court then went on in *Adarand Contractors v. Peña,* 515 U.S. 200 (1995), to subject federal-government affirmative-action programs to strict scrutiny as well.

The modern Court sees no distinction between benign and invidious discrimination for equal-protection purposes for the following major reasons:

✔ **The Court considers "searching judicial inquiry" to be necessary to "smoke out" unthinking or reflexive use of race** (as Justice O'Connor wrote in *Croson*).

✔ **The Court worries that affirmative action has the same risk as invidious discrimination — that a racial majority will use its political power to impose hardships on a racial minority.** Although many affirmative-action programs have been adopted by predominantly white policymakers willing to disadvantage some of their own race, the scenario in *Croson* seemed to confirm the Court's worse fears about racial politics. The city council of Richmond, Virginia, whose population and city council were both majority black, voted to set aside 30 percent of the city's public-contract funds exclusively for black- and other minority-owned subcontractors. To the *Croson* majority, this looked like a black majority using its political power to disadvantage whites.

✔ **Some justices take the position that equal protection requires government to generally be "color blind" — that is, to avoid race in drawing distinctions, except when government needs to adopt hiring quotas or other color-conscious measures to remedy its own past discrimination.**

A strong counterview on and off the Court contends that affirmative-action programs should have to pass a less strict standard. Among the various reasons put forward for a more government-friendly reception of "benign" discrimination is that it's more in keeping with the Fourteenth Amendment's basic purpose to improve the lives of African Americans and dismantle the effects of slavery and legal segregation.

Seeing strict scrutiny in operation: Split decisions on prominent affirmative-action programs

Because of strict scrutiny, governments have a much harder time sustaining affirmative-action programs against lawsuits claiming that they violate equal protection. Still, a split decision on affirmative action in education admissions shows that carefully designed programs can survive. In this section we overview three key decisions to sketch in the contours of the modern Court's mixed reaction to affirmative-action programs.

Hiring city contractors: Rigorous use of strict scrutiny in Croson

In voiding Richmond's 30 percent-set-aside program, *Croson* showed that strict scrutiny could be very strict indeed. Specifically, the majority held that

✔ **Interests were not compelling.** The only "compelling" interest that might justify affirmative action at the state and local government level was remedying past discrimination within the jurisdiction — either by the government or by private parties with whom the government was a "passive participant." The *Croson* majority rejected arguments that Richmond had an interest in enhancing minority participation to better match the racial makeup of the city, in providing "role models" for aspiring minority members, or redressing general discrimination in American society.

✔ **The law wasn't necessary.** After *Croson,* proponents of affirmative-action plans have to show lots of evidence that the plans are necessary to serve the compelling remedial purpose. In holding that Richmond did not meet the necessary burden of proof, the *Croson* majority rejected "conclusory" statements by officials familiar with past discrimination and the city's attempted reliance on federal government data. Instead, the city needed — but failed — to infer past discrimination from a meaningful statistical comparison between the number of qualified minority-owned subcontractors and the number who got city contracts.

✔ **Tailoring wasn't narrow.** The *Croson* majority said that programs like Richmond's can only survive strict scrutiny if governments conclude after appropriate study that their remedial goal can't be achieved by race-neutral means (for example, preferring all small subcontractors, regardless of the race of their owners), if the preferences given and the beneficiaries eligible for them are closely calibrated to past discrimination, and if the program is sufficiently flexible to account for situations in which there aren't sufficient qualified minority participants.

University admissions: The generous application of strict scrutiny in Grutter and the skeptical application in Gratz

More recently, in upholding the University of Michigan Law School's use of race as a factor in making admissions decisions, the majority opinion in *Grutter v. Bollinger,* 539 U.S. 306 (2003), applied a seemingly more generous version of strict scrutiny. Ways in which the *Grutter* majority seemed to apply a less-strict strict scrutiny include:

✔ **Finding compelling interests:** Even if public universities don't have a history of past discrimination, they have a second compelling interest for using racial preferences: achieving a diverse student body. This finding ended 27 years of speculation and much lower-court guessing about whether the Court would ever expand the category of compelling interests beyond remedying past discrimination.

✔ **Granting the necessity:** Public universities did not need to prove the benefits of diversity generally, or at their campuses specifically, through rigorous evidentiary showings. Instead, the Court "defer[red]" to the "educational judgment" of academics that "diversity is essential to its educational mission." The Court also credited arguments from "major American businesses" and "high-ranking retired officers and civilian leaders of the United States military" that today's increasingly diverse workforce and armed forces require leaders exposed during their educations "to widely diverse people, cultures, ideas, and viewpoints."

✔ **Recognizing sufficiently narrow tailoring:** Race-based admission programs in which race is just one of a number of factors considered during "a highly individualized, holistic review of each applicant's file" pass the requirement of being narrowly drawn without exacting hairsplitting. Nor is a program insufficiently careful in its tailoring if some public universities have found that they can enhance minority admissions by nonracial means (such as giving preferences for low socioeconomic status) or when the program fails to provide for regular periodic review to determine if it is still needed. (This latter requirement had seemed important in previous affirmative-action cases.)

What a difference a vote (or two) makes

On a multimember court — and especially on the Supreme Court — individual vote patterns often make crucial differences in case outcomes. *Grutter* and *Gratz* are perfect examples. Four justices (Rehnquist, Scalia, Kennedy, and Thomas) voted to strike down affirmative action in both cases. Three justices (Stevens, Souter, and Ginsburg) voted to uphold affirmative action in both cases.

What caused the *Grutter/Gratz* split verdict, then, were the votes of Justices O'Connor and Breyer, who voted to uphold the law school's affirmative-action program and to reject the undergraduate admissions policies. This split leads to two points:

✔ One vote can matter. (If either O'Connor or Breyer had voted against the law school, a five-justice majority would have coalesced for that result.)

✔ Individual judicial personnel decisions matter. (Justice Samuel Alito, who replaced O'Connor after *Grutter* and *Gratz* were decided, likely would have voted as she did.)

On the same day it decided *Grutter,* the Court invalidated a different race-based admissions scheme used by the University of Michigan's main undergraduate college. With a larger volume of applications, the college used a largely objective system in which each applicant automatically received a standard number of points for various factors. The undergraduate school gave an unusually large number of points for an applicant's race, which the majority in *Gratz v. Bollinger,* 539 U.S. 244 (2003), saw as "making 'the factor of race . . . decisive' for virtually every minimally qualified underrepresented-minority applicant." Without the individualized review the Court approved in *Grutter,* the undergraduate program flunked the requirement that affirmative-action admission programs be narrowly drawn.

Affording Significant Protection against Gender Discrimination

The Court also gives significant protection against discrimination to individuals when it comes to laws singling out a particular gender (although the degree of protection is less than with race). Keep in mind, however, that this refers to laws or policies drawing male-versus-female distinctions; it has nothing to do with sexual or transgender orientation. (For information on discrimination based on sexual orientation, see the later section "Flunking Rational-Basis Review: Hostility against a Disfavored Group.") In this section, we elaborate on court holdings about gender discrimination.

The Court came within one vote in *Frontiero v. Richardson,* 411 U.S. 677 (1973), of giving gender discrimination the same strict scrutiny afforded to race and national-origin discrimination. A four-justice plurality found gender discrimination similar in significant ways to race discrimination, as the following excerpt from the ruling explains:

> *There can be no doubt that our nation has had a long and unfortunate history of sex discrimination. . . . romantic paternalism which, in practical effect, put women, not on a pedestal, but in a cage. . . .*

Instead of equating race and gender discrimination, however, the Court settled on a middle-ground level of scrutiny in between strict and rational basis. This section first explains how *intermediate scrutiny* works in general. Then the discussion shows how two different unofficial tendencies — which we label *intermediate scrutiny heavy* and *intermediate scrutiny light* — can be detected in the modern case law relating to gender discrimination.

Understanding how intermediate scrutiny fits in theoretically

In theory, intermediate scrutiny operates in between strict and rational-basis scrutiny as follows:

- ✔ **The governmental interest asserted to justify gender discrimination has to be "important."** Not any old "legitimate" interest will work; specifically, "mere administrative convenience" or saving tax dollars are not sufficiently important to greenlight governmental policies disadvantaging an entire gender. But the interest can have less urgency than the kind of security-promoting and life- and property-protecting impulses that qualify as "compelling" for strict scrutiny.

- ✔ **The governmental interest has to be the "actual" interest really motivating government to discriminate.** Unlike rational-basis review, the Court will not imagine what purposes "might" have motivated government. Nor will after-the-fact justifications invented by clever attorneys fly. In this sense, intermediate and strict scrutiny are alike.

- ✔ **The discriminatory law or policy must "substantially further" the government's important interest.** The fit between means and ends must be "substantial" — in that a male/female distinction works in many (and maybe most) cases. Unlike rational-basis scrutiny, the law needs to do more than further the interest "in some way." On the other hand, the means don't have to be the least discriminatory ones or draw the narrowest possible distinctions. Unlike strict scrutiny, an insubstantial amount of over- or underinclusiveness is tolerated.

Table 10-1 shows the differing requirements of the three scrutiny levels.

Table 10-1	Three Scrutiny Levels for Gauging Discrimination		
	Rational Basis	*Intermediate*	*Strict*
The governmental interest(s) must be . . .	Legitimate	Important	Compelling
The claimed interest(s) must be . . .	What conceivably motivated the government	The actual interest	The actual interest
The discriminatory law must further the interest(s) . . .	In some way	Substantially	In the narrowest practical way
Over- and underinclusiveness is . . .	Totally allowed	Allowed as long as not substantial	Not allowed

Justifying sort-of-strict treatment of gender classifications

The Court has never officially justified providing heightened, but not fully strict, scrutiny for gender discrimination. Yet a common-sense rationale for "quasi-strict" scrutiny is that gender is "quasi-suspect" — meaning that *some,* but not all, of the reasons why race and national origin are strictly scrutinized apply to gender.

As the plurality noted in *Frontiero v. Richardson,* 411 U.S. 677 (1973), women are like racial minorities in that they have historically been the victims of serious and systematic legal and societal discrimination, including exclusion from voting and meaningful political participation. Gender, like race, is assigned by genetics and individuals do not generally choose the characteristics flowing from it.

On the other hand, racial minorities were the prime beneficiaries of Fourteenth-Amendment protection. (You'd have a hard time arguing that the amendment was intended to free women from the effects of discrimination.) Gender, and the biological and physical differences that go with it, also arguably are more relevant to traits government is legitimately be concerned about. Finally, of course, women are a majority — not a "discrete and insular minority" (classic language the Court has used to describe why racial minorities can't protect themselves well in the majoritarian political process). In theory, any time women want to engage in bloc voting, they can elect representatives to do their bidding!

The bottom line: Because some, but not all, of the major reasons for strictly scrutinizing racial and national-origin distinctions apply to gender classifications, the Court arguably applies *somewhat,* but not fully, heightened scrutiny.

Seeing intermediate scrutiny in action: Two unofficial tendencies

If what ultimately matters about legal rules is how they are actually applied, it is noteworthy that actual application of intermediate scrutiny for gender discrimination shows two different, yet not officially recognized, tendencies:

- ✔ **Intermediate scrutiny heavy:** This tendency requires an "exceedingly persuasive justification," in the words of *United States v. Virginia*, 518 U.S. 532 (1996), in which the Court invalidated Virginia Military Institute's male-only admissions policy. In intermediate scrutiny heavy, the courts skeptically examine the government's justifications (including any empirical data government cites). Courts are on alert for unnecessarily broad disabilities imposed on the disfavored gender.

  Courts seem to apply an especially rigorous brand of intermediate scrutiny when one or both of these factors are present:

  - Gender distinctions seem to reflect "archaic, overbroad stereotypes" about male/female differences.

  - The discrimination denies women important opportunities or benefits.

- ✔ **Intermediate scrutiny light:** This tendency is more forgiving of gender distinctions, which are tolerated on a common-sense basis. Not sensing old, tired gender stereotypes at work, courts use more tolerant intermediate scrutiny when one or both of these factors are present:

  - Gender distinctions reflect actual biological or other relevant differences between men and women.

  - Government seems to be employing a gender distinction in a sincere attempt to remedy past discrimination against women (that is, the court sees a bona fide affirmative-action program at work).

Checking out intermediate scrutiny "heavy"

In *Craig v. Boren*, 429 U.S. 190 (1976), the Court officially announced the intermediate-scrutiny standard for gender discrimination. In the process, *Craig* also provided a good example of intermediate scrutiny heavy.

Craig struck down an Oklahoma law allowing 18-to-21-year-old females — but not males in that age group — to purchase light beer. Assuming that the law represented vital traffic-safety interests (in light of data showing that Oklahoma males were arrested more often for drunk driving than females), the Court found the law not substantially related to the traffic-safety goal because of the following three reasons:

✔ The law only regulated beer *purchase,* not consumption (thus diluting its ability to prevent drunk driving).

✔ The law imposed a 100 percent burden on males in order to stop the 2 percent of them who were a drunk-driving problem.

✔ The statistics showing an 11:1 disparity between arrest rates for young males and females likely reflected gender stereotypes. (As the *Craig* majority explained, "'reckless' young men who drink and drive are transformed into arrest statistics, whereas their female counterparts are chivalrously escorted home.")

Another strong example of intermediate scrutiny heavy at work is *United States v. Virginia,* 518 U.S. 532 (1996). In striking down Virginia's male-only admissions scheme for the Commonwealth's only single-sex institution (the Virginia Military Institute), the Court rejected the argument that gender segregation was necessary to preserve VMI's "unique" educational methodology. The Court sensed that Virginia was engaging in sex stereotyping by assuming that women just couldn't handle VMI's in-your-face training method (known, appropriately, as the "adversative method"). The Court pointed to the experience of U.S. military academies, which had successfully integrated women recruits into previously all-male training regimens. The Court held that as long as "some women . . . are capable of all of the individual activities requested of VMI cadets," it was unconstitutional for Virginia to exclude all women.

TECHNICAL STUFF

Did the Virginia Military Institute case *really* employ strict scrutiny?

The majority in the VMI case purported to apply intermediate scrutiny. But critics of the decision both on and off the Court argue that it actually strayed into strict-scrutiny land.

Because the majority admitted that most women (probably like many men!) would not want to attend VMI's adversative training method, VMI's exclusion of women did seem to "work" in the vast majority of cases. A discriminatory classification that fits most cases would seem to be "substantially related" to the government's goals. In fact, in ruling that VMI could not exclude women as long as *some* women wanted to attend and would benefit, the Court seems to imply that even an insubstantial amount of overdiscrimination is enough to sink a discriminatory classification. But some overinclusiveness is supposed to be tolerated in intermediate scrutiny.

Adding fuel to the criticism is that Justice Ruth Bader Ginsburg, the author of the *VMI* majority decision arguably applying strict scrutiny, was the women's-rights advocate who had earlier come one vote short of getting strict scrutiny in *Frontiero.* Some wags say that *Justice* Ginsburg wanted to achieve what *Advocate* Ginsburg never did!

Discriminating against children of unmarried parents

Intermediate scrutiny also applies to any law or policy imposing a special burden on children whose parents were not married when the children were born.

For example, in *Clark v. Jeter,* 486 U.S. 456 (1988), the Court struck down a Pennsylvania law requiring paternity to be established (in order to claim child support) within six years of birth. The Court concluded that "the 6-year statute of limitations was not substantially related to Pennsylvania's interest in avoiding the litigation of stale or fraudulent claims." The Court noted that "increasingly sophisticated tests for genetic markers permit the exclusion of over 99 percent of those who might be accused or paternity, regardless of the age of the child."

Recognizing cases where the government gets off "light"

A case that helps illustrate the way intermediate scrutiny light plays out is *Michael M. v. Sonoma County Superior Court,* 450 U.S. 464 (1981). This decision upheld a California criminal law punishing the male but not the female participant in statutory rape (that is, consensual sex with a minor). Relying on the common-sense fact that females but not males can get pregnant, the Court held that California could legitimately think that its "criminal sanction imposed solely on males thus serves to roughly 'equalize' the deterrents on the sexes."

In *Califano v. Webster,* 430 U.S. 313 (1977), the Court thought that more favorable treatment of women, compared to men, bore a real relationship to past economic disadvantages suffered by women. *Webster* approved a Social Security Act provision allowing women to exclude more low-wage-earning years from figuring benefits than men could exclude. This gender discrimination, the Court declared, "operated directly to compensate women for past economic discrimination" in the workplace.

Do Facially Neutral Laws "Purposefully" Discriminate?

A difficult question arises when laws don't discriminate overtly against — but have a more burdensome effect ("disparate impact") on — members of certain groups. For example, a minimum-height requirement for police officers indirectly excludes more members of some racial minorities (who are on average shorter than their white counterparts) and more women (who are also generally shorter than men) from police jobs. Does this discriminatory effect make these laws subject to strict and intermediate scrutiny?

This section explores how the modern Court answers this question. As you find out, the decision depends on whether the discriminatory effect is the result intended by government; assessing this, in turn, requires analysis of all the relevant facts.

Acting because of an intention to discriminate

Antidiscrimination laws at times treat discriminatory *effects* as implying forbidden discrimination. For example, under Title VII of federal laws prohibiting employment discrimination, the "disparate impact" of an employment test or hiring/promotion policy can, if sufficiently severe, make a presumptive case for employment discrimination. The burden then shifts to the employer to prove that the disparity is not the product of discrimination.

But constitutional equal-protection rights only protect against purposeful discrimination. Intentional discrimination isn't hard to show when government draws overt racial, national origin, or gender distinctions. When government classifies neutrally and the *effects* are discriminatory, the challenger must show, in the words of *Personnel Administrator v. Feeney,* 442 U.S. 256 (1977), that government acted "'because of' not merely 'in spite of' [the] adverse effects on an identifiable group." (A desire to discriminate just needs to be "*a* motivating factor," not the sole or primary factor.)

Feeney is a good example of the because-of/in-spite-of distinction at work. *Feeney* upheld a law giving veterans a preference over nonveterans for state jobs. The law didn't draw an overt male/female distinction. But because most veterans were men, the law had the *effect* of discriminating against women job seekers. Although the state knew that a veterans preference would hurt women, the Court found that it adopted the preference "in spite of" this drawback, not as a cover for a desire to harm women. So the Court did not find *purposeful* discrimination and employ the intermediate scrutiny used for gender discrimination; rational-basis review instead was used and easily met.

Showing discriminatory purpose: Looking beyond the effects

Because well-intentioned (or at least not horribly evil!) government policies can have unintended disparate impacts on racial or other groups, disparate impact alone isn't usually sufficient to make courts use heightened scrutiny. Courts stick with rational-basis review unless, looking at all the circumstances, the disparate effect gives serious clues that the government's purpose was to discriminate.

As the Court put it in *Washington v. Davis,* 426 U.S. 229 (1976), purposeful race or other discrimination must be inferred from "the totality of relevant facts." *Davis* also clarified that, although usually not the "sole touchstone" for triggering heightened scrutiny, disproportionate effect is still an important starting point in a discrimination claim.

Village of Arlington Heights v. Metropolitan Housing Development Corporation, 249 U.S. 252 (1977), detailed the factors that may combine with a disparate effect to ring the "purposeful discrimination" gong:

- ✔ "The specific sequence of events leading up to" the law or policy

- ✔ "Departures from the normal procedural sequence" (which may suggest "that improper purposes are playing a role")

- ✔ "Substantive departures" from the "factors usually considered important by the decisionmaker"

- ✔ "The legislative or administrative history" of the law or policy (which may suggest that discrimination was a motivating factor)

But as with most legal rules, exceptions exist. Not every case of disparate effect needs additional evidence along these lines to be regarded as a result of government discrimination. Sometimes, as the *Washington v. Davis* Court noted, a law's disproportionate effect on a protected class "may for all practical purposes demonstrate unconstitutionality because . . . the discrimination is very difficult to explain" on any other grounds.

The classic example of disparate effect being strong enough on its own for the Court to find a law unconstitutional is *Yick Wo v. Hopkins,* 118 U.S. 351 (1886). The Court in *Yick Wo* saw as purposefully discriminatory a local ordinance prohibiting the operation, without governmental permission, of a laundry in a building made of materials other than brick or stone. Although the law didn't overtly discriminate based on the country of the laundry owner's ancestors, the evidence showed a clear pattern of discriminatory enforcement against "Chinese" laundries. Specifically, governmental authorities allowed all but one of the non-Chinese applicants to run a laundry in non-brick, non-stone buildings. Not a single applicant of Chinese ancestry got this privilege. The Supreme Court saw this as the legal equivalent of "well, duh!" and concluded that authorities engaged in purposeful discrimination based on national origin. They struck down the law.

Flunking Rational-Basis Review: Hostility against a Disfavored Group

The three-tiered system of equal-protection review — strict scrutiny, intermediate scrutiny, and rational-basis review — can seem insufficient to fully protect against inappropriate government discrimination.

After all, people have other *immutable* (unchangeable) characteristics they can't control (such as age, mental and physical health, and sexual orientation) that can be the basis for seemingly unfair discrimination. (True, important federal laws and regulations protect against some of the worst forms of discrimination in important areas of life. For example, the Americans with Disabilities Act protects mentally and physically handicapped people against discrimination in the public and private workplace and in important life opportunities, such as access to public places. Still, these statutory protections are incomplete.) Judges and other legal observers regularly call for constitutional protection against laws that, although rational in the low-level sense required by rational-basis review, still seem highly prejudicial.

Current equal-protection doctrines respond to this protective impulse by declaring that laws seeming to reflect "irrational prejudice" against a disfavored group flunk even low-level, rational-basis review. This principle, called the *animus doctrine* (to reflect the hostility it recognizes), is behind three decisions protecting three different groups:

- ✔ **Unrelated households:** In *United States Department of Agriculture v. Moreno*, 413 U.S. 528 (1973), the Court struck down a federal law discriminating, in the acquisition of food assistance under the federal food-stamp program, against people living together who are not related by blood or other family ties. The government defended its line-drawing as necessary to prevent fraud and assure that benefits went to the most needy people. But the Court read the law's legislative history as showing congressional prejudice against "hippie communes." The Court said that "if [constitutional equal protection] means anything, it must at the very least mean that a bare congressional desire to harm a politically unpopular group cannot constitute a legitimate governmental interest."

- ✔ **Developmentally disabled individuals:** In *City of Cleburne v. Cleburne Living Center,* 473 U.S. 432 (1985), the Court expressly declined to provide heightened scrutiny to laws discriminating against persons then called *mentally retarded.* That decision should have given a green light to the city ordinance in *Cleburne,* which selectively prevented group homes for the "insane or feeble-minded or alcoholics or drug addicts" from being located in certain city locations. (Although woefully over- and underinclusive, the city's zoning law was a partial response to legitimate concerns and would normally be considered rational.) Because the *Cleburne* Court saw the city ordinance as ultimately reflecting only an "irrational prejudice" against the developmentally disabled, the justices invalidated the law under rational-basis review.

- ✔ **Homosexuals:** The Court's latest use of the animus doctrine came in *Romer v. Evans,* 517 U.S. 620 (1996). Under supposed rational-basis review, *Romer* invalidated Amendment 2, a ballot initiative passed by Colorado voters. Amendment 2 prohibited local governments from adopting antidiscrimination laws to protect homosexuals, lesbians, or bisexuals. Dissenting Justice Scalia defended Amendment 2 as a rational measure to prevent dominance of city politics by powerful political organizations and assure that important political change would come at the state level. But the *Romer* majority found the amendment "inexplicable by anything but animus toward the class that it affects."

Part IV
Rights to Self-Expression and Political Participation

The 5th Wave   By Rich Tennant

In this part . . .

In making decisions, courts are constantly balancing an individual's rights and the greater public good. The right to self-expression is no exception. In this part, we discuss how courts tackle balancing this with other interests, including how they approach the difficult area of free exercise of religion — not interfering with individual rights while at the same time not allowing the government to favor a certain religion. We also discuss politics and voting, considering what practical realities resulted from constitutional provisions and subsequent cases in these areas.

Chapter 11

"Express Yourself!" Freedom of Speech

*T*he First Amendment guarantees the right of free speech. However, that doesn't mean government can't regulate speech to various extents. When legislatures pass laws or other governmental authorities adopt policies affecting speech, many agonizing and controversial questions arise. But luckily, a basic two-step (and, at times, three-step) approach can help you analyze many free-speech controversies.

When government sets out to regulate speech, the first step is to ask whether the speech in question gets *any* First Amendment protection. (Some kinds of speech are considered to be unprotected — that is, outside the scope of the protections the First Amendment provides.) If the First Amendment protects the speech at issue, the second step is to ask whether government is regulating based on the content of the speech or not. In many cases, answering these two questions tells you the *extent* of First Amendment protection and, significantly, the level of scrutiny by which you should assess the constitutionality of government's speech regulation. When government regulates speech in a particular location, you also need to further characterize the nature of the forum.

Of course, with an issue as important and controversial as freedom of speech, expect further complications. Judges are especially likely to find a constitutional violation when government censors speech in advance of its utterance ("prior restraint") or passes vague or substantially overbroad laws. On the contrary, courts provide lesser constitutional protection for conduct that "speaks," commercial speech, speech in special places (such as schools and prisons), and speech regulation designed to protect children.

Don't confuse speech being protected by the First Amendment with speech being immune (or *absolutely protected*) from government regulation. Individual Supreme Court justices have occasionally argued for an "absolute" right to speak, but free-speech case law has always disclaimed that. As you see in this chapter, even when government regulators are put to their highest test (when judges evaluate laws under the harshest test, known as *strict scrutiny*), lawmakers may restrict or even prohibit protected speech if they have a sufficiently strong justification for doing so and their speech restriction is carefully crafted.

In this chapter, you take a closer look at all these issues surrounding freedom of speech. You explore what the Constitution's framers intended by the phrase, and how modern cases expand on that. Then you examine in detail how to apply the two-step approach to determine protection. And because every rule has exceptions, we also give you an overview of special cases where more or less protection than usual is allowed. You may think this chapter is too long, but we just can't be silenced on the topic.

Expanding the Framers' Original Conception of "Free Speech"

Of course, any journey into Free-Speech Land must start with the constitutional text and the intent of the men who penned it.

"Congress shall make no law . . . abridging the freedom of speech." This First-Amendment phrase committed the U.S. government to tolerate a degree of freedom of expression then unknown in the world. Yet, looking back on the constitutional language from the perspective of the broad and robust free-speech protection Americans now take for granted, you may be struck by how far the modern doctrines you study in your constitutional-law course go beyond the original language and the conceptions of its framers. For example:

✔ **The prohibition on speech abridgment extends to all federal actors, not just Congress.** Despite the amendment's reference to "Congress," federal courts have logically inferred that the framers wanted to prevent any federal official or employee from suppressing speech. A "gag order" by a federal judge forbidding media coverage of a criminal trial is subject to First-Amendment limitations, and so is a presidentially ordered program of domestic telephone surveillance.

✔ **Constitutional protection extends beyond the most obvious ways in which Americans "speak."** As we note later in this chapter, modern free-speech decisions don't stop at protecting verbal or written communication. They extend constitutional protection to "symbolic speech," expressive conduct such as flag burning and (for a time!) nude dancing. And as we note in Chapter 13, the current justices obviously believe that "money talks!" They've afforded constitutional protection to money spent to support political campaigns, candidates, and issues.

✔ **A wide range of restrictions short of actually "abridging" speech is prohibited.** Although the literal language suggests that the First Amendment only prevents complete suppression of speech, modern doctrines kick in well before that. Laws simply making speech more difficult or expensive trigger skeptical scrutiny as well. For example, in *Minneapolis Star and Tribune v. Minnesota Commissioner of Revenue,* 460 U.S. 575 (1983), the Court invalidated a special state use tax falling disproportionately on large newspaper publishers because the tax made publishing the newspaper more difficult.

✔ **Protection is not merely limited to prior restraints on speech.** The First Amendment's framers likely followed the view of British jurist Lord Blackstone that the purpose of freedom of speech was to protect against governmental "prior restraints." That is, the evil to be stopped was governmental attempts to censor speech ahead of time. Specifically, the framers wanted to stop the notorious practice of the British crown and its colonial lackeys forbidding newspapers or books from being published unless they bore a governmental seal of approval.

What's surprising to many people is that the framers apparently didn't object to "subsequent punishment" after Americans speak or write. The framers generally weren't troubled by, for example, laws punishing authors for antigovernment sentiments amounting to "seditious libel."

As we discuss in the later section "Applying super-strict scrutiny to prior restraints," modern free-speech protectors remain *especially* troubled by subsequent punishments. Fortunately, current doctrines extend First-Amendment protection to a large spectrum of law, rules, policies, and enforcement actions restricting speech *after* it has occurred.

In fact, the actions of the framers and many later Americans didn't respect free speech the way we do today. Even the notorious Alien and Sedition Acts of the late 1790s — several laws clamping down on noncitizens and including a now-notorious prohibition on making false, scandalous, or malicious writings about the federal government or its officials — were objectionable in their time more because of the way they were applied than by general outrage over the notion that the federal government could pass antispeech laws.

Indeed, before the 1960s, Americans generally tolerated suppression, especially in times of political crisis, war, or social upheaval. The relatively robust (but by no means complete!) protection of a wide range of speech you and others now take for granted is the result of many recent, hard-fought efforts by a cadre of free-speech advocates and sympathetic jurists. (By the way, the strong modern protection for speech likely reflects the view that freedom of speech is one of the most important of all constitutional rights because it provides a foundation for other rights. For example, rights to vote and run for office would be meaningless without the widespread freedom to discuss public issues guaranteed by the First Amendment.)

Answering the First Key Question: Is the Speech Protected?

To understand free-speech jurisdiction, you must first master the distinction between protected and unprotected speech. This classic categorical approach assumes that speech is protected *unless it falls into one of the several categories of unprotected speech.* In this section, you become familiar with this "default rule" and then look at several classic situations in which courts have defined speech as unprotected. Finally, this section briefly canvasses two other categories of speech not receiving First-Amendment protection.

Don't assume incorrectly that if speech is unprotected by the First Amendment it is unprotected by the Constitution as a whole. As we discuss in Chapter 8, no government regulation can be arbitrary. (The legal system's test for arbitrariness is whether the law has a "rational basis" in that it serves a legitimate interest in some way.) This is even true for government regulation of speech "unprotected" by the First Amendment.

For example, as you see in the upcoming subsection entitled "Refusing to protect obscenity but strongly protecting indecency," hard-core sexual speech receives no First-Amendment protection. But even so, a governmental regulation of obscenity drawing arbitrary distinctions (for example, criminalizing obscene films with blue-eyed actors but not with brown-eyed actors, or only prosecuting obscenity purveyors whose last names start with the letters A–L) would violate the rule against arbitrary laws. This example is far-fetched, but it helps you see how the Constitution can provide protection in the area of speech even when the First Amendment doesn't.

The default rule: Presuming protection unless categorically excluded

Modern free-speech rules begin with a presumption that speech receives some degree of First-Amendment protection *unless* it falls into one of the narrowly defined categories of unprotected speech. Government officials bear the burden of showing why speech shouldn't be protected. Speakers don't have to justify the value of their speech — and it doesn't have to be as memorable as Patrick Henry's Revolutionary War cry, "Give Me Liberty or Give Me Death!"

Surveying the types of unprotected speech

All the unprotected-speech categories assume that the speech they include is so harmful that the need to prohibit it outweighs the Constitution's usually strong commitment to free speech. One group of unprotected speech categories concerns speech that is physically dangerous. Another category deals with the perceived moral dangers of highly sexualized speech. Still other categories of unprotected speech are based on other kinds of harm to individuals or society at large.

Denying protection to incitement of imminent lawlessness

The classic category of unprotected speech is *subversive speech,* which calls for the overthrow of the government or incites other law violations leading to death, personal injury, or property destruction.

Under the governing legal test formulated by the Supreme Court in *Brandenburg v. Ohio,* 395 U.S. 444 (1969), antigovernment speakers and other protesters are allowed to get caught up in the heat of the moment and support government overthrow or other illegal actions *except* when the speech meets *all* the following conditions:

- ✔ **Incitement:** The speaker's words are "directed to inciting or producing" action (for example, "Let's burn down city hall!"). Advocating government overthrow (for example, "The poor ought to burn down city hall!") or teaching the value or inevitability of government overthrow (for example, "If the city doesn't create jobs, it's only a matter of time before . . .") is *not* enough.

- ✔ **. . . of lawless action:** The speaker must incite "the use of force or of law violation." A passionate attempt to incite an economic boycott or legal political action is *not* lawless action — it's protected speech.

✔ **... in an "imminent" time frame:** The speaker must incite lawlessness now or in the imminent future. Calls for illegality at some vague later point in the future are constitutionally protected, in part on the theory that cooler heads may prevail or "counter-speech" (calls for moderation from authorities or political opponents) may succeed.

✔ **... under circumstances "likely to incite or produce" the lawless action called for:** Case law provides no ironclad standards for determining when circumstances are likely to lead to lawlessness. But this stipulation appears to turn on facts specific to the context of particular speech, such as

- The extent of the police presence

- The mood and mindset of the recipients of the inciting message

- Whether the recipients of the message have the capability to carry out the action called for (for example, a heavily armed crowd)

- Whether the target of the illegal action is close at hand and otherwise vulnerable to violence

Refusing to protect speech provoking antagonists to public disorder

The *Brandenburg* incitement test concerns the possibility that people who sympathize with the speakers may follow their lead and commit lawless action. Two other unprotected-speech categories are also concerned with imminent lawlessness, but from the opposite direction: from groups or individuals who are likely to react *against* the speaker's presence or message.

Continuing controversy over the *Brandenburg* test

Brandenburg v. Ohio, 395 U.S. 444 (1969), resolved decades of uncertainty and judicial wrangling over how to balance the need to protect antigovernment dissent against the importance of protecting the public. In *Brandenburg,* a Ku Klux Klan member was convicted for inciting violence at a media-taped rally in which he spoke vaguely about revenge against racial and religious minorities and people who supported them. The Court overturned Brandenburg's conviction because the statute he was convicted under allowed a jury to convict for "mere advocacy" of violence. (This is an application of the "overbreadth" doctrine, discussed in the section "Allowing special challenges for 'substantially overbroad' restrictions.")

But the *Brandenburg* answer — which requires "incitement" of likely immediate violence — remains controversial. In this Internet age, extreme messages spewing racial hatred and fanning disaffection with the American government can lay dormant on websites, waiting to appeal to troubled and psychologically vulnerable individuals (as apparently happened with the perpetrators of the mass shootings at Columbine High School and the bombing of the Oklahoma City Federal Building). Arguably, the *Brandenburg* standards made more sense in the context in which they were created — live speeches given to physically present audience members able to respond (or be talked out of responding) in real time.

The hostile-audience exception to protected speech

Under the "hostile audience" rationale, an otherwise protected speaker can lose the right to continue speaking because of a threat of violence not caused (incited) by the speaker. Also unlike the *Brandenburg* doctrines, the hostile-audience category lacks a neat multi-element test. But justices and scholars have combined recent cases into a workable doctrine in which otherwise protected speech loses its protection because

- ✔ Under all the circumstances, there is a clear and present danger of an immediate breach of the peace by people reacting to the speech.

- ✔ Reasonable police protection (including threats to arrest the hostile audience members) cannot quell the danger.

Like the *Brandenburg* "incitement" test, the hostile-audience doctrine takes into consideration common-sense factors relating to the size, mood, and armed or unarmed nature of the crowd, and the strength of the police presence.

In theory, whether the speaker does anything to fan the fires of hostility shouldn't matter for hostile-audience analysis. After all, if what makes otherwise protected speech unprotected is the danger of a riot, whether the speaker abetted that danger — or strove unsuccessfully to avoid it — seems immaterial. The danger is present, and it justifies government suppression.

But the reality is that courts are influenced by judgments about the speaker's role in creating the danger and the speaker's justification in speaking. For example, the Court's sympathy with the cause of civil-rights protesters may have led it to minimize, in *Gregory v. Chicago*, 394 U.S. 111 (1969), the threat potential from a march on Chicago streets that drew more than 1,000 increasingly unruly white opponents, who in several cases attempted to block marchers physically and threw rocks and eggs.

A hostile audience of one: "Fighting words" as unprotected speech

A different unprotected-speech category also hinges on a risk of public disorder. In the classic "fighting-words" case, a speaker crosses the line of speech protection by directing words to an individual which, when addressed to the ordinary citizen, are inherently likely to provoke a violent reaction. What makes fighting-words cases especially problematic is that speech does not lose its protection merely because it is provocative, coarse, or involves profanity. It also doesn't help that the Court has given little guidance on where to draw the line.

Refusing to protect obscenity but strongly protecting indecency

A different kind of unprotected speech is harmful for a different kind of reason. "Obscenity" has long been regarded as beyond First-Amendment protection because of its harmful effect on the morals of society. As with constitutional law generally, the law of obscenity seeks to achieve a delicate balance. Government should be able to protect community morals against hard-core sexual speech, but frank presentations of sexual matters as part of legitimate literary, artistic, and scientific activities must be protected. The devil is in the details, and since 1971 obscenity prosecutions and prohibitions have proceeded under the three-element test of *Miller v. California,* 413 U.S. 15 (1973). *Miller* makes written or pictorial sexual speech unprotected *only* when that speech meets the following criteria:

- **Appeal: The work "as a whole, appeals to the prurient interest."** This element commits judges, juries, and other censors to distinguish between a "normal" interest in sex and a *prurient* (deviant, abnormal) concern.

- **Manner of depiction: As a whole, the work "depicts or describes, in a patently offensive way, sexual conduct specifically defined" by the relevant law.** After state or federal antiobscenity laws define the range of potentially prohibited sexual conduct (sexual intercourse or practices short of that), juries then decide whether the manner in which that conduct is depicted is highly offensive.

- **Value: The work "as a whole lacks serious literary, political, or scientific value."** *Miller* specifically intended this less obscenity-friendly standard to replace a previous "utterly without redeeming social value" approach, in which isolated portions of value could turn an otherwise unprotected work into a protected one.

Application of the preceding three aspects of the *Miller* test is subject to the following nuances:

- **Elements 1 (appeal) and 2 (manner of depiction) are permitted to vary across the nation, depending upon the "contemporary community standards" at work in each jurisdiction.** *Miller* definitely responded to criticism that prior obscenity decisions overused national standards, requiring "the people of Maine or Mississippi to accept public depiction of conduct found tolerable in Las Vegas, or New York City."

- **Element 3 (value) is assessed under a unitary national standard administered by courts.** This policy reflects the assumption that a work's intrinsic value doesn't vary by community. And it preserves the right of courts to correct decisions by unrealistically prudish juries.

If all these conditions sound complicated and uncertain, then you understand well the demands of this particular categorical doctrine. *Miller* calls upon decision makers, in highly charged environments, to navigate a series of subjective distinctions (for example, "patently" offensive versus not-so-obviously offensive; appeal "as a whole" versus appeal in isolated parts). Obscenity prosecutions also pose other difficult questions, such as what the relevant "community" is for allegedly obscene materials distributed on the World Wide Web and whether a song (such as those on 2 Live Crew's album *As Nasty as They Wanna Be*) can ever be "obscene."

Huge stakes ride on whether sexual-speech producers end up on the "obscene" side of the categorical dividing line — subject to serious criminal penalties, hefty fines, and forfeiture of product inventories — or make it safely to the "non-obscene" side, where they benefit from the strong First-Amendment protection applied to "indecent" or "pornographic" speech. That's one reason why courts so carefully scrutinize obscenity statutes to make sure that they don't "chill" edgy artists and social commentators by causing them to play it safe and self-censor.

Reno v. American Civil Liberties Union, 521 U.S. 844 (1997), provides an especially — you'll pardon the pun — *graphic* example of what's riding on the obscenity/indecency distinction. *Reno* considered the constitutionality of the Communications Decency Act of 1996. In essence, the Act provided substantial criminal penalties for the knowing communication of (1) "obscene" and (2) "indecent" and "patently offensive" Internet messages to minors. The provisions about obscene communications were constitutional, because obscenity is unprotected speech. But the limits on indecent communication generated debate among the justices because indecency is protected speech being regulated based on its (patently offensive) content. The majority of the Court applied "strict scrutiny" (which we discuss in "Applying the relevant level of scrutiny") and invalidated two provisions; the justices found the law unacceptably vague and broad, and they said Congress could have accomplished its objectives through less-speech-restrictive alternatives, such as parental software controls.

Reviewing two other unprotected-speech categories

This survey of unprotected speech would be incomplete without a brief review of two other categories:

- ✔ **Defamation (slander/libel):** Going back to its English common-law roots, American law allows criminal penalties and substantial civil damages for false statements damaging an individual's reputation in his community (including his standing within his chosen profession).

  Yet legitimate free speech often involves criticism by the media, public officials, and other public figures. These elites could use defamation prosecutions and civil lawsuits to retaliate against such criticism and chill political dissent. This possibility led the Supreme Court in the 1964 case of *New York Times v. Sullivan,* 376 U.S. 254, to develop additional First-Amendment-based limits on the ability of public figures to sue for defamation. The *New York Times* case requires the allegedly defamed public figure to show that the defendant acted with "actual malice" — that is, with knowledge that the statements were untrue or with "reckless disregard" for their truth or falsity. (By contrast, if the person claiming to be defamed is a private figure, the defendant can be liable with having acted maliciously.)

✔ **Threats:** No one has a First-Amendment right to use words to threaten unlawful violence against a particular individual or group of individuals. Whether Tony Soprano likes it or not, "Pay me what you owe me or I'll hurt you!" clearly is unprotected speech.

The difficulty comes when speakers make threats as part of valid protests or protected free-speech activities. This requires courts to distinguish between "true threats" and mere "hyperbole" (that is, speakers getting carried away and using rhetoric not seriously intended to threaten).

NAACP v. Claiborne Hardware Company, 458 U.S. 886 (1982), posed the question of whether an official for the NAACP (National Association for the Advancement of Colored People) lost First-Amendment protection when he made the following statement to his audience during a speech supporting a lawful boycott of stores in a Mississippi community: "[I]f we catch any of you going into any of them racist stores, we're gonna break your neck." The Court concluded that, in the context of an otherwise long and legal speech, the official's threat was mere over-the-top hyperbole.

By contrast, in *Virginia v. Black,* 538 U.S. 343 (2003), the Court held that defendants who burned a cross at a Ku Klux Klan rally and in a neighbor's yard had engaged in "true threats." The burning cross's long association with Ku Klux Klan violence led the Court to find it "a particularly virulent form of intimidation." (We explain in "Protecting conduct that 'speaks'" why such nonverbal actions are protected "symbolic speech.")

Lower courts have also wrestled with whether speakers must have the apparent ability to carry out the threats themselves and the legitimacy of gauging threats by the reactions of their targets.

Answering the Second Key Question: How Much Protection Does Speech Get?

If the speech that government is regulating doesn't fall within an unprotected category (as discussed in the previous section), it is protected — meaning that the First Amendment requires government to justify any suppression of that speech.

The protection available to protected speech has varying degrees, depending on a several considerations. This section explores the two main questions to ask to determine how much protection protected speech gets:

✔ Is government regulating speech based on its *content* (or based on factors unrelated to content)?

✔ If speech regulation is specific to a "forum" (that is, a specific location), *what kind of forum* is it?

Answering these two questions leads the analyst to three possible levels of scrutiny (also addressed in this section): strict, intermediate, and reasonable.

Distinguishing content-based from content-neutral speech regulation

Whether or not government is regulating speech on the basis of its content or not is very significant. Ignoring for now the "public forum" complication (explored in the next section), content-*based* speech regulation is usually put to a "strict" test, in which government must show that it is pursuing a first-order concern in the narrowest way. (Most laws flunk strict scrutiny.) Content-*neutral* regulation of speech, by contrast, usually only requires government to meet a middle-ground ("intermediate") level of review accepting a less weighty government interest and allowing a broader regulation of speech than strictly necessary. (More laws pass this middle-ground scrutiny.)

So if the distinction between content-based speech regulation and content-neutral speech regulation is so important, how can you tell one from the other? The best way to do it is to put yourself in the shoes of the government official responsible for determining whether a speaker has violated the law. Then ask whether you need to know about the content of the speech or not.

You also need to be familiar with these possibilities of regulation, because each type of speech gets different levels of protection:

✔ **Content regulation based on *viewpoint:*** This kind of content-based speech regulation seeks to control speakers with particular points of view. For example, the 1996 Communications Decency Act may be best understood as regulation of Internet messages based on their "indecent" and "patently offensive" point of view.

✔ **Content regulation based on *subject matter:*** In this type, the subject itself, not the speaker's slant on it, is objectionable to government. For example, a law prohibiting the posting of any Internet message referring to sexual intercourse would be "subject matter" regulation. Proper application of the law would depend on whether the message's *subject* is sexual intercourse or something else, not on the message's viewpoint ("indecent" or "decent") about sexual intercourse.

✔ **Content-neutral (time, place, and manner) regulation:** Governments often regulate speech regardless of its viewpoint or subject matter. Instead, governments typically restrict the timing of speech ("No one may speak in the park after 10 p.m."), the place it occurs ("No one may speak on the lawn in front of the park bandstand"), or the manner in which it occurs ("No one may use a megaphone to speak in the park").

A Chicago ordinance subjected speakers to convictions for disorderly conduct if they picketed or demonstrated "on a public way within 150 feet of [any] school building while the school is in [session]." The ordinance regulated speech in a content-neutral way based on time (while school is in session), place (on a public way; within 150 feet of school), and manner (picketing or demonstrating). So far, just a content-neutral restriction, right? Not so fast.

The ordinance also contained an exception that stated that there would be no prosecution for "peaceful picketing of any school involved in a labor dispute." This portion of the ordinance addressed content. To faithfully apply the ordinance, a police officer called to the scene or a prosecutor later deciding whether to press charges would have to know the content of a picketer's speech; whether she was addressing the subject of a school-specific labor dispute, in which case she wouldn't fall within the ordinance's scope, or another subject, in which case she would.

So, viewing the ordinance as a whole, the Supreme Court in *Police Department of Chicago v. Mosley,* 408 U.S. 92 (1972), treated its regulation of speech as "content based." (The Court went on to measure the ordinance by strict-scrutiny standards, and it failed.)

Characterizing the forum where speech is being regulated

The next main question for determining how much protection the First Amendment provides is whether government's speech regulation is happening within a set *forum* (a specific location), and, if so, what kind of forum it is. Ordinarily, when speech regulation is *not* forum specific, after you figure out whether it is content based or content neutral, you're ready to move on to the relevant level of First-Amendment scrutiny (illustrated by the following example and further discussed in the next section).

In *Time v. Regan,* 468 U.S. 641 (1984), *Time* magazine objected to the U.S. Treasury Department's attempt to enforce a federal anticounterfeiting law against its editorial activities. The law made it generally illegal to "print, photograph, or in any other manner" depict U.S. dollar bills or coins. *Time* objected that over a 15-year period the magazine had used illustrations of United States currency "to symbolize the toll of inflation, to represent the economic issues

at stake in a presidential election, [and] to comment upon political scandals."
(Such visual commentary on public issues is clearly "protected" speech.)

The federal law under review in *Time v. Regan* was not "forum-specific" — it
applied everywhere in America. An edition of *Time* magazine with, say, an
exposé about gambling abuses in amateur basketball (accompanied by an
eye-catching illustration of a basketball hoop stuffed with dollar bills) would
have violated the law just sitting on your living-room table. After the Court
decided which parts of the law were content based and which were content
neutral, it was ready to analyze the parts under the relevant scrutiny levels
(as explained in the later section "Choosing between strict and intermediate
scrutiny"). The Court rejected the parts of the law subject to strict scrutiny
and upheld the parts subject to intermediate review.

When speech regulation is restricted to a particular location, however, you
must climb a further analytical step. In determining which kind of forum is at
issue, you have three possibilities:

✔ **A law may regulate speech in a "traditional" public forum.** These
  are places that, in the poetic words of *Hague v. Committee for Industrial
  Organization,* 307 U.S. 496 (1939), "have immemorially been held in
  trust for the use of the public and, time out of mind, have been used for
  purposes of assembly, communicating thought between citizens, and
  discussing public questions." Although this noble phrase can in theory
  apply to a variety of public places, free-speech cases pretty much restrict
  the "traditional" public-forum label to streets, parks, and sidewalks.

✔ **A law may regulate speech in a "nontraditional" public forum
  (also called a "public forum by designation").** As explained in *Perry
  Education Association v. Perry Local Educators' Association,* 460 U.S. 37
  (1983), a nontraditional forum consists of other public property that the
  government "has [voluntarily] opened for use by the public as a place
  for expressive activity." *Perry* and other public-forum cases make clear
  that the relevant "voluntarily opening up" can be shown by official governmental policies or by a long-standing pattern (but not just isolated
  instances) granting *the public at large* access to exchange views. Another
  relevant factor is whether the nature of the forum is "compatible" with
  general public-speech exchange. Two prominent examples of nontraditional public forums are state fairgrounds, which for a limited period
  operate like public parks, and municipal auditoriums, which are open to
  a broad range of artistic programs and public events.

✔ **A law may regulate speech in a "nonpublic" forum.** This designation
  is the default; if the forum in which speech is being regulated does not
  qualify as a traditional or a nontraditional public forum, it is a nonpublic forum. (Courts sometimes confusingly refer to it as a "limited public
  forum," to denote that a limited group of speakers, and not the public at
  large, is granted access.)

In *Perry Education Association v. Perry Local Educators' Association,* 460 U.S. 37 (1983), a rival teachers' union sought to replace the officially certified union representing teachers in a local school district. The district rejected an attempt by the rival union to communicate with the teachers by leaving messages in the internal school mailbox system. Because the officially certified union had the right to use the internal mailbox system, the rival union claimed that the district was discriminating against it in violation of the First Amendment.

The success of the rival union's claim depended in significant part on showing that the internal mailbox system was a "nontraditional" public forum. In rejecting this argument, the Court noted that the nature and purpose of the school's internal mailboxes was to ease communication among school officials and inform teachers about events and organizations especially relevant to their duties. That didn't mean the district was opening them up as a forum for general public communication.

When in doubt, bet on courts deciding that a not-previously-litigated location for speech regulation is a nonpublic forum. This is the trend in the case law, as illustrated in the following lineup of selected "public forum" decisions:

- ✔ **Nontraditional public forums:** Municipal auditoriums (1975), state fairgrounds (1981)

- ✔ **Nonpublic forums:** Advertising spaces in publicly owned buses (1974), publicly accessible parts of military bases (1976), individual mailboxes in residential areas (1981), internal mailboxes in public schools (1983), federal-employee charitable solicitations (1985), internal sidewalks on post-office property (1990), public access areas in airport terminals (1992), public-TV-sponsored candidate debates (1998)

Applying the relevant level of scrutiny

Depending on how you answer the content-based-versus-content-neutral and public-forum questions, the speech regulation at issue will face one of three levels of scrutiny explained immediately below. (*Note:* Our description of the different scrutiny levels may just sound like a bunch of words. But those words reflect different levels of judicial willingness to second-guess speech regulators. And they have *very* practical consequences.)

- ✔ **Strict scrutiny:** This level is the highest hurdle for government to jump through. Strict scrutiny requires that government be pursuing an interest of the most compelling nature and that the speech restriction be *narrowly drawn* to accomplish this compelling governmental interest. To be narrowly drawn, the speech regulation must not be overly restrictive (that is, it must not restrict more speech than practically necessary) or underinclusive (that is, it must not leave out speech that is important to regulate to accomplish government's compelling interest).

✔ **Intermediate scrutiny:** This level is a significantly easier but still mean-ingful barrier to government speech regulation. Government must be pursuing a significant, though not compelling, government interest. Also, some over- or underinclusiveness is allowed as long as the law is not *substantially* more (or less) restrictive than necessary. Finally, the regu-lation must leave open ample alternative channels for communication by the speaker.

✔ **Reasonableness review:** Similar to the baseline rationality requirement for all government action (established in Chapter 8), this scrutiny level merely demands, as the Court put it in *Perry,* that speech regulation "is reasonable and not an effort to suppress expression merely because public officials oppose the speaker's view."

We compare these three scrutiny levels in Table 11-1.

Table 11-1	Examining Government Regulation of Speech	
Level of Scrutiny Applied to Regulation	*For Regulation to Be Constitutional, Government's Interest Must Be . . .*	*To Be Constitutional, Regulation Must Be . . .*
Strict	Compelling	Narrowly drawn (not over- or underinclusive)
Intermediate	Significant	Not substantially over- or underinclusive/ Leaves ample alterna-tive forums
Reasonableness	Legitimate	Connected in some way (not arbitrary)

Choosing between strict and intermediate scrutiny

When government is regulating speech without reference to its location — or when government regulates speech in a traditional or nontraditional public forum — two levels of scrutiny are possible depending on whether content is relevant:

✔ For content-based regulation, *strict scrutiny* is used.

✔ For content-neutral regulation, *intermediate scrutiny* is used.

Note that in most cases the level of scrutiny dictates the result. The government usually flunks strict scrutiny; even if you find or assume that the governmental interest is compelling, usually the government can regulate speech and accomplish its interest in narrower ways. Intermediate scrutiny is more likely to go either way; government has more leeway to succeed by showing a less substantial interest and a less precise method of achieving it.

Time v. Regan, 468 U.S. 641 (1984), is a great example of how the government can fail to make the grade on the strict scrutiny test. The Supreme Court viewed part of the federal anticounterfeiting law as content based because the ban on depictions of U.S. currency varied depending on the content of the depictions. (For example, "newsworthy" or "educational" publications were exempt.) Applying the requisite strict scrutiny to this content-based restriction, the Court found that, although government had a compelling interest in preventing counterfeiting, the content-based provisions were drastically overinclusive (for example, they banned "non-educational" beach towels with dollar-bill likenesses even though they were unlikely to be of any use to counterfeiters!). The content-based provisions were also underinclusive because they exempted, for example, currency-depictions in magazines for coin collectors — even though those magazines are likely to contain especially accurate depictions of great use to counterfeiters.

Another part of the law disputed in *Time v. Regan* was content *neutral.* This provision allowed currency depictions if they were in black and white and significantly over- or undersized. This regulation of the *manner* of depiction was content neutral, so the Court applied intermediate scrutiny, easily upholding this provision.

Applying reasonableness review for nonpublic forums

A different scrutiny pattern applies if government regulates speech in a nonpublic forum, as follows:

- **Even in a nonpublic forum, viewpoint-based regulation still triggers strict scrutiny.** Maintaining a higher hurdle for regulating any viewpoint-based speech — even in a nonpublic forum — reflects the core First-Amendment value against government disfavoring speakers based on their position about issues.

- **For all other types of regulation, mere reasonableness review is all that's required.** The regulation just has to have some common-sense logic behind it (and not be arbitrary!). Because the government interest doesn't have to be especially weighty and inexact speech regulations are okay, reasonableness review is much less rigorous than the strict or intermediate scrutiny tests. This requirement holds even for content-based regulation based on *subject,* reflecting the view that government officials may have good reason to keep the distracting influences of certain subjects from much public property. For example, the Court found in *Lehman v. Shaker Heights,* 418 U.S. 298 (1974), that a city-owned bus company had good reason to decline to accept "paid political advertisements" while displaying a wide range of nonpolitical ads; the no-political-ads stance avoided the appearance of government favoritism in elections and protected the privacy and peace of mind of bus patrons.

Whether the forum where government is regulating speech is a public forum or not makes the biggest difference when the regulation is based on subject matter. The level of scrutiny falls from strict scrutiny (for public forums), which government almost certainly loses, to reasonableness review (for non-public forums), which government almost always passes. For content-neutral regulation, the drop-off is less precipitous but still major — from intermediate scrutiny (for public forums) to reasonable. (The forum issue is irrelevant for viewpoint-based regulation, which always gets strict scrutiny.)

Determining When Speech Should Get Extraordinary Protection

The basic rules for determining how much protection speech should get probably seem complicated enough already. But wait — speech gets even stronger protection in three particular contexts:

- ✔ When government seeks to restrict speech in advance of it occurring *(prior restraint),* strict scrutiny becomes *super* strict.

- ✔ When an unprotected speaker is being validly prosecuted under an appropriately narrow law, the law can be invalidated because of the way it may apply to someone else in different circumstances. This doctrine, which demonstrates the Constitution's special regard for speech, is called *substantial overbreadth.*

- ✔ When vague laws limit speech, the *void for vagueness* doctrine, a general prohibition against vague laws, applies with special force.

The following sections discuss each of these contexts in greater detail.

Applying super-strict scrutiny to prior restraints

First-Amendment protection is no longer limited to prior restraints (as it may have been in the Constitution's early days), but speech that hasn't yet been uttered does continue to get special treatment.

Not that the official level of scrutiny is any different. But in deciding whether the injunction served a compelling government interest in the most narrowly drawn way, you can be especially skeptical.

This special concern about prior restraints surfaces in a variety of contexts. Among the most typical or intriguing are the following two:

✓ **Judicial injunctions affecting speech rights:** When courts issue orders forbidding or limiting future speech, special concern arises.

✓ **Permit and licensing systems:** Laws requiring permits or licenses as a prerequisite for protest marches and other expressive activities are also prior restraints. Courts have developed special rules to ensure that sufficient standards and safeguards prevent officials from denying permits or licenses because they disapprove of the speaker's message.

Allowing special challenges for "substantially overbroad" restrictions

A second basis for especially strong speech protection arises when a law or other speech restriction applies to both unprotected speech and protected speech. Special rules allow speakers to admit (or at least assume for purposes of argument) that their speech is unprotected, but to nevertheless escape prosecution because the laws under which they were convicted are "substantially overbroad."

The state law at issue in *Gooding v. Wilson,* 405 U.S. 518 (1972), made it a misdemeanor for a person to utter "opprobrious words or abusive language" to or about another person when the words tend "to cause a breach of the peace." The Court overturned a demonstrator's conviction under the statute even though he arguably uttered unprotected "fighting words" to police officers. The Court reasoned that in several ways the state law covered lots of speech not meeting the fighting-word definition. Most significantly, a lot of protected speech uttered with strong feeling could be considered abusive or opprobrious (conveying disgrace) without causing an immediate fight (which is what Supreme Court decisions require). The Court invalidated Gooding's conviction and the state law in total because it was "substantially overbroad."

These two points about overbreadth are important for you to keep in mind:

✓ **Overbreadth is a special speech-protective exception to the general rule that litigants cannot raise the rights of others.** The general ban on "third-party standing" (as discussed in Chapter 6) would normally prevent one person (the *unprotected* speaker) from asserting the rights of someone else (hypothetical *protected* speakers) not before the court. The substantial overbreadth doctrine reflects, however, a special concern that a protected speaker will self-censor instead of violating the statute and challenging its constitutionality at trial. To avoid such "chilling" of legitimate speech by overbroad statutes, the case law lets only the party with an incentive to challenge the statute (that is, the unprotected speaker already tangled in its web) do so. This exception is yet another example of the "preferred position" speech rights hold.

✔ **Deciding cases on overbreadth grounds allows courts to avoid having to make difficult decisions about protected and unprotected speech.** For example, in *Gooding,* the antiwar protester called police officers seeking to clear him from the door to an army induction center dirty names and said, "I'll choke you to death." The Court found the statute used to convict Gooding void because it was substantially overbroad. The Court thus avoided deciding whether Gooding's own speech was unprotected "fighting words." (The Court would have had to decide that issue if the statute been narrower and therefore constitutional.)

As this example shows, one downside of the substantial-overbreadth doctrine is that, by avoiding individualized factual assessments, it leaves certain important free-speech questions unanswered.

Understanding the special problem of "vague" free-speech restrictions

The due-process clauses of the Fifth and Fourteenth Amendments invalidate any law that is so vague that a person of reasonable intelligence wouldn't have "fair warning" whether their planned conduct would violate the law. But given constitutional law's special regard for speech, the Court has stated that vague speech regulations raise special concerns, including the same concern not to "chill" speech that inspires the substantial-overbreadth doctrine.

Of course, legal terms are often subjective, and, even in the free-speech context, much vagueness is inevitable. (For example, as noted in "Refusing to protect speech provoking antagonists to public disorder," the *Brandenburg* test hinges on less-than-precise distinctions between "incitement" and "mere advocacy" and "imminent" and non-imminent lawless action.) But courts are more likely to find statutes vague when they brush up against free-speech rights rather than other rights.

In *Smith v. Goguen,* 415 U.S. 566 (1974), the Court struck down on vagueness grounds a law prohibiting any person from treating the American flag "contemptuously." Because arguably disrespectful flag treatment could be a constitutionally protected way to dramatize strong objections to American government policy, the law implicated free-speech principles. Thus, the Court was especially concerned with the law's failure "to draw reasonably clear lines" between protected and unprotected flag treatment. (As noted in the later section "Protecting conduct that 'speaks,'" the Court later held that the strongest form of flag mistreatment — burning the American flag — is protected speech that cannot be prohibited to promote "respect" for the flag.)

Giving Some Speech Less Protection

Not all speech gets the protection discussed so far in this chapter. In this section, we discuss the following three notable exceptions:

- ✔ Certain *types* of speech (namely expressive conduct and commercial speech) do not get protection fully paralleling their more classic (political and artistic) counterparts.

- ✔ Speech in particular settings, such as in public schools, may get less protection.

- ✔ Sometimes — though not always — free-speech cases bend the rules in order to protect children.

Protecting conduct that "speaks"

Sometimes, as the saying goes, actions speak louder than words. Some conduct, whether it's burning a draft card during the Vietnam era, burning the American flag at a political convention, or wearing a black armband to protest the deaths of American soldiers, is *expressive conduct* functioning like words.

If the conduct in question contains a legitimate *communicative element* and therefore is expressive conduct, First-Amendment protection is available to such symbolic speech. In determining how much protection is available, the key question becomes whether government is regulating the expressive conduct in order to suppress the message behind it. If so, classic strict scrutiny applies.

In *Texas v. Johnson,* 491 U.S. 397 (1989), the Court struck down a state law forbidding the burning of the American flag. The Court first found that the flag burning in question (which took place at a demonstration in front of the Republican national convention at which President Ronald Reagan was renominated) was expressive conduct designed to protest Reagan's policies. Texas argued that its anti-flag-burning law was necessary to prevent undermining the flag's value as a symbol of national unity and to avoid offending patriotic Texans. Because this justification turned on "the likely communicative impact" of the flag burning, the majority viewed the law as content based. Subjecting the law to strict scrutiny, the majority found that it was not narrowly drawn to accomplish Texas's one compelling interest (preventing a hostile audience reaction) because it did not limit its prohibition to only those flag burnings likely to arouse an immediate breach of the peace.

If the government's regulatory interest is *unrelated* to message suppression, however, then a modified version of the standard intermediate scrutiny applies. The modified test is similar to classic intermediate scrutiny in requiring a government interest of middling importance and requiring that government's restriction be not substantially more restrictive than necessary. However, the modified intermediate test contains no requirement that "ample alternative avenues" for communication be preserved.

Giving strong, but not full, protection to commercial speech

Once thought not to be protected at all by the First Amendment, advertising and other economically motivated speech has achieved substantially enhanced First-Amendment protection in a series of cases starting in 1976. Nowadays, speech that is primarily about "proposing a commercial transaction" may be regulated based on its commercial content via the following four-element test:

1. The speech must be *truthful, nonmisleading speech* concerning a lawful commercial activity.

2. The government's interest in regulating the speech must be substantial.

3. The regulation must "directly" advance the governmental interest

4. There must be a "reasonable fit" between the governmental interest and the means chosen to accomplish it.

In *Central Hudson Gas & Electric Corporation v. Public Service Commission,* 447 U.S. 557 (1980), the decision establishing most of the four-part commercial-speech doctrine just quoted, the Court invalidated an energy-crisis era regulation preventing public utilities in New York from promoting the use of electricity. The Court first found the obvious — that buying and selling electricity was a lawful commercial activity and that utilities were not promoting it in a misleading way. Because New York's interest in promoting energy conservation was "substantial" and a law forbidding advertising of a product was a "direct" way to lower its consumption, the Court noted that the "critical inquiry" was about the means-end fit. The Court found that a complete ban on advertising was unreasonable because the state could instead allow advertising but require disclosure of relative energy efficiencies and expenses. (This is consistent with the general trend in modern decisions, which prefer allowing commercial speech, but ensuring that it is accurate through government regulation, to banning the speech altogether.)

Allowing more restriction when speech "goes to school"

Students do not "shed their constitutional rights to freedom of speech or expression at the schoolhouse gate," as the Court memorably stated in *Tinker v. Des Moines Independent Community School District,* 393 U.S. 733 (1969). (*Tinker* upheld the right of students to wear black armbands at school to protest the Vietnam War.)

However, free-speech law recognizes that students must go to school up to a certain age, and school officials must look after student needs as substitute parents. Special concerns about the education, moral development, and welfare of students give school officials more leeway to restrict student freedom of speech at school than would be allowed either for adults or for students away from the reach of school.

Following are some examples of the greater restriction on speech at school:

✔ **School officials can restrict the freedom of speech and press of students writing for school newspapers and other school publications in ways that would be unthinkable for adult writers.**

✔ **School officials can discipline students for "indecent" remarks that would be fully protected, non-obscene sexual speech if uttered by an adult.** In *Bethel School District No. 403 v. Fraser*, 478 U.S. 675 (1986), the Court allowed school officials to place a negative notation on the permanent record of a student who made remarks full of sexual innuendo when giving a speech at a school assembly.

✔ **School officials can rely on school disciplinary policies to punish a student for speech that may "reasonably be regarded as encouraging illegal drug use."** The Court applied this principle in *Morse v. Frederick*, 551 U.S. 393 (2007), to a student holding up a large sign extolling "BONG Hits 4 JESUS" on a city street adjacent to his school. *Morse* held that student speech can even be restricted away from school boundaries if the student is participating in a school-sponsored activity.

Lesser First-Amendment protection for prisoners and government employees

All the complications emerging from various cases cannot be canvassed here, but one important detail is that, like students, prisoners do not forfeit their First-Amendment rights entirely when they are incarcerated. But both their diminished moral status and the special security needs of modern correctional facilities lead to relaxed free-speech protections. For example, prison officials may for valid, non-arbitrary security reasons limit prisoners' access to media interviews and contacts and deny access to certain publications.

A series of cases drawing complicated lines also gives government employees diminished free-speech room to "speak their mind" on and about their jobs. The free-speech rights of government employees require especially difficult balancing acts when employees "blow the whistle" on perceived abuses by their bosses and other governmental officials. Difficult line-drawing also looms when government employees (especially public-school teachers) engage in provocative speech in their private lives and arguably "on their own time." Because of the need for government employees to remain politically neutral, their right to engage in political activities, such as participating actively in political campaigns, is also more limited than private employees.

Protecting kids through diminished free-speech protection

Finally, free-speech law at times shows a pattern of relaxed protection when especially important *nonspeech interests* are at stake.

One good example of this phenomenon is the tendency to allow greater speech restriction when the interests of minors are at stake. (This tendency is seen in the *Fraser* case discussed in the preceding section.) Part of the reason why the Court allowed punishment of student sexual innuendo was a desire to protect minors "from exposure to vulgar and offensive spoken language."

Following are other examples of bending free-speech protections in the interests of children:

- ✔ **Actual child pornography:** Films or other pictorial representations of sex involving actual underage children may be punished even though this child pornography doesn't meet the three-element *Miller* obscenity test applicable to sex films involving adults (as discussed in the earlier section "Refusing to protect obscenity but strongly protecting indecency"). In *New York v. Ferber,* 458 U.S. 747 (1982) the Court justified "relaxing" the *Miller* test in three ways to allow more aggressive prosecutions of child pornographers based on the fact that child pornography captures illegal child abuse. The Court also credited the goal of regulators to stop the "economic motive" for child sexual abuse by drying up the "advertising and selling" of child pornography.

- ✔ **Indecent speech broadcast at child-accessible times:** *Cohen v. California,* 403 U.S. 15 (1971), which reversed the conviction of a young man who wore a jacket, in the corridors of the Los Angeles courthouse, using the "F word" to dramatize the depth of his opposition to the Vietnam war and the draft. *Cohen* held that the price of free speech is that Americans must generally put up with "offensive" speech in public. Yet the Court distinguished *Cohen* in its narrow ruling in *Federal Communications Commission. v. Pacifica Foundation,* 438 U.S. 726 (1978). *Pacifica* upheld the right of the FCC to discipline a broadcaster playing comedian George Carlin's satirical monologue "Filthy Words" on an afternoon radio program. Relying in part on the more limited free-speech rights of broadcasters, the Court's concern that "broadcasting is uniquely accessible to children, even those too young to read" trumped the station's right to poke fun at American "prudery" about profanity.

Don't get the idea that children's concerns always win out over free-speech rights. The examples of special sensitivity to children's interests just discussed are counteracted by these contrary examples:

✔ The diminished constitutional protection afforded to actual child pornography does not extend to "virtual child pornography" (for example, images made by computer manipulation not involving filmed sex with actual children) or to simulated child pornography using young-looking adults pretending to be children. The Court drew this line in *Ashcroft v. Free Speech Coalition,* 534 U.S. 234 (2002).

✔ The special concern for protecting children against indecent broadcasts dries up when additional barriers make it less likely that children will accidentally access this content. In later cases the Court limited *Pacifica* to broadcasts that come "unbidden" and without warning. For example, *United States v. Playboy Entertainment Group,* 529 U.S. 8003 (2000), declined to extend *Pacifica* for "premium" cable channels that could be blocked at the request of parents "on a household-by-household basis."

Chapter 12

The Constitution and Religion

· ·

In This Chapter

▶ Distinguishing two (potentially conflicting) facets of religious neutrality

▶ Finding out why achieving religious neutrality is easier said than done

▶ Making sure that the government doesn't restrict free exercise of religion

▶ Preventing government from establishing or promoting religion

· ·

*T*he First Amendment requires that government neither disfavors religious free exercise nor favors religion. In theory, these two requirements are reconcilable if government just treats religion neutrally. But as you can see throughout this chapter, a graceful government-and-religion balancing act is very difficult to achieve in practice.

Despite the difficulties, the modern Court has developed a number of relevant, if often conflicting, doctrines. In this chapter, we examine these doctrines and also provide some upfront explanation as to why practicing government neutrality toward religion is easier said than done. And to get started, we take a look at the First-Amendment framers' disagreement on how to practice this neutrality.

Understanding the Framers' Diverse Views on Religion and Government

The First Amendment has two distinct clauses defining how government should interact with religious institutions and their believers. In essence, the two clauses say that governments may not *disfavor* or *favor* religion:

✔ **The "free exercise" clause** forbids governments from "prohibiting the free exercise" of religion.

✔ **The "establishment" clause** provides that governments "shall make no law respecting an establishment of religion."

Clearly the drafters of the two religion clauses intended to prevent the newly created national government from following the English practice, carried out in several American colonies, of having an officially sanctioned church supported by taxes paid by many people who did not believe in that church. As for religious free exercise, the drafters clearly opposed laws punishing believers for having their beliefs or expressing them in typical ways, such as praying or coming together to worship. But beyond these clear intentions, the intentions of the drafters remain highly debatable today.

Some framers believed in the more-religion-friendly theory today called *nonpreferentialism*. They were satisfied if government just didn't play favorites *among* religious sects (and, perhaps, just not among *Christian* religious sects). Government could *accommodate* or even foster religion generally and recognize its key place in American life. For example, soon after being sworn in as America's first President, George Washington took the accommodationist step of proclaiming "a day of public thanksgiving and prayer" to gladly acknowledge "the many and signal favors of Almighty God."

By contrast, some First-Amendment framers believed in a very high "wall of separation" between church and state. The phrase (which many Americans mistakenly think is in the Constitution itself) was coined by colonial religious leader Roger Williams and reflected in the Bill for Establishing Religious Freedom that Thomas Jefferson penned for the State of Virginia. *Separationists* believed that government and religion had a mutually corrupting influence on each other. Religion would tone itself down to curry government's favor. Government and public unity would suffer as religious factions competed to turn government power to their advantage.

Not surprisingly, the framers' lack of consensus is reflected in a lack of unity on the modern Court. In recent establishment-clause decisions, a four-justice bloc has typically taken the *accommodationist/nonpreferential* view. A staunch four-justice bloc has typically taken a more *separationist* view. With this 4–4 split, case outcomes often depended on how one "swing voter" justice viewed the case.

Grasping the Difficulty of Putting Religious Neutrality into Practice

In theory, governments can honor both the free-exercise clause and the establishment clause by remaining *neutral* towards religion. (After all, if you're neutral with respect to chocolate ice cream — although, really, who is? — you neither disfavor nor favor it.) In practice, however, complying with both clauses is very difficult for government. Courts and others also have difficulty defining the exact boundaries of constitutionality and unconstitutionality. The trouble stems from two main issues:

✔ **Neutrality is in the eye of the beholder.** Suppose that during a war in which young persons are drafted into the armed forces, the national draft law exempts religious *conscientious objectors* (potential draftees whose religious beliefs require them not to participate in any war). From one standpoint, this exemption protects the free-exercise rights of religious conscientious objectors by keeping federal law from forcing them to violate their religious scruples. From another point of view, however, granting an exemption from military service to religious conscientious objectors but not to people opposing war on deeply felt nonreligious (philosophical and moral) grounds is unconstitutionally favoring religion over nonreligion. The practice establishes religion in a preferred position.

Luckily for the justices confronting this dilemma in *Welsh v. United States,* 398 U.S. 333 (1969), they found a creative way to satisfy both clauses. Specifically, they reinterpreted existing statutory language so that a draft exemption was granted to all persons whose pacifism was "spurred by deeply held moral, ethical, or religious beliefs." (The Court's statutory transformation was an arguably arrogant assertion of judicial power. But that's another issue, pursued in Chapter 6.) Religious conscientious objectors still got draft exemptions (thus preserving their free-exercise rights) while the Court avoided preferential treatment for *religious* pacifists by also exempting *nonreligious* pacifists (thus finessing establishment-clause difficulties). Most of the time, such easy escapes are not so readily available.

✔ **Staying within the boundaries of the clauses has become much harder because those boundaries have significantly expanded.** If restricted to its core application, the establishment clause would only require government to avoid supporting a particular church or religious denomination. And government could narrowly avoid "prohibiting" free exercise as long as it didn't forbid prayer, church attendance, or other core religious practices. If staying neutral only meant avoiding these evils, government compliance with the Constitution's religion clauses wouldn't be an especially tall order.

But as you discover in this chapter, the scope of both religion clauses has significantly broadened, especially through expansive Supreme Court decisions. The modern anti-establishment-clause principle kicks in when government favors *religion in general* over nonreligion. Subtle symbolic associations (for example, governments' inclusion of religious symbols or songs in holiday celebrations and displays) can trigger difficult decisions splitting the nine-member Court down the middle. Until recently, the Court also read the free-exercise clause expansively — as covering laws that merely *burden* (negatively affect or work against) religious observance in ways less stark than outright prohibition.

Protecting Religious "Free Exercise"

Of the First Amendment's two religion clauses, the one with the most clear-cut rules and relatively little disagreement among the framers is the free-exercise clause. The main distinction you need to keep in mind in this area is between the following two categories of law:

- ✔ **Laws that discriminate against religious exercise:** These laws must pass strict scrutiny (a difficult test in which government must show compelling reasons for the law) and are likely to be invalidated.

- ✔ **Nondiscriminatory laws that only *incidentally burden* (that is, have the effect of disproportionately affecting) religious exercise:** These laws only have to be rational in order to be valid.

In this section, we detail the main modes of analysis under these two options. Then we consider complications in the seemingly straightforward scheme.

Deciding which laws discriminate against religion and which laws merely burden it

With so much riding on the discrimination-versus-nondiscrimination distinction, you need to become adept at applying the standards set forth in modern case law.

Detecting discrimination

The leading modern case on discriminatory laws is *Church of the Lukumi Babalu Aye v. City of Hialeah,* 508 U.S. 520 (1993). There, the Court found a city ordinance prohibiting "animal sacrifices" (defined in part as the "unnecessary" killing of an animal "in a . . . ritual . . . not for the primary purpose of food consumption") unconstitutional after the church made a free-exercise challenge. The ordinance grew out of public controversy sparked when the Church of Lukumi Babalu Aye planned to establish a church, school, and cultural center for the practice of Santeria, a religion brought from Africa to America by slave descendants from Cuba and the Caribbean. (To invoke the protection of beneficial spirits, Santeria adherents sacrifice a wide variety of animals as part of birth, marriage, and funeral rituals.)

In analyzing the Hialeah ordinance, the Court indicated that strict constitutional scrutiny is required for a law that "discriminates against some or all religious beliefs or regulates or prohibits conduct because it is undertaken for religious reasons." Admittedly, the Hialeah ordinance didn't overtly discriminate against Santeria. (It didn't say, "No member of Santeria may sacrifice animals.") But the Court found that the ordinance was motivated by public outcry against the religion and seemed carefully designed to outlaw only Santeria animal killings, while exempting nonreligious animal killings (such as hunting or pest extermination) and the ritual killing involved in kosher butchering to render food consumable by observant Jews. The ordinance failed the strict scrutiny the Court's rules said was applicable once the law was labeled discriminatory.

Finding a mere incidental burden on religion

The flip side of a law *discriminating* against religious exercise is one merely restricting religiously motivated conduct as the "incidental effect" of a "generally applicable and otherwise valid" law. (As you see in the next section, a merely burdensome law is not strictly analyzed and will more likely be found valid.)

The language just quoted comes from *Employment Division, Department of Health Resources of Oregon v. Smith,* 494 U.S. 872 (1990), which also provides a prominent example of the distinction between discriminatory and incidentally burdensome laws. In *Smith,* two members of a Native American church were fired from jobs with a drug-rehabilitation center when they used peyote (a hallucinogenic drug made from cactus) in a religious sacrament. Oregon denied the fired church members unemployment benefits because state law prohibited benefits to workers fired for "misconduct." Church members claimed a denial of their free-exercise rights, arguing that the state's failure to exempt sacramental drug use from its antidrug laws penalized them for following the teachings and rituals of their religion.

A 6–3 majority in *Smith* found that Oregon's laws were not discriminatory against religion. Unlike Hialeah's anti-animal-sacrifice ordinance, for example, Oregon's laws were not adopted to target religious practices, Native American or otherwise. Rather, Oregon's criminal laws were "valid" antidrug enactments "generally applicable" to all Oregonians. The laws *unintentionally* ended up having an "incidental burden" on certain religions whose sacramental practices happened to involve illegal drugs.

Applying strict (or easy) scrutiny

After you successfully determine where a questioned law or policy falls on the discrimination/incidental-burden scale, you are ready to apply the appropriate level of scrutiny as follows:

> ✔ **Strict scrutiny for discriminatory laws:** You also encounter this scrutiny test in Chapter 10 (in dealing with race discrimination and laws drawing lines affecting fundamental equal-protection rights), in Chapter 11 (in understanding content-based regulation of protected speech), and in Chapter 14 (in analyzing fundamental privacy rights under substantive due process). As in those areas, strict scrutiny works in the free-exercise context as follows:

> • First, government must show that its discriminatory law is actually necessary to achieve a highest order "compelling interest." In *Lukumi Babalu Aye* (discussed in the earlier section "Detecting discrimination"), the Court assumed that promoting public health and preventing animal cruelty would be "compelling" interests in the abstract.

A different answer before *Smith:* Strict scrutiny for some substantially burdensome laws

The *Smith* case (introduced in the section "Finding a mere incidental burden on religion") did much more than just deny benefits to two fired Native American church members. A bare majority of justices (that is, the fewest possible necessary for a decision — usually five) used *Smith* to chart a new course for free-exercise law.

For almost three decades before *Smith*, the Court had applied the strict scrutiny it now reserves for *discriminatory* laws to a *subset* of laws burdening religion — namely, legal restrictions reaching the level of *substantial* burden. For example, in *Sherbert v. Verner,* 374 U.S. 398 (1963), the Court invalidated a South Carolina law denying unemployment benefits to a woman fired because she would not work on Saturday. (The woman declined to work on this day because her Seventh-Day Adventist religion held this day as God's prescribed day for humans to rest.) Viewing the state's law as one forcing a Saturday-Sabbath believer to choose between "following the precepts of her religion" and forfeiting benefits versus "abandoning [a] precept[ ] . . . to accept work," the Court applied strict scrutiny and invalidated the law.

Application of strict scrutiny in the pre-*Smith* era did not always invalidate the law in question. Sometimes the Court found that laws met

strict scrutiny. For example, in *United States v. Lee,* 455 U.S. 252 (1982), a unanimous Court found that a federal law making all employers pay Social Security taxes was narrowly drawn to accomplish a compelling interest — even though paying such taxes substantially burdened the religious free-exercise rights of Amish employers. (The simplicity-seeking Amish religion teaches self-reliance and mutual support, values at odds with government-mandated social-welfare obligations.)

Still, with two rather complicated exceptions we spare you the details of, the *Smith* majority's about-face eliminated even the *possibility* that nondiscriminatory laws could be reversed if they substantially deterred religious exercise. This result was highly controversial at the time and remains so to this day. In 1993, Congress took the unusual step of passing the Religious Freedom Restoration Act, which would have reinstated the pre-*Smith* regime of strict scrutiny for substantially burdensome law. Yet the Court stuck to its guns, invalidating the Act on the ground that Congress lacked authority to pass it. (We address this controversial view of congressional power in Chapter 4.)

And so *Smith*'s bright-line distinction between discriminatory laws and merely burdensome ones lives on!

- **Second, the law must be narrowly drawn to accomplish the compelling interest(s).** As in other areas applying a narrow-tailoring test, laws discriminating against religious free exercise must not be overinclusive (that is, they must avoid covering conduct not necessary to accomplish the interest) and must not be underinclusive (that is, they must not leave out conduct that should be included).

   The *Lukumi Babalu Aye* Court found the Hialeah ordinance incomplete because (as noted earlier) the city failed to prohibit many unnecessary, cruel, or unsanitary animal killings. The ordinance went too far, in that the city prohibited religiously motivated sacrifice without regard to its cruelty or health risk.

The bottom line, to quote *Lukumi Babalu Aye,* is that a discriminatory law challenged as a free-exercise clause violation "will survive strict scrutiny only in rare cases."

✔ **A rational-basis default for incidentally burdensome laws:** Quite a different fate awaits laws not considered discriminatory. Because strict scrutiny is generally inapplicable, the key becomes whether there's a rational basis for thinking that the challenged law furthers a legitimate governmental interest. For example, the *Smith* majority (discussed in "Finding a mere incidental burden on religion") easily agreed that Oregon had a legitimate reason for prohibiting drugs and not giving unemployment benefits to employees fired for misconduct. The majority also thought that Oregon had a rational reason for penalizing religiously based drug use; putting an exception in the law would have created an unacceptable loophole.

Avoiding Government "Establishment" of Religion

We hope that after the relative clarity of the free-exercise clause doctrines, you're in the mood for dealing with uncertainties and complications — because, alas, the establishment-clause case law is rife with them. Part of the problem is that the dividing lines between cases upholding and invalidating governmental enactments seem fuzzy. Another contributing factor is that the Court has been fractured on establishment-clause doctrines for several decades — and remains in disagreement today.

To provide some useful structure, we divide the various cases into three groups and discuss:

✔ **Limits on government promoting prayer and injecting itself into other matters of religious orthodoxy:** Here, the lines are clear but the results are highly controversial.

✔ **Restrictions on government funding of religious institutions (especially religious schools):** Here, one line of authority is clear (the rules governing aid flowing *indirectly* to religious schools) and another one is not (the principles applying when government gives *direct* aid).

✔ **Boundaries on government associating itself with religious symbols (especially on public property):** On this topic, the rules vary and Court coalitions shift. To explain it, the best we can do is discuss a variety of alternative approaches that may carry the day.

Staying away from prayer and religious orthodoxy

The clearest — although by no means the least controversial! — group of establishment-clause decisions prevents government from "officially prescribing a particular form of religious worship," as the Court put it in *Engel v. Vitale,* 370 U.S. 421 (1962). *Engel* invalidated the then-frequent practice in many public schools of starting the day with an officially led prayer. More broadly, *Engel* ushered in the modern era of strong establishment-clause skepticism "when the power, prestige, and financial support is placed behind a particular religious belief."

As we note below, a series of cases leaves clear guideposts as to how religion can and can't go to school. As we observe at the end, however, the rules are different when government-sponsored or government-enabled prayer occurs outside of school and involves adults.

Forbidden practices in schools

Engel and later cases elaborating its concerns establish that governments must not subject public-school students to any of the following religious activities or materials:

✔ **Officially written or endorsed prayer:** This prohibition applies in all the following situations:

• **Even if the prayer is nondenominational or broadly representative of many religious traditions:** The *Engel* Court objected to this fairly innocuous, generic prayer: "Almighty God, we acknowledge our dependence upon Thee, and we beg Thy blessings upon us, our parents, our teachers, and our country."

- **Even if saying the prayer is voluntary:** The *Engel* Court was unimpressed that authorities permitted students to remain silent during the prayer or even leave the room. The Court still found it "plain" that there would be "indirect coercive pressure upon religious minorities to conform to the prevailing officially approved religion."

- **Even if school officials use a prayer originating from another source:** *Murray v. Curlett,* 374 U.S. 203 (1963), invalidated a requirement that the school day begin with a recitation of the Lord's Prayer.

- **Even if the prayer occurs at a school function before or after the normal school day and at a location other than the school grounds:** *Lee v. Weisman,* 505 U.S. 577 (1992), applied the prayer prohibition to a nondenominational "invocation" and "benediction" at a high-school graduation ceremony, even though it occurred off-campus and attendance was optional for students. The Court noted that students would feel strong family and peer pressure to attend. And in *Santa Fe Independent School District v. Doe,* 530 U.S. 290 (2000), the Court applied *Lee* to the opening prayer at a nighttime high-school football game.

- **Even if the prayer is said by a student or private religious official to which the school merely gives access:** *Lee* and *Santa Fe* also illustrate this point. The prayers at graduation in *Lee* were written and said by a Jewish rabbi selected by the school principal, who advised the rabbi to make the prayer "nonsectarian" and provided a copy of a "Guidelines for Civil Occasions" pamphlet. In *Santa Fe,* students chose the person who would deliver the prayer over the school-owned microphone before the game.

✔ **Bible verses (or other religious texts):** *Abington School District v. Schempp,* 374 U.S. 203 (1963), (decided along with *Murray,* referenced above), invalidated a Pennsylvania requirement that "at least ten verses from the Holy Bible be read . . . at the opening of each public school day." The Court called this practice a government-sponsored "religious ceremony," prohibited even under the following conditions:

- **Even if the texts are read "without comment"**

- **Even if students are excused from attendance during it**

- **Even if special accommodations are made for varying versions of the official texts**

✔ **The Ten Commandments (or other religious texts) posted on school-room walls:** In *Stone v. Graham,* 449 U.S. 39 (1980), the Court ruled against a Kentucky law requiring this display. The Court saw the Commandments as an "undeniably sacred text in the Jewish and Christian faiths." Posting was intended to cause school children "to read, meditate upon, perhaps to venerate and obey, the Commandments," thus wrongly mixing government into "a matter of private devotion." *Stone* specifically addressed posting on the school wall, but the ruling's logic would make a similar posting unconstitutional anywhere in the school.

✔ **"Silent meditation" opportunities skewed toward prayer:** Alabama had a statutory requirement that schools begin the day with a period of silence "for meditation." So when the legislature amended the law to add the phrase "or voluntary prayer" as part of what the legislative sponsor called an effort to return such prayer to public schools, the Court in *Wallace v. Jaffree*, 472 U.S. 38 (1985), was not impressed. The later amendment had "the sole purpose of expressing the State's endorsement of prayer activities . . . as a favored practice." Government flunked the establishment-clause requirement of "complete neutrality toward religion."

✔ **Religiously motivated bans on the teaching of evolution — or requirements that "creation science" be taught alongside secular evolutionary theories:** Building on *Epperson v. Arkansas*, 393 U.S. 97 (1968) (establishing the first limit), in *Edwards v. Aguillard*, 482 U.S. 578 (1987), the Court struck down a state "creationism" law as one that "advances a religious doctrine" by "present[ing] a religious viewpoint."

It's not just a government-coercion (or money) thing

When it comes to injecting religion into public school situations, the government doesn't need to be *actually* coercing unwilling students for a law to be struck down. In *Engel* (discussed in "Staying away from prayer and religious orthodoxy"), the Court stated that "direct governmental compulsion" is not required to violate the establishment clause. Merely having government bring its "power and prestige" into religious matters is objectionable. And the cases summarized in the section "Forbidden practices in schools" show that even elaborate efforts to excuse students from participating or even being in the same room as are other participating colleagues have not helped prayer schemes survive invalidation.

Furthermore, in *Lee v. Weismann*, Justice Kennedy wrote that it was enough for school officials to create a context in which "public pressure, as well as peer pressure" would cause graduation attendees to feel that they at least needed to stand silently during opening prayers. Justice Kennedy also worried that "given our social conventions, a reasonable [religious] dissenter in this milieu could believe that the group exercise signified her own participation or approval of it."

Nor is the issue mainly about the small amounts of tax dollars teachers and school officials are being paid to say or write prayers, coordinate the participation of rabbis, and so on. Individual justices have emphasized the money element, citing the core establishment-clause concern about no taxpayer being forced to support a religion he or she doesn't believe in. But most justices think the small amounts of taxpayer money spent aren't the big problem. Instead, what's troubling is the direct or indirect presence of government officialdom when government involves itself with religious ceremonies.

Acceptable inclusions of religion at school

Even as the Court invalidated school prayer in *Engel* and other cases, its opinions stress that governing rules do not require "hostility to religion" *(Engel)* or a "religion of secularism" *(Abington School District)*. Specifically, governments may bring religion into the public schools in the following ways:

- ✔ **The Bible, other texts, or any religious content may be "presented objectively as part of a secular program of education."** The *Abington School District* opinion suggested that one's education might not be "complete" without "a study of comparative religion or the history of religion and its relationship to the advancement of civilization." And "the Bible is worthy of study for its literary and historic qualities."

- ✔ **Religious songs and holiday materials may be included in holiday assembly programs and concerts held in the public schools, as long as it is clear from the context that government is not sponsoring a religious ceremony.** This in part applies the Court's "endorsement" line of analysis (discussed in "The varying approaches and shifting coalitions").

- ✔ **Students can pray at their own initiative during "true" moments of silence (that is, ones not skewed toward prayer as in *Jaffree*) and at any other times and venues (before, during, and after school) where prayers are not inconsistent with other educational goals.** School officials may prevent students from praying out loud during a teacher's lecture. But officials may not prevent students from praying publicly over meals in the school cafeteria or silently while the teacher is passing out an assignment. Such heavy-handedness would violate the free-exercise rights students retain.

 Next time some politician or pundit says that the Supreme Court "took God out of the classroom," don't believe it. The applicable doctrines instead take officials out of the promoting-God-and-religion business. Case holdings leave room for God and religion when they are pursued educationally or when individual student consciences generate the pursuit. As the old joke goes, "as long as there are math tests, there will be prayer in school."

Prayer outside of school (and involving adults)

The Court brings a more tolerant approach to prayer and religious touches at public ceremonies outside of the school context. Prayers and invocations at civic events, opening each legislative day with a prayer by a government-paid chaplain (approved in *Marsh v. Chambers,* 463 U.S. 783 [1983]), having the motto "In God We Trust" on American currency, and even beginning Supreme Court oral arguments with the phrase "God save this Honorable Court" are considered appropriate modern heirs to George Washington's tradition of proclaiming a national day of prayer and thanksgiving.

Beyond reflecting the accommodationist inclinations of the First Amendment's framers and modern justices, these traditional religious touches are thought by many to be less objectionable for these reasons:

> ✓ **Because they are "part of the fabric of our society" (as the *Marsh* Court described legislative prayer), the likelihood is less that they will send a message of government endorsement.** Especially because they invoke the deity generally, they will not be understood as favoring any particular religious sect or tradition.

> ✓ **Adults are thought to have more of an ability than school children to put ceremonial religious traditions in context.** Adults are less likely, the theory goes, to jump to the conclusion that, because a revered authority is reciting a prayer to God, the government as a whole must support and believe in God. Adults can put in context, for example, the president ending a speech with "God bless America."

Whatever the reason for this school-child-versus-adult distinction, its implications are important. For example, it will help you understand decisions such as the one rendered by a federal circuit court in *Newdow v. United States Congress,* 328 F.3d 466 (2003). The Supreme Court nullified the *Newdow* decision on grounds that the challengers lacked standing to pursue their claim, but until then the appeals court found that it was unconstitutional for public-school teachers to lead their students in the Pledge of Allegiance. Because the Pledge included the phrase "one nation under God," the Ninth Circuit had found that school children would infer an unconstitutional religion-supporting message.

The *Newdow* case was widely — and wrongly — reported as striking down the Pledge of Allegiance. Yet the decision only prevented the saying of the two words "under God" *in public schools.* Nothing in the ruling prevented government officials and any American adult from reciting the Pledge with the reference to "God" in any nonschool setting.

Defining when government may fund religious teaching

Another major intersection of religion and government in the school context occurs when government funds flow to *religious* private schools as part of general aid-to-education programs. In these programs, government goes beyond the familiar pattern of running public schools, supported by local taxes and other revenue sources; government uses public funds to support the efforts of *private* schools, many of which are operated by religious institutions. Government aid to private schools inevitably brings government support to institutions fostering religious belief as well as teaching reading and math.

In this context, the verdict is mixed on case law clarity:

- ✔ **Direct aid:** For government aid flowing directly to private religious schools, the Court continues to follow a confusing, highly fact-specific inquiry focused significantly on whether government has done enough to avoid supporting religious teaching and to separate itself from identification and involvement with religious matters.

- ✔ **Indirect aid:** By contrast, when taxpayer dollars flow indirectly through thousands of parents making "private choices" to send their kids to private religious schools, current precedents now allow substantial aid to support their religious mission as long as the program makes aid broadly and neutrally available (at least in theory) to nonreligious schools.

In this section, you see how the Court devised a three-part test (called the *Lemon* test, after the name of the case in which it was announced) and then used that test to render a series of hair-splitting, hard-to-reconcile decisions. A later line of cases then split off from the *Lemon* test (Lemon twists?) and ripened into the current broad acceptance for school-aid flowing indirectly. Finally, you see that the Court has done some twisting of *Lemon* in the direct-aid context as well, although the current state of the law remains in flux.

Introducing the Lemon test

In 1971, the Supreme Court sought to bring order to chaotic previous cases by deciding cases challenging school-funding programs from Rhode Island and Pennsylvania. Rhode Island's program used tax dollars to give salary increases of up to 15 percent above average salary levels to teachers of nonreligious (secular) subjects in private elementary schools. Pennsylvania directly reimbursed private elementary and secondary schools for some of their expenditures on teacher salaries, textbooks, and other instructional materials. Accounting safeguards and other restrictions sought to ensure that aid went solely to secular teachers and subjects, not to those teaching religious topics.

In *Lemon v. Kurtzman,* 403 U.S. 602 (1971), the Court invalidated both programs after subjecting them to this three-prong analysis:

- ✔ **The aid program "must have a *secular purpose.*"** Both the Rhode Island and Pennsylvania programs do, answered the Court: The state aid programs sincerely seek "to enhance the quality of secular education" in all private schools, nonreligious and religious. The Court recognized that our nation's tradition of private education means that private schools will continue to educate substantial numbers of any state's students on subjects other than religion (without using public taxes, by the way!). The public has a big stake in ensuring that private schools sufficiently prepare students for their roles as productive citizens. (Note that, as this inquiry has developed, the government aid program does not have to *only* have a secular purpose; a secular purpose just has to be *among* the purposes government is pursuing.)

✔ **The program's principal or primary effect must "not Advance . . . religion."** This inquiry recognizes that "church-related elementary and secondary schools have a significant religious mission and that a substantial portion of their activities is religiously oriented." If aid flowed in significant measure to these religious aspects of the church-school day, the "primary effect" would be state funding of religious teaching and exercise in violation of the establishment clause.

On this prong, the *Lemon* Court left readers hanging. The Court agreed in the abstract (but not specifically based on the facts of this case) that the secular and religious aspects of private religious education are "identifiable and separate." The Court noted that the programs at issue approached territory that is forbidden by the Constitution — because even government money given to secular teaching would help religious schools by letting them spend more of their own funds on *religious* teaching. But the Court moved on to a third prong without deciding the "primary effect" issue.

✔ **The program "must not foster *excessive government entanglement with religion.*"** Here's where the *Lemon* Court had major problems with the Rhode Island and Pennsylvania programs. As to teachers, the Court worried that "a dedicated religious person, teaching in a school affiliated with his or her faith" and operated to teach the faith to the next generation, "will inevitably experience great difficulty in remaining religiously neutral." In order to make sure that, say, the history teacher at a Catholic school, who may be eligible for aid under the Rhode Island program, does not unconsciously teach from her religion's perspective, the government will need "comprehensive, discriminating, continuing . . . surveillance." This in turn fosters an "excessive and enduring entanglement between state and church."

Even for the inanimate textbooks and instructional materials covered under the Pennsylvania program, the Court feared excessive government intrusion into religious matters. Judging whether textbooks had forbidden "subject matter expressing religious teaching" might require government officials to entwine themselves in the "morals or forms of worship" of religious sects. Ongoing auditing accompanying government subsidies could inject government officials inappropriately into the affairs of religious schools.

Finally, the *Lemon* Court worried that state aid to education would foster political divisiveness, as "[p]artisans . . . will inevitably champion" religious education and opponents "will inevitably respond and employ all of the usual political campaign techniques to prevail."

All these problems convinced the Court that the Rhode Island and Pennsylvania programs were unconstitutional. (Notice that the *Lemon* test works like many "elementized" legal tests: Because government action must meet *each* element to be judged constitutional, failing any one element dooms the action to a negative judicial verdict.)

Making a Lemon into . . . ?

The *Lemon* test seemed to bring clarity to constitutional analysis of government aid to private religious education. But in practice, different justices split significantly on how to apply it.

This highly selective summary illustrates the arcane distinctions the Court made in post-*Lemon* cases — often within different parts of the same case:

- Public schools can loan textbooks to private nonreligious and religious schools — but cannot give them counseling, testing, remedial classes, or other ancillary services (*Meek v. Pittenger,* 433 U.S. 229 [1975]).

- Government can provide diagnostic and therapeutic testing services but can't fund field trips (*Wolman v. Walter,* 433 U.S. 229 [1977]).

- Government can't directly reimburse religious schools for some record-keeping and testing services (*New York v. Cathedral Academy,* 433 U.S. 125 [1977]) but can pay for other recordkeeping and testing expenses required by state regulation (*Committee for Public Education and Religious Liberty v. Regan,* 444 U.S. 646 [1980]).

Twisting Lemon to allow substantial indirect aid to religious schools

A dozen years after *Lemon,* the Court began pursuing a contrary analysis when, under the government aid program in question, aid flowed to religious schools "only as a result of numerous, private choices of individual parents of school-age children." Starting with the relatively minor tax deduction for educational expenses upheld in *Mueller v. Allen,* 463 U.S. 388 (1983) (the source of the quote in the preceding sentence), this separate line of precedent now allows substantial dollars to end up supporting the *religious* mission of private schools, in apparent violation of *Lemon*'s "effect" prong.

The interesting (and, to staunch church-state separationists, alarming) case progression leading to this separate establishment-clause strand happened as follows:

- **First, the Court upheld a state law allowing parents to receive a $500/child tax deduction for expenses they incur for "tuition, textbooks, and transportation."** In reaching this result, the *Mueller* Court was not worried that the great majority (96 percent) of tax benefits went to parents whose kids went to *religious* private schools. It was enough that, in theory, parents of kids attending public schools could have claimed the deduction (even though such schools rarely charge any of the deductible expenses).

Note that, at least for transportation costs, government funding was not restricted to secular school activities. (The same bus carrying religious-school students to math classes carried them at taxpayer expense to religion classes.) The ability to segregate secular from religious was a constitutional requirement in *Lemon* but not in *Mueller*.

✔ **Next, the Court significantly extended the green light for indirect aid by allowing state-vocational-education funds to assist a blind student in studying for the ministry at a private Christian college.** *Witters v. Washington Department of Services for Blind,* 474 U.S. 481 (1986), approved this expansion of *Mueller* despite strong objections that requiring taxpayers to fund *religious officials* of faiths they did not believe in strikes at the heart of the establishment clause.

✔ **Then the Court took another significant step by allowing authorities to send a government-paid employee (a sign-language interpreter) into a religious high school to assist a deaf student's studies.** The Court in *Zobrest v. Catalina Foothills School District,* 509 U.S. 1 (1993), did not see this government aid as an inappropriate extension of *Mueller* and *Witters,* despite a dissenting argument that establishment-clause values are especially trampled when "government furnishes the medium for communication of a religious message." (As the dissent noted, at the Roman Catholic high school in question, "[a] state-employed sign-language interpreter would be required to communicate the material covered in a religion class" and at daily Communion rites.)

✔ **Ultimately, the Court okayed a voucher program paying up to $2,250 of the tuition costs for very-low-income students to attend their choice of public or private school, including private religious schools.** The Court gave the green light in *Zelman v. Simmons-Harris,* 536 U.S. 639 (2002), despite 96 percent of the voucher money going to religious schools, despite the program's $8.2 million annual price tag, and despite the fact that the government voucher check (which parents signed over to their chosen school) would indiscriminately support secular and religious educational costs.

Thus, by steady steps over almost 20 years, the Court's indirect-aid cases have led to this result: Substantial taxpayer funds can be spent to support private religious education, without any *Lemon*-type restrictions to prevent government money from supporting religious instruction, as long as both of the following stipulations are met (quotes are from *Zelman*):

✔ **By its terms and as implemented, the aid program provides aid "to a broad class of individuals" on a "neutral" basis.** (That is, it doesn't restrict benefits to, or encourage beneficiaries to choose, religious schools.)

✔ **The program is "of true private choice."** Broadly granted government aid must reach religious schools only as a result of the "genuine and independent private choice" of citizens.

Ongoing uncertainty for direct aid to religious schools

Recent years brought a loosening of restrictions in programs providing aid directly to religious schools (as opposed to aid flowing indirectly through parent and student decisions, as just discussed in "Twisting *Lemon* to allow substantial indirect aid to religious schools").

But the Court's greater tolerance for direct aid to religious schools lacks the clarity of the *Mueller*-to-*Zelman* case line. Specifically, a majority of justices has not really settled on any one approach. Instead, unstable alliances have led to the following messy situation: The Court still checks direct financial aid and in-kind assistance (for example, loaning teachers or textbooks) to make sure that they won't be diverted to religious teaching and that mechanisms for preventing diversion don't create "excessive entanglement." But *application* of these *Lemon* factors is more forgiving, allowing more governmental involvement with religious schools than in previous cases.

In its 1997 decision in *Agostini v. Felton,* 521 U.S. 203, the Court revisited a New York City program it had struck down a dozen years earlier. The 1997 decision reversed course, upholding the legitimacy of sending public-school teachers into private religious schools to provide remedial education for disadvantaged children.

Attributing the changed result to a different "understanding" of the principles it had previously used, *Agostini* said the following:

✔ The Court would no longer presume "that the placement of public employees on [religious] school grounds inevitably results in . . . impermissible . . . state-sponsored indoctrination. . . ."

✔ The Court would no longer automatically worry that public-school teachers "would be tempted to inculcate [instill or promote] religion" when on religious school grounds. This new stance makes "pervasive" monitoring, beyond monthly unannounced visits from public-school supervisors, unnecessary and avoids "excessive entanglement."

The Court also employed a looser attitude in *Mitchell v. Helms,* 530 U.S. 793 (2000). In allowing state education agencies to lend computers, software, and library books to private schools (including private religious schools), the *Helms* Court downplayed a concern looming large in previous cases — that in-kind forms of aid could be diverted to religious uses.

Four — but not yet the critical five — of the current justices are ready to abandon the distinction between indirect and direct aid altogether. Writing for three colleagues in *Helms,* Justice Thomas found the distinction "arbi-trary." Thomas argued that as long as direct aid is neutral and broadly avail-able, the government should not be "thought responsible for any particular indoctrination" a religious recipient engages in. If another justice were to join this plurality, the picture would become clearer, and all aid to religious edu-cation would play by the *Zelman* rules of neutrality and breadth. The distinc-tion between "true private choice" programs and direct aid would become irrelevant.

The strange staying power of the *Lemon* test in the lower courts

The Court has moved away from the three-prong *Lemon* test in the context of govern-ment funding for religious schools. For several decades, the Court has also attempted to down-play *Lemon* as a useful tool for defining the limits of government's symbolic association with religion. (That's why you don't find *Lemon* included in the later section "The varying approaches and shifting coalitions," in which we discuss how the Court defines acceptable government/religion interaction.)

The story of "*Lemon* dissed" at the Supreme Court has several stages. At times, the Court has decided cases without mentioning *Lemon*. At times, it has expressed doubts about the util-ity of *Lemon*. (For example, in his plurality opin-ion in *Van Orden,* Chief Justice Rehnquist wrote: "Whatever may be the fate of the *Lemon* test in the larger scheme of Establishment Clause jurisprudence, we think it not useful in dealing with the sort of passive monument that Texas

has erected.") At other times, individual justices have called for *Lemon* to be overturned. (In a concurring opinion, Justice Scalia once color-fully referred to *Lemon* as akin to "a ghoul in a late-night horror movie that repeatedly sits up in its grave and shuffles abroad, after being repeatedly killed and buried" (*Lamb's Chapel v. Center Moriches Union Free School District,* 508 U.S. 384 [1993]). But *Lemon* has survived all the Supreme Court slights and attacks.

More important as a practical matter is that because lower federal courts are often the last stop for many constitutional cases, they often use *Lemon*'s three-element approach as the main template (or at least one of several alternative approaches) for decision. Perhaps its appeal is the apparent sense of order and certainty its 1-2-3-step process provides. In any event, *Lemon* remains significant for anyone wanting to understand how the establishment clause is really interpreted in court.

Confronting a lack of consensus on symbolic association with religion

The third major strand of establishment-clause restriction developed out of the presence of religious slogans or symbols on government property (such as public parkways and building entrances) and other symbols of government authority (such as dollar bills bearing the phrase "In God We Trust"). The best way to explain this subject, and the series of rulings and analytical tests relevant to it, is to first catalogue a few case results and then explain the various theories the Court used to get there.

"Monumental" mistakes versus allowable inclusions

Under different theories elaborated in the next subsection, governments may not

- Display a crèche (portraying Christ's birth) by itself in the hallway of a city building during the Christmas season (*County of Allegheny v. American Civil Liberties Union,* 492 U.S. 573 [1989]).

- Display the Ten Commandments by themselves or in the company of secular historical documents whose religious content is emphasized (for example, Thomas Jefferson's reference in the Declaration of Independence that all men are "endowed by their Creator" with rights) (*McCreary County v. American Civil Liberties Union,* 545 U.S. 844 [2005]).

Under the same varied theories, however, governments may

- Include a crèche in a broader city-sponsored park display including Santa Claus, giant candy canes, and other secular Christmas symbols (*Lynch v. Donnelly,* 465 U.S. 688 [1984]).

- Include a menorah symbolizing the Jewish festival of Hanukkah as part of a display outside a government office building that included a Christmas tree and a salute to religious and cultural diversity (the companion case in *County of Allegheny*).

- Include a monument containing the Ten Commandments among 16 other secular monuments on the grounds outside the Texas Capitol building (*Van Orden v. Perry,* 545 U.S. 677 [2005]).

The varying approaches and shifting coalitions

No one unifying theory produced the results in the preceding section. With the present Supreme Court personnel, their varying interpretations of what the establishment clause means in symbolic-association cases mean that no single theory is likely to produce a majority in the next case, either.

In order of importance, the results in this area have been produced by a combination of the following approaches:

✔ **The endorsement test:** This more focused version of the second prong of *Lemon* (primary effect) was first floated in Justice O'Connor's concurring opinion in *Lynch* (the crèche-in-the-public-park case).

The endorsement test focuses on whether the religion's symbolic association with government "sends a message to non-adherents that they are outsiders . . . , and an accompanying message to adherents that they are insiders, favored members of the political community." The relevant focus is the interpretation of facts made by a hypothetical "reasonable observer" who is "aware of the history and context of the community" and the "general history" of the place the religious symbol is displayed.

Different application of the endorsement test led to the conflicting results in *Allegheny*. The reasonable observer confronting only a crèche symbolizing God taking human form through the Christ child would perceive a government statement that Christianity is the favored "insider" religion. That same observer would read the Hanukkah menorah in light of the overall display, which included other nonreligious symbols sending "a message of pluralism and freedom to choose one's own beliefs."

✔ **The purpose test:** The justices have also enlisted the first prong of *Lemon* (secular purpose) to make symbolic-establishment decisions.

The *McCreary County* majority faced three distinct displays of the Ten Commandments in the county courthouse. The majority found that the first display, which showed the Ten Commandments accompanied by a resolution extolling their religious significance, had only a religion-promoting purpose and not a secular purpose. (As noted in the earlier section "Forbidden practices in schools," this same reasoning was used by the Court in *Stone v. Graham* to invalidate the display of the Ten Commandments in public schools.)

To the *McCreary County* majority, a second post-lawsuit display modified the first display in a way that *aggravated* the County's religious purpose. This second display included various documents important to America's founding, but highlighted the *religious content* of these documents. (As noted in "'Monumental' mistakes versus allowable inclusions," one of these religion highlights was the "endowed by their Creator" phrase in the Declaration of Independence.)

Unholy alliances on holy matters

The Court often achieves establishment-clause decisions by putting together a coalition of divergent viewpoints. Nowhere is this more evident than in cases involving government's association with religious symbols.

In *Lynch v. Donnelly,* 465 U.S. 688 (1984), the very first modern case of this sort, the Court validated a Nativity scene erected by the City, on property owned by a nonprofit organization, in Pawtucket, Rhode Island. Four justices emphasized the presence of a secular purpose in commemorating the holiday season, whereas the fifth justice making the majority (Justice O'Connor) emphasized that the reasonable observer would not read a message of endorsement into the presence of a crèche alongside many secular seasonal symbols.

The "unholy alliance" phenomenon can be found in *Van Orden v. Perry,* 545 U.S. 677 (2005), where the Court found a Ten Commandments monument, given to the state by a national civic organization and displayed by the state at the Capitol, did not violate the establishment clause. Eight justices were equally divided.

Four accommodationist justices wanted to uphold the Capitol monument, which they saw as nonpreferentially standing for historically important Judeo-Christian (and perhaps Islamic) traditions. Four justices believing in a strong separation of church and state objected to the "pervasively religious" nature of the Ten Commandments and found a clear message of religious endorsement. It took Justice Breyer to make the majority upholding the monument.

Significantly, Breyer thought that the case was a much closer "borderline" case than the four accommodationists. Breyer took them to task for too easily accepting the Ten Commandments monument as a neutral, ceremonial recognition of religion. Charting a very different course under the endorsement test, Breyer relied on such factors as the significant "secular" content of the Ten Commandments (as a contributor to the American legal system), the fact that the monument had been on Capitol grounds for 40 years without triggering any objection, and the "divisiveness" that would have come from ordering the monument's removal.

The County ultimately displayed a third version of the Ten Commandments that associated them with various documents of historical importance; this time the County emphasized their nonreligious (secular) aspects. Viewed newly, this third display might have passed both the secular-purpose test (because it showed the contributions of the Ten Commandments to the development of American law) and the endorsement test (because the religious parts of the Ten Commandments — principally the first five strictures about how humans should interact with God — would be neutralized in the overall secular context). But the *McCreary County* majority held that, under the circumstances, the County's third display was not sufficiently dissociated from the illegal religious purpose of the previous displays. The invalid purpose continued throughout, and made the third display unconstitutional.

✔ **The accommodationist/nonpreferentialist test:** This view is now in vogue with four members of the current Court. The accommodationist view sees past establishment-clause cases as permitting government to recognize "the strong role played by religion and religious traditions in our Nation's history," as Chief Justice Rehnquist put it in his plurality opinion upholding the Ten Commandments monument on the Texas Capitol grounds in *Van Orden v. Perry.* As long as government doesn't prefer one religion over another or coerce people to believe in and practice any religion, accommodationist justices think that government should have a relatively free hand in ceremonial and other acknowledgments (such as the "In God We Trust" motto on American money) of religion's historical importance.

Chapter 13

Getting Involved: Voting and Becoming or Supporting a Candidate

. . . .

In This Chapter

▶ Making sure that districts, voters, and votes are treated fairly

▶ Giving candidates and parties equal opportunities to get on the ballot

▶ Protecting (but regulating) campaign donations as free speech

. . . .

Constitutional democracy in the United States depends on active citizen involvement in electoral politics. Unsurprisingly, therefore, constitutional law contains specialized legal rules to protect political activities ranging from voting to becoming or supporting a party or candidate.

This chapter pulls together several lines of judicial authority applying standard equal-protection and free-speech analysis in special ways to protect political rights. We discuss voting rights, summarizing the current rules that prevent manipulation of electoral districts, limit most restrictions on the right to vote, and remedy arbitrary miscounting of votes. We also summarize constitutional doctrines protecting the rights of candidates and political parties to get on the ballot.

We then note how the Court applies strict First-Amendment scrutiny to protect the rights of political candidates and their supporters to spend money to advance their electoral prospects. By contrast, the Court generally upholds limitations on direct campaign contributions, disclosure requirements, and voluntary systems of public funding for candidates for certain races. These campaign-finance cases provide an important (though sometimes complicated) backdrop to efforts to promote meaningful deliberations about candidates and issues.

Promoting Equality in Voting Districts, Voting, and Vote Counting

The equal-protection guarantees of the Fifth and Fourteenth Amendments work in three main ways to protect voting rights:

- ✔ By preventing electoral boundaries from being manipulated numerically, based on the racial composition of potential voters or (in especially extreme cases) the partisan makeup of voting blocs

- ✔ By invalidating any governmental restrictions on the fundamental right to vote that can't withstand strict scrutiny

- ✔ By rejecting (to an admittedly uncertain degree) unfair distinctions among voters during vote counting

This section examines each of these protections in turn.

Preventing manipulation of voter districts

The landmark case of *Reynolds v. Sims,* 377 U.S. 533 (1964), recognized the important link between fairly drawn voting districts and the right of voters to influence electoral outcomes in proportion to their voting power. *Reynolds* held that the failure to redraw state legislative-district boundaries despite decades of population growth in urban areas — resulting in a rural minority electing a majority of state legislators and ensuring their lock on state power — unconstitutionally violated equal-protection guarantees. The *Reynolds* decision stated that dilution of urban votes denied "equal participation by all voters in the election of state legislators." The majority wrote, "in a society ostensibly grounded on representative government, ... a majority of the people of a state [should] elect a majority of that State's legislators."

Reynolds and the cases it inspired have led to constitutional protections of three different kinds. In this section, we cover court decisions on how voting-district lines can and cannot take the quantity, race, and political party of voters into account.

Considering the number of voters in each district

The *Reynolds* Court took on the task of deciding what kind of equality the equal-protection guarantees require in order to make voting districts constitutional. States divided into equal areas? Equal representation for each major city? Equal representation for each major industry or interest? *Reynolds* held that each district within a government jurisdiction must be "compact and contiguous" and must as far as "practicable" have an equal numbers of voters.

Although the *Reynolds* ruling generally requires that districts be numerically equal under the famous "one man, one vote" standard, the *Reynolds* majority recognized that other "legitimate considerations" may make giving each legislative district the exact same number of residents impossible. For example, the Court stated that district line drawers could deviate from strict numerical equality to ensure that cities and other "political subdivisions" were represented in the legislature. Still, at the end of the line-drawing, numerical equality had to be the primary consideration.

In addition to their authority to draw *state* legislative districts, under the Constitution, state legislatures draw districts for members of the House of Representatives every ten years based on new census data. The grant of state authority to draw congressional districts is consistent with the Constitution's more general authority to states to set the initial conditions for holding national elections for senators, representatives, and the president.

Consistent with the federal government's greater interest in and authority over the national legislature, the Court has been very strict about numerical disparities among the *congressional* districts drawn by states. For example, in *Karcher v. Daggett,* 462 U.S. 725 (1983), the Court invalidated a New Jersey plan for drawing congressional districts in which the total variance of population among districts was less than 1 percent. By contrast, deference to the judgments of state officials appears to be behind the Court's greater tolerance for disparities among *state* legislative districts. For example, in *Mahan v. Howell,* 410 U.S. 319 (1973), the Court upheld a maximum population difference of 16.4 percent between the most populous and the least populous districts in the map drawn by Virginia officials. The Court found this much greater variance justified by the state's consistently following the boundaries set by local governments.

Drawing racial lines

Use of race as the "predominant factor" in drawing electoral districts is only allowed if districting lines are narrowly drawn to serve a compelling interest. Chapter 10 explains how the modern Court uses such "strict scrutiny" to determine whether governments can draw racial lines — whether they hurt or help minorities. In similar fashion, various Court decisions invalidate race-based legislative redistricting unless it meets strict scrutiny.

In *Gomillion v. Lightfoot,* 364 U.S. 339 (1960), the Court struck down redrawn voting boundaries that changed the city limits of Tuskegee, Alabama, from a square to an "uncouth 28-sided figure." The new boundaries, adopted after previous laws overtly barring blacks from voting became invalid, effectively moved all but a few minority voters out of the city, completely disenfranchising them.

More recently, states have used race-conscious congressional districting to *enhance* minority voting power. As with other uses of race for affirmative action, the Court has strictly scrutinized government's well-meaning efforts. Several difficult-to-reconcile cases have established the rule that race can only be the main factor of line drawing if the government's interests are compelling. However, the cases leave a number of basic questions unresolved.

A bare majority of justices in *Bush v. Vera,* 517 U.S. 952 (1996), invalidated Texas's deliberate creation of three congressional districts in which voters from racial minority groups would have majority voting power. None of the several opinions commanded a majority, however. This left two matters up in the air: whether Texas had a compelling interest in complying with federal Voting Rights Act prohibitions, and what it takes to meet the requirement that a minority-protecting districting plan be narrowly drawn. Nor has the Court clearly decided whether strict scrutiny even applies when district creators use race as just one of a number of traditional line-drawing considerations.

Following party lines

Political gerrymandering — that is, manipulation of voting districts to assure a statewide advantage for one political party or faction — is tolerated unless it continuously reduces the other party's or faction's "influence on the political process as a whole." But judging from the fact that the Court has never found a political gerrymander to violate this limit (as we discuss immediately below), the reach and relevance of this rule remain unclear.

For the 25-plus years since *Davis v. Bandemer,* 478 U.S. 109 (1986), the Court has insisted that courts would strike down any voting-district manipulation if "the electoral system is arranged in a manner that will consistently degrade" the influence of voters of a certain party or faction. The Court reasserted this rule in 2004, in *Vieth v. Jubiler,* 541 U.S. 267.

The problem with taking this anti-political-gerrymandering stance too seriously is that, so far, the Court has never found that any challenged districting plan violated equal protection. And at least one modern case appeared to many observers to be ripe for invalidation. In *League of United Latin American Citizens v. Perry,* 548 U.S. 399 (2006), the Court rejected a challenge that political gerrymandering in a redistricting plan drawn by the 2003 Texas legislature was unconstitutional. Despite evidence that the Republican-party-dominated redistricting was payback for a prior pro-Democratic-party districting scheme and seemed designed to assure continued Republican dominance, the Court found the evidence insufficient. Critics say that if these and similar examples of political gerrymandering are not beyond the pale, few if any will likely be.

<hr>

Four-and-a-half votes to overrule *Davis*

The *Davis* political-gerrymandering limit (stating that courts will strike down districting plans that consistently degrade the voting rights of a given political party) appears so toothless that four justices in *Vieth* sought to overrule it officially. Speaking for himself and three colleagues, Justice Scalia's *Vieth* opinion noted that the justices have never been able to settle on any one standard for determining when political manipulation violated the equal-protection clause. (Scalia noted how justices used two different definitions in *Davis* and three in the *Vieth* case itself.)

This uncertainty, plus the fact that "essentially pointless litigation" had never overturned any politically manipulative districting plan, led Scalia and his three colleagues to conclude that the *Davis* limit was "incapable of principled adjudication." *Davis* is still theoretically on the books only because Justice Kennedy, also highly skeptical of the *Davis* limit, was unwilling to "foreclose all possibility of judicial relief."

<hr>

Protecting fundamental rights to vote

By its express terms, the Constitution doesn't offer a broad protection to voting rights *generally*. As part of abolishing slavery and providing equal rights for racial minorities, the Fifteenth Amendment, adopted in 1868, prohibits discrimination in voting "based on race, color, or previous condition of servitude." And as we note in Chapter 1, other provisions grant special voting-rights protections, including the Nineteenth Amendment (1920), which gave women the right to vote in national elections, and the Twenty-Sixth Amendment (1971), which gave voting rights to young adults age 18 to 21.

In 1966, the Court found that the Constitution's equal-protection guarantees protect a general *implied* right to vote in state and federal elections. As the Court in *Harper v. Virginia State Board of Education,* 383 U.S. 663 (1966), explained, "once the [right to vote] is granted to the electorate, lines may not be drawn which are inconsistent with the Equal Protection Clause." Three years later, the Court in *Kramer v. Union Free School District,* 395 U.S. 621 (1969), held that restrictions on the fundamental right to vote are unconstitutional if they aren't "necessary to promote a compelling state interest" and therefore don't meet strict scrutiny.

Kramer shows how restrictions on voting rights can flunk strict scrutiny. Some New York school districts only allowed property owners or residents with school-age children to vote in school-board elections. Governmental authorities argued that this limitation on the voting base was necessary to ensure that decisions about educational policy and taxes to support education were made by citizens who were "primarily interested" or "primarily affected." The Court rejected this argument, stating that New York voting-rights restrictions didn't "accomplish this purpose with sufficient precision" to justify denying the right to vote to the challenger, a bachelor who didn't own property or have school-age children. Under standard strict-scrutiny analysis, the law was overinclusive to the extent it allowed voters no more interested than the challenger to vote and underinclusive by excluding some highly knowledgeable and committed voters.

Post-*Kramer* cases yield relatively clear (if seemingly arbitrary) dividing lines between constitutional and unconstitutional voting-rights restrictions. In the following sections we explain some useful contrasting examples.

Property-ownership limits in general and special elections

States may generally *not* limit elections to property owners, even when property-owning taxpayers will bear the major financial burden if the electoral proposals are adopted. Thus, in *Phoenix v. Kolodziejski,* 399 U.S. 204 (1970), a six-justice majority rejected an Arizona law limiting the right to vote on "general obligation bonds" to property owners. The Court saw the fact that property owners would mainly foot the bill for repaying the bonds as "not sufficiently substantial to justify" excluding non–property owners. After all, reasoned the majority, these non–property owners had a direct interest in the services and policies that would be financed by the bonds.

On the other hand, for "special-purpose government districts" the Court upheld a scheme giving the right to vote exclusively to property owners (in *Salyer Land Company v. Tulare Lake Basin Water Storage District,* 410 U.S. 719 [1973]). In *Ball v. James,* 451 U.S. 355 (1981), the Court also okayed giving greater voting power to landowners based on the acreage of their holdings — even though the water-reclamation district holding the election served the electric-power needs of several hundred thousand residents, many of whom didn't own property and therefore couldn't vote.

Preregistration requirements for primary elections

Courts allow states to require voters to register at least 30 days before a general election (that is, the election at which candidates from different parties vie and an officeholder is selected) in order to vote in the next primary election (the election at which a party's nominees are chosen). The Court in *Rosario v. Rockefeller,* 410 U.S. 752 (1973), found that restriction a constitutionally valid means of preventing *party raiding,* the process "whereby voters in sympathy with one party designate themselves as voters of another party" to try to choose a candidate for the other party who will be easier to beat. The *Rosario* majority found this interest sufficiently important, even though the law could impose a voting restriction as long as 11 months.

Equal protection and voter-challenge laws

Recent years have seen a rise in state laws requiring voters to produce picture IDs, empowering party representatives to challenge voter registrations on election day, and the like. Depending on the observer's point of view, these laws either prevent fraud and promote confidence in American elections or seek to advance the Republican party's agenda by discouraging voting by poor or immigrant voters who usually vote Democratic.

In 2008, the Supreme Court encouraged at least some voter-challenge laws by upholding, against an equal-protection challenge, a controversial Indiana law requiring voters to produce a driver's license or other official identification card when voting. Rejecting arguments that the law unconstitutionally discriminated against the state's poor, minority, and especially homeless voters, the lead opinion found the ID-requirement was not "a significant increase over the usual burdens of voting" and that Indiana's interest in preventing vote fraud won out.

Only several months after *Rosario,* however, the Court in *Kusper v. Pontikes,* 410 U.S. 752 (1973), invalidated a longer restriction, which could have locked voters out of primary voting for up to 23 months.

Limits on voting by new residents

Restricting voting rights of new residents is also apparently a matter of timing. A state may not use "crude" presumptions against voters newly arrived in the state. Despite the state's interest in preventing fraud and ensuring knowledgeable voting, the Court in *Dunn v. Blumstein,* 405 U.S. 330 (1972), struck down a law preventing new residents from voting until they had lived one year in the state and three months in the relevant county.

By contrast, two cases decided the same day, *Marston v. Lewis,* 410 U.S. 679 (1973), and *Burns v. Forston,* 410 U.S. 686 (1973), upheld requirements that new residents live in the state for at least 50 days. The Court saw these as necessary to serve the important interest of ensuring voter-list accuracy.

Preventing arbitrary vote counting

All but the youngest of our readers probably remember *Bush v. Gore,* 531 U.S. 98 (2000), a momentous decision in which a 5–4 majority stopped the Florida vote recount and made George W. Bush the 43rd president.

The presidential election of 2000 was so close that whoever won Florida's electoral votes would also win a majority of electoral votes — and therefore the presidency. Given the closeness of Florida vote margins and allegations of irregularities in ballot construction and voting-machine performance, candidate Gore sued in the Florida courts. Several stages of state judicial rulings resulted in a partial vote recount of *undervotes* (ballots on which no vote was registered during an initial voting-machine count). After failing to convince Florida courts that the recount was illegitimate, Bush brought federal-law challenges in the federal courts.

Bush v. Gore is one of the most controversial decisions in modern times. Average Americans tend to approve or disapprove of the Court's decision based on who they wanted to win the presidential election. Legal scholars fall victim to this too, but some admirably note that, regardless of its political result, *Bush* raises serious questions about whether the federal courts should have gotten involved in such a classically and controversially political matter.

As a voting-rights case, *Bush* holds (with uncertain reach) that equal protection stops governmental authorities from counting different votes in an arbitrary manner. Seven *Bush* justices had substantial concerns about the fairness of the recount. As the five-justice majority opinion saw it, the recount was proceeding "in the absence of specific standards to ensure equal application" and with "varying standards" at work within a county and between counties. The recount therefore didn't "satisfy the minimum requirement for non-arbitrary treatment of voters necessary to secure the fundamental right" to vote. (In separate opinions, Justices Souter and Breyer sounded similar concerns.)

Whether *Bush* is only a "one off" decision affecting a unique set of facts remains to be seen. The majority noted that its decision was "limited to the present circumstances, for the problem of equal protection in election processes generally presents many complexities." The majority emphasized that it was not addressing "whether local entities, in the exercise of their expertise, may develop different systems for implementing elections."

But as you know by now, a narrow decision today can be expanded tomorrow — or at least litigants can try to expand it. For example, until the entire Ninth Circuit court overruled them, a three-judge panel of appellate justices thought the *Bush* precedent gave them authority to postpone California elections in 2003. The appellate trio saw the prospect that antiquated voting machines would result in a higher error rate as "present[ing] almost precisely the same issue as the Court considered in *Bush*." (The three-judge opinion in *Southwest Voter Registration Education Project v. Shelley* is reported at 344 F.3d 882 [2003]). The *en banc* court's reversal is reported at 344 F.3d 914 [2003].)

Questioning the Court's willingness to decide "the mother of all political questions"

The Court has crafted a *political question* doctrine (see Chapter 6) to keep the relatively apolitical federal courts from inappropriately wandering into controversial political matters. By many measures, having the federal courts directly meddle in the election of the highest-ranking political official in America would seem to qualify as inappropriate. *Bush v. Gore* certainly threatened the Court's appearance of being "above politics," and many observers think the Court should have tread cautiously, carefully considering the political-question implications before proceeding.

Yet only one justice in *Bush* (Justice Breyer) seriously discussed the validity of federal judicial intervention. The other eight justices disagreed mightily on how constitutional and statutory provisions applied to the Florida recount, whether it was fixable by follow-up Florida judicial remedies or needed to be stopped at once, and whether the federal courts should have been more *deferential* to state courts. But those eight justices failed to address, much less decide, whether the federal courts should have *even gotten involved* in the controversy. Other than a few general disclaimers of any desire to become president-makers, the *Bush* justices generally acted as though the appropriateness of federal-court involvement was clear.

As much as this debate concerns people who take judicial restraint seriously, in one sense the Court's blasé attitude is understandable. After all, in the leading political-question case of *Baker v. Carr*, 369 U.S. 186 (1962), the Court held that challenges to urban/rural mal-apportionment based on equal protection were not off limits. That ruling paved the way for *Reynolds v. Sims* and its "one man, one vote" rule. Giving equal-protection challenges a green light in the context of districting may have blinded the justices to the serious political-question implications of *Bush*.

But the Supreme Court didn't step into the *Southwest Voter Registration* controversy, and the Court has steadfastly avoided reviewing other recent lower-court opinions invoking *Bush v. Gore*. So the reach of *Bush*-style protections when vote-count irregularities are alleged remains unclear. In every election cycle, the prospect of lawsuits inspired by *Bush v. Gore* looms.

Protecting Ballot Access for Candidates and Parties

In addition to protecting the right to vote, modern equal-protection decisions recognize a fundamental right to run for office. (After all, what good is the right to vote if there aren't candidates the voter wants to vote *for?*) Here too the cases draw relatively clear (and at times seemingly random) lines. In this section we discuss third parties (parties other than the Republican or Democratic parties), independent candidates (candidates affiliated with no party at all), and incumbents (officeholders running for reelection).

Requiring petitions for "minor" parties

States may grant automatic ballot access to candidates from major parties (that is, parties achieving some minimum percentage of votes in a prior election — typically Republicans and Democrats). Meanwhile, states may require new or minor parties to show political support through signatures on voter petitions. But the signature requirements can't be set so high as to make it "virtually impossible for a new political party [to] be placed on [an upcoming] ballot." The quoted language is from *Williams v. Rhodes,* 383 U.S. 23 (1968), which struck down a requirement that minor parties file petitions nine months before a presidential election, signed by a number of voters equal to 15 percent of the vote count in the last gubernatorial election.

By contrast, the Court upheld a requirement for petitions to be signed by 5 percent of voters five months before the election in *Jeness v. Forston,* 403 U.S. 431 (1971). Several other cases also uphold petition requirements less daunting than *Williams.*

Restricting independent candidates

In *Storer v. Brown,* 415 U.S. 724 (1974), the Court upheld a ballot-access restriction stopping any candidate from running independently of a political party if he or she had been a registered party member within the last six months. Six justices saw the law as validly protecting the electoral process by preventing candidates losing in their primaries from suddenly turning independent out of "short-range political goals, pique, or personal quarrel."

Nine years later, however, the Court rejected (on free-speech grounds heavily influenced by equal-protection cases) a state law requiring independent candidates to file nominating petitions almost eight months before the election. The majority in *Anderson v. Celebrezze,* 460 U.S. 780 (1983), concluded that the state's asserted interests in "voter education, equal treatment for partisan and independent candidates, and political stability" failed to justify such a major limitation on independent runs.

Preventing current officeholders from running for election and reelection

A bare majority in *Clements v. Fashing,* 457 U.S. 957 (1982), upheld provisions in the Texas Constitution preventing current state officials from running for the state legislature or for other state or federal office until they completed their current terms. By contrast, in *U.S. Term Limits v. Thornton,* 514 U.S. 779 (1995), a different bare majority rejected a state law denying a place on the ballot for members of Congress seeking reelection after having served three terms in the House or two terms in the Senate.

Equating Campaign Spending with Political Speech

The free-speech rights of Americans allow them to pursue political agendas by advocating for candidates and issues. In *Buckley v. Valeo,* 424 U.S. 1 (1976), the Court held that these rights included substantial rights to spend money to support candidates and issues. Equating the right to spend with the right to speak, the *Buckley* Court famously stated that "[a] restriction on the amount of money a person or group can spend on political communication during a campaign necessarily reduces the quantity of expression by restricting the number of issues discussed, the depth of their exploration, and the size of the audience reached."

Because campaign-finance limitations restrict protected political speech on the basis of its content, *Buckley* invoked strict scrutiny.

It would take an entire chapter (and maybe a separate book!) to do full justice to the twists and turns in the modern campaign-spending case decisions spawned by *Buckley.* Still, the following sections give you the basic outlines of the post-*Buckley* constitutional world.

Paying for their own campaign

Buckley held that candidates have an unlimited right to spend as much money as they want to pursue their own campaign victories. (That's why so many independently wealthy candidates run these days!) As the main

Court opinion stated, "The candidate, no less than any other person, has a First Amendment right to engage in the discussion of public issues and [to] advocate his own election." *Buckley* and post-*Buckley* cases generally reject any governmental effort to "equalize[e] the relative financial resources of candidates competing for public office" by limiting a candidate's own spending levels. (In fact, as we explore later, the Court recently rejected Arizona efforts to work the other side of the equation by favoring less-well-heeled candidates.)

Funding independent campaign messages

The logic equating free speech with free spending applies to noncandidates as well. Individuals and political-action committees (registered organizations that advance candidates, parties, or causes, often called *PACs*) — and, now, corporations and labor unions — have a right to spend as much as they want on efforts not coordinated with an official campaign. The First Amendment fully protects attempts to influence voters to elect or defeat certain candidates or adopt or reject certain policy initiatives. (We leave the details of how to make sure outsider electioneering is truly "independent," and how far the Constitution lets governments go to assure it, out of this discussion.)

Recognizing corporations' rights to free speech: The *Citizens United* bombshell

Citizens United has been heavily criticized as thinly disguised judicial activism perpetrated by conservative justices. Justice Stevens's objections, lodged in a very lengthy dissent, are typical of critics. He claimed that the majority inappropriately expanded the issues of the case, and he wrote, "Essentially, five Justices were unhappy with the limited nature of the case before us, so they changed the case to give themselves an opportunity to change the law." He felt the case would have been more appropriately reviewed on much narrower grounds.

Citizens United has been heavily criticized on its merits as well. Detractors on and off the Court have argued that, as fictional entities holding money to benefit others, corporations and labor unions do not have the same free-speech rights as natural persons. It may be especially ironic, in fact, that the largely "originalist" justices in the *Citizens United* majority (that is, justices especially interested in achieving the original intent of the Constitution's framers) would create strong protection for corporate entities either unknown or distrusted by the framers — and which in this day and age can have strong multinational loyalties and interests outside of the United States.

Of course, the most problematic aspect of *Citizens United* is the idea that corporate money will flood the electoral process, drowning out anyone trying to limit or regulate corporations. Whether the electoral sky has truly fallen remains to be seen.

Cases draw a generally broad swath of protection for truly independent speech while giving government some room to ferret out advertisements and other electioneering activities that are in reality coordinated with an official campaign. One of these cases (and also one of the most heavily criticized Supreme Court decisions in recent memory) is *Citizens United v. Federal Election Commission,* 130 S.Ct. 876 (2010). *Citizens United* overruled a 1990 decision and held that corporations and labor unions have the same right as individuals to spend unlimited funds from their general funds on independent campaign advocacy. These newly freed-up entities can either fund their own campaign messages or pool their resources with like-minded entities and work through special political-action committees (dubbed "Super PACs").

Limiting direct contribution to campaigns

Governments may limit the amounts of money individuals, associations, corporations, and labor unions can donate directly to political campaigns — if the limitations are themselves limited. Government's restrictions can't be "so radical in effect as to render political association ineffective, drive the sound of a candidate's voice below the level of notice, and render contributions pointless." The quoted language is from *Nixon v. Shrink Missouri Government PAC,* 528 U.S. 377 (2000), which upheld contribution limits ranging from $1,075 for candidates to statewide office and $275 for candidates for the state legislature or offices representing small jurisdictions.

Nixon specifically reaffirmed *Buckley,* which earlier upheld the $1,000-per-candidate-per-contributor limits in the Federal Election Campaign Act of 1971 against an argument that they too severely limited candidate fundraising. The *Buckley* Court reasoned that limiting an individual (or group) contribution is only a small restriction on that person's (or group's) free speech. And that diminished impact on free speech is justified by the need "to limit the actuality and appearance" that "large individual financial contributions" corrupt the political process by buying access and favorable action from grateful public officials. (Under the same logic, *Buckley* also upheld a $5,000 limit on contributions to political committees and a $25,000 limit on total political contributions by an individual during a single year.)

Coming down hard on "soft money"

Another part of constitutional restrictions on campaign donations involves *soft money,* or contributions made indirectly in an effort to avoid federal regulations. Governments may prevent evasion of valid contribution limitations by prohibiting soft-money contributions.

Congress regulated soft-money contributions in the Bipartisan Campaign Reform Act (BCRA) of 2002. Seeking to plug loopholes in the earlier 1971 campaign-finance legislation, Title I of BCRA put major restrictions on the ability of individuals and entities to contribute large sums to national, state, and local political parties. The parties would then spend it on voter-registration drives, efforts to get voters to the polls on election day, and campaign ads stopping just short of calling for the election or defeat of a particular named candidates. In *McConnell v. Federal Election Commission,* 540 U.S. 93 (2003), the Court applied a "less rigorous standard of review" to give "proper deference to Congress' ability to weigh competing constitutional interests in an area in which it enjoys particular expertise."

Bringing transparency through disclosure

As part of allowing governments to restrict campaign donations, Courts allow them to impose disclosure requirements. For example, requiring candidates to reveal where their financing comes from is designed to enforce valid prohibitions on contributions and otherwise equip voters to assess whether candidates and issue proponents are inappropriately beholden to large donors. Political-action committees and other organizations involved in independent expenditures also face extensive disclosure requirements. The *Buckley* majority saw disclosure as generally "deter[ing] actual corruption and avoid[ing] the appearance of corruption."

Allowing public candidate funding

Buckley also held that governments may provide public funding for candidates — and restrict spending levels for candidates accepting public funds — as long as funding is offered equally to all qualified candidates and they can decline it. Public funding intends to free candidates of the need to raise extensive private donations so that candidates will be less dependent on "special interests." Public funding can also, in theory, induce candidates to voluntary agree to limit their overall campaign expenditures, dampening the ever-skyrocketing costs of elections in America. (Whether this is even possible after *Citizens United,* summarized in "Funding independent campaign messages," is open to question.)

The *Buckley* majority saw provisions in federal law offering public funding to presidential candidates, provisions which have inspired some even more ambitious state programs of public funding for state offices, as an effort "not to abridge, restrict, or censor speech, but rather to use public money to facilitate public discussion and participation in the electoral process." The Court called such goals "vital to a self-governing people."

Other First-Amendment protections for candidates and parties

As Americans know only too well that political candidates speak . . . and speak . . . and speak. Thus, First-Amendment principles come into play in a special way when candidates speak orally or in written form to voters. For example, in *Republican Party of Minnesota v. White,* 563 U.S. 765 (2005), the Court struck down a clause in the Minnesota code of judicial conduct prohibiting candidates for elected judgeships from taking sides on disputed legal and political issues.

Recent decisions also protect the right of political parties to decide with whom they will exercise their First-Amendment right of association. Thus, in *California Democratic Party v. Jones,* 530 U.S. 567 (2000), a majority struck down a voter-initiated reform replacing the state's previous "closed primary" system (in which only a political party's members can vote in primary elections listing only that party's candidates) with a "blanket primary." In this system, every candidate appears on the primary ballot regardless of party affiliation and voters choose freely among them. The *Jones* majority held that the "blanket primary" unconstitutionally interfered with a political party's right *not to associate* with voters not aligned with the party's views and goals. As the majority put it, "In no area is the political association's right to exclude more important than in the process of selecting its nominee" to run in the general election.

It isn't that states can't regulate primaries at all without violating the Constitution. As the *Jones* Court noted, past cases let states require parties to select candidates through primaries rather than by party activists and candidates appearing on primary ballots to have minimal support.

In a very recent decision, however, the Court struck down a feature in Arizona's public-funding system. Arizona offers public funds to candidates for seven statewide executive offices and for state legislative seats, provided that they agree to limit overall campaign spending and participate in at least one public debate, all of which is constitutionally valid. However, another provision in Arizona's system increased the amount of funding for publicly supported candidates when their privately and independently funded opponents spent more. The Arizona plan matched additional contributions dollar for dollar in an attempt to continue to keep public funding attractive. Sensing both an unconstitutional indirect attempt to interfere with the absolute right of candidates to spend as they see fit and an illegitimate attempt by government to compensate for disparities in the financial resources of different candidates and parties, the majority in *Arizona Free Enterprise Club's Freedom Club PAC v. Bennett,* 131 S.Ct. 2806 (2011), declared the law in violation of the First Amendment.

Part V

Understanding Privacy Rights

The 5th Wave   By Rich Tennant

In this part . . .

Privacy rights under the Constitution involve both civil and criminal settings. In this part, we discuss substantive due process and how the courts analyze cases in various civil contexts. We also discuss the ever-important criminal protections under the Fourth and Fifth Amendments, exploring the prohibition against self-incrimination, the right to be free from unreasonable searches and seizures, and related rights.

Chapter 14

Implied Privacy Rights — Fundamental and Otherwise

....

....

A very important aspect of modern constitutional law is the strong but selective protection given to fundamental rights relating to privacy.

The theory that privacy is an inherent and important aspect of the liberty protected by due process of law has fueled modern case law strongly protecting rights relating to marriage and family, reproductive freedom, and the right to die. Yet the privacy-rights resurgence has passed by some less "traditional" rights also seemingly tied to privacy, such as the rights of homosexuals to enter legally recognized relationships and the rights of Americans to keep important information out of governmental databanks.

In this chapter we look at what's at stake for the Court and its justices in the current fundamental-rights approach. We explain how labeling a challenger's right as *fundamental* triggers strict scrutiny and usually invalidates the law; a label of *nonfundamental* instead triggers deferential rational-basis review and usually upholds the challenged law. Finally, we look in detail at various decisions and trends in key areas of fundamental-privacy case law.

(Note that this Chapter deals with privacy rights in the *civil* context; the next two chapters focus on privacy-based rights arising in the *criminal* arena.)

Understanding the Various Ways the Constitution Protects Privacy

In this section you see how the Constitution affords some express rights with significant privacy implications, as well as some implied rights via substantive due process. (*Substantive due process* in general is the concept that the government can't take away certain rights — including rights relating to "liberty" — without adequate justification. See Chapter 8 for more details.)

These express and implied rights form the foundation upon which modern constitutional law erects the strong but selective protections for privacy. Reviewing the constitutional landscape gives you a good foundation before becoming immersed in the details of modern privacy-rights analysis.

Going over the express privacy protections in the Constitution

The Bill of Rights applies directly to the federal government and indirectly to state and local governments through Fourteenth Amendment "incorporation." Through either avenue the Bill of Rights ends up protecting rights affecting privacy in both civil and criminal contexts. These rights include the following:

- ✔ **The right *not* to associate with unwanted individuals, as granted by the First Amendment:** In *Roberts v. Jaycees,* 468 U.S. 609 (1984), the Court recognized that the First Amendment's grant of a right to associate included the right *not* to associate. For a voluntary organization, this means not being forced "to accept members it does not desire."

- ✔ **The right of organizations involved in controversial speech and activities to keep their members' identities confidential from government examination (also granted by the First Amendment):** In *NAACP v. Alabama,* 357 U.S. 449 (1958), the Court allowed the civil-rights organization to ignore a state law and keep names and addresses of its Alabama members private. Noting the "vital relationship between freedom to associate and privacy in one's associations," the Court worried that fear of being outed to less tolerant peers might "induce members to withdraw" and "dissuade others from joining."

- ✔ **The right not to have troops forcibly "quartered" (housed and fed) in your home, as granted by the Third Amendment:** You didn't have the

Third Amendment on the tip of your frontal lobe? Not to worry — no court case has ever had to address this one.

✔ **The right against "unreasonable searches and seizures," as granted in the Fourth Amendment:** This protection is important and complicated enough to deserve its own chapter (Chapter 15). Here we just want to note that protecting homes, persons, and other spaces from prying government operatives is centrally about preserving privacy.

Although people mainly think of search-and-seizure guarantees in the setting of criminal investigations and trials, these guarantees also have important civil implications. As we explain in the next chapter, random drug testing or the search of workspaces, lockers, or communication devices of government employees can lead to public-school students being disciplined or public employees being fired or disciplined.

✔ **The right not to be forced to incriminate oneself, as granted in the Fifth Amendment:** As we explain in Chapter 16, this protection is centrally about the right to keep misdeeds secret from government (and, by extension, the public and the media).

Implying privacy rights as due-process liberties

Constitutional law protects privacy-based rights in a second, more indirect way. As you find out in Chapter 8, the due-process clauses of the Fifth and Fourteenth Amendments protect liberty (along with life and property) against arbitrary deprivation. Because privacy is one important aspect of liberty, due process ends up imposing on governments a baseline requirement to act "rationally" — that is, to further a legitimate interest in some way — whenever it limits any privacy-based right.

Specifically, any governmental law, policy, or practice depriving anyone of privacy — say, New York's law requiring doctors to release drug-prescription info to public-health officials — must be rationally related to a legitimate interest that may conceivably have motivated government. Thus, even as it declined to fully mark out the extent to which the right to privacy protected citizens against governmental data collection, the Court in *Whalen v. Roe,* 429 U.S. 589 (1977), upheld this disclosure law as rationally furthering the state's legitimate desire to control illegal drug distribution.

And as you see later in this chapter, substantive due process affords more-significant protection to other aspects of the right to privacy.

Appreciating What's at Stake in Fundamental-Rights Analysis

To fully understand all the twists and turns in privacy-rights decisions, you need some background. This section first shows you what's at stake practically in deciding whether privacy rights are fundamental. Then we explain why the substantive-due-process/fundamental-rights cases reflect a heightened concern for the dangers the issues pose for courts. Finally, we cover the importance of how an arguably fundamental right is phrased.

Getting practical: Why the "fundamental" label matters

Most of this discussion focuses on high fallutin' but important questions of constitutional interpretive theory and judicial legitimacy. But first we want to get very practical by underscoring how, in most cases, what's at stake in whether an asserted liberty right is found to be fundamental is *nothing less* than whether the challenger or the government will win the day.

Bottom line: If government must pass the strict scrutiny usually afforded to fundamental rights, it usually loses. If government only needs to meet the rationality baseline, it almost always wins.

Griswold v. Connecticut, 381 U.S. 479, the 1965 case kicking off the modern era of strongly protecting certain privacy rights under substantive due process, is a very good example of the practical importance of a right being treated as fundamental. At issue in *Griswold* was Connecticut's extreme version of moral laws of the period; the state's law forbade any person from using "any drug, medicinal article, or instrument for the purpose of preventing conception." The *Griswold* challengers asserted that, as applied to married couples, the law undermined privacy rights in violation of substantive-due-process restrictions.

Had the *Griswold* challengers not persuaded the Court that the privacy rights at issue deserved special protection, they would have lost. Applying the standard rational-basis scrutiny applicable to most social regulatory laws, the Court would have found that Connecticut's asserted interest in protecting marital fidelity was conceivably (you'll pardon the pun!) legitimate. And, giving Connecticut the deferential benefit of the doubt as to whether its law furthered its legitimate end, the Court would have likely found that the state could rationally think that making contraception unavailable created a threat of pregnancy, persuading at least some would-be marital cheaters not to give into their impulses. (Again, you have to put yourself back in the mind-set of a bygone era to fully understand this thinking.)

However, the *Griswold* Court broke ground by more highly valuing the right of married couples to access contraception. This upped the ante. Using what later courts would recognize as "strict scrutiny" for a "fundamental" right, the majority held that the law was too inexactly drawn to be constitutional. The law went too far by restricting the rights of married couples who wanted contraception to avoid or delay getting pregnant with each other, not have sex with someone else. (Plus, Connecticut already had laws against fornication by unmarried persons.) The law was woefully incomplete because it exempted condoms (referred to in the words of the day as "devices for the prevention of disease"). This created a huge loophole, undermining the law's effectiveness.

Seeing why substantive-due-process analysis seems especially risky

Modern courts — and their critics and defenders — worry that substantive-due-process analysis comes with special risks. The following discusses three principal dangers of using this right as the basis for strong privacy protection.

Fewer objective guideposts for decisions

Justices and commentators frequently suggest that expanding rights through substantive due process is a special problem because, as Chief Justice Rehnquist reiterated in an important right-to-die case, "guideposts for responsible decision making in this uncharted area are scarce and open-ended" (*Washington v. Glucksberg*, 521 U.S. 702 [1997]). A lack of objective guideposts can mean that the Court will be seen as making social policy decisions, which is a controversial thing for unelected judges to do!

The concern about unusual danger starts with uncertainties in the term *liberty* as a basis for strongly protecting privacy rights. The phrase has a broader potential scope than, say, the First-Amendment terms *freedom of speech* or *establishment of religion*. And the framers of these terms more likely had at least some core protective intentions in mind. As we note in Chapter 8, the overt focus of constitutional protections for due process is *procedural* protection (the procedures government must provide when impacting rights). It therefore takes some creative extension of the term *process* to find *substantive* rights protections. (Substantive due process probes whether government can even regulate a given area in the first place.)

Is substantive due process *really* different?

Some critics on and off the Court doubt that substantive due process raises "special dangers" of judicial policymaking and constitutional rootlessness compared to other constitutional rights. These critics argue that even the express constitutional text relating to freedom of speech, freedom of religion, equal protection, and so on is often very brief and general. Especially when the Court takes those brief and general terms beyond their clear meaning and the relatively clear vision of their framers, the enterprise is arguably quite like substantive due process.

For example, as we point out in Chapter 11, the constitutional command against "abridging the Freedom of Speech" is very general, and yet modern judicial doctrines have taken free-speech protections far beyond the limited focus of the First Amendment framers. Especially as the Court has developed rules to protect commercial advertisers, corporations making general campaign expenditures, and (for a time at least) nude dancers, critics argue that the First Amendment lacks guideposts for responsible decision making as much as the Constitution's due-process language. Such critics argue, therefore, that the more explicit constitutional provisions pose as much a risk that justices will read their policy preferences into law, as with substantive due process.

These differences lead to extra concern that, in the substantive-due-process arena, judges and others lack objective, external indicators for decision. As the Chief Justice wrote in *Glucksberg,* the Court "must . . . 'exercise the utmost care whenever we are asked to break new ground in this field,' lest the liberty protected by the Due Process Clause is subtly transformed into the policy preferences of the members of this Court." The fear is that judges will inject their own personal feelings about policy rather than apply external principles. As we discuss in Chapter 6, such judicial policymaking raises concerns about the separation of powers and judicial legitimacy.

Vague criteria for identifying fundamental privacy rights

The problem of a lack of guideposts when considering matters of privacy is compounded by the vague two-part test the modern Court uses to determine whether a liberty interest is fundamental or not.

Lifted from a 1937 case arising in the different context of defining when the Bill of Rights applies to the states, this *Palko* test — named after *Palko v. Connecticut,* 302 U.S. 319 — declares that a right is "fundamental" if it is

✔ "Deeply rooted in this Nation's history and tradition," and

✔ "Implicit in the concept of ordered liberty," such that "neither liberty nor justice would exist if [the right] were sacrificed."

Both parts of this definition are subjective. The first part's reference to history and tradition looks objective by suggesting consultation of musty history books, past statutes, and case decisions. But even these sources are subject to much interpretation and dispute. For example, Justice Blackmun's majority opinion in the landmark abortion-rights case, *Roe v. Wade,* 410 U.S. 113 (1973), noted that American law didn't make abortion illegal before and during the time frame when the Fourteenth Amendment drafters penned the due-process clause's protection of "liberty." Does this suggest a "tradition" of allowing women to choose abortion, in consultation with their doctors, free of governmental interference? (As we shall see, this is what *Roe* decided.) Or, does it suggest a tradition of no special protection for abortion rights — a tradition that democratic majorities are free to change? (This is how anti-abortion-rights justices have consistently seen the relevant "tradition.")

And, of course, the second part of the *Palko* test is even more subjective. A lively dispute has always bubbled in and outside the pages of Supreme Court opinions about what standards should be used for determining the essential prerequisites of liberty and justice.

A checkered history with due process and economic rights

A third reason for special judicial skittishness when handling substantive due process is how the doctrine badly burned the Court in the early decades of the 20th century. In those years, in reviewing routine business regulations challenged on the basis of substantive due process, the Court gave these regulations much harsher treatment than now seems appropriate. Even though the Court actually upheld the majority of federal, state, and local laws challenged as violations of the so-called "liberty of contract," the justices discredited themselves in modern eyes by interfering in high-profile cases with legislative efforts to protect workers, tenants, mortgagors, and consumers in a burgeoning era of economic expansion.

The poster case for judicial arrogance in economic substantive due process is *Lochner v. New York,* 198 U.S. 45 (1905). In *Lochner,* a divided Supreme Court struck down a law making it illegal for bakery workers to work more than 10 hours a day or 60 hours a week. (That a *law* was needed to stop such a practice seems crazy, but modern notions of fair labor standards have progressed beyond those dark days.)

To critics at the time and since, the majority erred by letting its policy view that workers are "able to assert their rights . . . without the protecting arm of the state" blind it to the reality that bakers had very little bargaining power and were in an especially dangerous profession.

Lochner has come to stand for an arrogant judiciary enacting its political opinions into constitutional law. As Justice Holmes's famous dissent put it,

> *[A] constitution is not intended to embody a particular economic theory, whether of paternalism and the organic relation of the citizen to the State or laissez faire. It is made for people of fundamentally different views, and the accident of our finding certain opinions natural and familiar or novel and even shocking ought not to conclude our judgment upon the question of whether statutes embodying them conflict with the Constitution.*

To this day, justices accused of substituting their policy preferences for those of elected officials are blamed for *Lochnerizing.* (In fact, one judge accusing another judge of this is the closest judges come to calling each other out for a fight!) The ghost of *Lochner* and similar economic-substantive-due-process cases haunts modern cases when litigants invite the justices to expand protections for a different liberty — privacy.

Highlighting the importance of how the right at issue is defined

Another important, related source of angst in substantive-due-process analysis is how specific to be in defining the privacy right at issue.

The battle over specifically versus more generally framing privacy rights almost always determines the practical outcome. A narrow definition usually pulls for the right being labeled *not fundamental,* resulting in a government win. Broader definitions are more likely to attain the coveted *fundamental* label, invoking strict scrutiny that the government usually loses.

The modern Court has written that the special dangers posed by substantive due process justify a "careful description," as Chief Justice Rehnquist put it in *Glucksberg,* of the liberty interest a challenger claims is fundamental. Unfortunately, that's where the agreement among the justices ends.

A vivid example of both the Court's disagreement about rights framing and the stakes involved is *Michael H. v. Gerald D.,* 491 U.S. 110 (1989). In this case, a closely divided Court elevated the rights of a child's father by marriage over the rights of her biological father. In *Michael H.,* the man who was very likely the biological father of a daughter from an adulterous affair asserted his parental rights against the girl's now-reconciled parents of record. This brought the biological father into direct conflict with a California family law conclusively presuming that the father of a child born within a marriage is the husband. The biological father argued that, by cutting off his paternity rights entirely, California's law deprived him of his "constitutionally protected liberty interest in his relationship" with his daughter.

As noted in the next section, *Michael H.* shows a badly split Court finding a paternal right *not* fundamental. Here, the point is that the Court couldn't agree on how to define the liberty right the father was asserting.

Justice Scalia argued in the lead opinion that the Court could avoid the iffiness of substantive-due-process analysis only by defining the right at "the most specific level at which a relevant tradition protecting, or denying protection to, the asserted right can be identified." This approach would mean defining the father's right as the right "of an adulterous natural father." But only one other justice endorsed Scalia's define-the-right-specifically theory; two others generally joining Scalia's opinion wrote a separate opinion specifically distancing themselves from his narrow-description principle. Three dissenting justices argued for a broader definition of the right asserted — the right of a parent to a relationship with his or her child.

Lest this debate seem like an arcane judicial food fight over verbal formulations (but of course, much of law is exactly that!), notice the critical practical significance of this definitional wrangling:

 ✔ If the question is whether our history and traditions have deeply and consistently valued rights of adulterous fathers from episodic affairs, the answer is an emphatic no. The right is not fundamental. California wins.

 ✔ If the question is whether protection for parental rights *in general* is "deeply rooted" in American history and tradition and whether "liberty and justice would exist" in a society where government breaks the parent/child bond, the right seems fundamental. The challenger wins.

Charting Selective Protection for Marriage and Family Rights

This section looks at how the Court affords strong but selective protection to marriage and family rights. This branch of protecting privacy-based rights through substantive due process has the oldest pedigree. As far back as 1923, the Court stated that the right "to marry, establish a home, and bring up children" was an important part of the "liberty" protected by the due-process clauses. The language is from *Meyer v. Nebraska,* 262 U.S. 390 (1923), which protected parental rights to direct their children's education by striking down a law against the teaching of modern foreign languages in the state's public and private schools. (If you hated your French class, you probably think *Meyer* was wrongly decided.)

Fundamental marriage and family rights

Case law now protects marriage and family rights as fundamental aspects of privacy, triggering strict scrutiny. This high degree of protection means that government can't restrict the following rights, except through laws narrowly drawn to advance an interest of compelling importance:

✔ **The right of heterosexual adults to marry without direct and substantial governmental interference:** In *Zablocki v. Redhail,* 434 U.S. 374 (1978), the Court recognized the "fundamental importance" of the right to marry. The *Zablocki* Court invalidated a Wisconsin law requiring any parent under a valid child-support order to get "a prior judicial determination that the support obligation has been met" before marrying. The Court sympathized in the abstract with the state's concern that a new marriage may jeopardize the welfare of existing children, especially if the new marriage produces more children or other financial demands. But the statute was viewed as not narrowly tailored to accomplish child protection; it didn't guarantee that any money would end up going to existing children and because "the state already has numerous other means for exacting compliance with support obligations [that] do not impinge upon the right to marry."

✔ **The right of family members — even extended family members — to live together:** In invalidating a zoning law limiting the kinds of families that could live together to "a few categories" of traditional parent-child family arrangements, *Moore v. City of East Cleveland,* 431 U.S. 494 (1977), wrote broadly that "the Constitution protects the sanctity of the family precisely because the institution . . . is deeply rooted in this Nation's history and tradition." Seeing the family as "pass[ing] down many of our most cherished values, moral and cultural," the Court said that traditional regard for the family wasn't limited to the "nuclear family." Rather, "[t]he tradition of uncles, aunts, cousins, and especially grandparents sharing a household . . . has roots equally venerable and equally deserving of constitutional protection."

Giving careful scrutiny to the zoning law doomed it. Even if the city's justifications — "preventing overcrowding, minimizing traffic and parking congestion, and avoiding an undue financial burden on [the] school system" — were strong enough to be "compelling" (doubtful), these goals could have been met through less "intrusive regulation of the family." (For example, traffic and parking congestion could be dealt with by the zone parking-permit systems many cities employ, with per-household limits on the numbers of automobiles, and the like.)

✔ **The right of *unmarried* fathers in long-standing, stable relationships to continue to live with their children:** In *Stanley v. Illinois,* 405 U.S. 645 (1972), the Court held that "the interest of a parent in the companionship, care, custody, and management of his or her children" is not the exclusive province of parents who were married when the children were born. The Court invalidated a state law providing that, upon the mother's death, the children of unwed fathers automatically became wards of the state. By taking away paternal rights without any showing that the father was an unfit parent, the law "risk[ed] running roughshod over the important interests of both parent and child."

Marriage and family rights not considered fundamental

On the other hand, case law treats the following aspects of marriage and family rights as not fundamental — and therefore subject to government interference as long as it is minimally rational:

- ✔ **The right to marry without facing more modest (that is, not direct and substantial) interference:** In limiting "direct and substantial" interference with the right to marry, the *Zablocki* Court (discussed in the preceding section) disclaimed the idea "that every state regulation which relates in any way to the incidents or prerequisites for marriage must be subjected to rigorous scrutiny." This limitation on the *Zablocki* holding seems to allow more traditional restrictions on marriage, such as blood-test requirements and rules against marriage by first cousins.

- ✔ **The right to marry without facing financial deterrents:** This point was made by *Califano v. Jobst,* 434 U.S. 47 (1977), which upheld as rational a provision making it financially risky for disabled people to marry. (The law terminated federal benefits for a disabled child who marries, even if the spouse is also disabled.)

- ✔ **The right of a father to a relationship with his child, conceived in a casual extramarital relationship, when the mother and her husband object:** In the *Michael H.* case, discussed previously in "Highlighting the importance of how the right at issue is defined," the Court thought that Michael H.'s situation as the father of a child conceived in an adulterous affair was critically different from that of the unmarried father with a long-standing relationship with his three children over 18 years (see *Stanley,* discussed in the previous section).

- ✔ **The right of grandparents to continue to visit with their grandchildren if the custodial parent objects:** The Court spoke highly of grandparents as extended family members in *Moore* (see the preceding section). But that didn't matter when a state law pitted grandparent rights *against* parental rights. The Court in *Troxel v. Granville,* 530 U.S. 57 (2000), rejected a law allowing a judge to order grandparent visitation over parental objections if the judge determined that visitation was in the children's best interest. The *Troxel* Court ruled against the grandparents' rights, seeing the law as a "breathtakingly broad" switch from "the traditional presumption that a fit parent will act in the best interest of his or her child."

Taking Different Routes to Protecting Reproductive Freedom

The Court has identified several fundamental privacy-based rights relating to pregnancy and its consequences. A fairly straightforward and stable line of cases protects fundamental rights on both sides of the procreation coin — the right to get pregnant and the right to avoid (or delay) procreation through contraception. Much less consistent and logical are the several dozen cases since 1973 drawing and redrawing boundary lines for the fundamental (and still highly controversial) right to choose abortion.

Establishing the fundamental right to become (and avoid becoming) pregnant

Current substantive-due-process case law affords strong protection to pregnancy rights. The Court established the right to conceive a child indirectly through cases involving the right to avoid compulsory sterilization. The right to avoid pregnancy — represented by a strong Court stand that access to contraception is a fundamental right — stems from the landmark case launching the modern substantive-due-process era and later cases expanding on that beginning.

Recognizing the fundamental right to avoid compulsory sterilization

Any law or policy seeking to interfere substantially with any citizen's right to procreate faces strict scrutiny associated with fundamental substantive-due-process rights. However, the road to that result wasn't smooth.

The Supreme Court's first decision about the right to have a child was not promising. The infamous precedent in *Buck v. Bell,* 274 U.S. 200 (1927), saw none other than respected jurist Oliver Wendell Holmes leading the Court to uphold a law allowing compulsory sterilization of institutionalized persons found to have inherited insanity or some other mental defect. The result is shocking in modern times, as is the Court's rationale requiring a citizen to permanently sacrifice her reproductive capacity so that "society can prevent those who are manifestly unfit from continuing their kind." Worst of all was Holmes's callous statement that "three generations of imbeciles is enough."

The Court recovered from *Buck* without formally overruling it in *Skinner v. Oklahoma,* 316 U.S. 535 (1942). The *Skinner* Court struck down a law allowing a court or jury to determine that a defendant is a "habitual criminal" deserving compulsory sterilization based upon conviction for at least three felonies involving "moral turpitude" (that is, felonies supposedly showing an immoral and antisocial character). The Court used an equal-protection theory (that people who are alike should be treated that way) to overturn the selective way the law defined the crimes potentially leading to sterilization.

Most observers consider *Skinner* to really be a substantive-due-process case in equal-protection clothing. Neither of the equal-protection theories we note in Chapter 10 — that government line-drawing discriminates against a "suspect class" (such as a racial minority) or that it restricts the fundamental rights to vote, access certain judicial forums, or travel interstate — applies to laws treating different types of criminals differently. So what really bothered the *Skinner* Court was that the questioned law violated "a sensitive and important area of human rights," the "the right to have offspring."

The Supreme Court has never decided the issue, but modern laws seeking to sterilize repeat "three strikes" offenders, require chemical castration for sex offenders, or force drug-addicted women of childbearing years to wear contraceptive patches (all of which have at one time or another been proposed by legislators) would be unlikely to survive strict scrutiny after *Skinner.*

Endorsing and expanding the fundamental right to access contraception

The Court took a very different tack for the opposite right, the right to avoid (or at least postpone) becoming pregnant by using contraception.

As mentioned earlier in this chapter, the 1965 case of *Griswold v. Connecticut,* 381 U.S. 479 (1965), kicked off the modern substantive-due-process era of strong protection for some fundamental privacy rights. *Griswold* saw the strong interest of married persons to control conception free of state legal restraint. Although *Griswold* only decided the contraceptive-access right of *married persons,* later cases expanded the right to:

- **Unmarried persons:** Claiming to reach its result through an equal-protection analysis, the Court struck down a statute forbidding distribution of contraceptives to unmarried persons in *Eisenstadt v. Baird,* 405 U.S. 438 (1972). As with the *Skinner* case discussed in the previous section, equal-protection analysis does not provide a ready way to strongly protect what the *Eisenstant* Court viewed as "the right of the individual, married or single, to be free from unwarranted governmental intrusion into matters so fundamentally affecting a person as the decision whether to bear or beget a child."

- **Minors under the age of 16:** The Court extended contraceptive rights to minors in *Carey v. Population Council,* 431 U.S. 678 (1977). The justices saw the state's asserted interest in deterring illicit sexual activity by minors as insufficient to justify denying them contraception (and imposing the risk of pregnancy on them!).

- **Anyone seeking to access contraceptives from someone other than a pharmacist:** The Carey decision also struck down a requirement that only licensed pharmacists could distribute contraceptives. The Court applied strict scrutiny, which the law failed because it "clearly imposes a significant burden" on the right to contraception.

Transforming reproductive liberty rights into abortion rights

The Court's most important and controversial venture into reproductive liberty is its involvement in abortion-rights cases, begun in the landmark case of *Roe v. Wade,* 410 U.S. 113 (1973), and continuing to this day.

It could take an entire chapter (and maybe an entire *For Dummies* book!) to detail all the twists and turns in the dozens of abortion cases the Supreme Court has decided since *Roe.* These cases show complicated changes in legal rules and shifting coalitions of justices. This judicial back-and-forth-ing reflects larger national social and political trends, which the abortion decisions have implicitly responded to and sometimes directly referenced.

In this section, we cover the most important outlines of the Court's abortion jurisprudence. For convenience, we discuss these developments in chronological order, making general observations along the way.

Moving from no constitutional protection to strict protection: Roe's Revolution

The dramatic, rights-changing result of *Roe v. Wade* can best be understood in the context of how law and society handled abortion rights before 1973.

Before the late 1800s — and certainly when the framers wrote the Fifth and Fourteenth Amendments' due-process clauses protecting liberty — federal and state laws largely ignored abortion. As part of a broader concern about the moral fabric of society, however, federal and state laws began to adopt a more restrictive approach. In the first half of the 20th century, most abortions became subject to serious criminal penalty (always on the doctors performing them, but sometimes also on the women seeking them).

In the 1950s and '60s, several abortion-law reform movements made progress mainly by focusing on giving doctors greater authority to decide that particular abortions were "therapeutic" (that is, because they would prevent physical or psychological injury to a pregnant woman). In several prominent states, including California and New York, the right to abortion was significantly liberalized. It appeared that a gradual process of enhancing access to abortion could spread to other states and the federal government.

The 1973 ruling in *Roe* cut across these developments in one momentous judicial swoop. In holding that any adult woman has a fundamental right during her first six months of pregnancy to choose abortion, in consultation with her doctor, *Roe* marked a new chapter in reproductive rights. It also, to quote *Roe* dissenting Justice White, "constitutionally disentitled" the people of each state to weigh the pros and cons of abortion in the political process.

The *Roe* Court's ruling that the right to choose abortion is fundamental led directly to governments needing to meet strict scrutiny to deprive women of that right. (We show later how the Court significantly lowered the scrutiny level in 1992.) In considering the various governmental interests that might be compelling, and how government needed to design laws to make them narrowly drawn, the *Roe* Court divided pregnancy into three trimesters, in which government had the following lesser or greater regulatory authority:

✔ **In the first three months of pregnancy, governments had very little regulatory room.** Governments could limit abortion in a few ways typical of regulation of any other medical procedure — say, requiring that the procedure be performed by licensed physicians.

Otherwise, in this first pregnancy trimester, governments had no compelling interest to ban or regulate abortion. Getting an abortion was actually safer medically during this time frame than continuing to stay pregnant. (A concern for potential fetal life would not become compelling until the seventh month of pregnancy, because that was the point of medical viability — that is, the point at which a fetus had "the capacity for meaningful life outside the mother's womb.")

✔ **In the second trimester (fourth through sixth month) of pregnancy, government could regulate, but not ban, abortion through narrowly drawn measures necessary to protect maternal health.** Because in the fourth month of pregnancy abortion became riskier than staying pregnant, governments could then regulate to protect maternal health. Per the logic of strict scrutiny, though, regulations had to be narrowly drawn. For example, governments could require second-trimester abortions to be performed in licensed outpatient clinics. But they could not impose costly procedures only needed in special cases (such as requirements that a second physician be present for all abortions).

✔ **In the third trimester (seventh month of pregnancy to birth), government can ban abortion, except where necessary to save the life or protect the health of the mother.** The point of fetal viability finally gives governments a compelling interest to protect potential fetal life. Because allowing but regulating abortion compromises this potential life, governments may now ban abortion. Even here, though, *Roe* concludes that the fetus's right to *potential* life bows to the pregnant woman's right to *actual* life, when only one life can be saved.

The *Roe* Court said that it was not deciding when life begins. Noting that various religious and philosophical traditions had disagreed about that point (with several major religions believing that life begins at conception, making abortion morally equivalent to murder), the Court declared that it "need not resolve the difficult question." Critics have objected that *Roe* at least decided *implicitly* that life did *not* begin at conception; otherwise, a woman's right to abort what would then be a "human life" would have raised great difficulties.

Why *Roe* is an essential part of any abortion-rights discussion

As you see in this chapter, cases since the 1990s have departed substantially from *Roe v. Wade*. Therefore, the question may occur to you, why the detailed discussion of *Roe* here?

First, *Roe* is still worth discussing because its central abortion-rights holding has survived strong efforts to overrule it. And understanding its view of offsetting rights and its strict version of judicial scrutiny (now discredited after the 1992 *Casey* decision, discussed in the later section "Changing the rules") will help you make sense of the later law.

More broadly, *Roe* continues to be one of the most controversial decisions of the modern era, both on the Court and off. An example of off-Court controversy occurs whenever a new person is nominated to the federal bench and senators make repeated, fruitless efforts at nomination hearings to gauge the nominee's views on abortion. (This practice is, in turn, controversial. Many experts and regular Americans decry this waste of senatorial and nominee resources.)

The Court did rule that the fetus was not a "person" with a right to "life" under the due-process clauses. Justices read the limited meaning of "person" in other parts of the Constitution and the general lack of legal protection for fetuses during the framing period as negating legal personhood before birth. This holding prevented the argument that the fetus's right to life trumped a woman's right to liberty with respect to the abortion decision.

Preserving government's authority to avoid funding or otherwise supporting the abortion choice

Even as *Roe* and later cases were significantly increasing the constitutional protection afforded the right to choose an abortion, the Court generally upheld the right of governmental units to decide not to devote public funds and resources to making abortion more available.

Soon after *Roe*, the Court decided the trend-setting case on abortion funding. In *Maher v. Roe*, 432 U.S. 46 (1977), the Court declined to strictly scrutinize Connecticut's policy of refusing to fund nontherapeutic abortions (abortions not needed to protect maternal health) as part of participating in the federal program providing healthcare benefits to poor persons. The *Maher* Court held that government's duty after *Roe* not to place "obstacles — absolute or otherwise — in the pregnant woman's path to an abortion" did not require governments to affirmatively help women overcome barriers governments didn't create (such as a poor woman's lack of money to pay for an abortion).

Finding that the state's restrictive funding law did not contradict the fundamental right to choose abortion (and, therefore, should not be strictly scrutinized per *Roe*), the *Maher* Court applied baseline rationality and easily upheld the law. The justices found that not funding abortions for poor women rationally furthered the state's legitimate interests in "mak[ing] a value judgment favoring childbirth over abortion."

In a series of cases decided after *Maher* — and still retaining force today — the Court has held that governments may decline to support or facilitate a woman's abortion choice in the following ways:

- ✔ **Governments maintaining social-welfare programs may decline to fund nontherapeutic abortions (and even therapeutic abortions not compromising maternal life) — yet fund prenatal care and childbirth.** The first clause flows directly from *Maher*. The extension in parentheses comes from *Harris v. McRae,* 448 U.S. 297 (1980), which used Maher's logic to uphold the federal "Hyde amendment" denying funding for poor women who desire abortions even when necessary to avoid non-life-threatening health risks. The *Maher/Harris* line of cases also justifies present federal restrictions on funding for members of the military and their dependents.

- ✔ **Governments can prevent abortions from being performed in public hospitals and clinics and by government-funded healthcare employees — even when very few private hospitals or private doctors perform abortions in that state.** The leading case establishing this is *Webster v. Reproductive Health Services,* 492 U.S. 490 (1989).

The special case of minors' abortion rights

Although *Roe* afforded super-strong protection to the abortion choices of *adult* women, justices in the *Roe* era recognized that the abortion right of pregnant girls requires a different balancing act.

In general, of course, parents have more control over the medical choices of their minor children. So when governments stand *in loco parentis* (that is, in the parents' shoes, as with school programs and children in governmental custody), they can more legitimately restrict the healthcare choices of minors. At the same time, of course, *Roe*'s holding that the abortion decision is fundamental makes a girl's decision whether to terminate her pregnancy more deserving of protection than other medical and lifestyle choices.

A series of cases results in this balancing act: Governments may require parental *approval* of, or notification about, a minor's decision to seek an abortion — with the provision that a minor who is living independently or is legitimately afraid of the consequences of informing a parent may seek a prompt and confidential *judicial bypass* (which, as the name implies, permits a judge after a prompt hearing to give substitute approval for the desired abortion). And governments have the same ability to decline to fund or facilitate abortions for minors as they do for adults.

✔ **Governments may impose restrictions on abortion counseling and other separate-accounting procedures to ensure that funds to promote family planning do not end up furthering abortion.** In *Rust v. Sullivan*, 500 U.S. 173 (1991), the Court upheld the constitutionality of restrictions on doctors and other health professionals providing government-funded family-planning advice under a federal program. This so-called "gag rule," adopted by the Secretary of Health and Human Services, forbade these professionals from recommending abortions "as a method of family planning" or otherwise counseling regarding abortion.

Rust reached this result despite arguments that the regulation interfered with the doctor-patient relationship and doctor free speech in more significant ways than other funding limits and countered *Roe*'s emphasis on a woman's right to consult a doctor about her abortion choice.

Preserving but downgrading protection for the abortion right

Cases since *Roe* preserve substantial, but not all aspects of a woman's right to choose an abortion. We explore those cases in this section.

Changing the rules

By the time *Planned Parenthood of Southeastern Pennsylvania v. Casey,* 505 U.S. 833, reached the Supreme Court in 1992, many people predicted that *Roe* would be formally overturned. Two antiabortion presidents had appointed new justices thought to be unsympathetic to *Roe*. A majority of justices then on the Court had either called for *Roe*'s overruling outright or had written opinions highly disparaging its reasoning.

Note that that repeal of *Roe* wouldn't have meant the immediate end of available abortions. Only *special constitutional protection* for abortion would have ended. Whether abortion was freely or restrictively available would then have turned on the outcome of political fights in the states and in Congress.

Considering all the fears that *Roe* would be overruled outright, the *Casey* Court's statement that Roe's "essential holding" should "be retained and once again reaffirmed" was quite surprising. However, while stating that abortion rights remained fundamental, the Court worked some major changes in abortion-rights law:

✔ *Roe*'s **division of the first six months of pregnancy into two "trimesters" is replaced by the view that governmental interests in maternal health and potential fetal life exist "from the outset" of pregnancy (and grow in importance over time).** In significant part, this change reflects the previously expressed view of Justice Sandra O'Connor, the author of the critical *Casey* plurality opinion for three justices in the middle of the Court's alignment, that the *Roe* trimester system was "on a collision course with itself." As medical science advanced, the fetal viability point (at which abortion could be banned) would move earlier in pregnancy; progress in making abortion safer would move the point when abortion was no longer as safe as pregnancy (thus allowing government to regulate to promote maternal health) later in pregnancy. At some point, the lines would cross.

✔ **Abortion regulations before viability are now subjected to a single "undue burden" standard (which focuses on whether a law has "the purpose or effect . . . to place a substantial obstacle in the path of a woman seeking an abortion"), rather than strict scrutiny.** This "undue burden" language had been a relatively unnoticed part of the *Maher* abortion funding decision until Justice O'Connor began promoting it in pre-*Casey* concurring opinions.

✔ **Governments have more latitude to regulate abortion than under the previous *Roe* standard.** Specifically, as explained in the following section, restrictions that didn't pass the compelling interest/narrowly drawn test now survive under the undue-burden standard.

On the other hand, *Casey* preserved these features of *Roe*'s regime:

✔ **Governments can only regulate abortion, not ban it, before viability.**

✔ **Governments retain their authority to ban abortion after viability, except where necessary to protect the life or health of the mother.**

Applying the changed rules

The newly critical undue-burden standard (which is not as stringent as strict scrutiny; that is, the government doesn't have to show its abortion restriction will narrowly achieve a compelling interest) is quite subjective and wasn't explained in previous abortion cases. (That led dissenting Justice Scalia to strongly criticize it as an "ultimately standardless" test with "no principled or coherent" meaning.) Perhaps more light is shed by analyzing the provisions upheld in *Casey* with the one provision the justices invalidated.

Casey held that the following restrictions on abortion choice before viability (before the fetus can survive on its own) are *not* an undue burden on an adult woman's fundamental abortion right:

✔ **Informed-consent requirements going beyond disclosures customary for other operations:** Reversing past precedents, seven *Casey* justices upheld a requirement that doctors inform women seeking abortions of several matters unrelated to the classic disclosure of risks and benefits to which all patients facing surgery are entitled. Specifically, the law required that pregnant women be informed of the comparative risks of continued childbirth and "the probable gestational age" of the fetus.

These requirements went beyond the information necessary to protect a woman's health; they were designed, as the Court noted, "to persuade the woman to choose childbirth over abortion." Decisions after *Roe* and before *Casey* had struck such restrictions as not "narrowly drawn" to achieve a compelling maternal-health interest. But they were not an undue burden under *Casey*'s relaxed standard because, after listening to the disclosures, a woman could still decide to have an abortion.

✔ **A 24-hour waiting period:** Again reversing past precedents, seven *Casey* justices upheld a mandate that at least 24 hours pass between the informed-consent conversation and the abortion. Such waiting periods seek to allow women to take time to consider the information received.

Some *Casey* justices found the waiting period requirement a "closer case" constitutionally. Poorer women, women from rural areas, and women whose family situations are unsupportive of abortion may face special problems in having to miss work, be away from home, and potentially travel long distances more than once. Still, because the lower court's findings didn't clearly find that women would ultimately forgo abortion, the majority upheld the 24-hour waiting period as not an undue burden. (Because many women would not benefit from having more time to consider an abortion decision they had already thought long and hard about, an identical 24-hour waiting period had previously been rejected as not narrowly drawn under *Roe*'s strict-scrutiny standard.)

On the other hand, a different majority of *Casey* justices held that requiring a married woman to certify under penalty of perjury that she notified her spouse of her decision to have an abortion *is* an unconstitutional undue burden. As the lead decision noted, "There are millions of women in this country who are the victims of regular physical and psychological abuse at the hands of their husbands. Should these women become pregnant, they may have very good reasons for not wishing to inform their husbands." Forced to choose between informing their husbands and getting an abortion, "in a large fraction of cases [the spousal-notification requirement] will operate as a substantial obstacle."

Seeing what Casey suggests about applying the undue-burden standard in future cases

Although the *Casey* Court did not provide design criteria for applying its undue-burden test in future cases, comparing the reasoning from the main holdings seems to suggest that the following considerations are useful guides:

✔ The fact that a provision merely delays the time frame for getting an abortion or increases the cost doesn't make it an undue burden.

✔ That "some women" suffer special disadvantages doesn't disable state regulation. The key instead seems to be a demonstrated risk that (at least "a large fraction" of) women will completely forgo a desired abortion.

✔ In cases where the provision seems to paternalistically interfere with the woman's decisional independence — and especially interfere with the marital relationship — the undue-burden label may be more likely.

Providing limited and inconsistent guidance on undue burden

Given the uncertainties created by the introduction of *Casey*'s undue-burden standard, Court watchers expected the justices to quickly take new cases to add clarity. Surprisingly, the Court stayed on the sidelines while many states adopted new abortion regulations immediately challenged in court. Lower-courts judges were left on their own to decide the reach of the undue-burden standard. Not surprisingly, court-by-court differences arose.

Eight years later the Court decided *Stenberg v. Carhart,* 530 U.S. 914 (2000), a challenge that was not typical of the kinds of expanded regulations states generally sought to impose after *Casey.* The Court waited seven more years to decide *Gonzales v. Carhart,* 127 S.Ct. 1610 (2007), the only other decision to date shedding substantial light on the undue-burden standard, and one that also pertains to the same atypical kind of regulation.

Stenberg v. Carhart, 530 U.S. 914 (2000), struck down Nebraska's ban on a rarely used and gruesome form of late-second-term abortion generally known as *partial-birth abortion.* Controversial in medical circles as well as decried by abortion opponents, partial-birth abortion was also an awkward vehicle for clarifying *Casey.* After all, the constitutional fate of a law *banning one rare abortion procedure* was a very different question from the validity of a law allowing but *regulating* a *generally used* abortion method.

Still, the *Stenberg* decision seemed to signal that a majority of the Court would apply the undue-burden standard relatively strictly. The majority erred on the side of the pregnant women in the abortion equation. It found Nebraska's law an undue burden both because statutory uncertainties could make doctors unwilling to perform any late-term abortions and because the law didn't have a "maternal-health exception" for a small group of pregnant women whose best abortion alternative might be partial-birth abortion.

Seven years later the Court ruled in its only other post-*Casey* decision. Although the subject was again partial-birth abortion, this time a different Court alignment *upheld* a *federal* law adopted in 2003.

The decision upholding the law in *Gonzales v. Carhart,* 550 U.S. 124 (2007), partly turns on standard legal reasoning. The new majority held that, unlike the law in the *Stenberg* case, Congress had avoided statutory ambiguities threatening to deter doctors from using the more common abortion method. But with several new justices on the Court, a new majority did not err on the side of maternal health. Rather, a 5–4 majority saw insufficient evidence that partial-birth abortion "creates significant health risks for women." (Splitting hairs, the majority said that evidence that partial-birth abortion may be *safer* for some women is not the same as showing that making women rely on other methods is *unsafe.*) Instead, the Court gave governments "wide discretion to pass legislation in areas where there is medical and scientific uncertainty."

Limits to sexual privacy as a "fundamental" right

A major indication of the Court's tendency to go only a certain distance in protecting fundamental rights to sexual privacy is its unwillingness so far to provide (at least officially) strong protection to the rights of homosexuals to follow their romantic and sexual preferences.

True, the Court took a major step in 2003 in *Lawrence v. Texas,* 539 U.S. 558, by invalidating a law that had made consensual sexual relations between homosexual adults a crime. In the late 1980s a majority of the justices saw claims that the right of homosexuals to sexual privacy was a logical extension of past right-to-privacy decisions as "facetious." In *Bowers v. Hardwick,* 478 U.S. 186 (1986), a majority found that the rights of homosexuals could be overcome by a Georgia criminal law because it rationally reflected the moral views of the state's majority. *Lawrence* formally overturned *Bowers,* writing in much more sympathetic terms that the "liberty protected by the Constitution allows homosexual persons the right to choose to enter upon relationships in the confines of their homes and their own private lives and still retain their dignity as free persons."

Lawrence did not, however, hold that adult homosexuals had a "fundamental" right to follow their romantic and sexual preferences. (In fact, *Lawrence* used no descriptor to characterize the strength of the right.) And the Court's holding that Texas's law "furthers no legitimate state interest which can justify its intrusion into the personal and private life of the individual" left observers unclear about the level of scrutiny the Court applied. (Did Texas truly lack any legitimate interest — even including preventing sexually transmitted diseases — in discouraging homosexual sex? Or was the Court using some undeclared balancing test between rational basis and strict scrutiny to hold that the interest wasn't *strong enough* to "justify" homosexual rights?)

Perhaps *Lawrence* is a first (although largely unacknowledged) step in a typical gradual expansion of liberty and privacy rights. If so, it may lead to the ultimate rejection of state laws failing to recognize same-sex marriage and the federal Defense of Marriage Act, which purports to protect those laws. Other rights for homosexuals may also be recognized.

Whether *Gonzales* is a limited judicial reaction to an unusual abortion controversy — or is "alarming," as dissenting Justice Ginsburg put it, because a majority of the Court now "refuses to take *Casey* and *Stenberg* seriously" — remains to be seen. With no major post-*Casey* ruling from the Court on more typical laws regulating abortion generally, there is very little guidance for lower courts, advocates for pregnant women, and others.

Providing Some Clarity — and Many Questions — about the Right to Die

A last area of active right-to-privacy cases invoking substantive due process is what is commonly referred to as the right to die. Here the Supreme Court has drawn a bright-line distinction between a right to terminate medical care (strongly protected) and the right to have a physician assist in "dying with dignity" (not strongly protected). And the Court has made common-sense distinctions between the strength of the rights of competent adults (that is, adults who are conscious and can understand their medical conditions) and those who are incompetent (for example, because they're in comas).

The surface clarity in this area disappears, however, when the broad consensus rulings are broken into specialized questions.

First, here are three points about the right to die made clear by the Court:

- ✔ **A competent adult has a strong liberty interest in terminating medical care, even if that ends his life earlier than it would with continued care.** In *Cruzan v. Director, Missouri Department of Health,* 497 U.S. 261 (1990), the Court applied a general and long-established common-law right to resist unwanted touching by another person to well-intentioned doctors and nurses seeking to continue medical care. Although the Court never officially labeled this right as fundamental or applied strict scrutiny, governments clearly would need an especially strong justification for undercutting "the right of a competent individual to refuse medical treatment," even if it hastens that person's death.

- ✔ **An incompetent adult has a diminished liberty interest in terminating treatment, because this right must be exercised through a surrogate** (such as the parents in *Cruzan,* who sought to effect what they felt were the wishes of their daughter, who had persisted in a coma for four years). Given the stronger interests of government "to assure that the action of the surrogate conforms . . . to the wishes expressed by the patient while competent," *Cruzan* held that a state may require "clear and convincing" evidence before a judge orders hospital authorities to terminate care for a comatose patient. ("Clear and convincing" evidence is higher than the evidentiary standard used in most civil proceedings.)

- ✔ **In general, states may prohibit doctors from assisting patients in terminating their lives.** A unanimous Court held in *Washington v. Glucksberg,* 521 U.S. 702 (1997), that as a general matter the right of patients to "physician-assisted suicide" is *not* fundamental. Seeing a distinct line between the passive withdrawal of treatment protected in *Cruzan* and active assistance in dying, the *Glucksberg* Court found the relevant historical tradition was that "[i]n almost every State — indeed, in almost every Western democracy — it is a crime to assist a suicide." The *Glucksberg* Court found five legitimate interests rationally served by broad bans on physician-assisted suicide, including preserving medical ethics and "protecting vulnerable groups — including the poor, the elderly, and disabled persons — from abuse, neglect, and mistakes."

Despite their surface clarity, both *Cruzan* and *Glucksberg* leave much unresolved, including the following points:

✔ **Government's power to further limit surrogates in asserting the rights of incompetent patients remains unclear.** What if government held surrogates claiming that a comatose patient wanted to terminate treatment to an even higher burden of proof — say, the even-harder-to-meet "beyond a reasonable doubt" standard for criminal conviction? What if government denied the right of surrogates to speak for incompetent patients altogether, and instead required patients to write a "living will" or advanced directive before they became injured? *Cruzan* provides no definitive answers to these questions.

✔ **Although the *Glucksberg* justices agreed that states could criminalize physician-assisted suicide for their state's residents *generally*, individual justices wrote separately to support a greater liberty interest in more limited contexts.** Three justices indicated that terminally ill persons in great pain had a constitutional right to "palliative" (comforting) care, even if serious pain medications would end their lives prematurely. A fourth justice wrote that all terminally ill people (whether or not in great pain) had a greater right to control the manner of their inevitable death. A fifth justice, content for now to leave the physician-assisted suicide question to state legislatures, implied that in the future he might find a general right to die with dignity. Whether any of these more nuanced assertions of a right-to-die liberty will be recognized in future cases remains to be seen.

Other ducked questions regarding substantive-due-process and medical rights

Challengers have recently asserted other substantive-due-process rights relating to medical care. However, the Court's general failure to address these assertions leaves this part of medical/privacy-law undeveloped.

In *Gonzales v. Raich,* 545 U.S. 1 (2005) (discussed in Chapter 5, as an important case on Congress's ability to reach local non-economic activities through its interstate commerce power), the Court declined to decide the alternative substantive-due-process argument of a patient claiming that only medicinal marijuana eased her chronic pain from a debilitating illness.

The Court also declined to rule on the full D.C. Circuit's decision, in *Abigail Alliance for Better Access to Developmental Drugs v. von Eschenbach,* 495 F.3d 695 (D.C. Cir. 2007), that

terminally ill patients have no fundamental right to access experimental drugs once the drugs pass the first stage of federal testing. Patient advocates claimed, and some dissenting circuit judges agreed, that the patients had a fundamental constitutional right to try to save their lives.

The Court in *Gonzales v. Oregon*, 546 U.S. 243 (2006), protected Oregon's "Death with Dignity" law allowing physician-assisted suicide in carefully controlled cases. (The Court rejected the U.S. Attorney General's position that, under federal controlled-substance laws, doctors acting under the Oregon law faced legal sanctions.) However, this decision turned on nonconstitutional matters, so it has little to say about the constitutional right to physician assistance in dying.

Chapter 15

Preventing Unreasonable Searches and Seizures

*I*n this chapter, we explore privacy in a very important criminal-law context: when law-enforcement officials engage in searches and seizures before, during, and after arresting suspects. We explore why the founders developed the major constitutional amendment governing these areas (the Fourth Amendment) and how the law in this area has developed over the years.

We start with a brief look at the essence of Fourth Amendment protections and then explore the core concept that the courts developed to embody the amendment's protections in practice — the doctrine of "reasonable expectations of privacy." We see how privacy expectations play out in the classic Fourth-Amendment location, the home and surrounding areas. You then find out when the Fourth Amendment requires officials conducting a search to have a warrant, what that warrant must contain, and when warrant requirements can be dispensed with.

We then shift our focus to searches and seizures occurring in the context of a criminal arrest (which is in itself a "seizure"). Here, too, we explore the dividing line between legal and illegal law-enforcement activity.

Later in this chapter you also get to explore the "exclusionary rule." According to this rule, illegally obtained evidence must be excluded from criminal prosecutions of the suspect who was illegally searched or otherwise unconstitutionally treated. This important rule and its related "fruit of the poisonous tree" doctrine are relevant as well to the Fifth-Amendment rights discussed in Chapter 16.

Finally, we close by noting how Fourth-Amendment rights against unreasonable searches can arise in noncriminal contexts, such as administrative searches and searches at school and in the workplace.

By the time you finish this chapter, you'll know about the rules of search and seizure in different, important situations. You'll understand why we have certain rules related to search and seizure, and what's protected from government intrusion and what's not.

Understanding the Essence of Fourth Amendment Protections

The Fourth Amendment of the Constitution states,

> *The right of all people to be secure in their persons, houses, papers, and effects, against unreasonable searches and seizures, shall not be violated, and no Warrants shall issue, but upon probable cause, supported by Oath or affirmation, and particularly describing the place to be searched, and the persons or things to be seized.*

You can better understand this amendment if you remember where the drafters were coming from when they wrote it. (Taking this perspective also helps students analyze decisions by Supreme Court justices, who look to framer intent to reach their conclusions.) Remember, at the time the Bill of Rights was drafted, the framers were upset about many things the British monarchy was doing. They didn't like certain aspects of taxation, and they especially hated enactments like the Stamp Act, which required that legal and business documents, books, newspapers, and other materials be printed on a certain type of paper that was taxed.

But the key problem that likely inspired Fourth-Amendment protections was the way the British government went about enforcing the tax. Parliament would issue a writ of assistance sending inspectors into people's homes to search for "contraband," even in the absence of any evidence of a violation. The colonialists thought this government action was unwarranted — hence, a strong desire by some (though not all) colonialists to make sure that Americans would not be subjected to this kind of thing.

Diminished Fourth Amendment rights of convicts: Parole, probation, and jail-cell searches

The Fourth Amendment governs the legality of *almost* all searches. People convicted of crimes essentially give up their Fourth-Amendment rights until they serve their sentences and complete parole.

When an individual has a criminal case against them and he or she decides to plead guilty, in some states part of the plea agreement is that the guilty party forfeit Fourth-Amendment rights and submit to a search. Police sometimes conduct "Fourth searches" to make sure that a probationer or parolee is remaining law abiding.

And people in jail after being convicted have no Fourth-Amendment rights, and their jail cells can be searched at any time. Even people in jail awaiting trial have no Fourth-Amendment rights due to a lack of a reasonable expectation of privacy in the jail cell (see the section "Defining Reasonable Expectations of Privacy In and Around the Home"). Rest assured, however, that other provisions of the Constitution may afford prisoners, probationers, and parolees with avenues for recourse if they want to make a claim of unfair treatment.

So the Bill of Rights — focused on individual liberties — includes the Fourth Amendment to prohibit the new government from subjecting people to unreasonable searches such as those enforcing the Stamp Act. As you read this chapter, keep in mind that a search can be of a person or place, and a seizure can be of items of evidence, or of a person — an arrest. The Fourth Amendment and standards of reasonableness govern the legality of all searches and seizures.

Defining Reasonable Expectations of Privacy in and around the Home

Courts take into consideration a number of factors when it comes to privacy concerns. In this section, we discuss how Courts determine what constitutes a reasonable expectation of privacy, including at the one place most cherished: the home. We also look into what government must do to invade a person's privacy.

Understanding the two-prong test for weighing privacy expectations

The Fourth Amendment prohibits only *unreasonable* searches and seizures. Couched within that principle is the understanding that unless a person has a reasonable expectation of privacy in a given area, no warrant is required for law enforcement to conduct a search. For instance, as you see later in this chapter, a person has no reasonable expectation of privacy in a trash bin in front of their house. Police can therefore search the trash and use any evidence of a crime found in a later criminal case. As the Court stated in *Terry v. Ohio,* 392 U.S. 1 (1968), a person has a right to be free from unreasonable governmental intrusion, but the specific content and incidents of this right must be shaped by the context in which it is asserted.

Think about this just as an average citizen — you expect to have privacy in your home, but you don't have the same expectation while walking down the street, where what you are carrying may be in open view of untold members of the general public.

Under the landmark privacy case *Katz v. United States,* 389 U.S. 347 (1967), which established constitutional protections against telephone wiretapping, the following two-part test determines whether a person has a constitutionally protected reasonable expectation of privacy:

- ✔ Does the person have a subjective expectation of privacy in the area?
- ✔ Is society willing to say that expectation is reasonable?

These inquiries essentially constitute a common-sense approach, judging the reasonableness based on the facts and societal norms. The approach is used to decide a range of cases involving varied, and sometimes very particularized, circumstances.

Determining the reasonableness of privacy expectations at home

Most people would probably say that their home is the most "sacred" place to them — private and special — and would prefer that only people they invite should ever come inside. This desire is recognized in the Fourth Amendment and the cases interpreting that amendment and is one of the reasons we have the warrant requirement in the first place.

If law-enforcement officials have probable cause to believe, however, that evidence of a crime can be found at your residence, they can obtain a warrant and go onto your property and search wherever that evidence might be. And certain areas in and around your home (particularly your yard) may not be as private as you would think. Here are some examples of nonprotected areas around your home, based on actual court cases:

✔ **Garbage bins left out for collection:** The bin owner has no reasonable expectation of privacy under the holding of *California v. Greenwood,* 486 U.S. 35 (1988). The police had information that Greenwood was engaged in drug trafficking, so they collected and searched his trash. When police found evidence of narcotics use, they used the information to obtain a search warrant for the house, where they found quantities of cocaine and hashish. The Supreme Court held that the Fourth Amendment doesn't prohibit warrantless searches of trash left out for collection. Part of the Court's rationale was that trash left at the curb is accessible to "scavengers, snoops . . . and other members of the public" and that society would not accept as reasonable Greenwood's claim of a privacy expectation in the trash.

✔ **Other things left out in open view:** Similarly, property owners have no reasonable expectation of privacy in things they expose to discovery (including things that could be smelled or touched). But other items not in plain view can only be searched if the plain-view items give police probable cause for further investigation. This is known as the "plain-view" doctrine.

As Supreme Court decisions have refined the plain-view doctrine, evidence can now be admitted at trial only in cases where

- • Law-enforcement officers were lawfully at a place where the evidence could be plainly viewed (such as when officers are driving down the street and see something plainly visible on private property); *or* officers had a lawful right of access to the object (for instance, when they are in a place covered under a warrant); *and*

- • The incriminating character of the object is "immediately apparent."

Horton v. California, 496 U.S. 128 (1990), the case giving rise to the above three criteria, is a good example of evidence that may be seized under the plain-view theory. In *Horton,* police had a warrant permitting them to search for the "proceeds of a robbery." The police didn't find the stolen property, but while in Horton's house they did see weapons and seized them. Horton objected when prosecutors later sought to prove Horton's involvement in the robbery through the weapons. The Supreme Court held that the Fourth Amendment did not prohibit the seizure of the weapons despite the failure of the warrant to specify that they were looking for weapons. The Court reasoned that officers were validly at Horton's home in a location permitted by the warrant when they saw the weapons, which were of an incriminating nature under the circumstances.

By contrast, *Arizona v. Hicks,* 480 U.S. 321 (1988), shows the limits of the plain-view doctrine. In *Hicks,* police entered an apartment during an emergency to look for a shooter, possible other victims, and weapons.

While inside, officers noticed expensive stereo equipment that looked out of place. (The stereos turned out to be stolen in an armed robbery.) Hicks was later indicted for armed robbery, but the evidence of the stereos was suppressed because the search violated the Fourth Amendment — in part because officers moved the stereos to obtain the serial numbers.

✓ **Things that can be viewed from the air in flight over your home:** In *California v. Ciraolo,* 476 U.S. 207 (1986), police investigating a tip that Ciraolo was growing marijuana in his back yard flew over his property in a private airplane. Although the plants were shielded from view on the ground, the officers, who could identify marijuana by sight, were able to view the plants from the air. They then used photos they took from the plane as part of the probable cause to obtain a search warrant, and the marijuana plants were seized. The Supreme Court held that the officers' actions did not violate the Fourth Amendment because Ciraolo's subjective expectation of privacy was unreasonable. The fact that the backyard was within the "curtilage" (the perimeter) of the home (a more protected space) didn't matter. What mattered was that the officers were able to view the contraband from public airspace with the naked eye.

✓ **Open fields beyond the "curtilage" (that is, the area beyond the immediate outside perimeter) of the home:** Here, whether the expectation of privacy is reasonable depends upon the nature of the area and what is done to conceal it. For example, in *Oliver v. United States,* 466 U.S. 170 (1984), another marijuana-growing case, officers drove up to Oliver's property, to a gate marked "No trespassing." The officers continued traveling on a path along the perimeter of the property. From there they were able to view a significant number of marijuana plants. The Supreme Court held that Oliver had no reasonable expectation of privacy and upheld the "open fields rule."

Evolving technology and consequent challenges

Modern technology presents unique circumstances for law enforcement because items to be searched and seized must sometimes be described in terms of hard drives, memory, gigs, jpg files, and so on rather than describing desks, file cabinets, or other storage areas commonly found in a home or business. Technical items need very particularized descriptions; law enforcement must be very descriptive about why certain evidence will be found on things such as laptops and cellphones. Courts have had to recognize that although the storage method may be different in our times, the substance of the proposed intrusion is still the same. Case law is constantly developing to keep up with technology. The general rules still remain the same under prior case law, but the specifics dictate the outcome of these cases, as they do in any other case.

Probable Cause: Requiring a Warrant to Search

Probable cause is generally defined as a reasonable belief, justified by substantial evidence, that something is true. Under the Fourth Amendment, this standard of probable cause must be met before a warrant can be issued authorizing intrusion into someone's personal property. As the Court put it in one case, the question is whether there is a "fair probability that contraband or evidence of a crime will be found in a particular place." (The quote is from *Illinois v. Gates,* 462 U.S. 213 [1983], which validated a search of the defendant's home and vehicle based in part on a tip from a confidential informant which was corroborated by other facts).

This standard is also what must be met to force a criminal defendant to stand trial. Cases describe the probable-cause standard as a "strong suspicion that a crime was committed and the defendant [or in the case of warrants, the suspect] committed it."

To establish the necessary probable cause to justify a search warrant, law-enforcement officers must articulate certain facts. A judge is a check in the system, signing off on warrants to confirm that law enforcement has probable cause to conduct a search. A search warrant that goes before a judge for approval must include answers to the following basic questions:

- **What?** What exactly is law enforcement looking for at this location? If law enforcement is looking for large items, such as a boat or car, it can potentially limit the places to be searched — unless the search is for other smaller evidence (such as a key or an address book showing where the large item might be). Or, is law enforcement looking for small items (such as diamonds or a pocketknife used in a murder)?

- **When?** The *when* part of the equation is important because law enforcement must be reasonably certain that the things being searched for will actually be there when they arrive. A warrant must be served within a reasonable amount of time to make sure that the information isn't "stale." Whether the items will be present at a particular time may depend on what type of evidence is being searched for.

  For instance, if the warrant pertains to searching a residence or business location out of which illicit drugs are being dealt, the drugs may be gone when law enforcement gets to the location. So the warrant must describe details about when important information was received and what time frames are relevant to the total circumstances that gave law enforcement probable cause.

- **Where?** Before a judge or magistrate can sign off on a warrant, the place(s) to be searched must be described with sufficient particularity to allow any law-enforcement officer to execute the warrant. The scope of the intrusion must be sufficiently described. For instance, a residence should be described with the full address along with anything that would help someone identify the home with certainty, including possibly an apartment or duplex number, color of the outside, full description of the entire building if applicable, and any other details necessary depending on the circumstances of the location.

Also, the warrant must describe specific areas within the residence (or other location) that officers propose to search. This point goes back to *what* is being searched for — when searching for smaller items, the scope of the search might include every drawer and small storage space within the residence, whereas a search for larger items would justify a much narrower scope for the search. Guns may be hidden under a bed, but a vehicle isn't going to be under there!

✔ **Why?** The warrant must describe why officers believe evidence of a crime is at the location they are proposing to search. The warrant must explain all the facts surrounding this belief; any documents reviewed, activity observed, or witness statements taken should be set out.

Note: The person to be arrested must also be identified and described in an arrest warrant. And the other requirements as described above must be met to show why this person is connected to the crime that law enforcement believes was committed.

Warrants must be served between 7 a.m. and 10 p.m., unless nighttime authorization is obtained. Also, although police have a right to enter a premises under a valid warrant, they must knock and announce their presence before entering. These requirements were created out of respect for people who are law-abiding citizens, particularly in the event of an error.

All the requirements of a warrant are in place to protect people's privacy rights. But in some particular instances, warrants are not required or exceptions apply. Those parameters, discussed in the following section, are in place to address the needs of law enforcement and to protect society.

Determining When Criminal Searches without Warrants Are Allowed

In many situations, searches can be made without a warrant. In this section we highlight six typical instances when the Fourth-Amendment warrant requirement either doesn't apply or can be overridden due to the circumstances. Remember that the Courts are always balancing the needs of law enforcement (and consequently public safety) with the rights of individuals to privacy.

When the individual consents

Law enforcement doesn't require a warrant when the person consents to the search. The key is that the consent must be voluntary. Police aren't allowed to coerce someone into abandoning a reasonable expectation of privacy. Sometimes police officers obtain a written waiver of privacy rights by the person before beginning the search.

Conversely, though, law enforcement doesn't have to tell a person that she has the option not to consent; the person must know that she can "just say no." As a practical matter, law-enforcement officers usually approach the situation casually, saying something like, "Mind if we have a look around?" Many people simply consent, not realizing they have a choice.

Two caveats apply to consent searches:

✔ **A consent waiver may be challenged later and considered dubious.** Even a written waiver is not necessarily determinative. Courts look at all the circumstances to determine if the consent was truly voluntary.

✔ **The person consenting must have *authority* or *apparent authority* to consent to a search of the proposed place.** You can imagine dozens of scenarios in which a person may be asked to consent to a search of an area over which they have no authority. The police are required to act reasonably. Even if a person doesn't have actual authority over a proposed place to be searched, if the police reasonably believe the consenting person has authority, then the search is valid.

In *Illinois v. Rodriguez,* 497 U.S. 177 (1990), a woman who said she lived with defendant Rodriguez, and who had a key to his apartment, let the police into his apartment, where police found cocaine. After being arrested for possession of illegal substances, Rodriguez sought to suppress the evidence on the basis that the woman did not have authority to consent to the entry; Rodriguez claimed that she had vacated the apartment weeks earlier. The Court said that because police reasonably believed the woman had authority to consent, the search and seizure were valid — whether or not she actually had that authority.

Here is the practical bottom line: Consent is not really the best way to go. Not only can consent create messy situations for the police, but it can also be withdrawn at any time. The best way to conduct a search and seizure is through a warrant, assuming that there is time to do so.

When someone has been arrested

Another typical instance of warrantless searches occurs when police legally arrest suspects. After someone is under arrest, police can search him (and his vehicle, if he was driving immediately prior to arrest). Such searches are generally limited to places within the suspect's reach — unless further search is justified for officer safety or to preserve evidence (or, of course, another exception to the warrant requirement is relevant and justifies a further search). Police can always get a warrant to search additional areas if the facts justify it.

Case law determining when a search "incident to arrest" is constitutional has evolved in recent years. Following are three especially important cases:

- ✔ *Chimel v. California,* 395 U.S. 752 (1969), established the basic parameters of the search-incident-to-arrest doctrine. The police suspected Chimel of burglarizing a coin shop. They went to his home with a warrant for his arrest (but without a search warrant). When Chimel arrived home, police arrested him and then walked through the entire house, recovering numerous items that had been stolen from the shop. The Court held that the search was unlawful because the police went beyond merely searching Chimel's person and the immediate area within his reach. The Court ruled that such a broad search was not justified to protect officer safety or preserve evidence from destruction. However, *Chimel* still left room for appropriately conducted searches when police arrest someone.

- ✔ *New York v. Belton,* 453 U.S. 454 (1981), extended the "search incident to arrest" exception to include the passenger compartment and any containers in the passenger compartment of the vehicle the suspect is driving when arrested. Such a search, however, is limited to areas the arrested person could actually access or areas likely to contain evidence of the offense for which the person was arrested.

- ✔ *Arizona v. Gant,* 129 S. Ct. 1710 (2009), clarified the narrow reach of the incident-to-arrest exception after suspects are incapacitated. Police arrested Gant for driving on a suspended license. They handcuffed him and put him in the back of a patrol car. Then the police searched his car and found cocaine in the pocket of his coat, which was in the back seat. Because "only the area from within which he might gain possession of a weapon or destructible evidence" was appropriate to search, the Court held that the search-incident-to arrest exception did not apply. There was no longer a credible threat that the suspect represents a threat to law enforcement or could destroy evidence. After the threat has been removed (such as after the person has been handcuffed and placed in the patrol car, as Gant was), then searching even the immediate area (absent additional facts) may be unreasonable.

When law enforcement takes inventory

A third major exception to the Fourth Amendment's warrant requirement arises when a vehicle is legally impounded. In that case, the entire vehicle can be searched for inventory purposes.

These inventory searches are allowed to ensure officer safety (by making sure that nothing dangerous is in the car) and to catalog the belongings of a suspect so she can't make a claim later that her property has not been returned. An inventory search is reasonable if made in good faith, in accordance with standard procedures of the law-enforcement agency conducting the search.

When time is of the essence

Yet another exception to the warrant requirement is when *exigent circumstances* exist. This exception refers to situations in which law enforcement has probable cause to conduct a search but, for one of the following reasons, has no time to get a warrant:

- An immediate danger threatens the public or law-enforcement personnel.
- There's a risk that a felon may escape.
- Evidence of a crime is likely to be destroyed.

Where exigent circumstances are present, a search of potential wide scope may be valid. For example, the warrantless search of an entire vehicle could be valid if circumstances related to the car create part of the danger or if the vehicle's mobility triggers the danger that evidence may be destroyed.

Courts have limited the exigent-circumstances exception to the following conditions:

- Law enforcement is acting pursuant to clear evidence of probable cause.
- The crime is serious and destruction of evidence is likely.
- The search or seizure is limited in scope to the minimum intrusion necessary to prevent destruction of evidence.
- The indications of exigency are clearly defined and not subject to police manipulation or abuse.

Based on these requirements, the decision is more clear-cut in cases where law-enforcement personnel witness some act of violence or respond to a call about an ongoing crime, especially a violent incident. (For example, the Court held in *Welsh v. Wisconsin,* 466 U.S. 740 [1984], that no real exigency was present when police arrested a suspect in his home at night for having previously driven under the influence of alcohol.) On the other hand, cases involving destruction of evidence may be more difficult and require scrutiny of often-convoluted facts to determine such questions as whether law enforcement actually had time to get a warrant.

Why fixed checkpoints "check out" constitutionally

Even without a warrant, law-enforcement officers can stop cars and talk to occupants at fixed checkpoints. Selective referral of some vehicles to a secondary inspection area is acceptable (even if based on, say, appearance of Mexican ancestry). In *United States v. Martinez-Fuerte,* 428 U.S. 543 (1976), the Court held that the government and public interest is outweighed by the minimal intrusion made by being stopped at checkpoints.

However, without additional facts giving law enforcement a reasonable suspicion or probable cause, the scope of the intrusion even at fixed checkpoints is still limited as a practical matter

When you're on the border

Perhaps you have had your bags searched when at an international border, or at least have noticed other people's bags being searched by customs officials for no apparent reason. At all airports, citizens walk through scanners, put bags through other machines, and are sometimes asked to step aside for further scanning or searching of their person or bags — all without any suspicion of wrongdoing.

Suspicionless border searches are considered reasonable, based on national sovereignty, simply because they occur at the border. As stated in one case, the government has a "paramount interest in protecting the border" (*United States v. Flores-Montano,* 541 U.S. 149 [2004]). In essence, your Fourth-Amendment rights become subordinate when you cross the border or are in a place where you can potentially cross the border (the airport). Even when you fly within U.S. territory, a combination of federal authority to regulate the means of interstate commerce and the assumption that you voluntarily consent to search by entering airport security areas eliminates any requirement of a warrant based on probable cause.

When evidence is in plain view

A final exception to the warrant requirement relates to expectations of privacy in and around the home, which we introduce in the earlier section "Determining the reasonableness of privacy expectations at home." The plain-view doctrine states that police can seize evidence when it is in plain view and the illegal nature of it is readily apparent. We mention it here, however, to emphasize how often it comes into play in law enforcement's work. Not surprisingly, often when law enforcement is searching a location for evidence of one crime, they find evidence in plain view that the suspect committed additional crimes.

To illustrate a typical scenario, imagine that law-enforcement personnel are legally present at someone's residence executing a warrant related to a murder case. Upon arrival, they enter into the living room of the residence and it's filled with obvious counterfeiting materials — a bill printer, big sheets of hundred dollar bills, infrared machines, and the like. Those counterfeiting materials are in plain view, and even though that's not why law enforcement went to the residence in the first place, they don't need to get another warrant. The materials can be seized, and most likely the suspect will be arrested on charges of counterfeiting (if not yet for murder).

As always, many situations are not so cut and dried. Because a warrant has to sufficiently describe the items to be searched for and the places to be searched, if the items in plain view are not in a place where the police would logically be allowed according to the warrant, law enforcement's reliance on the plain-view doctrine is going to be called into question. For example, if police are looking for a stolen car at a suspect's home, they would likely not be able to claim the bags full of diamonds they found under the bathroom sink were in plain view.

Consider another scenario. Assume that law enforcement is executing a valid warrant at someone's home on a white-collar crime case — maybe for embezzlement or securities fraud. In a case like this, the warrant is (presumably) written so that the officers or agents can search *anywhere* in the individual's home where evidence of the crime may be found. If written properly, the warrant could extend even to the person's kitchen freezer. (You may laugh, but a colleague of ours once worked on a white-collar case where thousands of dollars in cash were found in the freezer.) If the cops open the freezer and find an illegal weapon, it's considered to be in plain view. Even if the weapon isn't related to the embezzlement case, it can be seized, and new charges would probably result (in addition to possibly another warrant for more evidence of a different crime, depending on the circumstances).

Sometimes an unnecessary warrant is wise

In practice, even if law enforcement can legally proceed without a warrant, getting one anyway may be the better move. This is always true when law-enforcement personnel executing a search warrant for one crime find evidence of a completely different crime.

In a case one of us worked on, multiple computers were seized lawfully as part of an investigation into a securities case involving fraudulent stock sales and operation of a pyramid scheme. When searching the computers, the forensic specialists found evidence of child pornography on one of the computers. This child porn was in "plain view," and would have been admissible in a later separate prosecution; arguably the computer analyst could have just kept moving forward with the securities-fraud investigation and any *further* evidence of child pornography would also be in plain view.

However, to be safe, investigators halted the imaging and investigation of the computer evidence until they obtained an additional warrant to search for additional evidence of possession of child pornography. Precautions like theirs are the best way to be safe in defending against later claims of Fourth-Amendment violations.

Limiting Arrests and Related Searches and Seizures

Beyond limiting the scope and circumstances of law-enforcement searches, the Fourth Amendment is a basis for limiting when a person can be arrested and their person (in addition to their property) can be seized.

Here, too, courts are always balancing the interests of law enforcement (and consequently the interests of the society law enforcement is charged with protecting) and the individual's rights. The Fourth Amendment embodies a preference to ensure that arrests and related searches and seizures are reasonable in light of all the circumstances. Although most people would rather not see a guilty person go free, they also don't want innocent people to have their privacy intruded upon or be harassed or humiliated.

Case law implements the Fourth Amendment by requiring probable cause for arrest, for indictment, and at preliminary hearings (or their equivalent) at which state judges conduct an initial review of the evidence against a suspect. Precedents define *probable cause* as a "strong suspicion that a crime was committed and the defendant committed it." It requires law enforcement to articulate specific facts about why they believe the suspect committed the particular crime or crimes. By contrast, *reasonable suspicion* is less specific. It only requires that law enforcement articulate facts causing them to inquire further (because of a belief that a crime *may* have been committed).

Armed with this key distinction, we can now look at several typical scenarios in which Fourth-Amendment issues arise during and after arrest.

Getting "frisky": Terry stops and reasonable suspicion

In *Terry v. Ohio,* 392 U.S. 1 (1968), the Court recognized the dangers facing police officers and the need to protect them and allow them to do their job of protecting the public. This case solidified a police officer's right to talk to citizens and even to make a "pat down" of a person based on a "reasonable suspicion that criminal activity is afoot."

In *Terry,* an experienced police officer in downtown Cleveland had been assigned for years to patrol the area for shoplifters and pickpockets. The officer proceeded to watch two men doing what he believed to be "casing a job" (that is, preparing to rob a store in the area). Terry and another man repeatedly walked back in forth in front of the store, peering in the window each time they went by. The officer became increasingly suspicious, and based on his observations and experience, investigated further.

The officer decided to talk to Terry and his companion, who had by this time started conferring with a third person on the street corner. The men responded to the officer's questions by "mumbling." The officer frisked Terry and found a pistol. The officer found another weapon concealed on one of the other men.

At his later trial on concealed-weapon possession charges, Terry tried unsuccessfully to have the evidence of the gun excluded on Fourth-Amendment grounds. The Supreme Court held that the gun was admissible because the officer's "pat down" of him was based on reasonable suspicion that criminal activity was afoot.

Thus, *Terry* gave officers the green light to talk to people without having probable cause, which would allow them to obtain a warrant. *Terry* stops give police leeway when, based on their experience, they believe someone may be about to commit a crime but the situation hasn't advanced to the point where the officer can articulate more than a suspicion based on a few facts and his experience. *Terry* stops typically involve circumstances similar to that of the *Terry* case.

Permitting vehicle stops and searches

The Fourth Amendment's relevance to seizures and related searches is not limited to suspects on foot, however. Police are allowed to pull vehicles over without a warrant. They cannot, however, pull someone over without some justification — such as a state vehicle-code violation. And an officer who pulls someone over only for a routine traffic infraction doesn't typically have the right to search the vehicle. (That is, the search-incident-to-arrest exception does not usually apply.)

Aside from vehicle-code violations, however, police may develop reasonable suspicion or probable cause based on particular circumstances, such as a vehicle fitting the description of one having just fled from the scene of an armed robbery. Or, erratic driving might give an officer a reasonable suspicion that the person might be under the influence; after a stop, probable cause may develop for arrest.

The constitutionality of sobriety checkpoints

Especially during holidays and other times when excessive drinking is likely, law-enforcement officials set up temporary DUI (driving under the influence) checkpoints to enforce laws against drunk driving. (Temporary checkpoints can also be used after a crime to identify witnesses and suspects.)

Such checkpoints raise Fourth-Amendment questions by allowing law enforcement to stop vehicles absent any particularized suspicion or justification for doing so. The law allows this practice based on society's interest in deterring driving while under the influence, essentially as long as it is conducted in a systematic,

fair manner. And the courts recognize that the intrusion (just like with other checkpoints) is minimal (well, at least to law-abiding citizens).

This rationale only justifies the initial brief stop. To inquire further or search beyond simply speaking to the vehicle occupants, law-enforcement personnel are required to have more specific suspicion (such as the driver responding with slurred speech) or to recognize circumstances that trigger another exception to the warrant requirement (for example, the questioning officer sees an open bottle of whiskey in plain view).

What is reasonable and allowable on law enforcement's part is always dictated by the totality of the circumstances. The same is true for police searching a vehicle after a traffic stop. Suppose an officer pulls a woman over because the taillight on her vehicle is out. When the officer approaches the vehicle, he notices the smell of marijuana in the vehicle or sees a bag of marijuana and a pipe on the passenger seat. Now the officer has justification to further look into the vehicle (though not to search the entire vehicle) and arrest the driver (assuming that the driver is the only one in the vehicle). However, the search is limited to a scope appropriate to the suspected crime, or to the needs of officer safety or preservation of evidence, as discussed in the earlier section "When someone has been arrested." As a practical matter, additional evidence may be found in an inventory search (see the earlier section "When law enforcement takes inventory.")

Excluding Evidence: "Fruits of the Poisonous Tree"

Only evidence obtained legally can be used in court. Therefore, evidence that law enforcement obtained in violation of Fourth- or Fifth-Amendment (against self-incrimination) or even Sixth-Amendment (right to counsel) mandates may not be used against an accused in later criminal proceedings. To implement this core protection against official illegality, courts have developed a legal concept called the *exclusionary rule* and a doctrine called *the fruits of the poisonous tree*. The exclusionary rule dictates that "tainted" evidence — that is, evidence obtained illegally — should be excluded from evidence in a court trial. Note that this is a court-created doctrine and doesn't actually appear in the text of the Constitution. "Fruits of the poisonous tree" refers to subsequent evidence that is tainted because it was obtained as a result of other illegally obtained evidence or an illegal confession or suspect statement. The exclusionary rule generally prohibits "fruits of the poisonous tree" from being used to convict.

As with all the constitutional doctrines in this book, in implementing the exclusionary rule, courts are always doing a balancing act between the rights of suspects and the need to make sure that law enforcement can do its job in protecting the public. Sometimes protecting people's civil liberties is the most important thing, even if it means important evidence could have been obtained if police ignored people's rights. Therefore, inappropriate conduct by the police must be deterred, especially if it is intentional.

Even so, courts have carved out exceptions to the exclusionary rule for when they perceive that constitutional lapses do not reflect bad intent, when a special public-safety need is present, or both.

Here are the main exceptions to the exclusionary rule:

- **The attenuation doctrine:** This exception applies when prosecutors seek to introduce illegally obtained evidence at trial and that evidence is thought to be sufficiently attenuated (or separated) from the initial illegal police activity. If separate enough, the later-discovered evidence is considered to be "purged of the primary taint" and may be used in court. An example of this exception is *Segura v. United States,* 468 U.S. 796 (1984), in which the Court held that problems with an initial illegal search of an apartment didn't require the suppression of evidence seized 19 hours later under a search warrant. The Court concluded that the later warrant was not based on evidence obtained during the earlier illegal search.

- **Inevitable discovery doctrine:** Under this doctrine, if law enforcement obtained evidence illegally but the facts and circumstances show that the evidence would have been obtained by other means (and not illegally), the evidence can still come in at trial. The prosecution has to show by a "preponderance of the evidence" standard (the standard for civil cases, not the "beyond a reasonable doubt" standard used in criminal cases) that the evidence would have been found by legal means (*Nix v. Williams,* 467 U.S. 431 [1984]).

In *Nix v. Williams,* police spoke to the defendant in violation of his Sixth-Amendment right to counsel. The defendant told the police where to find the body of a missing 10-year-old girl. A search team of 200 people was already searching the general area, but the team stopped operations when the defendant led police to the body. When the defendant tried to suppress the evidence relating to the condition and location of the body on the basis of the Sixth-Amendment violation, the Supreme Court held the evidence admissible because the search team had been systematically searching in the area and would inevitably have discovered the body.

✔ **Independent source doctrine:** If the source of the evidence a defendant seeks to suppress is separate from the illegal activity conducted by law enforcement, the evidence may still be allowed in court despite that illegal conduct.

In *Murray v. United States,* 487 U.S. 533 (1988), police arrested two people they saw entering and exiting a warehouse where they believed drug trafficking was taking place. The vehicles lawfully seized after the arrest of the first two individuals contained drugs. Thereafter, police unlawfully entered the warehouse and saw bags of marijuana. Police then obtained a warrant, without mentioning that they had illegally entered the warehouse before seeking the warrant. The *Murray* Court held that the illegal entry did not taint the warrant, because the warrant was based on facts independent of what police saw in their illegal entry. (That is, the warrant was based on suspicions formed based on the earlier lawful arrest.)

✔ **Good faith:** When police rely on a law that's later changed or declared unconstitutional or they rely on a defective search warrant, the good-faith exception can kick in and tainted evidence can still be admissible. The key to this exception is establishing that police did not intentionally disobey the law but instead made an honest, good-faith error.

A clear example of the good-faith exception is *United States v. Leon,* 468 U.S. 897 (1984). Police wrote an affidavit to search some premises for drug activity; several prosecutors reviewed the warrant and a judge signed it. After the warrant was executed and the searches yielded illegal drugs, the warrant was found to be invalid because the police had not established probable cause. However, because the error in issuing the warrant was the judge's in approving it, and because the police did not act recklessly but rather acted in reasonable reliance on a warrant signed by a neutral judge, the good-faith exception applied.

A strange case of mistaken identity

Interestingly, courts make an exception to the exclusionary rule even when the police "get the wrong guy." In *Hill v. California,* 401 U.S. 797 (1971), two men driving Hill's car were arrested because stolen items were found in the car. The two men admitted involvement in a robbery and described Hill to the police as having been involved as well. They gave police information on where Hill lived. Police went to the address given (which was in fact Hill's apartment) and arrested a man who fit Hill's description, even though the man denied that he was Hill (and it turned out he was not). A search incident to arrest yielded solid evidence against Hill and he was convicted of robbery. Over Hill's challenge, the evidence obtained in the search was found to be admissible because police had made a good-faith mistake — even though the police had arrested the wrong man!

Applying the Fourth Amendment in Noncriminal Contexts

Fourth-Amendment rights usually come into play in the criminal context. But in some other circumstances, governmental authorities need to search persons, their homes, their belongings, or storage areas outside of the traditional context of law-enforcement officials investigating and fighting crime. This section briefly explores three noncriminal contexts — administrative searches, searches at schools (including random drug testing), and searches at the workplace.

Administrative searches

When it comes to noncriminal searches, the rules under the Fourth Amendment are more relaxed. Administrative searches often involve businesses the government has a greater interest in regulating than the average "mom and pop" shop down the street. These heavily regulated industries (gasoline or alcoholic beverages, for instance) are connected to concerns about public protection, and government agencies usually have a statutory basis for searching them at least to some extent. That is, there are laws specifically outlining requirements for maintaining the particular type of business, as well as describing government's ability to search. Note, however, that often these searches result in nothing more than fines and a directive with a fixed time to correct violations.

If the government claims justification for a search without a warrant based on the type of industry or the activity in which a business is engaged, courts look at several factors, including the following, to determine legality:

✔ The strength of the government's interest in regulating the industry

✔ Whether the search furthers the regulatory scheme

✔ Whether the procedures include safeguards for ensuring that any search is not unnecessarily intrusive

New York v. Burger, 482 U.S. 691 (1987), is a classic case illustrating the more-flexible rules used to judge administrative searches. In *Burger,* the Supreme Court upheld a warrantless inspection of an automobile junkyard; the search uncovered stolen vehicles and parts. The state's regulatory scheme allowed inspections of automobile junkyards, particularly to check for proper licensing and other requirements. The Court said that the search of the premises after the owner failed to present a license was reasonable based on the state's interests in regulating the industry, including preventing legitimate businesses from contributing to automobile theft by serving as "chop shops" for refitting stolen cars for resale, and the fact that the time, place, and scope of the search was limited.

Note, however, that when an administrative search has more criminal characteristics, a warrant would be required. For example, in *Michigan v. Tyler,* 436 U.S. 499 (1978), the Court held that firemen who returned to the scene of a fire after it had been extinguished to investigate suspected arson needed a warrant.

School searches

Students' rights under the Fourth Amendment seem to be a subject of increasing debate in recent years. As with other Fourth-Amendment issues, the courts engage in a balancing act to determine the reasonableness of searches. Like with administrative searches, the rules are a bit relaxed due to the society's interests in protecting children, maintaining an atmosphere where learning can take place, and allowing school officials to enforce rules and disciplinary procedures. The Court has held that a probable-cause finding is not necessary, because it would interfere with these mandates. Further, students have a more limited expectation of privacy in the school context than they may have elsewhere.

The standard by which searches at school are judged is that of reasonableness. As the Court held in the key case of *New Jersey v. T.L.O.,* 469 U.S. (1985), a search at school is justified if there are reasonable grounds to believe it will yield evidence of whether a student has violated the law or a school rule. In *T.L.O.,* a school official searched a student's purse after receiving a report that the student violated school rules by smoking in a school restroom. The *T.L.O.* Court upheld the legality of that search and also allowed enforcement action to be taken based on drugs and drug paraphernalia found in plain view in the student's purse during the search for cigarettes. The *T.L.O.* Court said that such a search is permissible in scope when measures adopted are reasonably related to the objectives of the search and not excessively intrusive in light of the student's age, sex, and nature of the offense.

Random drug testing has been another hot topic in applying the Fourth Amendment at schools. As with other school searches, courts have held that students have more-limited privacy interests when at school than elsewhere. And government officials have especially important interests in detecting and preventing drug use among students. The Court referred to this as a "special needs" situation in *Board of Education v. Earls,* 536 U.S. 822 (2002).

In *Earls,* the Supreme Court upheld the school board's policy of random drug testing for students participating in extracurricular activities. The Court said that students participate in such activities voluntarily, thereby subjecting themselves to many of the same intrusions on privacy as student athletes endure. (These intrusions include off-campus travel and "communal undress," as well as other limits on their freedom not faced by students not participating in extracurricular activities.) The Court further stated that the invasion of the students' privacy was not significant in this case given the manner in which the samples were taken and the limited use for the test results (which were only used to determine continued eligibility to participate in the extracurricular activity).

Searches at the workplace

The Fourth Amendment does apply in the government workplace (remember, the Constitution limits *government action*). But an individual's rights are somewhat diminished here as well. Courts, as always, balance individual rights against legitimate needs to conduct business. In judging the constitutionality of a workplace search, courts review the scope of the search, the procedures used, the level of intrusion, and the individual employee's subjective expectation of privacy in a given place. For example, the appellate court deciding *United States v. Simons,* 206 F.3d 392 (2000), upheld a random workplace computer search for unauthorized activity. The search uncovered the employee's possession of computer files containing child and other pornography. After the initial search revealed activity that was not only unauthorized, but illegal, authorities obtained a warrant for further search. In the private workplace, employees have no Fourth-Amendment rights against their employers; these rights would not kick in until government gets involved (say, if law enforcement comes searching for evidence of a crime after the private employer tips them off). Employees may have other claims against an employer with respect to how they are treated — but those issues are subjects for another book!

The practical reality is that most workplaces these days, government and otherwise, have policies in place allowing employers to conduct searches based on business needs. Employees most often consent to these terms when accepting a position (whether they remember doing so or not). Courts such as *Simons* recognize that because employees typically use office-issued equipment and are supposed to be working during office hours, employers have a right to search.

Chapter 16

The Right against Self-Incrimination

*T*his chapter discusses the Constitution's Fifth Amendment and the right against self-incrimination. This right, which applies to all individuals in both criminal and civil contexts, is integrally connected to "privacy" in that it is about individuals' right to keep information to themselves — and, specifically, not to be forced to divulge it to governmental authorities.

The first section of this chapter reviews the background of and major rights granted by the Fifth Amendment. The next section zeroes in on the right against self-incrimination and the various contexts in which the right is triggered. Specifically, we examine the development of the *Miranda* warning and its use before, during, and after arrest. We discuss real-world examples in which the right has been asserted, including by suspects and witnesses seeking to avoid testifying at trial. You get a good idea how the right plays out in criminal cases — and what the limitations of the right are.

You then discover what happens when a person's right against self-incrimination is violated and how the courts have applied the "fruits of the poisonous tree" doctrine we introduce in Chapter 15, which discusses search-and-seizure law. That doctrine ensures that illegally obtained evidence can't be used inappropriately. You also find out how courts make exceptions to the "fruits" rules and how a lively debate is occurring about the validity of this "exclusionary rule."

Finally, you get an understanding of the benefits of the right against self-incrimination in the context of civil cases, where the benefits apply very differently than in criminal cases.

Understanding the Background and Essence of the Fifth Amendment

The Constitution wouldn't provide much in the way of individual rights without its amendments (and especially without the first ten amendments commonly known as the *Bill of Rights*). Specifically, the Constitution wouldn't provide much in the way of protection against arbitrary law enforcement action without the ever-important Fifth Amendment:

> *No person shall be held to answer for a capital, or otherwise infamous crime, unless on a presentment or indictment of a Grand Jury, except in cases arising in the land or naval forces, or in the Militia, when in actual service in time of War or public danger; nor shall any person be subject for the same offence to be twice put in jeopardy of life or limb; nor shall be compelled in any criminal case to be a witness against himself, nor be deprived of life, liberty, or property, without due process of law; nor shall private property be taken for public use, without just compensation.*

In this fairly short paragraph, the Constitution's framers laid the foundation for a number of rights — civil and criminal — and an unbelievable amount of case law. You can break down the Fifth Amendment into the following different rights:

✔ **Grand jury indictment:** Federal defendants can't be tried for capital and other serious offenses without the approval of a *grand jury,* a special body of community members convened to review the strength of the prosecutor's evidence. If the grand jury finds that the prosecutor has probable cause for proceeding further — a "reasonable belief" that a crime has been committed and the defendant committed it — the grand jury hands down an *indictment,* a formal document charging the accused with criminal violations.

By contrast, state prosecutors can opt to avoid the grand-jury route and instead initiate capital or other serious criminal cases by filing complaints and holding *probable-cause hearings,* sometimes called *preliminary hearings.* (Note that some states may refer to the hearing differently; also, some states go through a more drawn-out process.) A probable cause hearing or preliminary hearing is the functional equivalent of a grand jury, but it takes place in front of a judge; thus, the same essential Fifth-Amendment functions are met. Putting forth evidence of probable cause is the key.

The rules of evidence for state probable cause hearings are different from those for a grand jury, and prosecutors sometimes make the decision as to which way to go based on those differences. Sometimes a grand jury takes longer, which can be a consideration as well.

After a grand jury, the indictment is the *charging document* (the document containing the complete charges against the defendant). Generally, after a probable cause hearing, if probable cause is established, a different charging document is filed with the court. For instance, in California, if a complaint is filed, then after the preliminary hearing, an *information* is filed on the charges for which the judge found probable cause. (Note that this is true for felony cases; in *misdemeanor* cases, which are less serious, prosecutors can file complaints and then proceed to trial without the probable cause hearing.)

The right to a grand-jury indictment is the only right in the Fifth Amendment not applicable to state officials. (As you find out in Chapter 8, only a few rights in the Bill of Rights have *not* been "incorporated" and applied to the states. This right is one of those few.) Therefore, state prosecutors have options when instituting criminal actions.

✔ **No double jeopardy:** Defendants initially acquitted on criminal charges can't be retried for the same offense.

✔ **No self-incrimination:** Suspects can't be forced to confess or otherwise involuntarily rat themselves out.

✔ **Due process:** No person can lose his life, liberty, or property without both

  • Adequate *procedures* (that is, fair notice, an appropriate hearing, and any other procedures that are "due" under the circumstances)

  • A sufficient *substantive* justification for government's interfering with his or her protected interest

✔ **Just compensation for property takings:** Governments can take private property for a wide range of public uses. But governments must reimburse property owners for the fair value of the seized property. (And let's not forget, that means the public ultimately pays via their tax dollars!)

As with many other constitutional provisions, the framers drafted the Fifth Amendment in response to specific concerns troubling the colonialists. They knew about the checkered history of English kings, whose prosecutors often abused criminal proceedings to retaliate against political enemies and free thinkers. The framers specifically tried to ensure that people wouldn't be forced into confessions when accused of something. The framers had seen similar abuses continue under colonial governors and wanted to avoid such abuses in the newly reconstituted American states.

But as with many other constitutional provisions, later interpreters see the Fifth Amendment as a source of general legal concepts transcending the particular background and history of framer concerns. For example, modern courts have transplanted notions of self-*incrimination* from their original criminal-law settings into proceedings before important governmental institutions not technically in a position to impose *criminal* sanctions (see the later section "'Taking the Fifth' before legislative and regulatory bodies" for details).

Reconciling Police Interrogation, Constitutional Guarantees, and Miranda

You've undoubtedly heard of *Miranda rights,* but you may not know what this case was about or how the specific rights evolved. *Miranda v. Arizona,* 384 U.S. 436 (1966), involved multiple defendants convicted of various crimes after being questioned, confessing, and having the confessions admitted against them in court. Ernesto Miranda was arrested and charged with rape, kidnapping, and robbery. Police questioned him for two hours, and he confessed. The police had never told him he had a right to remain silent or that he was entitled to an attorney, and he did not have an attorney present when he was questioned by police. The Supreme Court heard the case and found in favor of Miranda and others, overturning Miranda's conviction (although he was later retried and convicted without the illegally obtained confession).

The ban on putting a defendant in double jeopardy doesn't apply when a conviction is overturned on constitutional (or other legal) grounds. The defendant who is retried after conviction is "twice put in jeopardy . . . for the same offense" in a practical *but not legally significant* sense. Case law assumes that overturning the past conviction puts the defendant and prosecutor back where they started. Retrying the defendant does not implicate the core concern of the self-incrimination clause: that, having once failed to convince a jury of guilt, the prosecution is trying to get a second bite at the conviction apple.

The *Miranda* Court enumerated certain things that police must tell people after they're arrested as a safeguard for people who may be wrongfully accused and/or who may not even be aware of their rights. The Court said that before "custodial interrogation" (questioning someone who is in custody and thus not free to leave), police must tell the suspect the following information:

- ✔ You have the right to remain silent.
- ✔ Anything you say [can and] will be used against you in court.
- ✔ You have a right to consult with a lawyer.
- ✔ You have the right to have a lawyer present during questioning.
- ✔ If you cannot afford an attorney, one will be appointed for you.

Often police want to talk to a suspect after an arrest. Before proceeding to question the suspect without an attorney present, police usually (and should!) verify that the person understands the rights and wants to waive them.

We often note that constitutional law requires reconciling competing interests. Miranda rights reconcile the competing interests of the individual suspect's rights (and the society's interests in avoiding police abuses and, ultimately, a police state) and the interests of law enforcement (which, as the Supreme Court has consistently recognized, is charged with protecting the public — no small task).

The challenge for the Court is to make sure that individual rights are protected while making sure not to frustrate law enforcement's efforts to the point where it can't do its job. As the Court acknowledged in *Miranda,* "Our decision is not intended to hamper the traditional function of police officers in investigating crime"; "the limitations on the interrogation process required for the protection of the individual's constitutional rights should not cause an undue interference with a proper system of law enforcement, as demonstrated by the procedures of the FBI and the safeguards afforded in other jurisdictions."

Case law continues to evolve in this area, considering a myriad of different circumstances and deciding whether certain scenarios violate the Fifth-Amendment right against self-incrimination. The following four subsections explore many of the most important wrinkles, depending upon the timing of questioning (pre-arrest, during arrest, and later in court) and other special contexts.

Answering questions before arrest: Terry stops

In *Terry v. Ohio,* 392 U.S. 1 (1968), the Court recognized law enforcement's need to protect police officers and the practicalities of a beat cop's job in protecting the public. This case solidified a police officer's ability to talk to citizens and even make a "pat down" of a person based on a "reasonable suspicion that criminal activity is afoot." A police officer is allowed to do this to prevent a potential crime from being committed and to protect the officer's own safety. As we discuss in Chapter 15, the main focus of the Court in *Terry* was the reality that the "pat down" and checking to see what the officer felt in the defendant's clothing (which yielded an illegally concealed weapon) amounted to a search.

The Court found that the officer's actions were acceptable under the Fourth Amendment, based on specific facts leading the officer to believe that Terry and his cohort might be about to commit a crime (justifying the officer's approach of the suspects) and could be armed and dangerous (justifying more specifically the "pat down" and search). This satisfied the requirement that the officers have a "reasonable suspicion that criminal activity was afoot" (articulable reasons for thinking a crime is about to occur).

Terry is worth noting here because it solidified the right of law-enforcement officers (assuming that they otherwise meet the *Terry* stop requirements) to talk to suspects without "Mirandizing" them. The *Terry* Court did not say a suspect in this situation must talk to police. But the key is that a suspect's failure to talk does *not* mean that police must stop questioning or call in an attorney. The police can keep attempting to talk to the suspect. In other words, the police do not have to follow the parameters set out in *Miranda* when making a *Terry* stop. An individual is free to talk or not talk in this situation, but the police do not have to advise them of their rights. Of course, if suspects say that they won't talk without attorneys, the questioning should stop; also, the suspects should be Mirandized at that point if the police are ready to arrest. But suspects' evasiveness in this type of scenario may give the police more suspicion.

Asserting the "right to remain silent" after arrest

Suspects in police custody can at any time assert their right to remain silent and their right to have an attorney present during questioning. Suspects decide for themselves when and how much they wants to speak — either during police interrogation or later after charges are filed. In *Miranda,* the Court stated, "If the individual indicates, prior to or during questioning, that he wishes to remain silent, the interrogation must cease; if he states that he wants an attorney, the questioning must cease until an attorney is present." The Court further explained that "Where the individual answers some questions during in-custody interrogation, he has not waived his privilege, and may invoke his right to remain silent thereafter."

As simple as that sounds, many cases have grappled with precisely when the right to silence has been invoked. That is, what exactly does the person have to say? In some cases a suspect or defendant may be too vague to be considered to have asserted the right. (For example, a suspect could mumble something about "talking to someone" or say something along the lines of "I really don't know. . . .") But as a practical matter, cops and prosecutors are generally (or should be!) very careful. Literally, as soon as a suspect utters the word "attorney" during questioning, regardless of whether he previously said he wanted to talk, the questioning should, and usually does, stop. Case law reinforces that this procedure is appropriate.

The right to remain silent is never completely waived. At any time, a suspect can assert the right to remain silent (and/or ask for an attorney), period.

The need to speak to claim the right not to speak

It may be ironic, but a recent Supreme Court case emphasized that a defendant wanting to claim his Miranda right not to speak must, well, speak! In *Berghuis v. Thompkins,* 130 S.Ct. 2250 (2010), the police had questioned Thompkins, a murder suspect, for a few hours after reading him his rights. He essentially sat silent for most of the time until police asked him if he prayed to God to forgive him for the murder and he responded, "Yes." This statement was admissible in court, and he was convicted.

Thompkins filed an appeal claiming that his silence should be considered an assertion of his right to remain silent. The Supreme Court found that because the defendant did not specifically say he wanted to remain silent or that he didn't want to talk to police, he had not

asserted his right. Had he made either of those simple "unambiguous" statements, the Court said, he would've invoked his right to cut off questioning. But because he had done neither, his right to silence had not been invoked.

Some argue that the *Thompkins* case flies in the face of *Miranda* and actually rewrites law established by that case. After all, the *Miranda* Court said that silence is not a waiver of an individual's Fifth-Amendment rights. But the other argument is that *Thompkins* just articulates that silence doesn't mean the police have to stop talking to a suspect — just as a waiver can't be presumed by silence, the person's silence also doesn't operate to automatically *invoke* a person's right to silence. In short, a suspect's silence neither invokes the right nor constitutes a waiver.

Concerning the right to counsel, the adjoining Fifth and Sixth Amendments interact in interesting ways. The Sixth Amendment affords a criminal defendant a separate right to counsel at every critical stage of a criminal case. The Fifth Amendment, in contrast, doesn't explicitly reference the role of counsel. The right to have one during interrogation is born out of and intertwined with the right not to incriminate oneself. Case law presumes that the presence of attorneys during custodial interrogation assures that Fifth-Amendment rights are not violated.

Extending the right to the courtroom

The right against self-incrimination is demonstrated in the criminal court-room in different ways, depending on whether the person asserting the right is the defendant or a witness.

Analyzing the self-incrimination rights of defendants

The general right of defendants not to be compelled to "take the stand" to testify in their own defense gives rise to three related prerogatives:

✔ **Most fundamentally, the defendant doesn't even have to put on a single witness as part of her case.** She can sit back (not that being a defendant in a criminal case is actually relaxing!) and just wait to see whether the prosecution actually proves its case.

✔ **Even if she does put on a case (with witnesses and documents), the defendant doesn't have to testify.** The prosecution can't issue a subpoena for a defendant the way it can issue subpoenas for other witnesses.

✔ **Going a step farther, prosecutors aren't allowed to do or say anything suggesting that the defendant should take the stand or comment on the fact that the defendant didn't take the stand.** In fact, to be especially protective of the defendant's right not to testify, judges instruct the jury in criminal cases not to place any significance on the defendant's failure to testify. Even some rather vague references to a lack of explanation of circumstances or presentation of evidence have been found to be prosecutorial error, though not necessarily enough to overturn a case.

The Court solidified these Fifth-Amendment rights in the landmark case of *Griffin v. California,* 380 U.S. 609 (1965). In closing argument, the prosecutor talked quite a bit about the fact that the defendant was seen with the victim in the alley where her body was found, and that the defendant had not taken the stand to explain or deny whether he had beaten her. The prosecutor's comments were acceptable under an article in the California Constitution specifically allowing attorneys to comment about a criminal defendant's failure to testify or explain away prosecution evidence.

The *Griffin* Court found, however, that such comments and the California Constitution's "comment rule" violated the defendant's Fifth-Amendment rights. In reversing the defendant's conviction, the Court stated that even innocent people may not want to take the stand and that commenting on the refusal to testify amounts to a penalty for exercising a constitutional privilege. Although the *Griffin* Court held back from deciding that the defendant was entitled to a jury instruction to infer no guilt from the defendant's failure to testify, case law now requires that such an instruction be given on request and courts routinely do so even without a request.

Analyzing the self-incrimination rights of witnesses other than the defendant

Distinct from a defendant's right not to take the stand is the general Fifth-Amendment right of all persons not to be forced to incriminate themselves through any kind of involvement in a criminal trial. Witnesses cannot be compelled to answer any questions tending to expose them to criminal penalties. This application of the right against self-incrimination has some interesting implications, including the following:

✔ **A witness exposed to self-incrimination on the stand needs to be advised by his own attorney.** Due to a conflict of interests, the prosecutor (and typically the defendant's attorney) can't advise the witness. (The prosecutor represents "the people," and the defendant's attorney has a client whose interests may or may not be aligned with the witness.) In such a case, a separate attorney will be appointed by the court to advise the witness before he takes the stand and represent him while he testifies if necessary.

✔ **Sometimes a witness's exercise of her right not to testify, lest she incriminate herself, may appear illusory.** In such a case, an attorney can challenge the witness, and the witness has the burden of showing that she really has a valid reason to refuse to testify. The court then determines whether the witness really will be put in a position of self-incrimination if she testifies. Usually this step consists of a brief probe by the judge as to what the line of questioning will be and very generally why the witness is claiming the privilege. This questioning generally takes place outside the jury's presence.

Note the interesting contrast to the defendant's right against self-incrimination. Like defendants, witnesses can't ultimately be forced to put themselves in legal jeopardy. But unlike defendants, who can simply assert the right not to testify, witnesses can be further scrutinized when they "take the Fifth." This difference points up both the Constitution's special emphasis on the rights of the defendant on trial and the reality that the primary focus of a criminal trial is on protecting the defendant while serving the interests of society; witnesses are a *means* to those ends.

✔ **The prosecution can usually eliminate a self-incrimination issue for a witness by granting immunity from prosecution.** After immunity is granted, the witness can be forced to testify upon penalty of being held in contempt of court.

Dave robs the corner store and then asks his friend Joe whether he can hide out at Joe's house. Joe says yes and thus becomes an accomplice in the robbery because he helped Dave hide from the police. Dave is later arrested and put on trial for the robbery, and the prosecution calls Joe to the stand. But Joe "takes the Fifth" because if he testifies he may incriminate himself and wind up getting charged for a crime (for being an accomplice). To eliminate the issue of self-incrimination, the prosecution offers Joe immunity from being tried as an accomplice in Dave's crime. Joe can then testify freely (from a legal standpoint, anyway).

Witness self-incrimination issues are always theoretically possible, but are more typical in gang or organized-crime cases involving witnesses who are often guilty of their own misdeeds. Sometimes prosecutors grant immunity to a witness for his crimes so he'll testify truthfully against the perceived more-culpable party without fear of later being prosecuted for his own crimes.

Understanding what the right of silence does (and doesn't) cover

Although an individual always has a right to silence, a person can't be shielded from anything and everything she says. Some circumstances do not trigger the right of silence, and some scenarios can disqualify a person from protection.

To begin with, *Miranda* doesn't protect a person who decides freely to speak "in the unfettered exercise" of his own will. In other words, the Court did *not* say the police have any obligation to *stop* a person from talking. So if an individual gets arrested and decides to blurt a host of information out to the police, it's not necessarily protected. The police do not have to elaborate on *Miranda* rights beyond telling a person, prior to custodial interrogation, that she has certain rights. Nor must police inform a suspect, for instance, "You know, if you tell us you did it, you're almost certain to be convicted" or anything like that. In addition, the police could arrest someone and wait a while to Mirandize them, and if the person in custody decides to ramble on to the police about what happened, what he says is still admissible in court. (Police can and do sometimes wait to Mirandize in situations where, for instance, they feel that their evidence is solid enough that they don't necessarily need to interrogate the suspect.)

Here is a good example of "unfettered exercise" of a person's own will to speak to the police: While working for a judge, one of the authors reviewed a *motion to suppress* (which asks the court to keep out evidence) brought by a young man who was arrested for bludgeoning his parents to death. While in the police car, unprompted by police, the defendant told the police he wanted to talk to them. They advised him of his rights, and he said he wanted to talk. Again, they told him of his rights but said he could talk if he wanted to. (Again, this case illustrates how *Miranda* does not protect against voluntary self-revelation.) The defendant blurted out a confession of how and why he killed his father and mother. After he was charged for the double homicide, the defendant filed a motion to suppress the statements, claiming that they were not voluntary and taken in violation of *Miranda*. The judge ruled that the statements could come in at trial, and of course the defendant was convicted.

Even when the statements were voluntary when made, defendants often later claim they were not. This denial is sometimes the only way defendants can try to challenge statements to prevent highly incriminating evidence from coming in at trial.

So remember, the courts can protect people from a lot of things, but they can't necessarily protect people from themselves!

In addition to cases of a defendant's unrestrained blurting, the right against self-incrimination also is inapplicable in the following circumstances:

- ✔ **When the defendant *specifically* waives the right:** The key to the prosecution using statements against a suspect is making sure that the suspect made a *voluntary,* or "knowing and intelligent," waiver of his Fifth-Amendment rights. As the *Miranda* Court emphasized, "Where an interrogation is conducted without the presence of an attorney and a statement is taken, a heavy burden rests on the Government to demonstrate that the defendant knowingly and intelligently waived his right to counsel."

  As a practical matter, a knowing and voluntary waiver mostly boils down to the police's making sure that the suspect acknowledges that he has been advised of his rights under *Miranda* and wants to answer questions anyway. And when questioning a suspect, especially in higher profile cases, the waiver may be videotaped along with the interrogation itself. In such a case, police may even break down the *Miranda* rights for the suspect and have him acknowledge and waive each aspect. Sometimes police take a written waiver from a suspect. But again, police don't have to stop a suspect from talking or tell him anything other than the standard advisements.

  Waivers, both written and on tape, are often either found to be valid or are never challenged. But courts still look at outside factors potentially invalidating a waiver. So, for example, the court considers everything that the suspect and the police said, what the physical surroundings were like when the waiver was made, what the attitude of the police officer(s) was, and anything else that happened around the time the waiver was made. For instance, coercion (which involves severe pressure by police) may invalidate a waiver.

- ✔ **When police have suspicion of a crime but have not yet made an arrest:** Suppose a police officer pulls over a driver for a traffic violation such as failing to signal before changing lanes or speeding. The officer then realizes the driver has had a few drinks, because he's slurring his speech or smells of alcohol. The officer now has a reasonable suspicion to believe that the person may be driving under the influence. The officer can then start asking questions about what the driver had to drink that night, how much he had, or where he was. The driver doesn't have to answer, but because the driver isn't under arrest yet, the officer doesn't have to read the driver his rights. Most people answer. (It may have something to do with the recklessness alcohol tends to bring on!) Everything the driver says can be admitted into evidence at trial.

- ✔ **When police seek "physical," as opposed to "testimonial," evidence:** Asking a suspect to do things like participate in a lineup for possible witness identification, or give a blood sample, do not trigger the right against self-incrimination (*Schmerber v. California,* 384 U.S. 757 [1966]).

The prosecution must meet certain technical requirements in order to be able to introduce a lineup identification later at trial. Also, a person is entitled to counsel at a lineup after criminal proceedings are initiated. These requirements exist to ensure that the lineup is not somehow biased against the suspect; the requirements help to support the credibility of a positive identification.

Similarly, a variety of courts, including *Johnson,* hold that fingerprinting a suspect at the time of arrest can be done regardless of whether the suspect has chosen to exercise his right to silence. This acquisition of physical evidence is done routinely as part of the process of booking individuals into jail after arrest.

Enforcing Miranda through the Exclusionary Rule

Violation of the Fifth-Amendment right against self-incrimination is akin to violation of the Fourth-Amendment right against unreasonable search and seizure (which we discuss in Chapter 15). It goes to the core of a person's privacy and the notion that you don't have to put everything out there for everyone's — especially the government's — knowledge or access. No more do Americans want someone forcing them to make a confession (or say something potentially incriminating) than they do having someone search their home without a legally justifiable reason.

Understanding the rule

Confessions obtained in violation of the *Miranda* rules and evidence found as a result of what police find out through these confessions are illegally obtained. So Fifth-Amendment law borrows the remedy that courts created to deal with Fourth-Amendment violations: the exclusionary rule and the "fruits of the poisonous tree" doctrine.

The *exclusionary rule* means that a confession obtained in violation of a person's *Miranda* rights is not admissible at trial against the defendant. And the *fruits of the poisonous tree doctrine* means that any evidence that was found due to that illegal confession is suppressed as well, unless an exception applies to the other evidence obtained. For instance, if the confession led police to evidence that the police would've found as a result of independent information learned later, the inevitable discovery exception may apply to ultimately make that evidence admissible.

To make a claim of violation of an individual's constitutional rights, a defendant first has to have *standing*. (*Standing* means that the challenger asserting constitutional rights has been personally injured and so has a sufficient "stake" in asserting his rights.) Generally, third parties can't complain when the rights of others are violated; people must assert their *own* constitutional rights when they have a reason (such as their own separate case) to do so. Standing has more application to Fourth-Amendment violations, as we discuss in Chapter 15.

Allowing the confession or fruits anyway: Exceptions to the rule

What's a rule without exceptions, right? As with so many other areas of law, the exclusionary rule and the fruits of the poisonous tree doctrine have several important exceptions.

Applying the Bill of Rights always involves a balancing act in protecting individual rights while not thwarting law enforcement's legitimate efforts to do its job properly, as the Court articulated in *Miranda*. The same balancing act is involved in the exclusionary rule and the exceptions to it. Courts always seek to encourage police to follow constitutional requirements — even if violation of constitutional rights would solve an important crime and be used to convict a wrongdoer — to protect individuals' rights. However, the courts don't want to punish police mistakes that stem from legitimate or "good faith" efforts gone awry.

As we explain in Chapter 15, courts recognize several exceptions to the exclusionary rule for evidence obtained in violation of the Fourth Amendment. Those exceptions are also applicable to Fifth-Amendment violations, at least theoretically. However, for example, one of those exceptions (which excuses "good faith" violations of the rules about searches and seizures) is really not applicable to the right against self-incrimination. As a practical matter, failure to Mirandize a suspect prior to custodial interrogation is always going to result in courts throwing out any self-incriminating statements or confessions, unless the scenario lends itself to a finding those statements were voluntary, which doesn't hinge on whether or not law enforcement had good intentions.

The main exclusionary-rule exception relevant to the Fifth-Amendment context is the *attenuation* exception, which kicks in when the confession is *attenuated,* or sufficiently separated from the illegal activity of police. This exception doesn't "forgive" the *Miranda* violation because police acted in good faith. Rather, the exception discounts the *Miranda* violation because it does not seem sufficiently connected to the later confession to say that the violation "caused" the later revelation of defendant secrets.

Ongoing controversy over the exclusionary rule: Is there a better way?

Over the years, the exclusionary rule has been the subject of much debate. Some critics argue that the exclusionary rule inappropriately interferes with the prosecution of guilty defendants, fails to effectively deter police misconduct, or both. Would police be more likely to follow the Fifth Amendment if they weren't immune from lawsuits by parties whose rights they violate? Or is more-effective discipline of police who violate the Fifth Amendment the answer?

Some disputants of the rule want disciplinary action or monetary sanctions against police in place of the exclusionary rule — or *in addition* to excluding "tainted" evidence. Opinions differ significantly depending on views about the proper balance between preserving defendants' rights and making sure not to deter police from performing their job properly. (For example, police may overcorrect out of fear that they'll be held personally liable for mistakes.)

Supporters of the status quo argue that, at present, the most egregious police behavior can be adequately addressed; police can be sued if their constitutional violations are in bad faith, or they can be disciplined in their jobs. Supporters argue that police do respond to

the exclusionary rule by avoiding interrogation practices that will place critical confessions at risk.

For now, the Courts and legislatures don't appear likely to change the rules that are in place. In fact, most observers were surprised that the Supreme Court decided to reaffirm *Miranda* in a 2000 case directly challenging its continued validity. In *Dickerson v. United States,* 530 U.S. 428 (2000), seven justices led by Chief Justice Rehnquist (himself no real fan of *Miranda*) invalidated a congressional statute seeking to return federal criminal prosecutions to a pre-*Miranda* world in which confessions may be deemed voluntary under a "totality of the circumstances" test (that is, looking at all circumstances surrounding the statements). Nor did the Court deem overruling *Miranda* appropriate — even though the justices could have said that *Miranda* was a Court-made remedy not expressly required by the Fifth Amendment. Among other reasons to stick with precedent, the majority noted that "*Miranda* has become embedded in routine police procedure to the point where the warnings have become part of our national culture."

If police arrest a suspect and start interrogating him without reading him his *Miranda* rights, any confession he makes is inadmissible in court. Change the circumstances, however, and assume that the suspect is arraigned on criminal charges, gets released from custody, and comes back days later and confesses. Now the confession is admissible, due to the attenuation exception. The Court held in *Wong Sun v. United States,* 371 U.S. 471 (1963), that the key question is whether the events leading to the confession are sufficiently distinguishable from the illegal arrest (or illegal confession) so that the new confession is "purged of the primary taint."

Applying Self-Incrimination Rights outside the Typical Criminal Context

Fifth-Amendment rights arise mostly in the context of a criminal arrest and later proceedings. But the right against self-incrimination is applicable in other contexts as well — although some critics find the Fifth Amendment's noncriminal reach incomplete. This section explores Fifth-Amendment rights in the context of civil litigation, testimony before regulatory and congressional officials, required administrative reports, and as a barrier to the enforcement of tax obligations.

"Taking the Fifth" in civil litigation

In courtroom disputes over civil matters (for example, over money or contract issues), parties and witnesses may risk disclosure of matters potentially exposing themselves to criminal penalty. Parties and witnesses retain their rights against self-incrimination. But the rights play out in civil cases in very different ways.

Unlike in criminal cases, civil parties and witnesses can be compelled to testify (in trial and at depositions). Although they may still "take the Fifth" when testifying to avoid particular risky self-disclosures, unlike in criminal cases, judges and juries can use the civil litigant's failure to answer questions against her, assuming that she is admitting the truth of what she doesn't deny.

The Court upheld this point in *Baxter v. Supreme Court,* 425 U.S. 308 (1976), in which a prison inmate accused of starting a disturbance faced 30 days of "punitive segregation" and having his release status downgraded. He failed to speak up in his own defense, and later challenged the ability of prison authorities to draw a negative conclusion from the inmate's silence. The *Baxter* Court held that, because the inmate was not exposed to criminal liability and because applicable rules relied on the disciplinary decision being based on other "substantial evidence" besides the inmate's silence, the Fifth Amendment was not violated. Later case decisions have consistently recognized that, in proper circumstances, silence in the face of a civil accusation can be part of the evidence used against the accused.

In a case one of the authors worked on, a school district was using its eminent-domain power to take a piece of property from homeowners to build a new school. The owners were extremely upset because the property had been in their family for many years. Two of the owners, who were brothers, decided that if their property was going to get taken, they would at least maximize the economic return. (The "fair market value" of the property, not the subjective value of the property to the homeowner, is all the government has to pay when taking someone's property.) The brothers conducted "straw man" transactions — sales of the property to and from different individuals for increasingly higher prices — to inflate the on-paper value of the property in an attempt to hike up the compensation the government would have to pay. One of the brothers testified at a deposition as part of the litigation disputing the value of the property. When asked about the straw man sales, the brother took the Fifth (on the premise that he might've exposed himself to potential criminal prosecution for conducting fraudulent real-estate transactions). In fact, other than responding to a few questions, his whole deposition transcript was him declining to answer on grounds that the answers could incriminate him. Needless to say, this refusal to answer did not bode well for him and his case.

Civil litigation also doesn't play by the criminal-case rule that the defendant need not take the stand himself or put on a single witness. Failure to do either can prejudice the Court against the civil litigant who takes the Fifth as much as any other civil litigant who fails to prove his case. And unlike in a criminal proceeding, the jury will know about the defendant's taking the Fifth and not wanting to answer tough questions.

"Taking the Fifth" before legislative and regulatory bodies

As in civil litigation, individuals participating in legislative or administrative proceedings (including as parties seeking or opposing legislative or administrative action) can prompt Fifth-Amendment self-incrimination issues.

When claiming Fifth-Amendment protection in these proceedings, the results are similar to those in litigation (see the preceding section). Witnesses can't decline to take the stand, but they can refuse to answer incriminating questions or to provide subpoenaed documents that could subject them to potential prosecution. (Of course, Congress or the state legislature has the power to grant "limited" immunity, thereby eliminating the criminal risk to the person by testifying, or the person can be jailed for contempt of court for refusing to do so.)

And no constitutional rule prohibits officials, the public, or the media from forming adverse impressions or taking adverse actions against a witness who clams up. (Think of the times you've seen athletes testify in front of legislative committees and take the Fifth when asked whether they used performance-enhancing drugs. What did you think? Pretty obvious the person had something to hide, right?)

Taking the Fifth before legislative and regulatory bodies presents special complications for corporate entities. The Court has held that corporations, as opposed to individuals (including corporate officers), do not have Fifth-Amendment self-incrimination rights (*United States v. Kordel,* 397 U.S. 1 [1970]). Basically, corporations do not have a "self" to incriminate. (Individuals who work for a corporation, however, maintain their individual right against self-incrimination.) This distinction can lead to difficult dilemmas, as when a person acting contrary to corporate policies takes the Fifth, prompting an adverse inference against the corporation. (The inapplicability of the Fifth Amendment to corporations also means that they don't have any right to resist compelled regulatory reports or requests to produce documents.)

Mandating reports of regulatory matters and violations

An individual's (but not a corporation's!) Fifth-Amendment right against self-incrimination may come up with regard to government's typical practice of requiring that regulated parties maintain records subject to inspection by administrative officials. In a very real sense, required recordkeeping obligates individuals to "rat themselves out" to the government by providing evidence of wrongdoing that only the regulated individuals know (or at least are in the best position to know). The nuances of these compelled reports are beyond the scope of this book. But note here that the specialized view courts bring to mandated administrative reports doesn't end up protecting regulated parties very much.

Under the formulation of *Shapiro v. United States,* 335 U.S. 1 (1948), Congress can require regulated businesses to maintain records to be inspected by enforcement officials. These required records can be the basis for civil sanctions (or even criminal penalties), notwithstanding the right against self-incrimination, as long as the records are of the kind "customarily kept" by the business owner and there is "a sufficient relationship between the activity sought to be regulated" and a matter of "public concern." In *Shapiro,* the required records established that store owners violated World War II–era criminal laws controlling the sale of groceries.

Required regulatory reporting also arises when individuals are required to report violations of public laws, such as environmental laws. Clearly, as the 2010 BP oil-drilling disaster in the Gulf of Mexico shows, industry sources are often in the best position to report law violations by company executives.

Taxing illegal activities and self-incrimination

Normal, law-abiding citizens earn legitimate income and file tax returns reporting their income and what it is from. But some people make substantial income from criminal activity — and not just the violent sort. Many drug dealers, white-collar criminals committing securities fraud and the like, and organized-crime members (a combination of violent mob types and white-collar criminals) make a lot of money. And they, too, are supposed to report their income — all of it.

The fact that the *source* of reported income is also requested on a tax return has been the subject of some case law. The argument is that requiring taxpayers to identify the sources of their illegally gained income necessarily forces them to incriminate themselves. Picture this: John reports $100,000 in income and then has to tell the government he got that money by dealing drugs. The courts have agreed that this requirement violates his right against self-incrimination under the Fifth Amendment, although they've said the remedy is for the person to refuse to identify the specific activity which yielded the income, simply writing "Fifth Amendment" in the space for identifying the source of income.

The protection offered by this solution may sound illusory, because that response on a tax form could obviously give the government a heads-up that the person may be engaged in illegal activity. But the IRS and state taxing agencies can't use such a response to get law enforcement to *initiate* an investigation into illegal activity. However, prosecutors do have access to people's tax returns if a case has been initiated independent of the response on a tax return.

Tax forms are available to law enforcement when a case involving that person is brought to them through other avenues. For instance, often prosecutors file tax-evasion charges, along with charges for things such as securities fraud, after complaints from investors who believe that they've been defrauded. In those types of cases, defendants usually do not report on their tax returns income that is considered to be stolen. (And they often actually don't file tax returns at all; in such a case, the Fifth Amendment does not come into play.) After tax forms are obtained as part of an investigation on a case, a response of "Fifth Amendment" as the source of income obviously reinforces the validity of the prosecution's case.

However, as a practical matter, individuals commonly don't report income from illegal activity at all. In *Marchetti v. United States,* 390 U.S. 39 (1968), the Court held that the Fifth Amendment was a complete defense to prosecution for a professional gambler's failure to register as a gambler (an illegal occupation) and pay a federal "occupational tax" on wagering. Because the "consistent practice" of the IRS at that time was to provide information derived from registration and tax paying to "interested prosecuting authorities," the Court held that gamblers had a "reasonable expectation" that registration and tax paying would "significantly enhance the likelihood of their prosecution" and would "really provide evidence [. . .] facilitate[ing] their conviction." Punishing taxpayers for failure to provide evidence of their own criminal conduct was unconstitutional self-incrimination. However, *Marchetti* suggests that if there are appropriate protections in place to assure a taxpayer that reporting illegal income will not trigger the interest of those responsible for enforcing the criminal laws, the Fifth Amendment would not be violated.

The *Marchetti* Court distinguished this reporting requirement from the typical regulatory-reporting mandate upheld in the *Shapiro* case because the records required of *Marchetti* were not the kind gamblers "customarily kept." There was no "public aspect" to the records the IRS required. More fundamentally, the *Marchetti* Court distinguished between "an essentially non-criminal and regulatory area of inquiry" (allowed!) and a targeted disclosure scheme aimed at a "selective group inherently suspect of criminal activities."

Part VI
The Part of Tens

The 5th Wave   By Rich Tennant

In this part . . .

Books on law could take up an unfathomable number of warehouses. And in the specific area of constitutional law, countless cases are important and worth discussing. In this part, we give you examples of cases covering just some of the important constitutional-law holdings. Just from reading this part alone, you'll have a good sense of the most important concepts in constitutional law today and how the courts arrived at their conclusions.

Chapter 17

Ten Landmark Court Decisions about Governmental Structure

In This Chapter

▶ Establishing the power of the federal judiciary

▶ Granting and limiting congressional and presidential power

*A*ny list of the top ten most important government-structure cases is inevitably going to be somewhat arbitrary (or biased!). As with other areas of law, the number of cases is vast and each case has its own importance, but we simply don't have room to fit them all in this book. Despite the obvious limitations, here is our list of the ten most important Supreme Court decisions regarding the structure of government. We cover key cases that granted and limited power of the federal judiciary, Congress, and the president. We have done our best to select cases that we think will give you the most benefit in terms of a quick reference of important cases in this area affecting American society today.

Authorizing Judicial Review: Marbury v. Madison

Marbury and others were appointed as justices of the peace for the District of Columbia. But President John Adams left office before Marbury and his fellow appointees were given their papers to take office. The new president, Jefferson, wanted to appoint new justices loyal to his party, and so ordered his secretary of state not to deliver the commissions. Marbury brought suit in the Supreme Court for a "writ of mandamus" (an order to perform an official duty) ordering the papers to be delivered, and the Judiciary Act of 1789 authorized the Court to issue these writs. The Court held in *Marbury v. Madison,* 5 U.S. 137 (1803), that it was unconstitutional for the Act to give the Supreme Court authority to issue writs of mandamus to public officers. In this case, the court famously stated, "It is emphatically the duty of the Judicial Department to say what the law is," holding for the first time that a law was unconstitutional.

You can't overestimate the impact of *Marbury* on the power of the federal judiciary and, even more broadly, the power of *Marbury* to preserve the limitations of the Constitution and keep elected officials in line (see Chapter 6 for details). Simply put, *Marbury* claimed for the federal judiciary an awesome power not necessarily fully justified by the Constitution's express provisions — namely, the power of *judicial review,* which establishes that the federal courts have the authority to consider the constitutionality of, and declare null and void, decisions by all other officials at the federal, state, and local levels.

In establishing this authority, *Marbury* ensured that the institution most immune from short-term majority political passions (that is, the Court) could protect and defend constitutional values. The Supreme Court and its federal lower-court brethren haven't always lived up to the task, but we have a freer and more orderly society, characterized by the "rule of law," because of *Marbury*'s holding.

Establishing Judicial Supremacy: Cooper v. Aaron

After the Court ordered school desegregation in *Brown v. Board of Education,* 347 U.S. 483 (1954), the school district in Little Rock, Arkansas, was under a court order to comply. Worried about violence after mob threats were inflamed by a defiant state governor, school officials sought court approval to suspend desegregation for a time. As presented to the Supreme Court, their case, *Cooper v. Aaron,* 358 U.S. 1 (1958), questioned whether the *Brown* decision was itself binding on state officials or whether a new round of litigation would be necessary to make *Brown* binding on state and local authorities. The Court found that the state and governor could not nullify federal law. *Brown* was the supreme law of the land, and the states were bound by it.

In hindsight, *Cooper* seems nothing less than a second *Marbury* (which we cover in the preceding section). *Marbury* didn't necessarily claim a "special" role for the federal courts. It could be interpreted as making the federal judiciary a constitutional equal, merely one of three branches with independent power to interpret the Constitution and act on that interpretation. Nothing in *Marbury* necessarily implies that the Supreme Court is the "ultimate" constitutional interpreter, whose decisions state and federal officials are obligated to follow in their official actions.

Cooper filled in that gap. In no uncertain terms, *Cooper* stated "the basic principle that the federal judiciary is supreme in the exposition of the law of the Constitution." *Cooper* reasoned that, by making the Constitution the "supreme law of the land," Article VI also makes "the interpretation[s] enunciated by this Court . . . the supreme law of the land." Thus, the Court equated constitutional supremacy with *judicial supremacy.*

The decision in *Cooper* logically implies that Congress and the president are obligated to bend to Supreme Court decisions as soon as they are made. After all, Congress and the president take an oath to support and defend the Constitution. If Supreme Court decisions are equivalent to the words of the Constitution itself, then Congress and the president must give supremacy to those decisions as well!

Marking Judicial Superiority in Enforcing Individual Liberties: City of Boerne v. Flores

Flores was the Archbishop of San Antonio. His congregation wanted to enlarge one of their churches to accommodate the number of parishioners attending masses. Their request for a permit to expand the church was denied (under a local ordinance limiting construction in historical districts). The congregation brought suit to get the permit, relying on the Religious Freedom of Restoration Act of 1993 (RFRA), and the case went up to the Supreme Court. The Supreme Court held in *City of Boerne v. Flores,* 521 U.S. 507 (1997), that Congress had exceeded its power in enacting RFRA.

Boerne signaled the end of an era in which the Court gave substantial deference to Congress when that body legislated to protect Bill-of-Rights liberties against state and local government violations. *Boerne* ushered in the continuing practice of more-searching judicial second-guessing of Congress, replacing a period in which Congress and the Court were copartners in protecting individual rights with a regime in which federal judges are the senior partners. Now Congress can't define new substantive rights. It can only remedy rights already defined, and when it does so, it must satisfy the judiciary that its remedial legislation actions are "congruent" and "proportional."

Limiting Standing to Sue: Allen v. Wright

Not all modern decisions expanded federal judicial power. As Chapter 6 explores, some modern Court-created "justiciability" doctrines limit access to federal courts; in the process, these decisions reduce federal-court interference with the discretion of elected officials. The most important of these restrictive standing cases is *Allen v. Wright,* 468 U.S. 737 (1984).

The plaintiffs in this case were the parents of African American children attending racially desegregated schools. The parents were upset because they did not believe the IRS was adequately enforcing its rules of denying tax-exempt status to racially discriminatory schools. A number of private (and allegedly racially discriminatory) schools had popped up in their area, which the parents felt was encouraged by the IRS's lack of diligent enforcement. The Supreme Court held that the parents did not have standing to sue.

Allen erected several potential barriers to individuals and entities wanting to challenge laws and policies at all government levels. Especially when governmental policies injure the litigant indirectly by restraining or failing to restrain other "third parties" subject to federal regulation, litigants risk a federal judge seeing their injuries as too "speculative" or occurring through a chain of causation that is too "attenuated" (that is, the person doesn't have an actual injury or the claimed wrong is too far removed from the person's injury). Such a judge would never reach the merits of the challenge (that is, make a decision on the substantive issue), and a serious legal violation could go unremedied. In other words, the case would be decided procedurally and not substantively, thus leaving the person's claimed injury or damages unaddressed.

Enlarging Federal Power Generally: McCulloch v. Maryland

Congress established a national bank and opened a branch in Baltimore, Maryland. Maryland then passed a law under which any bank not locally chartered could be taxed by Maryland. McCulloch, who ran the U.S. bank, refused to pay the tax, and litigation going up to the Supreme Court ensued. On its way to deciding whether Maryland could tax the bank, the Supreme Court first asked whether Congress had the right to set up the bank in the first place. In the ruling of *McCulloch v. Maryland,* 17 U.S. 316 (1819), the Court answered yes, on the theory that setting up the bank was a valid means of achieving several enumerated congressional powers.

The *McCulloch* Court's relatively generous conception of Congress's "implied powers" — that is, its endorsement of congressional authority to use any implied means that are "appropriate" and "plainly adapted" to fulfillment of an enumerated power — was crucial in giving Americans the large and multifaceted scheme of federal government regulation we have today. Had *McCulloch* embraced the other major theory (that Congress was limited to those implied means "necessary" to achievement of enumerated powers), the federal-government presence would be substantially less than it is today. Many governmental activities the Congress authorizes today are "appropriate" but arguably not exactly "necessary"!

Expanding Congress's Regulatory Power: NLRB v. Jones & Laughlin Steel Corp. and Wickard v. Filburn

Two closely-related-in-time decisions worked together to dramatically expand Congress's power to regulate interstate commerce. Although it's just one of Congress's 17 express powers, the interstate-commerce power is the one-stop source of most federal legislation in the economic, health and safety, and criminal arenas.

In *National Labor Relations Board (NLRB) v. Jones & Laughlin Steel Corporation,* 301 U.S. 1 (1937), the steel company challenged Congress's authority to enact a national law protecting the rights of workers to unionize. When Jones & Laughlin fired ten employees after they attempted to form a union, the NLRB ordered the employees rehired with back pay, and imposed other mandates. The Supreme Court held that the labor law was a valid exercise of Congress's power to regulate interstate commerce.

In *Wickard v. Filburn,* 317 U.S. 111 (1942), Mr. Filburn was a farmer who grew wheat in excess of what was allowed under the federal laws intending to stabilize the farm prices and restore solvency to the nation's famers during the Great Depression. Filburn objected that he was not selling the wheat; he was using it on his own farm. The federal government sought to have Filburn destroy his excess crop and pay a fine. The Supreme Court upheld that application of federal law to Filburn.

Both these cases reversed several decades of narrow "formalistic" commerce-power interpretation. *Jones & Laughlin* set the guiding principle for when Congress can use its interstate-commerce power as an implied means for regulating *local* activities. *Jones & Laughlin* held that Congress could reach any local activities that would have a "substantial" practical effect on the national economy. In so doing, *Jones & Laughlin* replaced the previous view that Congress could not regulate local activities — whatever their practical effect — if they fell outside narrow categories of activities "directly" related to interstate commerce.

Wickard followed up on the *Jones & Laughlin* expansion of congressional power with an even bigger enlargement of its own. Obviously, farmer Filburn's overproduction of wheat did not have a "substantial" economic effect by itself. (This contrasts with the named litigant in *Jones & Laughlin,* which as the then-fourth-largest steel producer in America clearly had its own substantial effect!) Not to worry, said the *Wickard* Court. The "cumulative" effect of thousands of farmers could be "aggregated" — in other words, the Court could take into consideration the possible effect of thousands of farmers doing the same thing as Filburn. If the cumulative effect of the class of activities is "substantial," Congress may regulate all the activities in the class. The *Wickard* Court's approach dramatically expanded the reach of federal commercial regulation into "small potatoes" activities.

Preventing Congressional Coercion of State Power: New York v. United States

New York v. United States, 505 U.S. 144 (1992), involves the Low-Level Radioactive Waste Police Amendments Act of 1985 and its "take title" provision. Under the Act, Congress was attempting to force state governments to regulate radioactive waste or be liable for damages for waste not disposed of within certain time frames. Although it upheld all but one provision of the Act, the Supreme Court held that the "take title" provision, which would have forced states to be responsible for any consequences of failing to dispose of the waste in a timely manner, was beyond Congress's power.

New York held that Congress acts unconstitutionally if federal law *requires* states to exercise their legislative or regulatory powers in federally dictated ways. Congress can encourage states to legislate/regulate by offering them federal funding if they do so; or Congress may pass national legislation and let states develop a parallel state regulatory alternative under federal guidelines. Both of these approaches protect political accountability and treat states like sovereigns, said the *New York* Court, because states ultimately determine whether to take the federal government up on its offer. (A state can "Just say no!")

What Congress can't do is "coerce" states to legislate or regulate against their will. (A later related case, *Printz v. United States,* 521 U.S. 898 [1997], extended this anticoercion principle to congressional efforts to force a state to use its executive powers to enforce federal law.)

Restricting Congressional Commerce Powers: United States v. Lopez

What the Court giveth in *NLRB v. Jones & Laughlin* and *Wickard v. Filburn* (see the earlier section "Expanding Congress's Regulatory Power"), it taketh away (in part) in *United States v. Lopez,* 514 U.S. 549 (1995).

In *Lopez,* a high school student brought a .38-caliber revolver to school. Authorities at the school questioned him and he admitted to having the gun, along with bullets. He was convicted under a provision of the federal Gun Free School Zones Act of 1990, which forbade any person taking a gun within 1,000 feet of a school. Lopez challenged his conviction on the basis that the Act was an unconstitutional exercise of the Congress's power under the commerce clause. The Supreme Court held that the issue of guns in schools was too far removed from commerce to fall under the purview of that clause.

Lopez (and *United States v. Morrison,* 529 U.S. 598 [2000], which reinforced the *Lopez* theory five years later) threw a potentially broad "monkey wrench" into almost 60 years of increasing federal commerce regulation. *Lopez/ Morrison* held that, no matter how significant local activities were, they could not be reached by federal power if they were not "part of a broader economic enterprise" and if regulating non-economic local activities was not "an essential part of a larger regulation of economic activity." These and other portions of the *Lopez* holding have led to substantial uncertainty and controversy (including a spate of lawsuits over whether the "individual mandate" provision in health-insurance-reform legislation is a constitutional exercise of Congress's commerce power.)

Developing the Competing Theories of Presidential Power: Youngstown Sheet & Tube Co. v. Sawyer

During the Korean War, President Truman issued an executive order to seize and operate the country's steel mills. The president argued that a threatened strike could have grave consequences to the country's national defense. The steel companies sued to declare the order unconstitutional, and the Court agreed in *Youngstown Sheet & Tube Company v. Sawyer,* 343 U.S. 579 (1952).

Although the Court ruled against presidential power in *Youngstown,* the longer-run value of the case is its laying down of two competing theories by which many assertions of modern presidential power are justified and upheld. The "formalistic" approach, used in the majority opinion, held that presidents not exercising authority as Congress's delegate must find authority in one or more of the express powers in Article II of the Constitution. The more "pragmatic" approach endorsed by two influential concurring justices recognized that, even in the absence of express authority, presidents can acquire expanded power by asserting it over time and not being challenged by Congress.

Limiting Executive Privilege: U.S. v. Nixon

In *United States v. Nixon,* 418 U.S. 683 (1974), President Nixon claimed an "executive privilege" not to comply with a federal district-court subpoena for tapes of conversations between him and other high-ranking officials in his administration. Special federal prosecutors sought the materials to aid in prosecuting a number of White House staffers and others implicated in the infamous Watergate break-in and coverup. The Court unanimously held that Nixon had to comply with the subpoena and ordered the district judge to subject particularized presidential claims of confidentiality in certain documents to a secret, *in camera* review. The Court said, "Absent a claim of need to protect military, diplomatic, or sensitive national security secrets, we find it difficult to accept the argument that even the very important interest in confidentiality of Presidential communications is significantly diminished by production of such material for *in camera* inspection. . . ."

The *Nixon* case turned out to be rather inconclusive on the general question of when presidents may assert executive privilege. (Presidents use this privilege not infrequently, typically in the face of congressional subpoenas for information about administration policy.) True, *Nixon* turned down the argument that presidents had "an absolute, unqualified" privilege to withhold documents. But *Nixon*'s narrow decision subordinating a president's generalized, conditional privilege to the need for "evidence that is demonstrably relevant in a criminal trial" leaves lots of executive-privilege law still unresolved.

Still, the enduring value of *Nixon* is its unanimous assertion that even the president exercises powers "in light of our historic commitment to the rule of law."

Chapter 18

Ten (Plus Three) Top Individual-Rights Cases

- -

In This Chapter

▶ Landmark cases that expanded rights for individuals

▶ Key criminal-rights cases: Balancing law-enforcement needs against personal privacy

- -

*I*n this chapter, we explore some of the top cases that have shaped individual rights, both in criminal constitutional law (more specifically, criminal procedure) and civil constitutional law. This chapter serves not only as a reminder of some of the cases and concepts discussed in other chapters but also gives you a quick reference guide of sorts.

Criminal procedure (that is, rights people are entitled to with respect to criminal cases), which is taught as an entire semester course in law school, is a vast subject. Likewise, the volumes of civil constitutional-law cases, which address civil rights like free speech, freedom of the press, and rights people are entitled to in civil actions, could fill a small warehouse. But this chapter gives you a summary of important cases that have shaped Americans' everyday lives with respect to individual rights — rulings that ensure people's basic rights, whether the person is suspected of a crime, or a member of the general public subjected to government action.

Given the spread of the terrain, we just couldn't limit the list of "top" individual rights and liberties to *ten* cases. In fact, we think we did well to narrow the list to a "baker's dozen."

As you read this list, please bear in mind that reasonable minds can differ on how important one case is versus another. Many scholars and/or law professors would argue the first criminal-rights case we cover — *Miranda v. Arizona* — is the most important case when it comes to individual rights, at least on the criminal side. But the cases are in no certain order of importance.

Extending the Bill of Rights to State and Local Governments: Palko v. Connecticut and Other Cases

From the standpoint of *both* civil and criminal constitutional rights, the most important development has likely been the extension to state and local governments of most of the "fundamental" rights expressly required of the federal government via the Bill of Rights. This development dramatically expanded the reach of the U.S. Constitution and the power of federal courts in ensuring that the Constitution's protections are vital and widespread.

This expansion of the Bill of Rights, originally intended to only bind the federal government, has been done through the Fourteenth Amendment's due-process clause. In a series of cases starting in 1908 and continuing to the present, the Court has considered whether particular Bill of Rights protections are so fundamental as to be "incorporated" and applied to state and local governments through the command that they not deprive persons within their jurisdiction of due process of law. Almost all the Bill-of-Rights protections are now incorporated.

The best representative of the development of binding the states to the Bill of Rights is *Palko v. Connecticut,* 302 U.S. 319 (1937). The defendant was convicted of second-degree murder, rather than first degree, and the state appealed. The case was reversed and defendant was brought to trial again; this time he was convicted of first-degree murder and sentenced to death. Over the defendant's objection that this violated the prohibition against double jeopardy, the Supreme Court affirmed his conviction. Ironically, the Court did not apply the Fifth Amendment double-jeopardy clause to the state of Connecticut. (The double-jeopardy clause is now incorporated and applied to the states, and prosecution appeals of innocent verdicts are unconstitutional.) But *Palko* established an important and enduring formula for determining when rights are fundamental — whether the right is "so rooted in the tradition and conscience of our people" as to be part of "the very essence of a scheme of ordered liberty."

Vigorously Protecting Subversive and Offensive Speech: Brandenburg v. Ohio and Cohen v. California

You may think we're cheating right off the bat by discussing these two close-in-time cases together in one section, but the pairing is logical. Each case in its own way ushered in the modern era of very strong protection — some critics would say overly strong protection — for potentially dangerous or highly objectionable speech.

Brandenburg v. Ohio, 395 U.S. 444 (1969), concerned the constitutionality of convicting an Ohio leader of the Ku Klux Klan (the militant white-supremacist organization with a long career of harassment and violence against racial minorities and other disfavored groups). After TV news stations covered and broadcast Brandenburg's racist and ungrammatical rant vaguely promising "revengeance" down the road if the nation's political establishment "continues to suppress the white, Caucasian race," Brandenburg was sentenced to a long prison term for the crime of "advocating . . . the duty, necessity, or propriety of crime, sabotage, violence . . . as a means of accomplishing . . . political reform." The Court unanimously invalidated the Ohio law, declaring that "mere advocacy" of future violence was constitutionally protected unless it met the high threshold of being "incitement of imminent lawless activity" in circumstances likely to produce the result. For better or for worse, *Brandenburg* made it very difficult to prosecute militant speakers whose hate speech may trigger violence at some future (but non-imminent) time.

Cohen v. California, 403 U.S. 15 (1971), did for offensive speech what *Brandenburg* did for violence-prone speech. During the Vietnam War, Cohen wore a jacket in the Los Angeles County Courthouse bearing the message "F*** the Draft." Convicted for "disorderly conduct," Cohen claimed that punishing him for speech that didn't fall into any narrow categories of "unprotected speech" was unconstitutional. (For example, because Cohen did not use the "F-word" in a sexually provocative manner, his speech was not unprotected "obscenity.") The Supreme Court agreed, holding that tolerating "offensive" speech was better than giving government a broad right to suppress speech based on a vague, undifferentiated fear of unrest or a generalized concern of elevating the dignity of public discourse. The Court's holding in *Cohen* that free-speech required offended viewers to simply "avert their eyes" set the standard for many later cases requiring Americans to tolerate coarse and offensive expression.

Protecting Flag Burners: Texas v. Johnson

Texas v. Johnson, 491 U.S. 397 (1989), indicated that the Supreme Court was willing to strongly protect the free-expression rights of people disrespecting core American icons. To protest the military policies of President Ronald Reagan, Gregory Johnson burned an American flag at the Republican convention being held in Dallas. The state of Texas convicted Gregory for violating its statute against flag desecration. Reviewing and overturning the conviction, the Supreme Court applied strict scrutiny on the theory that the prosecution was content-based regulation of "symbolic speech" (that is, Texas was prosecuting Johnson for conduct expressing a point of view *because Texas objected to that point of view*).

One of the most unpopular cases of modern times (at least measured by public-opinion polls and condemnations from political leaders), *Johnson* is emblematic of the modern trend of strong protection — by both conservatives and liberals on the Court — of the most outrageous and unpopular speech. This willingness to defend the indefensible can be seen in later cases about the rights of neo-Nazis, purveyors of Internet indecency, and antigay protesters at military funerals.

Keeping Government from Promoting Religious Belief: Engel v. Vitale

Speaking of unpopular cases (see the preceding section), certain segments of American society count the Court's series of school prayer decisions as among the most objectionable. *Engel v. Vitale,* 370 U.S. 421 (1962), started the series off by ruling that New York's requirement that its teachers start the public-school day off by leading their classes in prayer was unconstitutional. Even though the prayer was a short, bland, nondenominational prayer — and even though objecting students could be excused from saying it — the Court held that the Constitution's establishment clause forbade government from using its prestige and resources to promote religious teachings. Later cases extended this theory to a variety of efforts to foster religion among public-school students, including requirements that Bible verses be read, that the Lord's Prayer be recited, and that the Ten Commandments be displayed.

Interestingly, the *Engel*-inspired case law did not "take God out of the classroom" completely. The Court has emphasized that the *Engel* ruling still allows the study of religious texts (and even the Bible and the Ten Commandments), religious art, and other religious objects in the context of courses on literature, world history, and comparative religion. And religious music and traditions can be included in holiday programs and other activities. The key is that the religious items be included for educational reasons as opposed to religion-promoting reasons.

Limiting Protection of Religious Free Exercise: Employment Division, Department of Human Resources v. Smith

Before the decision in *Employment Division, Department of Human Resources v. Smith,* 494 U.S. 872 (1990), any federal, state, or local law that "substantially burdened" religion had to survive a rigorous judicial review under the "strict scrutiny" standard. Some laws did pass this test, but many didn't. *Smith* substantially restricted the reach of the constitutional protection for the free exercise of religion. It did so by generally limiting strict scrutiny to the much narrower category of laws deliberately "discriminating" against religious rituals or practices.

Smith concerned the validity of an Oregon law that denied unemployment benefits to employees fired for misconduct, such as drug use. Smith, a substance-abuse counselor, was fired from his job because he used peyote (a hallucinogenic plant) during a traditional Native American religious ceremony. He claimed that Oregon's failure to give him unemployment benefits substantially burdened his religion because, he said, the state forced him to choose between practicing his religion or keeping his job. Rejecting his claims, the *Smith* majority held that it was inappropriate to apply strict scrutiny to "generally applicable" laws that inadvertently have the effect of limiting some people's religion. Instead, the *Smith* Court held that rational-basis review, which is typically easy to satisfy, is all that's constitutionally necessary when the law is generally applicable and only inadvertently affects some.

Rejecting Racial Segregation: Brown v. Board of Education of Topeka

In an era in which official segregation of the races was entrenched throughout the South and other parts of the United States, *Brown v. Board of Education of Topeka,* 347 U.S. 483 (1954), unanimously and courageously established that official segregation of the races in allegedly "separate but equal" schools and other public facilities was inherently discriminatory in violation of the equal-protection guarantees in the Fifth and Fourteenth Amendments.

Brown capped a brilliant, multicase litigation strategy by the National Association for the Advancement of Colored People. Based in part on psychological evidence that making African American children attend separate schools sent an inherent message — and reflecting a modernized understanding that *separate* was inherently *unequal* for constitutional purposes — *Brown* mandated desegregation.

Compliance with this mandate was hardly immediate. Implementing *Brown*'s command to dismantle official racial segregation took years of protracted litigation in lower courts and active enforcement by the executive and legislative branches of the federal government. (The task is still incomplete today.) Yet *Brown* was a landmark step in implementing the motto chiseled in stone atop the Supreme Court Chamber, "Equal Justice Under Law."

Strictly Scrutinizing Affirmative Action: City of Richmond v. J. A. Croson Co.

For some time after the *Brown* case, the Court and the nation struggled with how to fit "affirmative action" (programs using race preferences to remedy the effect of past discrimination against disadvantaged minorities) into the law of racial discrimination. Did "equal protection" require government to be color-blind, so that reference to race in laws — even to help the racial minorities the Fourteenth Amendment was adopted primarily to benefit — should be subject to the same strict scrutiny applied to antiminority laws when evaluating challenges? Or should affirmative action be subject to a more forgiving standard?

After avoiding resolving the question for more than a dozen years, the Court in *City of Richmond v. J. A. Croson Company,* 488 U.S. 469 (1989), put a narrow majority together in favor of treating affirmative action like past discrimination against racial minorities. Invalidating a program in which the City of Richmond set aside 30 percent of its public contracting funds for minority-owned subcontractors, the Court found that Richmond had an insufficient evidentiary basis for assuming that past discrimination in local contracting needed to be remedied in this way. The Court stated that the city would have had to show a compelling interest in apportioning public contract opportunities on the basis of race in order for the law to be constitutional, and it had not.

Explaining its rationale, the Court said, "to accept Richmond's claim that past societal discrimination alone can serve as the basis for rigid racial preferences would be to open the door to competing claims for 'remedial relief' for every disadvantaged group; the dream of a nation of equal citizens in a society where race is irrelevant to personal opportunity and achievement would be lost in a mosaic of shifting preferences based on inherently unmeasurable claims of past wrongs." Whatever its other merits, *Croson* made pursuing affirmative-action remedies extremely difficult and expensive for governments.

Implying Fundamental Privacy Rights: Griswold v. Connecticut

You may have expected *Roe v. Wade*, the 1973 case establishing the fundamental right of a woman to choose abortion (thereby creating a political and legal cauldron still boiling to this day), to make this list. However, *Roe* and several other important decisions establishing fundamental rights to marry, have children, and live together as a family all owe their existence to an earlier case, *Griswold v. Connecticut,* 381 U.S. 479 (1965).

Griswold invalidated, as a violation of substantive due process, a Connecticut law prohibiting any person from using most contraceptives. The law, intended to discourage people from having sex outside of marriage, would have passed low-level rational-basis review. Giving the generous deference to officials that standard allows, the reasoning behind the law was rational. But *Griswold* held that the law had to be strictly reviewed because it implicated the fundamental right of married people to privacy — both in their home and with respect to this important life decision.

Even though the Constitution nowhere explicitly protects a right to privacy, the *Griswold* Court recognized it as an implied right "older than the Bill of Rights" yet protected within its due-process formula. *Griswold* thus gave birth (if you'll pardon the pun!) to the next four-plus decades of judicial decisions expanding (and sometimes not expanding) the orbit of personal liberties falling within the privacy rubric. (We summarize these cases in Chapter 14.)

Advising People of Their Rights: Miranda v. Arizona

In *Miranda v. Arizona,* 384 U.S. 436 (1966), the defendant was arrested on rape, kidnapping, and robbery charges, along with others. Miranda was questioned for a couple hours and ultimately confessed to the crimes. While he was being questioned, he did not have an attorney present. He was never told he had a right to an attorney, or that he had a right to remain silent. Miranda's initial conviction was overturned because his confession was admitted at trial even though he had not been advised of his rights beforehand. The Supreme Court said Miranda's rights were violated and the confession should not have been admitted.

This case strikes a balance between the powers of law enforcement and an individual's rights. The case held that a person must be advised of their rights to (1) remain silent, (2) to have an attorney appointed, (3) to have an attorney present prior to any custodial interrogation (police questioning when the person is not free to leave), and (4) that anything a person says can be used against them in court.

This case has major significance because someone unaware of his rights may be more likely to talk to police and potentially confess. "Mirandizing" also serves as a reminder to suspects who are aware of the rights they have under the Constitution (but who may not be thinking clearly after being arrested). Without these advisals, the protections afforded every individual in the Constitution in criminal cases would be devalued.

Allowing Police to Stop and Frisk: Terry v. Ohio

In *Terry v. Ohio,* 392 U.S. 1 (1968), a police officer in downtown Cleveland was patrolling the area when he saw two men "casing" a store, and he believed the men were preparing to rob it. The officer talked to the men and eventually patted them down because their behavior was still suspicious, and he found a gun in one man's shirt pocket. That man, Terry, was later convicted of carrying a concealed weapon and sentenced to a short prison term. Terry's request to have the gun excluded from evidence on Fourth Amendment grounds was denied. On appeal, the Supreme Court held that the gun was admissible, because the "frisk" was based on the officer's reasonable suspicion that criminal activity was afoot.

This case is significant because the Court recognized the needs of law enforcement in protecting the public, protecting officers, and trying to prevent crime. The case solidified a police officer's right to talk to citizens and even make a "pat down" of a person based on a "reasonable suspicion that criminal activity is afoot" without having to advise the person of their rights. It allows law enforcement a little more leeway than they have when an individual is actually being arrested.

Solidifying the Right Not to Testify: Griffin v. California

In *Griffin v. California,* 380 U.S. 609 (1965), the defendant, who was charged with murder, was the last person to see the victim lying in the alley where her body was found. The defendant chose not to take the stand. In closing, the prosecutor commented on the fact that the defendant did not take the stand to explain the circumstances or deny whether he was the one who had beaten the victim. The Court found the prosecutor's comments were improper and said the state's "comment rule" violated the Fifth Amendment, which is applicable to the states by the Fourteenth Amendment.

This case solidified a criminal defendant's absolute right not to testify in the case against him and in essence extends the right, which is explicitly granted in the Fifth Amendment. Without this ruling, the right not to testify was somewhat illusory; commenting on a defendant's refusal to testify implies that he *should* testify even though he technically doesn't have to and seems to take away the value the right is supposed to extend in the first place.

Determining When an Individual Has a Right to Privacy: Katz v. U.S.

In *Katz v. United States,* 389 U.S. 347 (1967), the defendant was conducting illegal gambling out of a telephone booth. The police had wiretapped the phone, and evidence that was consequently obtained was used to convict against Katz. He then appealed on Fourth Amendment grounds, but the lower court rejected his claim, because law enforcement had not made a physical intrusion into an area that the defendant occupied. He appealed and the Supreme Court reversed, holding that the defendant had a reasonable expectation that when he entered the phone booth and shut the door behind him, he was entitled to assume that his words would "not be broadcast to the world." The Court said that the Fourth Amendment protects people, not places, and the lack of a "trespass" with respect to the phone booth was not controlling.

Katz established a two-part test to determine whether a person has a constitutionally protected reasonable expectation of privacy. The test includes two questions:

✔ Does the person have a subjective expectation of privacy in the area?

✔ Is society willing to say that expectation is reasonable?

This approach uses common sense, judging the reasonableness based on the facts as to whether the person really had an expectation of privacy and whether most (reasonable) people would agree with him. In this way, the test considers the subjective aspect (the individual's expectation) and the objective aspect (the public's view).

Katz broadened an individual's rights under the Fourth Amendment by clarifying that the Fourth-Amendment's protections follow you wherever you go, because it protects individuals, not places. This holding basically affords people extended individual rights, requiring additional circumstances in which the police must have probable cause and obtain a warrant before making such an intrusion.

Establishing Exceptions to the Exclusionary Rule: Wong Sun v. U.S.

In *Wong Sun v. United States,* 371 U.S. 471 (1963), a string of events and information from other people led police to the defendant, and he was arrested without probable cause. Wong Sun was arraigned on drug charges and then released on his own recognizance (which means he didn't have to post bail).

Days later, he confessed to the charges. The defendant was convicted of narcotics transportation and concealment. He challenged his conviction, claiming that his unsigned confession, admitted against him at trial, was a "fruit of the poisonous tree" (as discussed in Chapter 15). Although the Supreme Court agreed that his arrest was illegal, his confession was not a direct result of the illegality and was therefore admissible.

In this case, the court clarified that the exclusionary rule bars only evidence obtained as a direct result of illegal activity on the part of law enforcement. The Court said, "a court need not hold that all evidence is 'fruit of the poisonous tree' simply because it would not have come to light but for the illegal actions of the police." Instead, if the police do something illegal, the question of whether the evidence is admissible depends on whether it was gained by "exploitation" of the illegality. The Court said that in this case, Wong Sun's unlawful arrest and the admitted confession were so unconnected that the statement did not constitute a "fruit of the poisonous tree."

If the means by which the evidence was obtained is sufficiently distanced from the illegal action that it is "purged of the primary taint," the evidence can be used. The holding in this case gives an obvious advantage ("freebies") to law enforcement (and consequently to the prosecution) in that certain evidence is still admissible even though the police have violated some constitutional guidelines in handling the case.

Index

• *E* •

• *T* •